THE COLLEGE GUIDEBOOK ENVIRONMENTAL ENGINEERING AND SCIENCE

College Admissions & Profiles

Rachel A. Winston, Ph.D.

Lizard Publishing is not sponsored by any college. While data was derived by school, state, or nationally published sources, some statistics may be out of date as published sources vary widely based upon the date of submission and currency of numbers. Attempts were made to obtain the best information during the writing of this book from, NCES, U.S. Census Bureau, U.S. Department of Education, Common Data Set, College Board, U.S. News & World Report, college, and organizational sites. Descriptions of colleges are a compilation of college website information as well as student, faculty, and staff interviews with individuals and often from unique experiences and impressions. Attempts were made to triangulate multiple points of light. If you would like to share program information, data, or an impression of a specific college, please write to Lizard Publishing at the address below or at the e-mail address: *collegeguide@yahoo.com*

ISBN 978-1958558478 (paperback); 978-1958558461 (e-book)

LCCN: 2024926989

© Copyright 2025 Lizard Publishing. All rights reserved.

All rights reserved. No part of this work may be reproduced or transmitted in any form or by any means, including, but not limited to, photocopying, recording, image capture, electronic, mechanical or any other information storage and retrieval systems, without the express written permission from Lizard Publishing.

Lizard Publishing, 7700 Irvine Center Drive, Suite 800, Irvine, CA 92618 *www.lizard-publishing.com*

Lizard Publishing creates, designs, produces, and distributes books and resources to provide academic, admissions, and career information. Our mental process is fueled by three tenets:

- Ignite the hunger to learn and the passion to make a difference
- Illuminate the expanse of knowledge by sharing cutting edge thinking
- Innovate to create a world that makes the transition from dreams to reality

We work with academic leaders who transform the educational landscape to publish relevant content and advise students of their educational and professional options, with the aim of developing 21st-century learners and leaders. We also work with students to publish their books and present widely diverse ideas to the college/graduate school-bound community. With headquarters in Irvine, California, Lizard Publishing works virtually with authors to edit, publish, and distribute both hard copy and paperback books.

This book was published in the U.S.A. Lizard Publishing is a premium quality provider of educational reference, career guidance, and motivational publications/merchandise for global learners, educators, and stakeholders in education.

Book design by Michelle Tahan *www.michelletahan.com*

Book formatting by Obinna Chinemerem Ozuo

Book website: *www.collegelizard.com*

This book is dedicated to Shauna Bahri, Corina Lee, and Camus Hu whose commitments to the environment and a positive vision for humanity will energize and transform society.

ACKNOWLEDGMENTS

There is never enough room to acknowledge every person. Numerous people contributed to my perspective about environmental science, environmental engineering, and alternative energy. Students, faculty, counselors, and researchers assisted in enhancing my knowledge base or taught me indelible lessons. Over a lifetime of experiences working with students, I am wiser and more worldly.

I gratefully acknowledge Michelle Tahan, Jasmine Jhunjhnuwala, E. Liz Kim, Jacqueline Xu, and Chenoa Robbins as well as my family, friends, colleagues, and professors. With profound gratitude, I also acknowledge those I have known in the universes of design and engineering.

As a faculty member in the UCLA College Counseling Certificate Program, I met many dedicated counselors who spend their life serving and supporting students. Meaningful contributions to the book have been made indirectly by admissions representatives, college counselors, and faculty members who took a special interest in this book's success.

> *"If I see so far, it is because I stand on the shoulders of giants."*
> — Isaac Newton

I would also like to thank the thousands of students I have taught, counseled, or supported in my nearly four decades of service.

Isaac Newton once said, "If I see so far, it is because I stand on the shoulders of giants." A few of those giants whose broad shoulders lifted me higher and helped teach invaluable lessons include Nadia Aluzri, Patrick Bayeh, Regina DeBilio, Marina Eryan, Heather Ferraro, Cindy Grieder, Gracie Hare, Alyssa Ing, Peter Liang, Jennifer Pearson, Eesa Quraishi, Ida Ramazani, Taya Salman, Lisa Salvi, Sophia Tazerouni, Michelle Temby, Harrison White, Harrison Woodruff, and Emily Yates.

Finally, there would be no book on universities focused on environmental engineering and alternative energy and no career in college admissions counseling without the support of Robert Helmer, whose tireless efforts support me every single day.

ABOUT THE AUTHOR

Dr. Rachel A. Winston is a tireless student advocate. She has served the educational community as a university professor, college advisor, statistician, medical researcher, chemist, cryptanalyst, quality control analyst, motivational speaker, author, educational leader, and lifelong student. As one of the leading experts in college counseling and an award-winning faculty member, Dr. Winston has spent her lifetime learning, teaching, mentoring, and coaching students. Her counseling practice centers around college admissions, college essays, portfolios, and intellectual conversations about life and career pursuits.

She started college at thirteen and graduated from college in widely ranging disciplines including chemistry, mathematics, computers, liberal arts, international relations, negotiation, conflict resolution, peacebuilding, business administration, higher education leadership, interpreting, college counseling, and publishing. Throughout her education, she attended and graduated from Harvard, University of Chicago, University of Texas, GWU, UCLA, Syracuse, CSUF, CSUDH, Pepperdine, Claremont Graduate University, and Gallaudet University.

Her position working in Washington, D.C. on Capitol Hill and with the White House in the 1980s took her to approximately a hundred universities training campaign managers at colleges from Colorado to California, thoroughly dotting the western states. Later, she led college tours with students and their families on road trips throughout the United States. She has taught or counseled thousands of students over her career and speaks at conferences and academic programs throughout the world.

As a professor and avid writer for numerous publications, she won the 2012 McFarland Literary Achievement Award, Bletchley Park Cryptanalyst Award, and numerous other writing, research, and leadership awards, including Faculty Member of the Year, Leadership Tomorrow Leader of the Year, and college service and leadership awards. While studying Human Capital at Claremont Graduate University, she was a scholarship recipient at the Drucker School of Management. She was also elected to the statewide Board of Governors for the Faculty Association for California Community Colleges, where she served on the executive committee.

She also served as a faculty member for the UCLA College Counselor Certificate Program, Embry Riddle Aeronautical University, Chapman University, Cal State Fullerton, Brandman University, where she also served as the Director of Mathematics, and a handful of California Community Colleges, including Cerro Coso College where she represented the faculty as the Academic Senate President and retired in 2016. Over her career, she taught mathematics online, on television, live interactive satellite, telecourses, and in large and small lecture halls.

AUTHOR'S NOTE

You are reading this book because you are considering admission to colleges where you open the doors to the world of research, engineering, and creativity. Whatever route you took to get to this point, you are in the right place. Right now, you need to gather information to make informed decisions.

While many people offer advice, suggestions differ. Friends will tell you the 'right' way or the way their neighbor was accepted. Graciously accept this anecdotal information, while pursuing innovative projects, AI, big data analysis, and engineering with your heart and mind as you commit to learning more.

Dig deeper to consider both expert and current information from counselors who have worked with hundreds of students. Changes in programs, curricula, requirements, and links happen each year.

Doublecheck each program yourself. Each school's profile information is current as of March 2024. However, since researching this book, changes may have taken place. There are other guidebooks written by talented and experienced counselors, though none like this book on college programs for environmental engineering and alternative energy. Nevertheless, I admire and cheer on their efforts.

> *"We are what we think. All that we are arises with our thoughts. With our thoughts, we make the world."*
> *— Buddha*

This book, providing lists of colleges, admissions information, and profiles, is different in that it also offers unique tidbits. I hope you find the information valuable. Your job is to begin early by assembling lists of possible schools to consider. Create a road map and set yourself on a clear path.

If you see an error in this book or even a suggestion for a future edition, please write to Dr. Rachel A. Winston at collegeguide@yahoo.com. We will fix the entry with the next printed version. All of that said, this book was written with you in mind.

This book contains a wealth of information. The Internet offers free downloads, FAQs, testimonials, and appeals from "experts" to help you with your applications. Some "advisors" are knowledgeable and provide valuable assistance. Unfortunately, some are not legitimate. Further, students and parents hunt around the web, searching for a tremendous number of hours to find the information they need. This book aims to resolve this problem with college admissions data and profiles to make your search easier.

For now, though, I will assume you want to attend college to study environmental engineering or alternative energy and are exploring this book to find programs that will get you on your way toward your goal. You are undoubtedly a talented candidate who is willing to work very hard. Creative mental exploration is virtually a prerequisite for engineering and STEM programs.

As you investigate colleges, you might find that some programs are found in different departments. Either way, this book will help you reach your goal. Applying to college and writing essays for each application will require research to determine which program is right for you and the specific reasons you are a good fit.

While you might believe that engineering-focused colleges are relatively similar, each program's nuances make them very different. These small differences may seem confusing. My goal with this book is to demystify the information and process.

CONTENTS

Chapter 1: Environmental Engineering Past, Present, & Future   1

Chapter 2: Expectations, Training, & Competitions   13

Chapter 3: Academic Preparation & Career Options   31

Chapter 4: Summer Programs & Internships   45

Chapter 5: University Options for Environmental Engineering & Environmental Science   85

Chapter 6: College Degrees   105

Chapter 7: College Admissions   115

Chapter 8: Financial Aid & Scholarships   143

Chapter 9: Employment Outlook   159

Chapter 10: Preparation & Real-World Skills   171

Chapter 11: Region One - Northeast   188

Chapter 12: Region Two - Midwest   210

Chapter 13: Region Three - South   230

Chapter 14: Region Four - West   252

Chapter 15: Profiled Environmental Engineering Programs   274

Chapter 16: ABET Accredited Environmental Engineering Programs   276

Chapter 17: ABET Accredited Environmental Engineering Technology, Fire Protection, & Environmental Science, Health, & Safety ... 280

Chapter 18: ABET Accredited Geological, Mining, & Ocean Engineering Programs ... 282

Chapter 19: ABET Accredited Nuclear Energy Programs ... 286

Chapter 20: ABET Accredited Civil Engineering Programs ... 290

Chapter 21: ABET Accredited Chemical Engineering Programs ... 300

Chapter 22: ACT-SAT Concordance Table ... 304

Index ... 310

CHAPTER 1

ENVIRONMENTAL ENGINEERING PAST, PRESENT, & FUTURE

"The Earth is what we all have in common."

– **Wendell Berry**

The world needs forward-thinking individuals dedicated to resolving society's most pressing problems. Some of humanity's daunting crises include climate change, pollution, and access to clean water, food, and shelter. Passionate students committed to overcoming these challenges and eager to make a difference can change the future. As an environmental engineer, you will envision and invent sustainable systems that protect the health of our planet and its inhabitants, ensuring a brighter tomorrow for generations to come.

Civilization's earliest ancestors created roads, buildings, aquifers, filtration, roads, and bridges out of necessity. Human progress began with the need to solve problems. In the desert, people would have died without water. Surprisingly, though, when they dug deep enough into the ground they found swells of groundwater. While some breakthroughs were made by trial and error, others required sophisticated calculations. Complex buildings were constructed with few tools and massive boulders that literally weighed a ton. As with many other challenges, progress led to extraordinary solutions.

There is a running joke in engineering circles that engineers can construct a bridge across the most difficult terrain but cannot figure out how to sew on a button. While this is not always true, engineers do take pride in their ability to comprehend, compute, and resolve some of the most challenging problems. Furthermore, certified engineers develop essential skills in managing both projects and people.

ORIGINS OF CIVIL & ENVIRONMENTAL ENGINEERING

Civil and environmental engineering's emergence 4,000 to 6,000 years ago mirrored humankind's development with transportation, buildings, water, and resource needs. As people left their cave dwellings, abandoned their nomadic lifestyle, and sought permanent shelter, civil and environmental engineering took root. In Egypt, Mesopotamia, and the Indus Valley, rafts aided in crossing rivers. Cutting and chopping tools were developed to slice tree trunks, while vines strapped slabs together to make more sophisticated boats.

Civil engineers and architects were basically the same individuals. The pyramids represent one of the greatest engineering feats of all time. More than 100 pyramids remain in Egypt today. The oldest pyramid was constructed more than 4,000 years ago. Additionally, the demand for water in the Egyptian desert necessitated the engineering of innovative storage facilities. Similarly, in ancient Mesopotamia, water channels, called qanats, built 3,000 years ago, transported water from wells and aquifers for agriculture and human consumption.

ENGINEERING ARCHITECTURAL MARVELS

Some of engineering's marvels include the seven wonders of the world - Chichén Itzá, Christ the Redeemer, Colosseum, Great Wall of China, Machu Picchu, Petra, and the Taj Mahal – and numerous others from centuries past when modern tools, transportation, materials, and machinery were unavailable.

Brazil - Christ the Redeemer – 1931 – 2,340 ft – This 13-story reinforced concrete, soapstone-coated sculpture sits atop Corcovado Peak where lightning damaged two fingers, but the rest remains for millions to see.

China – The Great Wall of China – 220 BC – 13,171 miles (highest elevation 4,722 ft) – Constructed over 2,000 years, this impressive brick and stone structure has 25 ft high walls with 40 ft towers constructed approximately every 700 ft.

China – Leshan Giant Buddha – 803 CE – 232 ft tall - This Buddha is the largest stone carving in the world, complete with a complex drainage system.

China (Tibet) – Potala Palace – 1645 CE – This 13-story structure with 1,000 rooms, 10,000 shrines, and 200,000 statues served as the winter palace of the Dalai Lama until 1959. Copper, poured into the foundation, protects against earthquakes.

Ethiopia – Underground Churches of Lalibela – 12th century – 11 connected churches were carved from a single rock, using aquifers, drainage ditches, and subterranean passageways, built after the Muslim conquest of Jerusalem. This site

is a spiritual pilgrimage for those who are Ethiopian Orthodox with approximately 100,000 visitors each year.

Greece – Parthenon – 432 BC – This Athenian temple, dedicated to the goddess Athena, was constructed with marble columns and lead metal connectors, protecting the iron from rust while also absorbing shocks from earthquakes.

Guatemala – El Mirador – 300 BC – 230 ft tall, 2,800,000 m³. This pre-Columbian Mayan settlement on 500,000 acres with 35 pyramids contains La Danta, the world's largest pyramid by volume.

India – Chand Baori – 800 CE – 62 ft deep – Constructed near the Thar Desert, the Chand Baori is one of the world's deepest stepwells with 3,500 zigzag steps descending 13 stories below the earth surface to provide water supply to the people.

Italy – Colosseum – 72 CE – This iconic Roman structure, capable of holding 80,000 spectators was constructed with travertine limestone, tuff, and brick. The colosseum is the largest amphitheater ever built.

Jordan – Petra – 300 BC – This former capitol of the Nabatean Kingdom, nicknamed 'Rose City', contains tombs and temples carved into iconic pink sandstone cliffs.

Mexico - Chichén Itzá - 8th – 12th century – This Mayan complex includes the Pyramid of Kukulkan, a massive Mesoamerican step pyramid, that dominates the ancient city. With sophisticated geometry and numerous carvings, the structure casts a shadow of a serpent descending the pyramid's stairway on the fall and spring equinoxes.

Mexico – Teotihuacan – 100 BC – Ancient urban pyramidal structures with temples and residences for 200,000 people.

Pakistan – Lost City of Mohenjo Daro – 3,000 BC – Planned Indus Valley community with wells, baths, and drainage system for 35,000 residents.

Peru - Machu Picchu – 1420 - 1532 CE – 7,970 ft. – A masterpiece in architecture and engineering, this Inca citadel was constructed with polished stone cut together without mortar. The site's advanced civil engineering design and construction include trails, buildings, water supply, canals, fountains, and terraces.

Peru – Sacsayhuamán (Saqsaywaman) – 1438-1471 CE – Elevation 12,142 ft - Precisely-fit stone-walled citadel built outside of the Incan capital of Cusco. The largest boulder weighs approximately 120 tons.

Sri Lanka – Jetavanaramaya – 273 CE – 400 ft – Buddhist stupas are mega-sized hemispherical brick structures that house earthly remains and sacred texts. The structures are protected against lightning, corrosion, and wear. Ironically, stupas predate Buddhism.

United Kingdom - Stonehenge - 3,000 BC – While iconic, little is known except its relationship to the solstice and possibly a burial ground.

FIRST COLLEGES TO TEACH CIVIL ENGINEERING

The first college to teach civil engineering (1741) was the Royal Military Academy in England. Meanwhile, in France, the Ecole des Ponts et Chaussees (National School of Bridges and Roads) opened to train civil engineers. In 1802, the U.S. Military Academy at West Point was established. In 1817, the Academy created a program to teach students how to construct bridges, roads, canals, and fortifications. Norwich University, founded in 1819, created its first civil engineering program. However, the first degree in civil engineering in the U.S. was conferred in 1835 at Rensselaer Polytechnic University in Troy, NY. Nora Stanton Blatch, Cornell University graduate in 1905, was the first woman to earn a civil engineering degree in the United States.

FIRST COLLEGES TO TEACH ENVIRONMENTAL ENGINEERING

Environmental engineering also has its origins in chemical engineering since pollutants, water testing, energy, and soil science require an understanding of chemistry. Initially, chemical engineering focused on industrial chemistry - medicine, munitions, and manufacturing. The field took shape at the University of Giessen, near Frankfurt Germany, where chemists trained and spread the knowledge of inorganic and organic processes. The publication of *Chemical Technology* in 1848 and an 1887 Manchester Technical School (later the University of Manchester) course in chemical engineering furthered the burgeoning field.

George E. Davis, considered the "father of chemical engineering", published his lectures on chemical engineering in the *Chemical Trade Journal*. These writings inspired Lewis M. Norton, professor at MIT, to offer his own chemical engineering course. Seven students graduated from MIT with a degree in chemical engineering in 1891. Frank H. Thorpe formed MIT's Department of Chemical Engineering and published the first chemical engineering textbook in 1898, *Outlines of Industrial Chemistry*. In 1904, Davis published A *Handbook of Chemical Engineering* in the UK.

Davis formed the Society of Chemical Industry in 1881 in the UK. In the United States, scientists created the first formal group of chemical engineers, American Institute of Chemical Engineers (AIChE), in 1908. These groups united chemists and engineers to develop more efficient and effective industrial processes, while also considering the impacts of new developments on the environment.

FORMALIZATION OF ENVIRONMENTAL ENGINEERING IN ABET

Before environmental engineering took hold, chemical engineering progressed as a discipline, joining the Accreditation Board for Engineering and Technology (ABET), originally founded in 1932 as the Engineers' Council for Professional Development (ECPD) to certify, approve, and oversee engineering departments and degrees. California Institute of Technology was the first chemical engineering program to be accredited. Presently, there are approximately 4,307 accredited engineering programs in 846 institutions and 41 countries. The current ABET-accredited programs in chemical engineering are listed in the back of this book.

Environmental engineering was not recognized as a distinct discipline by the Accreditation Board for Engineering and Technology (ABET) until 1965. Initially, environmental engineering was incorporated within civil engineering programs. The establishment of environmental engineering as an independent discipline

reflected the growing awareness of distinct environmental issues, particularly regarding waste management, water treatment, and air pollution. The changes in society's mindset, public discussions about climate change, and public health concerns opened the doors for more specialized education and research in conservation, sustainability, energy, pollution, and environmental hazards. These issues helped align academic programs more closely with the technology changes, humanity's challenges, industrial processes, and governmental regulations.

Meanwhile, minerals, metals, and new materials took centerstage as bottles, cans, paper products, and disposable appliances and technology required resources with environmental impacts. A pressing need emerged to envision sustainable materials, devices, and vehicles. Materials science gained increasing importance as a separate area of research, distinct from chemical, metals, and ceramic engineering.

Materials science did not gain widespread recognition until the late 20th century, the first ABET-accredited programs were accepted in 1936 under different names. For example, Carnegie Mellon University was accredited in Metallurgical Engineering and Materials Science in 1936, Penn State was accredited in Ceramic Science and Engineering in 1938, while Georgia Tech and the University of Washington were accredited in the closely related field of Ceramic Engineering in 1936 and 1942, respectively. Other early universities to be accredited in materials science include Case Western Reserve, Lehigh, the University of Michigan, and Washington State in 1936 and Purdue in 1941.

USING ENGINEERING METHODS TO AWE AND INSPIRE

Committed to solving complex societal challenges while constructing buildings, developing infrastructure, and producing efficient technologies, engineers invent the future with an eye to sustainability, energy conservation, and the environment. Innovations in technology, energy, clothing, wellness, and agriculture are rapidly changing daily life and lifestyles. One day, people will no longer put gas in a car or pick up an office telephone in much the same way as they no longer depress keys on a manual typewriter.

Quantum computing and nanotech biomaterials, aided by engineering innovations, will further advance society as robots perform lawn maintenance, body functions will be monitored by wearable devices, and waste will be readily adapted into usable alternatives. Our walls will become massive computer monitors, bathroom mirrors will have embedded televisions, and building materials will be stronger, thinner, and more durable than ever. Technological innovation is disrupting every facet of life. Thus, we live in a time when rapid change will require that we think differently. This moment is exciting!

You live at a critical juncture where 5G, 6G, and 7G will mesh with digital currencies and Metaverse spaces. Innovation is the solution to affordable housing, overcrowded cities, and land depletion. The future of humanity and all other living things on Earth (and soon outer space) depends on environmentally conscious engineers, architects, and city planners.

You will barely recognize our current existence by 2050. Much of that transformation will happen as a function of engineers who will design tomorrow's transportation corridors and skylines while ensuring efficiency, conservation, and sustainability. Harnessing alternative energy and artificial intelligence, engineers will imagine the future with the foresight and power to transform society into a place we want to live.

Materials scientists will collaborate with bioengineers and computer engineers to invent novel nanoelectronics, quantum dots, surgical tools, filiments, fibers, fabrics, wearable devices, cements, plastics, alloys, and renewable materials. Aerospace engineers will create transportation corridors on earth and in space while computer scientists transform device technologies and robotics with augmented and virtual realities. With efficiencies in transportation, manufacturing, automation, healthcare, and construction, our next-generation live-learn-work-evolve environment awaits.

A city's twinkling lights, dimmed after a long bustling day of work, retain their magic in a process that takes place around the dials of a timepiece. Like clockwork, urban centers electrify. The energy of people rushing to and fro may be hushed for now but will awaken soon enough. This process begins and ends in our living spaces where we, too, dim the lights in the evening and wipe our eyes in the morning, refreshed from our necessary moments of rest.

In workshops and labs, creativity is unleashed. Engineers are inspired to invent the future, blending vision and wonder with technological analysis. In class projects, students learn to overcome obstacles and invent what has not yet been imagined. Engineers set free the barriers of their mind's-eye and imagine what has yet to be considered.

Why? Change is inevitable. Barriers must be surmounted. Quick, sharp, and creative minds will lead the rapid transformation of society while resolving any problems along the way.

TRIFECTA OF SOCIOCULTURAL & TRANSFORMATIONAL CHANGE

The tsunami of uncertainty can be summed up in the trifecta of sociocultural and transformational progress.

1. Climate Change
2. Political Strife
3. Engineering Innovation

Overwhelming evidence portends dynamic changes on the horizon. Sea levels are rising. Social tensions rage in cities and countries. A wave of engineering advances are rapidly percolating in university and industrial research labs. You live and study at this most exciting, yet harrowing juncture. You can make a difference. Your role is to envision and create tomorrow today.

CHALLENGES AHEAD

Climate change is one of the most significant challenges facing materials science engineers today, particularly regarding infrastructure damage. According to the Environmental Protection Agency (EPA), while absolute sea levels are rising 0.12 – 0.14 inches per year, relative sea levels are not uniform. New York City has

578 miles of shoreline with most of its inhabitants within a mile of its waterfront. Planning agencies in New York are mitigating for "managed retreat". While sandbags, berms, dams, and barriers may work in the short term, city planners, architects, and engineers are working with agencies to mollify this problem.

The National Oceanic and Atmospheric Administration (NOAA) estimates the prognosis for Miami is worse. So, how can engineers help create entirely new cities in the wake of unprecedented flooding? In envisioning a new tomorrow and rebuilding the cities of today, engineers must prepare for climate change, population growth, delivery pipeline disruptions, and sustainable practices with innovative fuels, efficient energy, faster processing speeds, and cleaner industrial technologies that improve people's lives and livelihoods.

Furthermore, today's unsustainable waste practices must shift toward reuse and repurpose options which pose opportunities and challenges for engineers. For many, financial and physical security rank next in priority next to health and wellness as global citizens protect their living, learning, and working environments. As a result, college academic programs offer a myriad of ways to view today's safety and protection, while designing next-gen possibilities for a new tomorrow.

A FEW FACTS TO CONSIDER

- Poverty, inflation, war, and disease increase global food insecurity.
- Africa's population is expected to double by 2050.
- Supply chains, transportation mechanisms, and limiting factors of nonrenewable resources are likely to threaten populations.
- Oceans are dying due to overfishing, pollution, ocean warming, acidification.
- Sea levels will rise. Many islands and some U.S. cities are likely to be partially underwater by 2050. According to NOAA, Miami's sea level is 8 inches higher now than in 1950.
- Extreme weather events like droughts, heatwaves, hurricanes, tornadoes, cyclones will increase causing water scarcity, flooding, and deaths.
- Agriculture will be impacted by climate change limiting food supply in some regions and displacing millions of people.
- Global angst, propaganda mechanisms, and philosophical divisions threaten to widen the fissure between people.
- Since the beginning of time, societies relied on wood, stone, iron, steel, minerals, cement, and now plastics, semiconductors, nanomaterials, and quantum dots. Yet, today, nations compete and even go to war over raw materials. The competition is likely to intensify.

HOPE AND PRAGMATISM

An engineer's work exists at the intersection of hope and pragmatism. While resolving transportation and mechanization problems, engineers will develop stronger, lighter, and more efficient materials, functionality, processes, tools, and designs. The possibilities are limitless. Engineers harness the raw materials for foods, medicines, energy, and technology necessary for civilization's future. Begin this journey by stepping into the possibilities of today and developing the augmented realities of tomorrow.

There are numerous directions you can take with an educational foundation in engineering. The engineering programs available at the universities profiled in this book offer varied paths to licensure, design, planning, development, and management.

The future is yours. Choose the path that makes sense for your life goals. The information contained within this book will lead you on your way and, hopefully, inspire you as a leader to empower others along their educational pathway.

The ideal engineer is a composite ... He is not a scientist,
he is not a mathematician, he is not a sociologist or a writer;
but he may use the knowledge and techniques of any or all of these disciplines
in solving engineering problems.

— **Nathan W. Dougherty**

CHAPTER 2

EXPECTATIONS, TRAINING, & COMPETITIONS

"A nation that destroys its soils destroys itself."

– **Franklin D. Roosevelt**

The environment faces serious challenges. Today, strong forces push society toward an uncertain future. Competing pressures, economic interests, and human consumption tug and pull on the planet's limited land, air, and resources. Yet, expanding populations demand more. As harmful gases are emitted from fossil fuels, livestock, and industrial manufacturing, they absorb infrared radiation from the planet's surface, trapping heat in the Earth's atmosphere. Rays return to the planet like those trapped in a greenhouse.

Thus, greenhouse gases like carbon dioxide threaten the planet. The resulting increase in the Earth's temperature and change in climate outcomes produce extreme weather conditions, rising sea levels, and loss of biodiversity. Furthermore, the resulting outcomes impact human health, water systems, and agricultural output while disrupting ecosystems and economies.

The greenhouse effect and changing climate patterns impact society in various ways, including heat waves that affect human health and agricultural productivity. Extreme flooding threatens countries globally. Moreover, rising sea levels threaten coastal communities. Intense and frequent natural disasters like hurricanes and floods strain infrastructure, communities, and ecosystems, necessitating adaptation and mitigation strategies to cope with the evolving climate challenges.

Even if you never have the chance to see or touch the ocean, the ocean touches you with every breath you take, every drop of water you drink, every bite you consume. Everyone everywhere is inextricably connected to and utterly dependent upon the existence of the sea.

– **Sylvia Earle**

COMMON GREENHOUSE GASES

Carbon dioxide (CO_2) – Carbon dioxide is emitted during the burning of fossil fuels and forest biomass, as well as during decomposition when trees are cut down and left to rot. This leads to a reduction in CO_2 absorption due to deforestation.

Methane (CH_4) – Methane gas is released into the atmosphere through various sources such as livestock farming, fossil fuels, and waste decay in landfills.

Nitrous oxide (N_2O) – Nitrous oxide is a byproduct of fertilizer use, industrial chemical production, and the burning of fossil fuels.

Fluorinated Gases – Nitrogen trifluoride, perfluorocarbons, sulfur hexafluoride, and hydrofluorocarbons are commonly used in manufacturing and refrigeration.

SOCIETY'S ENVIRONMENTAL CHALLENGES

1. Climate Change
2. Greenhouse Gases
3. Deforestation
4. Manufacturing/Industry
5. Plant/Animal/Land Use
6. Urbanization
7. Fossil Fuel Extraction
8. Transportation
9. Coal Emissions
10. Waste/Trash
11. Plastics
12. Hydrofluorocarbons
13. Water Quality/Pollution
14. Air Pollution
15. Renewable Energy
16. Health Hazards
17. Sustainability/Conservation
18. Technology Disposal
19. Biodiversity/Nature
20. Recycling/Reuse/Repurpose

ENVIRONMENTAL SCIENCES

Environmental sciences play a crucial role in addressing the challenges of greenhouse gas emissions, climate change, and sustainability. By developing innovative technologies and practices, environmental scientists aim to reduce greenhouse gas emissions, manage waste, protect water and air, and remediate contaminated environments. Today's students generate innovative solutions in renewable energy, pollution control, and resource management, which are essential in mitigating climate change's impact and safeguarding the planet for future generations. Environmental engineers and scientists build resilient societies that can adapt and thrive in a changing climate.

With environmental issues at the forefront of society's consciousness, those in social science, engineering, geology, architecture, agriculture, energy production, transportation, and manufacturing seek eco-friendly solutions. Environmental engineers and scientists search for answers to prevent the rise in temperatures, increase in water levels, mismanagement of land, hazardous impact of waste, and depletion of the Earth's non-renewable resources. These interdisciplinary fields encompass public health, waste management, sustainable development, and the protection of natural resources. By working together, policymakers and scientists will create a tomorrow that thrives for millennia to come.

Environmental scientists aid in the production of humanity's food and water supply while supporting the industries that produce the housing, infrastructure, and technologies we need to live. Environmental science departments are closely linked to those in policy, chemistry, and engineering in many colleges. Additionally, courses in environmental management and sustainability are found in nearly every environmental science program. Environmental scientists work with environmental engineers to design clean energy systems, improve building performance, and encourage sustainable business practices.

Alternative energy is another hot topic among environmental scientists. Humanity relies on energy for nearly every aspect of life, from heating and cooling to powering technology, machinery, and transportation. Yet, whether the energy is dug from the ground, powered on a grid, or captured from natural sources, more efficient, effective, and sustainable options are necessary.

POLLUTION & WASTE

Pollution, waste, and contaminants may contribute to the greatest overall destruction. Environmental Protection Agency data show that approximately 35% of waste results from the use of paper or cardboard, 12% from landscaping disposal items, and 11% from food waste. The remaining 42% comes from plastic, metal, glass, and textiles. Across the world, waste and waste disposal pose a significant problem. The World Bank estimates that 2.24 billion tonnes of waste was created in 2020, with 3.88 billion tonnes in 2050. Below are the twenty countries that produce the greatest amount of yearly per capita waste.

1. United States – 25,163.8 kg
2. Armenia – 17,470.1 kg
3. Ukraine – 11,306.2 kg
4. Japan – 4,470.8 kg
5. China – 3,643.1 kg
6. Australia – 3,158.3 kg
7. Montenegro – 2,265.4 kg
8. Norway – 2,130.7 kg
9. Switzerland – 2,020.4 kg
10. Thailand – 1,986.0 kg
11. Malta – 1,978.0 kg
12. Iceland – 1,705.5 kg
13. Iran – 1,696.1 kg
14. Kuwait – 1,653.7 kg
15. Qatar – 1,554.6 kg
16. Malaysia – 1,553.6 kg
17. Albania – 1,477.7 kg
18. Jordan – 1,452.3 kg
19. Algeria – 1,375.7 kg
20. Egypt – 1,311.7 kg

COMPETITIONS AND PRIZES

In addition to school projects and challenge opportunities, there are numerous K-12 science competitions students can pursue.

1. ***Regeneron ISEF - International Science & Engineering Fair*** – Started in 1950, this competition is one of the largest international high school science competitions for students to present their research and discoveries and win one of hundreds of prizes in multiple categories. Grand Awards – 17 ISEF categories; each has first, second, third, and fourth place. There are also special awards given by public and private organizations.

2. ***NASA Competitions*** - Cube Quest, Break the Ice, Deep Space Food, and Watts on the Moon – These offer prizes totaling $5,000,000 to teams.

3. ***Google Science Fair*** – First launched in 2011, this online science and engineering competition is open to students 13 to 18 who pose a question, develop a hypothesis, and conduct research. Regional finalists compete to be global finalists. These students are invited to Google's headquarters for the final round. Prizes are given in different age-specific and thematic categories.

4. ***Regeneron Science Talent Search*** – Started in 1942 by Westinghouse and later Intel, Regeneron continues the legacy as the oldest U.S. science talent competition. From 300 scholar semifinalists, 40 finalists are chosen to present their research in Washington, D.C. where they compete for awards.

5. ***3M Young Scientist Challenge*** – Sponsored by 3M and administered by Discovery Education, this competition for middle school students has been in existence since 1999. Students create an innovation to improve people's lives. Ten finalists are chosen based on communication, creativity, originality, potential, and a short video explaining their project. Finalists are paired with 3M scientists who mentor them through the development process. One national winner is selected.

6. ***ExploraVision Science Competition (Toshiba & the National Science Teaching Association)*** – Started in 1992, this is one of the world's largest K-12 science competitions. Students use futuristic thinking and innovative solutions to develop and explore technology that may exist in 20 years. National, regional, and honorable mention winners are selected each year in four grade-level categories.

7. **Broadcom MASTERS (Math, Applied Science, Technology, and Engineering for Rising Stars)** – This prestigious middle school science and engineering competition, in existence since 2011, gives prizes for innovative STEM projects and teamwork. Thirty finalists are selected to participate in a team-based, hands-on STEM competition which showcases the most practical and extraordinary science fair projects.

8. **Junior Science and Humanities Symposia (JSHS)** – Established in 1958 by the U.S. Army, Navy, and Air Force, this program challenges high school students to conduct STEM research in regional events. Winners advance to the national competition. Students present original research to professionals. The winners receive scholarships.

9. **Conrad Challenge** – This competition was started in 2008 by the Conrad Foundation, continuing the legacy of former astronaut Charles "Pete" Conrad Jr. (third to walk on the Moon). This multi-phase competition focuses on innovation and entrepreneurship. Teams of 2-5 high school students pitch ideas to solve global challenges. Successful teams are invited to the Innovation Summit to present their ideas to a panel of judges. Winners who develop a viable, scalable, solution with real-world impact span a range of discoveries.

10. **Lexus Eco Challenge** – The goal of this middle/high school Land & Water Challenge and Air & Climate Challenge is to develop and implement real-world environmental solutions. Sixteen winning teams (8 from middle school and 8 from high school) are awarded prizes and participate in the Final Challenge, where the grand prize winners are selected.

11. **Shell Science Lab Challenge** – In 2010, the Shell Oil Company began sponsoring this contest, administered by the National Science Teaching Association for middle and high school science teachers who approach science in an innovative way. Approximately 18 winners receive a lab makeover with equipment and resources.

12. **Microsoft Imagine Cup Junior** – Introduced in 2020, this technology and innovation competition for high school students was created as part of Microsoft's broader Imagine Cup for university students. This junior level seeks to encourage students to pursue technology and computer science by developing global solutions for social impact. Winners are selected by their participation and development of technology like machine learning, virtual reality, artificial intelligence, and augmented reality.

13. **Samsung Solve for Tomorrow** – Established in 2010, this contest for middle and high school students encourages students to use STEM solutions to address real-world issues. State winners are selected and then national finalists are chosen to receive prizes, technology, and resources.
14. **BioGENEius Challenge** – This internationally recognized competition for high school students started in the early 1990s to focus on STEM solutions to biotechnology problems. Categories include Healthcare, Agriculture-Biotechnology, and Industrial-Environmental Biotechnology. Winners are chosen in each category.
15. **eCYBERMISSION** – In 2002, the U.S. Army Educational Outreach Program began sponsoring this online STEM competition for middle school teams that propose a solution to a real-world challenge. Along with regional winners in each grade level (6,7,8, and 9) with one national winner.
16. **Genius Olympiad** – Established in 2011, this international high school project competition coordinated by the Terra Science Education Foundation focuses on environmental issues. Based in New York, students compete worldwide in areas of Science, Visual and Performing Arts, Writing, Business, and Robotics. Awards are given in each category.
17. **Moody's Mega Math (M3) Challenge** – M3, started in 2005, is a mathematics competition for high school juniors and seniors. Over a 14-hour period, teams of students use models to solve real-world challenges. The top four to six teams are awarded scholarships. Typically held in March, students have 14 hours to submit their solutions.
18. **American Rocketry Challenge** – This is the world's largest student rocket contest. Started in 2002 and sponsored by the Aerospace Industries Assn and the National Assn of Rocketry, this Design-Build-Fly rocketry contest for middle and high school students is designed to increase interest in STEM subjects. Typically, the top 100 teams are invited to the National Finals where prizes are awarded. The American Institute of Aeronautics & Astronautics holds Design-Build-Fly contests on the collegiate level.
19. **FIRST Robotics Competition (FRC)** – Started in 1992, FIRST (For Inspiration and Recognition of Science & Technology) sponsors the international high school FRC. Teams design, build, and program robots for competitions, promoting education, teamwork, and innovation at different levels.

20. ***International Olympiad on Astronomy & Astrophysics (IOAA)*** – The annual IOAA international high school competition started in 2007. Recently, 52 countries competed. National teams of up to five members (two team leaders) are selected by the participating country, typically from its national competition. The IOAA includes theoretical, observational, and practical exams. Individual and team awards are presented.

21. ***International Physics Olympiad (IPhO)*** – This high school competition, started in 1967, recently hosted students from 90 countries. Each country selects its national team of up to five members (two team leaders) in internal competitions. Team selection process varies by country. The IPhO includes theoretical and experimental exams that test knowledge and problem-solving. Individual and team awards are presented.

22. ***International Chemistry Olympiad (IChO)*** - This annual high school competition started in 1968 with three European teams and now represents about 90 countries. Each participating country selects its national team of up to four members (two team leaders) through its internal competition process. Team selection process varies by country. The IChO includes a 5-hour laboratory practical exam and a 5-hour written theoretical and experimental exam. Individual and team awards are presented.

23. ***International Biology Olympiad (IBO)*** – Started in 1990, more than a million students begin the trek through their country's individual competitions to participate in this prestigious event with more than 75 countries participating with four contestants in their National Biology Olympiad's local, regional, and national competition rounds.

24. ***American Society of Human Genetics Essay Contest*** – This is a high school writing competition on topics of human genetics (no more than 750 words). For example, the 2024 question said, "Provide an example of how the interplay of genetics and environment can shape human health."

25. ***Bioethics Essay Contest*** – This STEM writing competition allows high school students to explore ethical issues in science and technology.

26. ***National Bioethics Bowl*** – This U.S. intercollegiate competition debates ethical issues in medicine, biotechnology, and healthcare. Teams of five compete in rounds where each team is given a case and presents arguments to the other team and judges.

27. ***Engineer Girl Writing Contest*** – This writing contest, sponsored by the National Academy of Engineering, is primarily for girls and focuses on how engineering impacts the world.

28. ***Young Naturalist Awards (American Museum of Natural History)*** – This essay competition for middle and high school students is an inquiry-based approach to scientific research and writing.
29. ***Ocean Awareness Contest (Bow Seat Ocean Awareness Program)*** – This high school art, writing, and advocacy competition invites students to present their art, research, and essays to win awards.
30. ***NASA Scientist for a Day Essay Contest*** – Students are challenged to write an essay about a topic related to space and planetary science.
31. ***Living Rainforest International Schools Essay Competition*** – This essay contest challenges students to write about a topic involving sustainable living and human's relationship with nature.
32. ***Society for Technical Communication High School Writing Contest*** – This contest challenges students to write essays on topics regarding science and technology.

IMPORTANCE & VALUE OF COMPETITIONS

Competitions not only inspire new ideas but they they develop skills in adaptability, creativity, and teamwork. Students must consider factors such as safety, functionality, sustainability, efficiency, and viability. Students learn how to create a plan, organize a set of procedures, and implement a project. In math and science competitions, students acquire vast amounts of knowledge.

Similarly, environmental engineers must incorporate diverse topics and consider mitigating circumstances that may confound or alter a plan or solution. New tools and techniques are ideated that help companies develop aesthetic, efficient, and utilitarian technologies. Each new group implements unique project designs, programming strategies, management methods, and evaluation process. The point is not to copy previous teams but to build upon the seeds of success.

ACADEMIC ROAD TO LICENSURE

Engineering applies mathematics and science to the creative exploration of solutions to real-world problems. Bridging physics, chemistry, geology, and environmental science with situational challenges, engineers apply their knowledge as idea-generators and inquisitive problem solvers. Advanced topics in mathematics and physics provide the foundation for future coursework.

Bachelor's-level university engineering training programs require a minimum of 45 engineering-focused semester hours. The master's level requires one to two additional years. With the need to master concepts across a broad set of subjects, continually expanded due to technology innovation and regulations, engineers must develop numerous proficiencies. Starting with theoretical underpinnings, students consider societal needs and emerging consequences. College workshops and labs offer the space to imagine and invent unique designs.

After gaining experiences from internships, co-ops, and working on job sites, engineers can apply for the Professional Engineering (PE) license. Only licensed engineers can take on higher roles in project management for public projects. With this licensure, professional engineers may also gain credentials and certifications in a variety of specialty areas to enhance their abilities, work on more complex projects, and take senior-level positions.

Thus, engineers must balance multiple, and often conflicting objectives. Safety, budget, and policy knowledge are required to determine the feasibility of overall plans. Taking the lead, professional engineers are responsible for technical knowledge, troubleshooting, and contingency considerations. Working with city and regional planners, engineers are part of a larger group of experts including surveyors, project managers, and construction-site developers.

Project management is another focal point of an engineer's work. On the job, bottlenecks occur due to environmental, geological, and societal challenges that may impact a coordinated plan. Since professional engineers sign off on design and construction documents, they must be organized, monitoring, evaluating, and ensuring compliance during the construction phase.

Furthermore, engineers often coordinate complex sets of activities on multiple projects simultaneously. Thus, engineers must be able to multitask with several teams as a problem-solver and a decision-maker on different job sites where the specifications have different requirements, possibly even in different countries.

Effective communication is a foundational requirement for the job. Translating complicated scientific information to individuals with a wide range of literacy and technical expertise on all levels of a project is essential. Thus, written and oral communication skills must include the ability to modulate appropriate language for machine operators, surveyors, construction managers, elected officials, urban planners, architects, and engineering team members.

ENGINEERING PROGRAM LEARNING OBJECTIVES

Communication – Engineers must present clear, engaging writing and speaking that transmits information appropriately and effectively to those with no technical or scientific background. However, effectively translating complex scientific topics into written text is not as easy as it sounds. Listening is equally important since team members may offer valuable suggestions to complete tasks. By encouraging team projects, college engineering programs train students to communicate with a wide range of audiences in group presentations, poster sessions, and outcome delivery.

Teamwork - Engineering projects not only provide opportunities to develop effective group communication, but also the necessary skill of team membership, leadership, and inclusivity. As such, students get to know each team member's strengths and weaknesses while establishing group goals, dividing tasks, and creating a plan for the delivery of performance outcomes.

Creativity – Engineers must think differently. In the development of new products, creativity is essential to envision and create new and better options. Often engineers must rely on workarounds using existing equipment. Collaboration stimulates ideas, offering new avenues to accomplish the same task.

Problem Solving – Students identify problems in society that need to be resolved. With a solutions-oriented approach, engineers formulate best-fit alternatives by applying lessons learned in math, science, and engineering classes. Furthermore, since multiple options may achieve an optimal solution given critical variables and project specifications, consensus is necessary.

Analysis – Students are taught design thinking for functionality, feasibility, and aesthetics while also ensuring factors like health, safety, environment, and costs.

Engineers rely on holistic analysis, experimentation, and testing. To improve judgment, engineers must understand, harness, and apply statistical analysis and data-informed decision-making.

Ethics – Engineers have an ethical responsibility to society and a professional responsibility to clients. Thus, engineers must use good judgment and transparent communication, while also considering political and societal consequences.

Lifelong Learning – Students soon discover that their knowledge and skills are quickly outdated. From the moment a student begins college until the moment they graduate, technological transformations take place that require information renewal like learning new software and using state-of-the-art materials. Yet, like a time warp, some industry projects or processes may use decades-old equipment.

DESIGN SCIENCE OF ENGINEERING

As an engineering student who will play a role in inventing the future, you should expect to spend long hours developing your projects. The synergy and energy of collaboration can be electrifying as projects take shape and masterful designs propel ideas to a whole new level. However, there is much to learn by widening your scope regarding society, innovation, and trends.

Despite the structure of science, creativity is fundamental to the work. Ultimately, the jigsaw puzzle of chemical, physical, and software elements, magnificently blending art and science, will seamlessly fit together, connecting its moving parts. Yet, with a limited timeframe and compact lab space, clarity and design have their bounds.

You will learn how to manage time and quickly evaluate the status of your projects. Collaboration can be both challenging and exhilarating at the same time. Each member must listen attentively and conceptualize options in 2-D and 3-D space while proposing ideas, accepting alternative viewpoints, and creating a clear line of communication. By discussing opportunities for improvement, pitfalls in design elements, and financial and spatial limitations, the team can efficiently and effectively cooperate to craft the best representation of the design.

Within the engineering design process, students devise systems, components, or processes given a specified set of constraints. Realizing that customers provide terms and conditions that need to be fulfilled, engineers must budget time, costs, and materials as required. Engineering, thus, is both a creative and analytical process. Coursework leads students from the basic sciences to solutions-oriented development and the implementation of engineering design.

Students learn to spot opportunities where problems need to be overcome. Then, by exploring alternatives and evaluating multiple solutions, students identify the optimum plan to remedy the problem. The process requires considering risk-reward trade-offs. Some considerations might include LEED (Leadership in Energy and Environmental Design) rating requirements and the ability to accomplish the specified objective within the legal requirements of regulation, functionality, and accessibility.

LEED (LEADERSHIP IN ENERGY AND ENVIRONMENTAL DESIGN) RATINGS: CERTIFIED (40-49 POINTS); SILVER (50-59 POINTS); GOLD (60-79 POINTS); AND PLATINUM (80+ POINTS)

As students infuse environmental consciousness into society and research centers develop stronger and more durable materials, engineers inject noticeable improvements in design, efficiency, and sustainability. LEED projects undergo a systematic verification and review process through a 'green' rating system, awarding points corresponding to a LEED certification level. Engineers may become involved with one or more of the seven LEED areas of concentration: Sustainable Sites, Water Efficiency, Energy & Atmosphere, Materials & Resources, Indoor Environmental Quality, Innovation in Design Process, and Regional Priority.

THE INCREASING IMPORTANCE OF MATERIALS SCIENCE

Chemistry may seem dry, pardon the pun, but there is an immense amount of research transforming tomorrow's materials into those that are lighter, thinner, stronger, conductive, and absorbent. Carbon is one of the most intriguing elements in the research sphere today. When graphene grabbed the attention of scientists and global citizens, researchers clamored to discover its many uses.

Graphene is a one-atom-thick sheet of carbon that conducts heat and electricity along its plane, absorbs light of all visible wavelengths, is 100 times stronger than the strongest steel, and nearly transparent. The possibilities for graphene are endless, including building materials, electronics, medicine, transportation, and military uses. Companies have already begun using innovations in material science to construct the foundations of buildings, fix damaged structures, and design computer screens that lay flat like wallpaper on your wall. You could be part of some very big and potentially profitable innovations.

In civil and environmental engineering, one way graphene is consistently used today is in concrete additives for construction. Graphene increases strength, reduces carbon footprints, and increases the longevity of finished products. With graphene's strength and ability to decrease a structure's permeability, completely new fabrications can be made. Graphene acts as a mechanical support and a catalyst surface for initial hydration reactions, better bonding, and nanoscale foundation for durability and corrosion resistance.

In 2010, two Russian scientists were awarded the Nobel Prize in Physics for their discovery and groundbreaking research in graphene. This nanomaterial offers high tensile strength, electrical conductivity, and transparency. Earlier, in 1996, two Americans and one British researcher won the Nobel Prize in Chemistry for their discoveries regarding another carbon-based molecule, fullerene.

Fullerene, C_{60}, a hollow cage of atoms or cylindrical mesh, has similarly fascinating properties with a tremendous number of possible uses including nanotubes, nanorods, and other nanotechnologies like tumor therapy. Presently researchers believe that C_{60} is not only an antioxidant, but the molecule has healing properties that may slow down aging, boost immunity, increase energy, reduce wrinkles, inhibit fat cell production, and provide stronger mental capacity.

OPPORTUNITIES TO ENGINEER SOCIETY'S FUTURE

The world faces significant environmental, transportation and technological challenges. Intelligent, human-centered design thinking is essential to resolve living, learning, technological, and supply chain problems. Smart, broad-minded engineers gain the multidimensional training necessary for research, rendering, and fabrication. In turn, they will produce, test, and present solutions.

Remember, everything in our sphere exists in a system. Interfaces and functionality must be compatible. Thus, engineers must be aware of people's surroundings and what might support or interfere with functionality. For example, while drones may eventually repair supply chain issues, software glitches, delivery errors, and nefarious instigators must also be considered. Weather, like sand or dust storms, hurricanes, tornadoes, or heat, can also cause significant problems. Nanomaterial medical technologies may save a person's life, but will the materials be rejected by or interfere with natural human body processes?

Additionally, what solutions will make industrial work safer, cleaner, healthier, or more productive? Considering sustainability, are the newly-developed products environmentally friendly? In metal fabrication workshops, you may mold, laser-cut, and weld material after rapid prototyping. In a modeling shop, you may experiment with materials like foam, plastic, and wood. A woodshop assignment may require you to reinvent an ergonomic massage chair, creating code to include safety specifications.

On a transportation engineering project, you may use design software to convert sketches and orthographic drawings into renderings. You may create innovative motion-sensored toys for children, delivering your vision and prototype in an industry presentation. You might even translate your ideas into the next nifty and popular toy.

From your first-year experiences to sponsored workshops, college research labs are abuzz with activity. You will survey consumer needs, translating proposals from concepts to physical products using aesthetic appeal and engineering design. There are no limits to what you can imagine.

For your senior project or capstone, you might choose to create drug delivery systems, fuel cells, organic photonics, cancer diagnoses, quantum dots, or laser-sensing systems. Projects might include the super-propulsion of insect urination to discover how to expel water from smart-watches, anti-microbial adhesive properties in cicadas, and synthetic nanoparticles to stop internal bleeding.

You will also need to know the law. In patenting your inventions, you must be extremely detailed, while also mastering the nuances of intellectual property. College classes will push you into the deep end, but you will learn how to swim using your instincts and problem-solving skills to make products more functional and attractive. Ultimately, you will produce your unique vision and improve society.

Emerging technologies, UX design, and software adaptations will force you to swim faster to say ahead of the next wave of new tools coming your way. Virtual Reality (VR), Augmented Reality (AR), Artificial Intelligence (AI), and machine learning opportunities are here and they are taking society by storm.

Lean into AI's potential. The opportunities are astounding, swiftly intensifying innovation. A tsunami of changes are on the horizon that will smother those who ignore the rapidly rising tide. Research and development in next-gen uses captivate the minds and attentions of students, faculty, and independent researchers. Full force innovation and implementation are right around the corner.

Surf on the wave's crest!

NEVER-ENDING FASCINATION

You will study history, social structures, and computer science while building eco-friendly tools, machinery, energy products, and vehicles. By learning variations in local, state, national, and international policy, you will discover that every region holds its unique opportunities and challenges. Furthermore, restrictions can be a big factor in the success of a project. Securing materials, mitigating obstacles, and obtaining permits can be impediments or open doors to new possibilities.

The journey you are taking will have its ups and downs, but you will be filled with stories to tell for the rest of your life. Your education may also include unpredictable events. Pitfalls may lay in your path. Since you have endured a pandemic and the repercussions of a war, you are imbued with a few doses of resilience.

Even so, your engineering studies will test and retest your mettle. Your science courses and laboratory projects provide you with much to learn in a short amount of time. You are embarking on a thrilling, demanding, and disciplined pursuit. You will work with extremely skilled and brilliant students who participated in summer programs since elementary school and also took courses, workshops, and individual training in programming, engineering, and technical drawing each year.

Some classmates have interned in engineering firms and will blow you away with their abilities. However, rarely are there engineering students equally skilled in all areas. Some of your work will be a team effort where everyone will contribute what they know. You will too. Some students will be amazingly talented. Do not let their abilities bring you down or make you feel as if you are not good enough.

You will add your element and learn more during college. Besides, your enthusiasm for engineering will show through in your work and effort. Recognizing your potential, commitment, and attitude, people will be awed at your creations as you also step back to appreciate your work.

CHAPTER 3
ACADEMIC PREPARATION & CAREER OPTIONS

"Water is the best of all things."

– **Pindar**

Studying engineering will challenge you in multiple ways. You will never be bored. You will use design software and prepare models using prototyping machinery. You will work together with others while also spending long hours working alone. Engineering is not for the faint of heart. You have to want this and work hard at each project. However, If you like drawing, modeling, building, fixing, and solving problems, you will get plenty of practice.

EXPECT TO PULL A FEW ALL-NIGHTERS.

You will not be alone resolving last minute problems on the nights before projects are due. Collaboration is at the core of engineering. You will work on projects with people in your major, but you are likely to consult with students in chemical engineering, civil engineering, electrical engineering, industrial engineering, and materials science. You will also need to be practically obsessed with inspecting fine details since the smallest crack, melted sheath, or defective metal piece will hang your project out to dry. Plan ahead!

If you fail to plan, you are planning to fail.

- Benjamin Franklin

ACADEMIC PREPARATION

The moment is now. You are full STEAM ahead on a course toward engineering mastery. To gain admission you must be smart in science, analytical in math, and talented in design. Even if the admissions requirements do not demand that you have experience in robotics, laboratory work, 3-D printing, or engineering design, you should prepare with summer activities or school year projects since many of your future classmates will have dabbled in research projects and engineering.

Students should develop preliminary skills before applying. Admissions committees may find it difficult to justify selecting an applicant without research experience, summer engineering programs, or computer programming skills. Applicants often take two years of coding, interned with an engineering firm, dabbled in robotics, participated in an engineering magnet program, worked in a lab, entered engineering contests, and/or competed in hack-a-thons. While engineering may sound fun and offer a high income, it takes real work and certain skills are necessary.

Plan for your future now. Some applicants have competed in bridge-building, egg drops, paper skyscraper constructions, robotics clubs, concrete canoe events, solar oven competitions, rope and wood bridge contests, engine design, automobile construction, solar car racing, or water balloon challenges. High school students must build solid computational and critical thinking skills. AP Physics, AP Chemistry, and AP Calculus are almost always a prerequisite. More is better. However, you must also be a talented and creative thinker. High school students must build solid computational and critical thinking skills. AP Physics, AP Chemistry, and AP Calculus are almost always a prerequisite. More is better. However, you must also be a talented and creative thinker.

Talent is only the beginning!

HARDWARE AND SOFTWARE SKILLS

You will spend significant time on laptop computers and digitized machinery. The more you know, the better prepared you will be. Computer science classes in high school, community college, or summer programs are extremely valuable. Hardware and machinery classes are a definite plus.

You will benefit from taking classes in graphic design, CAD, or robotics. You are entering a future where AI, AR, VR, and machine learning will require greater technology skills than applicants ten years ago when most engineers created 2-D renderings that were difficult to visualize. Yet, as you enter college, technology's rapid advancements will transform from primarily 2-D drawings to primarily 3-D virtual reality graphics or holograms.

VISUALIZE, COMMUNICATE, EXECUTE

The promise of 5G, 6G, and 7G combined with artificial intelligence will advance engineering in revolutionary rather than evolutionary ways. Computing power, many times faster than today, will allow for quick permutations of design options and animations never before possible. Teams will collaborate, contributing data and graphs to holograms of disrupted environments, mechanical systems in vehicles, and biomedical technologies that detect cancer.

Clearly visualized 3-D animations using virtual reality will allow foremen and customers to digitally walk through a manufacturing facility, power plant, or wastewater treatment facility. Augmented reality will add to this experience by providing the viewer a user experience, possibly, one day, in the Metaverse.

These synchronous and asynchronous environments can be fully automated with computer design and programming tools. Groups will adapt designs in quick iterations, allowing for a near-real visualization of the physical model as each team member analyzes the form and function without being physically present.

Implementation of a design or experiment, can be witnessed and managed in real time, since every aspect will be computerized and visualized without the necessity of manual paper and audio call updates. Automated processes will be more efficient and effective without the necessity of frequent in-person site visits.

A 3-D PRINTER IN EVERY SCHOOL

While 3-D printing machines were initially developed in the 1980s for rapid prototyping, more than two decades ago, the broader public got a glimpse of a desktop model by MakerBot, a company, that envisioned a 3-D printer in every home. More than a hundred thousand guests at the 2012 Consumer Electronics Show (CES) witnessed the creation of plastic parts printed for the first time. CES is held in Las Vegas each January.

As a future industry member committed to cutting edge ideas, I recommend attending CES as soon as you can to view products not yet on the market. The show is three days of tantalizing inspiration for the maker in you. Nevertheless, what started as an expensive novelty, Stratasys, changed the market focus of the 3-D printing machines when it purchased MakerBot and realigned its sales and distribution strategy toward the technology and education markets.

By 2024, almost every engineering school had 3-D printers in their fabrication labs. At one point or another, while studying engineering, 3-D printing will come into play. Fabrication projects will likely include vehicle parts, heating and cooling systems, semiconductor chips, glass panels, furniture, biomaterials, prosthetics, human organs, and robotic arms for surgeons to conduct hands-free surgery.

You may also be asked to design machinery using filament in a wide variety of colors with matte, silk, shiny, or transparent and finishes resembling wood, cardboard, and an assortment of metals. Some filaments even glow in the dark while others change color based on temperature. Imagine the extraordinary possibilities.

COMPELLING REASONS TO STUDY ENGINEERING

1. Freedom of creative expression and scientific investigation
2. Mind explosion of possibilities for research and development
3. Desire to experiment and bring cutting edge ideas to fruition
4. Keen understanding of science and math, undaunted by tough questions
5. Love for problem-solving in a fast-paced, dynamic environment
6. Interest in learning new technologies and computer software
7. Desire to work with groups toward a common goal
8. Inquisitive hunger to test, shape, mold, and adapt materials
9. Emotional feeling that beckons you toward engineering design
10. Opportunity to turn your passion for engineering into a lifetime career

In this constantly changing profession, continually upgrading and evolving, environmental engineers must keep pace with rapid technology advancements. Today, new materials and power sources are swiftly reinventing what remained relatively constant for many decades. As a result, the ever-conscious, forward-thinking engineer will need to think five paces ahead.

Highly regarded professors who are often successful outside of academia will suggest ways for you to find your niche in engineering companies. A few brilliant faculty members whose experiences and knowledge are outdated, may not use the latest equipment or software since technology changes so rapidly.

You might get frustrated with their 'lack of knowledge'. Don't. The basic principles of engineering rarely change. Some well-connected college professors may even link you to their contacts for internships and jobs. Throughout college, you will discover your brand of professionalism along with a calling card of experiences that allow others to understand the talents and abilities you offer.

GAINING VALUABLE EXPERIENCES

Train now in the application of 3-D printing, holograms, virtual reality, and augmented reality spaces. Anything you learn now will help you be better prepared to immerse yourself in power generation, vehicle development, CAD, and computer science. Find avenues where you can experiment with new technologies, conduct research or volunteer at an engineering firm. Even if all you do is get coffee and volunteer without pay, you will gain invaluable lessons as you watch how companies tick. For now, you need experience navigating engineering spaces.

While engineering classes may not be offered at your school, summer camps, short-term programs, online training, maker clubs, and college classes will help you immensely along the way. Additional science classes would not hurt you either. Knowledge of chemistry and physics is imperative. The more you understand analytical tools, computational methods, and design options, the more you will be able to access the information necessary to be an engineering guru.

Additionally, there is no way to understate the value of basic understanding of robotics. Building, programming, and working with robots in high school will help you understand design thinking in college. Join or create a robotics team. See if there is a regional robotics club or league. If neither of these is available, find an avid robotics student and have them help you start from scratch.

Enjoy the experience.

Don't judge each day by the harvest you reap but by the seeds that you plant.

- Robert Louis Stevenson

"THERE IS NO ROYAL ROAD TO GEOMETRY" - EUCLID

When a student asked Euclid if there was an easier way to learn geometry, he cautioned that discipline and persistence are essential. Hard work is absolutely necessary. Additionally, there is no one way to succeed, just as there is no one way to enter the fields of engineering design and manufacturing.

You may choose to produce new technologies for a company, test devices, prepare drugs, devise biomaterials, or work on large integrated team-based projects. Either way, engineering design is a versatile skill. Related professional options with your skills include engineering management, entertainment, education, forestry, beach management, government policy, and much more. You could manage an engineering firm or create an innovative start-up with some friends. You might enjoy consulting or helping engineers market their services.

TEACHING, EDUCATION, AND TRAINING

Kids clamor to create. Their imaginations run wild with ideas. Self-expression and exploration through design and engineering offer people young and old the chance to put their ideas onto a paper, computer, or still/moving medium. LEGO projects, robotics, and scientific experiments offer limitless possibilities for the STEAM (Science, Technology, Engineering, Art, and Math) student. As a result, there are numerous jobs in private and public education.

Schools everywhere employ science teachers. Families hire math, science, engineering, and robotics tutors and coaches. College professors can make six-figure salaries for teaching and research while mentoring, publishing, and traveling to conferences. Of course, you would need to attend graduate school, but a master's degree in engineering or business would also take you to the next level of your profession. Furthermore, a doctorate opens additional doors if you choose the research route. There is so much to innovate that you will always stay engaged.

In 2024, there were 97,568 public and 32,461 private K-12 schools in the U.S. according to the National Center for Educational Statistics. In 2024, there were 10,375 K-12 public schools and another 3,840 private schools in California alone. On the college level, in 2024, there were 2,010 public and 4,230 private degree-granting higher education institutions. In California, there were 177 public colleges (including 10 UC campuses, 23 California State Universities, and 116 community colleges) and 521 private institutions of higher learning. Other major college hubs include New York with 439 colleges, Texas with 425, and Florida with 412.

Finally, private companies conduct workshops and hold training programs. You might choose to work for a management consulting firm like Bain, McKinsey, or BCG.

COLLABORATION IN ENVIRONMENTAL SCIENCES

Environmental scientists work in the field or at computers collecting data and analyzing results, while environmental engineers design processes. Environmental science is a field that considers the relationship and interaction between the environment and external factors, such as climate change, pollution, urbanization, industrialization, agriculture, deforestation, resource extraction, and waste generation. Environmental scientists collect and analyze data from the natural environment and humanity's development to assess risks.

Meanwhile, environmental engineers apply scientific principles. experimental procedures, and regulatory policy to develop methods that conserve the natural environment and rehabilitate land, sea, and sky. They employ technology like AI, GIS, CAD, and programming. Using physical, chemical, and biological methods along with socioeconomic, political, and demand-side considerations, environmental engineers help mitigate destructive forces.

Environmental scientists collect and analyze samples, data, and field research to inform their decision-making process, while engineers develop remediation plans. Both professions require a minimum of a bachelor's degree, though their academic approach differs in fieldwork and design. Environmental science programs typically include specializations in natural resources and conservation, while environmental engineering majors take more math and physics-based courses like fluid mechanics and thermodynamics. The median annual pay for environmental engineers is around $100,00, while environmental scientists earn about $20,000 less.

ENVIRONMENTAL STUDIES: EXPLORING THE RELATIONSHIPS BETWEEN HUMANS & NATURE

The field of environmental studies focuses on humanity's interaction with the environment. The major considers how human actions impact nature and centers around the relationships between people and their surroundings. Environmental studies is broad and interdisciplinary, embracing elements of diverse fields, including psychology, sociology, anthropology, and statistics. With expanding urbanization, population, and resource needs, this data-centered social science approach allows student researchers to better understand environmental changes using statistics, problem-solving, and critical reasoning. Experts in environmental studies collect data from nature, communities, and industry to evaluate risks arising from pollution and contamination. Experts evaluate soil quality, water supply, and other parameters.

COMPANIES FOCUSED ON ENVIRONMENTAL ENGINEERING

Environmental engineering companies play a critical role in addressing environmental challenges, including water and air pollution, waste management, and sustainability. These companies are engaged in various projects worldwide, from consulting on environmental impacts and sustainability to designing and implementing solutions for water treatment, waste management, and pollution control.

Environmentally-focused companies are instrumental in driving the transition towards a more sustainable energy future by innovating and expanding the use of alternative and renewable energy sources worldwide. Here are 15 companies that specialize in various aspects of environmental engineering and consulting:

AECOM – Headquartered in Dallas, Texas (relocated from Los Angeles), this company's projects include One World Trade Center, Port of Los Angeles Waterfront, and Mercedes Benz Stadium in Atlanta. The diverse group of approximately 52,000 employees includes infrastructure consultants, sustainable project designers, and innovation experts working in the areas of clean water, energy, and environmental restoration.

Arcadis – Headquartered in Amsterdam, Netherlands, Arcadis has more than 29,000 employees who work on consulting and design projects involving water, environment, and urban infrastructure. Projects include the London City Airport, Millau Viaduct in France, and the Tietê River Project in Brazil.

Brown and Caldwell – Started in 1947 and based in Walnut Creek, California, this privately-held company has 1,600 employees focused on resolving complex environmental problems in the United States and abroad in 52 locations. Projects include habitat restoration, infrastructure, water protection, wastewater management, and construction.

Burns & McDonnell – Headquartered in Kansas City, Missouri, Burns & McDonnell employs 7,000 people for projects in construction and engineering. Projects include power plants, transmission lines, and environmental restoration.

Cardno – Focused on infrastructure and environmental services, this Queensland, Australia-based company has 4,400 people working on projects like the Environmental and Social Impact Assessment for Papua New Guinea Liquefied Natural Gas, USAID Indonesia Urban Water, Sanitation, and Hygiene project, and the Health and Pollution Action Plan for Madagascar.

CH2M Hill (acquired by Jacobs Engineering Group) – Now headquartered in Dallas, Texas (formerly Englewood, Colorado) CH2M Hill was one of the largest engineering firms in the U.S. specializing in environmental, energy, water, and infrastructure projects. Jacobs Engineering Group has approximately 60,000 employees. Its projects included one of the world's largest environmental cleanups of Washington's Central Plateau. Internationally, CH2M Hill provided project management for Iraq's Seawater Supply Project and the Panama Canal Expansion.

Dewberry – With headquarters in Fairfax, Virginia and 2,500 employees, Dewberry conducts environmental assessments, infrastructure projects, disaster response, water resources, and preservation methods. Projects include the Hudson River Feasibility Study, Wacissa Springs Florida restoration, coastal protection in New Jersey, and those at the University of Pennsylvania, University of Waterloo, and the University of Maryland.

ERM (Environmental Resources Management) – This London-based company has about 8,000 employees who work in environmental impact assessment, compliance, ESG reporting, sustainability, climate change, and offshore wind power, including the UK's Project Dolphyn. Other projects include those in African manufacturing, U.S. farms, and digital services with a host of companies.

HDR – Headquartered in Omaha, Nebraska, HDR's 12,000 employees work on complex engineering projects. Some of these include Project Neon road and urban infrastructure project in Las Vegas, the NJ-NYC Bayonne Bridge raising project, and the design and development of Cleveland Clinic Abu Dhabi's state-of-the-art medical facility.

Kimley-Horn – With headquarters in Raleigh, North Carolina, the company's 4,300 employees consult, plan, and design transportation, water, and environmental projects, including urban development and infrastructure projects across the United States.

Mott MacDonald – This global engineering, sustainability, and development company with 18,000 employees is headquartered in Croydon, UK. A few of its major projects include the second heightening of the Aswan High Dam in Egypt, the Hampton Roads Bridge-Tunnel expansion in Hampton, VA, and London's Elizabeth Line, a hybrid urban-suburban railway.

Stantec – This Edmonton, Alberta, Canada-based company with 28,000 employees designs and develops projects across the globe, including the Panama Canal Expansion and the 66-story Stantec Tower in Edmonton, which serves as their global headquarters. Stantec offers consulting and project design in engineering, architecture, and environmental services.

Tetra Tech – Headquartered in Pasadena, California, Tetra Tech employs approximately 27,000 people in consulting and engineering services. Focused on the environment, the company works on water, sustainability, infrastructure, energy, aviation, management, and development. Projects included the Global Clean Water Fun, partnering with Engineers w/o Borders, and sustainable design in the U.S., Canada, Europe, Asia, and Australia.

TRC Companies – TRC, headquartered in Windsor, Connecticut, employs approximately 8,000 on environmental, infrastructure, transportation, technology, and renewable energy projects. Two of these projects include the UK HS2 high-speed railway environmental impact assessment and a geospatial technology expansion.

WSP Global - This Montreal-headquartered engineering company offers environmental engineering services. WSP Global acquired Golder Associates to create a company with 66,500 employees. Projects include those in construction, environment, and energy such as buildings and railways in London and New York.

ALTERNATIVE ENERGY-FOCUSED COMPANIES

Alternative energy solutions complement sustainable development. Companies whose primary projects focus on alternative energy are at the forefront of developing next-generation solutions to meet the world's growing energy needs. These 20 companies specialize in solar, wind, hydroelectric, geothermal, and bioenergy.

1. **Acciona** - A global provider of renewable energy solutions, including wind, solar, hydro, and biomass.
2. **Bloom Energy** - Specializes in solid oxide fuel cell technology, offering a clean and reliable alternative to conventional electricity generation.
3. **Brookfield Renewable Partners** - Operates one of the world's largest publicly traded, pure-play renewable power platforms, including hydroelectric, wind, solar, and storage facilities.
4. **Canadian Solar** - Manufactures solar photovoltaic modules and runs large-scale solar projects.
5. **Covanta** - Provides sustainable waste and energy solutions, focusing on converting waste into energy through advanced technologies.
6. **Enel Green Power** - Part of the larger Enel Group, it is dedicated to developing and managing energy production from renewable sources globally.
7. **Enercon** - German wind turbine manufacturer known for its innovative and reliable technology.
8. **First Solar** - An American company that manufactures solar panels and provides utility-scale PV power plants and supporting services.
9. **GE Renewable Energy** - A division of General Electric, focusing on wind, hydro, and solar power solutions.
10. **Iberdrola** - A Spanish multinational electric utility company, focusing on wind, solar, and hydroelectric power.
11. **JinkoSolar** - One of the largest and most innovative solar module manufacturers in the world.
12. **NextEra Energy** - The world's largest generator of renewable energy from the wind and sun, also involved in battery storage.

13. **Nordex Group** - Focuses on the development, production, servicing, and management of wind energy turbines.
14. **Ørsted** - A Danish company that focuses on offshore wind farms, bioenergy plants, and waste-to-energy solutions.
15. **Rockwell Automation** - Industrial automation projects include graphene-based battery manufacturing and electric vehicle/battery plant automation.
16. **Siemens Gamesa Renewable Energy** - Specializes in wind power generation with a strong focus on sustainable energy solutions.
17. **SolarEdge Technologies** - A global leader in smart energy technology, providing inverter solutions for solar photovoltaic arrays.
18. **Sunnova** - Offers residential solar and energy storage services, including solar lease, PPA, and purchase with battery options.
19. **SunPower** - Designs and manufactures high-efficiency solar panels and systems for residential, commercial, and utility markets.
20. **Vestas** - A global leader in manufacturing, installing, and servicing wind turbines.

"Philosophy is written in that great book which ever lies before our eyes — I mean the universe — but we cannot understand it if we do not first learn the language and grasp the symbols, in which it is written. This book is written in the mathematical language, and the symbols are triangles, circles, and other geometrical figures, without whose help it is impossible to comprehend a single word of it; without which one wanders in vain through a dark labyrinth."

- Galileo – The Assayer (1623), translated by Thomas Salusbury (1661)

CHAPTER 4
SUMMER PROGRAMS & INTERNSHIPS

"He that plants trees loves others besides himself."

— **Thomas Fuller**

Start early to gain software, design, and engineering experiences. Internships and summer programs are as important in your educational pathway as coursework. The lessons you learn from working collaboratively and collegially with design-focused mentors is equally important. Historian and scholar, W.E.B. DuBois (1868-1963), a founding member of the NAACP and the first Black American to earn a Ph.D. at Harvard said, "Education must not simply teach work - it must teach life." Your college, experiential, and life education go hand-in-hand, driven by purpose and foresight since life truly is a journey, not a destination.

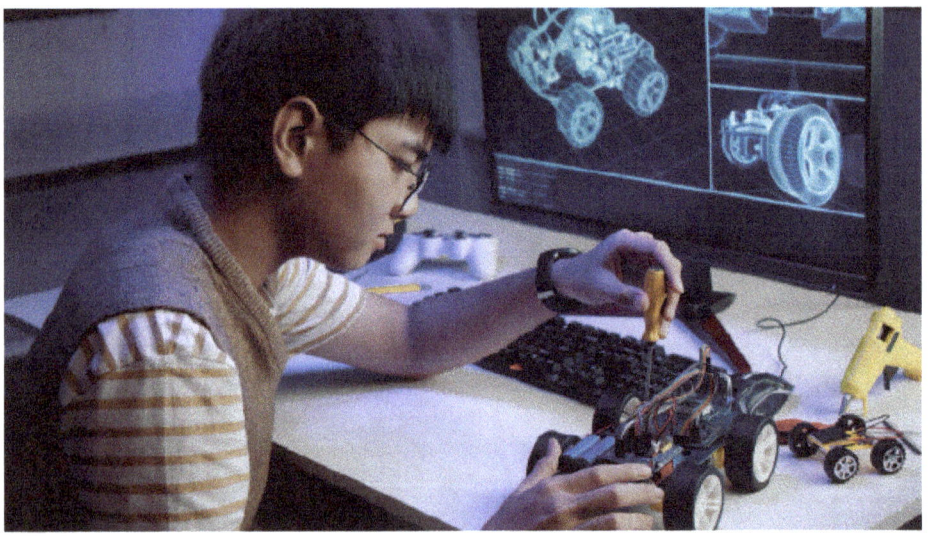

WHY PARTICIPATE IN SUMMER PROGRAMS/INTERNSHIPS?

You should participate in summer programs and internships. While some students participate to look good and show dedication, the real reason should be to develop skills with critique and feedback from specialists in the field. Discussions, seminars, and portfolio development are immensely valuable for your future pursuits. However, merely living on a campus and getting a feel for what college would be like cannot be understated. Some immersions like Girls Who Code, Code Connects, Veritas AI Scholars, NextGen Boot Camp are completely online. Other programs like iD Tech camps offer robotics, AI, and tech programs at 65 locations.

Consider attending MIT's Splash November weekend event, where high school students choose from 250+ hands-on classes. The cost was $50 in 2024.

Note: The following list is not exhaustive nor an endorsement of any program. Dates, camps, internships, descriptions, and length may change yearly.

SUMMER CAMPS & PROGRAMS FOR ART, ARCHITECTURE, COMPUTER SCIENCE, ENGINEERING, & SUSTAINABILITY

Alabama

Auburn University – Engineering Camps - STEM - Architecture Camp – Creative Writing – Industrial Design - Multiple Sessions/Scholarships Available

Work w/professors. Counselors support/supervise students. Engineering Summer Expo (9th-11th); Senior Engineering Expo (12th); Computing/ Robotics for All (7th-8th) Minority Intro to Engineering (11th- 12th); Paper & Bioresource Engineering Camp (12th); Computer Science, AI, Cybersecurity (9th-12th)

Cyberpatriot - Air Force Assn National Youth Cyber Education Program - 1 Week

HS Students - Multiple camp locations, incl Calhoun CC & the Univ. of Alabama

GenCyber – 5-day Nat Security Agency-Sponsored Cybersecurity Camp for HS Students - Univ. of Alabama, Huntsville - Taught by Cyber Industry Professionals

Engaging & Dynamic - Role-playing, visual aids, activities, discussions: Computer networking, systems security, cyber operations, defense, AI, virtual reality

Tuskegee University Taylor School of Architecture & Construction Science

Virtual Preview of Architecture and Construction at Tuskegee (V-PACT) 3-hour Virtual Program. Preview Architecture & Construction Science 2-Week Program

Alaska

GenCyber – 5-day Nat Security Agency-Sponsored Cybersecurity Camp for HS Students - Univ. of Alaska, Anchorage – Taught by Cyber Industry Professionals

Engaging & Dynamic - Role-playing, visual aids, activities, discussions: Computer networking, systems security, cyber operations, defense, AI, virtual reality

Arizona

Arcosanti – Re-Imagined Urbanism – 6-week discussion-based classes - AZ

Architecture & ecology (arcology)' learn in the World's First Prototype Arcology. Core values: (1) Frugality & Resourcefulness, (2) Ecological Accountability, (3) Experiential Learning, (4) Leaving a Limited Footprint, Arcosanti is juxtaposed to mass consumerism, urban sprawl, unchecked consumption, & social isolation.

Cyberpatriot - Air Force Assn National Youth Cyber Education Program - 1 Week

HS Students - Multiple camp locations, incl Cochise CC & the Univ. of Arizona

Earthwatch Teen Expeditions - 15-18 year olds - Portal, AZ - 8 days

Following Forest Owls in the Western U.S. - Learn how climate change threatens the routine of species as tree cavities and food sources disappear; study habitats

Engineering Education Outreach - at ASU - 1-wk day camp for 11th/12th Graders

Train, collaborate, & compete in the National Underwater Robotics Competition Fun, hands-on training ground in buoyancy, electricity, & autonomy. No Exp Nec.

GenCyber – 5-day Nat Security Agency-Sponsored Cybersecurity Camp for HS Students - Grand Canyon University – Taught by Cyber Industry Professionals
Engaging & Dynamic - Role-playing, visual aids, activities, discussions: Computer networking, systems security, cyber operations, defense, AI, virtual reality

National Institute of Health – 8-week Paid Internship Program – Phoenix, AZ
Biomedical research internship for students 17 years or older by June.
HS-SIP for high school juniors & seniors June to August hands-on research.

Science and Engineering Apprenticeship Program (SEAP) – US Navy - Flagstaff
8-weeks, 300 openings, 30 research labs nationwide, $4,000-$4,500 salary. HS students must be 16+ years old. Apply starting in August for following summer.

Arkansas

University of Arkansas – In Person & Virtual Design Camp – Fayetteville, AK
Grades 9-12 - design projects, studio gps, tours, & meetings w/local designers. No fee; design camp; students are paired w/faculty member in a studio group. Advanced Design Camp for students in Grades 11-12, 2 weeks in Fayetteville

California

Academy of Art University – 4-6 Week Pre-College Art/Design/Fashion/Film - SF
Advertising, Animation/VFX, Architecture, Fashion, Game Devt, Graphic Design. Illustration, Ind Design, Motion Pictures, Music Prod, Photo, Writing for Film/TV

Boeing Summer Internship – High School & College – Seal Beach & Palmdale, CA
Hands-on Industry Experience - Aviation and Engineering Internships

California State Summer School of the Arts (CSSSA) Sacramento - Grades 9–12
Rigorous 4-week, visual/ perf arts - 2D & 3D, painting, printmaking, sculpture, ceramics, digital media, & photography; scholarship opp for CA residents.

Cal Poly Pomona Engineering Summer Program - On-Campus, Hands-On
Workshops, labs, team projects, lectures & speakers - mechanical, civil, electrical

Canon Insights Summer Internship – Canon USA – Irvine, CA
Computer Science Major – 2nd or 3rd year; Position: Computer Vision Tech Assist with Quality Assurance Engineers; Digital Imaging Solution Division

COPE Scholars Program – Healthcare Internship – 280 Training/Experience Hrs
Locations: Anaheim/Orange, Bakersfield, Covina/Glendora, Hanford, Irvine, L.A., Mendocino County, Mission Viejo, Newport Beach, Oxnard, Riverside, Simi Valley, Tulare, Woodland Hills

Health Scholars must be 18+. Students assist w/basic healthcare for medical or nursing school, etc. Certificate of Completion - Keck Graduate Institute.

COSMOS – UC - California State Summer School for Math & Science – 4 weeks
Hands-on research program for California high school students (9-12) pursuing STEM fields; students live on campus and work with UC researchers. Application opens in January and closes in Feb. Topics from biomedical to space science.

Cyberpatriot - Air Force Assn National Youth Cyber Education Program - 1 Week
HS Students - Multiple camp locations, including Consumnes River Col & LBCC

Edwards Air Force Base - Lancaster, CA - Air Force Research Labs - 8-12 Weeks
Students participate in mentored ongoing research. Paid internship: comp sci, physics, materials science, & aerospace. Workshops, seminars, presentations.

Edwards Lifesciences Summer Internship Program – BS, MS, Ph.D., MBA - Irvine, CA
Currently Enrolled in College - Interested in Healthcare Related Programs Proficient in Engineering Drafting Software, Writing, or Business/Leadership

GenCyber – 5-day Nat Security Agency-Sponsored Cybersecurity Camp for HS Students at CSU Bakersfield & CSU San Bernardino – Taught by Cyber Industry
Engaging/Dynamic: Role-playing, visual aids, activities, & discussions: Computer networking, systems security, cyber operations, defense, AI, & virtual reality

Getty Museum – Paid Student Gallery Guide – Los Angeles, CA
Paid summer internship for teens ($2,400 in 2022). Learn the fundamentals of museums and public speaking while leading visitors around the grounds.

Also available – Open Call for teen photographers to share images, 8-week paid STEAM internship, and Summer Latin Academy at the Getty Villa to learn Latin.

Great Books Summer Program - Stanford University - Grades 6-8 and 9-12
Great Books & Big Ideas, Writer's Workshops, and Literary Travel Programs Read, Write, & Discuss Big Ideas in Literature and Philosophy with scholars

Golden Gate National Parks Conservancy - Linking Individuals to their Natural Community (LINC) 6-Week Summer Program for HS Students - San Francisco, CA
Trail work, habitat restoration, community clean up, wildlife monitoring, outdoor fun

Harvey Mudd Annual Future Achievers in Science & Technology (FAST) Program
All-expenses paid fly-in program for high-achieving college-bound HS seniors September or October weekend. Apply in August - speakers, presentations

Keck Graduate Institute (KGI) - 3-Week High School Summer STEM Program & Summer Undergrad Research Experience (SURE) - Claremont, CA - 16+ yrs old
Hands-on research experience w/KGI faculty mentor; seminars & workshops

Laguna College of Art & Design Pre-College Program – Laguna Beach, CA
Animation, Sculpture, Drawing Fundamentals, Figure Drawing, Graphic Design

Los Angeles Air Force Base - L.A., CA - Air Force Research Labs - 8-12 Weeks
Students participate in mentored ongoing research. Paid internship: comp sci, ysics, materials science, & aerospace. Workshops, seminars, presentations.66   ph

NASA Jet Propulsion Laboratory – Pasadena, CA (Apply by March 31)
Paid Internship - Must be in an undergraduate in a STEM subject

NatureBridge Summer Programs - Yosemite National Park - 1-2 weeks
Environmental science education, & hands-on fieldwork while backpacking for students in 7th - 12th grades. Connect to nature with trail building, habitat restoration, and wilderness exploration.

Otis College of Art and Design Summer of Art Intensive - 4 Weeks– Los Angeles
Portfolio/studio training for students 15+ - art, architecture, design, digital and printmaking; lectures and critiques. Merit/need-based scholarships available.

Parker Hannifin Corporation – Paid Summer Internship – Irvine, CA
Mechanical or Industrial Engineering Major – Flight Control, Aircraft Systems

Rady Children's Hospital - Summer Medical Academy - San Diego, CA
Students 15-19 years old attend this 2-week medical training camp

Rosetta Institute for Biomedical Research - 2-Week Middle/High School - Alameda
Molecular Biology of Aging, Cancer, Immunology, Neuroscience, Medicinal Chemistry, Bioinformatics of Cancer, Intro to Cellular & Molecular Medicine

Santa Clara University Summer Engineering Seminar (SES) – 10th and 11th Grade
4-day program introduces students to engineering practice, research, and education

School of Creative & Performing Arts (SOCAPA) – Occidental College (13-18-yr-olds)
2-week, 3-week - learn Filmmaking, Screenwriting, Dance, Music, Photography

SCI-Arc (Southern California Institute of Architecture) Immersive 4-week Summer Program (Design Immersion Days) – Los Angeles
Introduction to the academic and professional world of architecture – Grades 9-12

Science and Engineering Apprenticeship Program (SEAP) – US Navy Camp Pendleton, Port Hueneme, Pt. Mugu, San Diego, Monterey, Corona
8-weeks, 300 openings, 30 research labs nationwide, $4,000-$4,500 salary. HS students must be 16+ years old. Apply starting in August for following summer.

Sierra Club's Summer Outings - Channel Islands
Kayaking and hiking - families can go together to explore scenic areas

SpaceX – Summer Engineering/Co-op – Hawthorne, Irvine, & Vandenberg AFB
Paid Internship - Must be in an undergraduate in a STEM subject

Stanford University Summer Programs for HS Students - Apply by March
Art & Architecture Exploration Program - 3 Weeks - Architecture, Art, Drawing, Dance, Creative Writing, Music, and Photography

Earth & Environmental Sciences - HS research program w/labs, tours, field trips, discussions, speakers, & research methodology at the Doerr School of Sustainability

Humanities Institute - 3-Weeks On-Campus, 11th & 12th Grade - Explore politics, literature, and philosophy with Stanford professors and graduate students

ID Tech (on-campus, not sponsored by S.U.) - Courses in coding, Minecraft game design, and other aspects of computer, VR, AR, & AI technology

Math Circle - 10-Week Accelerated Math Program - Online w/groups for advanced students in grade levels from 1st to 12th grade - year round

Middle School Scholars Program (SMSSP) - Free - Low-Income Students Grades 6 & 7 - Selective & rigorous for exceptional students - 3 Weeks

Stanford Anesthesia Summer Institute (SASI) - 2 Week medical internship for HS students & pre-med undergrads seeking careers in clinical medicine

Stanford Medical Youth Science Program (SMYSP) 5-Week Medical Research Program for Juniors & Seniors (US Citizens or Permanent Res) - Highly competitive

Stanford Summer Engineering Academy (SSEA) - 4 weeks - Fully Funded Exceptional students engage in hands-on engineering - highly competitive

SUMaC – Stanford University Mathematics Camp - Highly selective & intensive program in advanced mathematics & problem solving.

TeenNat - Grades 10-12, 6-Week, Hands-On Research - Pepperwood Preserve
Scientific inquiry, data collection, & statistical analysis. The program develops a sense of stewardship and appreciation for the natural environment.

Tesla Internships – Average $33/hour – Dozens of Positions Throughout CA
Full-Time Automotive Design, Engineering Technologies, Vehicle Service Research/Training

University of California, Berkeley Summer Programs for HS Students

Academic Talent Development Program (ATDP) & Explorations - Students can take 2 Berkeley courses w/small classes & hands-on activities

AI4ALL @ UC Berkeley - 9th & 10th Grade Underrepresented Students - Learn about computer programming & artificial intelligence - Free, On Campus

Computer Science Academy - 2 Weeks - Rigorous immersion into coding, & problem-solving. Intense exploration of "big ideas". Apply by March.

Environmental Design (CED) Program - Students pursue environmental studies hands-on, immersive experiences in urban planning and sustainable design

ID Tech (on-campus, not sponsored by UCB - Courses in coding, Minecraft game design, and other aspects of computer, VR, AR, & AI technology

University of California, Davis - Young Scholars Program (YSP) - Apply in March

6-week STEM Summer Research Program - Rising juniors and seniors

University of California, Irvine Engineering Summer Academy &AI Camp

The on-campus engineering academy includes guest speakers, holds interactive workshops in robotics, computer science, mechanical engineering

AI Camp 1-wk - NSF funded "Privacy IoT and AI" - create Alexa-like assistants using Raspberry Pi, Python, and OpenAI interfaces

UCLA Computer Science Intro Track - 6 Week Boot Camp - Apply by June 1

This coding boot camp includes college-level classes & labs in computer science, design, coding, and computational techniques (strings, lists, structures, and functional decomposition. No experience necessary.

UCLA SummerJumpstart Summer Art Inst, Digital Media Arts Inst, Digital Filmmaking Institute, Game Lab Institute. Computer Science Summer Institute

2-week program - Portfolio development– college credit available
Drawing, Painting, Photography, Sculpture, Video Art, Animation, and Game Design

University of California, San Diego - Academic Connections - HS Students

Lab and academic programs/projects in STEM subjects - 3-week program

University of California, Santa Barbara - Research Mentorship Program

6-week STEM Summer Research Program - Rising juniors and seniors

University of California, Santa Cruz HS Student Science Internship Program

10-week research internship for high school students in STEM fields. Conduct research with a faculty/doctoral student mentor. Apply in March.

University of Southern California Viterbi Discover Engineering - HS Students

Hands-on program in designing, 3D printing, building, & testing projects, Field trips to JPL, Hyperion Treatment Plant. Topics include aerospace, biomedical, chemical, computer science, electrical, environmental, industrial, and mechanical engineering.

USC Summer Film, Writing, Drama, and Architecture Programs – 2-4 Weeks
Creative Writing Workshop, Comedy Performance, Exploring Architecture

Colorado

Catalyst Campus - Colorado Springs, CO - Air Force Research Labs - 8-12 Weeks
Students participate in mentored ongoing research. Paid internship: comp sci, physics, materials science, & aerospace. Workshops, seminars, presentations.

Colorado School of Mines Summer Programs for HS Students - Golden, CO
Engineering Design Camp - 10th - 12th - Real world problem solving and engineering design while living on the Mines campus.

SUMMET (Summer Multicultural Engineering Training) - 11th & 12th - Program for ethnic/racial minorities, women, and first-gen college students

Cyberpatriot - Air Force Assn National Youth Cyber Education Program - 1 Week
HS Students - Training at the National Cybersecurity Center, Colorado Springs

GenCyber – 5-day Nat Security Agency-Sponsored Cybersecurity Camp for HS Students - Univ. of CO Denver & Colorado Springs – Taught by Cyber Industry
Engaging & Dynamic - Role-playing, visual aids, activities, & discussions: Computer networking, systems security, cyber operations, defense, AI, & virtual reality

National Security Agency (NSA) – Paid Computer Internship – Aurora
Students must be at least a junior in high school with interest in business, engineering, or computer science. Apply between September 1 and October 31.

University of Colorado, Boulder - Summer STEM Program - K-12 Options
STEM programs for all age levels - topics include AI, computer science, DNA, biomedical engineering, biotechnology, geology, technology design, LEGOs, math, medicine, programming, rockets. microbes, and video games

University of Colorado Summer Science Program Intensive - HS Students 5-6 Wks
Biochemistry and molecular biology research - experimental design/synthesis; advanced lab techniques, lectures, collaborative workshops - highly competitive

Connecticut

GenCyber – 5-day Nat Security Agency-Sponsored Cybersecurity Camp for HS Students - Univ. of New Haven – Taught by Cyber Industry Professionals
Engaging & Dynamic - Role-playing, visual aids, activities, discussions: Computer networking, systems security, cyber operations, defense, AI, virtual reality

Science and Engineering Apprenticeship Program (SEAP) – US Navy – Groton
8-weeks, 300 openings, 30 research labs nationwide, $4,000-$4,500 salary. HS students must be 16+ years old. Apply starting in August for following summer.

Summer Studio: Discovering Graphic Design (AIGA) – Bridgeport, CT
Free 4-week hands-on program for Bridgeport rising juniors and seniors
Week 1 – Music Festival Poster, Week 2 – Digital Media Poster
Week 3 – Animating Your Ideas, Week 4 – Portfolio Art for College Applications

Yale Summer Program in Astrophysics (YSPA) - Rising HS Seniors
Research/enrichment at the Leitner Family Observatory & Planetarium; 2-week online prelim & 4-week on-campus program w/ research project

Yale Young Global Scholars - 2-Week HS Program; 150 countries; 50 states
Residential sessions June, July, & August - Apps due in January - Environmental Studies/Issues, Innovations in Science & Technology, Literature, Philosophy, & Culture, Politics Law & Economics, and Solving Global Challenges

District of Columbia

American Chemical Society - Project SEED Program - Washington, D.C.
Hands-on summer research/mentor chemistry prog. for low income students; 8-week program - Virtual summer opp. for 11,000 students in 40 U.S. states

Catholic University School of Architecture and Planning
Summer High School Program - 2-week Residential (Two Session Options)

Federal Summer Internship Program - Paid - High School & College Students
National Institutes of Health (NIH) - Biomedical, behavioral, and social science research for 11th grade to grad school. Interns work w/a Principal Investigator
Pathways Internship Program - HS to grad school - Hands-on w/govt agencies.
U.S. Fish & Wildlife Service Internships - Work in wildlife conservation and visitor services. Practical experience may lead to permanent federal positions.

GenCyber – 5-day Nat Security Agency-Sponsored Cybersecurity Camp for HS Students - Gallaudet University – Taught by Cyber Industry Professionals
Engaging & Dynamic - Role-playing, visual aids, activities, discussions: Computer networking, systems security, cyber operations, defense, AI, virtual reality

George Washington University Digital Storytelling Pre-College Program – July
Produce stories w/smartphones, learn storyboarding, & social media broadcast craft ideas, capture images, & create compelling content, w/character devt.

Georgetown University – 1-week – Creative Writing – Publishing
Fiction, Short Story, Poetry, and Professional Writing; visit literary hubs

National Air and Space Museum in Washington, D.C. – HS and College Students
The Explainers Program offers ~$15/hr year-round paid position for students to help visitors better understand the Museum and its artifacts and exhibitions.

U.S. Department of Education - Internships for HS & College - Fall, Winter, Spring, & Summer; Must be 16+; 8-Week Program

Human Resources/Project Mgmt, Educational Policies, Data Analytics, Training/Development; Grants Management; Communications; Information Technology

Florida

Cyberpatriot - Air Force Assn National Youth Cyber Education Program - 1 Week

HS Students - Multiple camp locations, incl FL SW Col, DoD StarBase, & USF

Earthwatch Teen Expeditions - 8 days - 15-18 year olds - Sarasota, FL

Tracking Sharks and Rays - Conduct research alongside scientists in one of the oldest and largest shark and ray programs; consider overexploitation and environmental threats. Mote Marine Laboratory & Aquarium

Eglin Air Force Base - Valparaiso, FL - Air Force Research Labs - 8-12 Weeks

Students participate in mentored in ongoing research. Paid internships: comp sci, physics, materials science, & aerospace. Workshops, seminars, presentations.

Florida Atlantic University School of Architecture - Boca Raton & Ft. Lauderdale

July 3-week program for HS students & first 2 years of college - Portfolio development, fabrication, architectural education, portfolio display, & critiques

Certificate of Completion Awarded – Enrollment is first-come, first-served basis.

Florida International University - Journalism Jumpstart - FREE - Miami, FL

Partnership & grant from the Dow Jones News Fund, Student work is showcased on the Jumpstart Journal Webpage; promotes a diverse national media; participants get to work closely with media professionals.

GenCyber – 5-day Nat Security Agency-Sponsored Cybersecurity Camp for HS Students - Florida Inst of Technology, FL International University, Innovation Tech Academy, Univ. of West Florida – Taught by Cyber Industry Professionals

Engaging & Dynamic - Role-playing, visual aids, activities, discussions: Computer networking, systems security, cyber operations, defense, AI, virtual reality

Ringling College of Art and Design –Sarasota, FL - Intensive 4-week Program

Art/Design - computer animation, virtual reality, creative writing, digital sculpting, entertainment design, fabrication, film directing/production, game art, game design, illustration, painting, photography, and storyboarding

Science and Engineering Apprenticeship Program (SEAP) – US Navy Patrick SFB, Jacksonville, Orlando, Panama City

8-weeks, 300 openings, 30 research labs nationwide, $4,000-$4,500 salary. HS students must be 16+ years old. Apply starting in August for following summer.

SpaceX – Summer Engineering/Co-op Program – Cape Canaveral, FL

Paid Internship - Must be an undergraduate in a STEM subject

University of Florida Design Exploration Program (DEP) - 3 Weeks

On-campus immersion into architecture. Construction of studio design projects, teamwork, seminars, field trips, architectural theory.

University of Florida - Student Science Training Program (SSTP) 6-Weeks

Rising seniors; 16+ years old; UF-SSTP is a rigorous, fast paced program for academically talented, and self-motivated students

University of Miami Summer Scholars, Explorations in Architecture & Design

3-week Residential program; 6 college credits; Design, Graphics, and Theory. Architecture, Landscape Architecture, Historic Preservation; Urban Planning. Studio experience with drawing, model making, drafting, CAD, visual analysis.

Georgia

Centers for Disease Control - Atlanta, GA - CDC Disease Detective Day Camp

11th & 12th Grade - Lectures on global health, interventions, infectious diseases, chronic disease, & injury prevention. Students participate in mock press conferences, re-created outbreaks, lab sessions, & disease surveillance

Cyberpatriot - Air Force Assn National Youth Cyber Education Program - 1 Week

HS Students - Multiple camp locations, including GA Cyber Innovation/Training Center, Middle GA State U., Ft Valley State U., & Wesley Community College

Emory University – Atlanta, GA – 2-, 4-, 6-Week Writing Programs

Journalism, Dramatic Writing, Media & Politics, Psychology & Fiction

GenCyber – 5-day Nat Security Agency-Sponsored Cybersecurity Camp for HS Students - Columbus State Univ., Savannah State Univ. , Univ. of North Georgia, Westminster Schools of Augusta - Taught by Cyber Industry Professionals
Engaging & Dynamic - Role-playing, visual aids, activities, discussions: Computer networking, systems security, cyber operations, defense, AI, virtual reality

Georgia Institute of Technology Pre-College Design Program – Atlanta, GA
2-week Residential program – College of Design – Grades 11 & 12 (Two Sessions); Architecture, Building Construction, Industrial Design, and Music Technology

Georgia Tech Summer Engineering Institute - Atlanta, GA - 3-Week
Residential engineering/tech prog. Grades 11-12, underrepresented students

National Security Agency (NSA) – Paid Computer Internship – Augusta
Students must be at least a junior in high school with interest in business, engineering, or computer science. Apply between September 1 & October 31.

Savannah College of Art & Design – 5-Week Rising Star & SCAD Courses
2-week College of Design Residential program –- Grades 11 & 12 - Courses include Advertising, Animation, Virtual Reality, Illustration, Storyboarding, Photography, Painting, Fashion, Digital Film, Graphic Design, and Industrial Design

University of Georgia - Women Experience Creativity, Excitement, & Learning (ExCEL)
1-Week - Engineering Discovery Laboratory & Fabrication Studio

Hawaii

COPE Scholars Program – Healthcare Internship – 280 Hrs Training in Kailua
Health Scholars must be 18+. Students assist w/basic healthcare for medical or nursing school, etc. Certificate of Completion - Keck Graduate Institute.

GenCyber – 5-day Cybersecurity Camp for HS Students - UH, Hilo, UH Kahului, UH Kaunakakai, UH Lihue-UH Wahiawa: Taught by Cyber Industry Professional
Engaging & Dynamic - Role-playing, visual aids, activities, discussions: Computer networking, systems security, cyber operations, defense, AI, virtual reality

Maui Optical & Super Computing Site - Maui, HI - Air Force Research Labs: 8-12 Wks
Students participate in mentored ongoing research teams. Paid internship: comp sci, physics, materials science, & aerospace. Workshops, seminars, presentations.

National Security Agency (NSA) – Paid Computer Internship – Oahu
Students must be at least a junior in high school with interest in business, engineering, or computer science. Apply between September 1 and October 31.

Science and Engineering Apprenticeship Program (SEAP) – US Navy – Honolulu
8-weeks, 300 openings, 30 research labs nationwide, $4,000-$4,500 salary. HS students must be 16+ years old. Apply starting in August for following summer.

Science Camps of America - Land & Sea Camp - 9-day HS Residential Camp
   Practical exploration of volcanos, turtles, fish, & geological/marine conservation

STEMworks Innovation Internship Program - HS Students - $2,000 stipend
   Focus areas include: 3D design, architecture, biomedical tech & engineering

University of Hawaii, Manoa College of Engineering Summer HS Student Program
   Hands-on engineering & STEM program in robotics and interactive learning

Idaho

GenCyber – 5-day Nat Security Agency-Sponsored Cybersecurity Camp for HS Students - Boise State University – Taught by Cyber Industry Professionals
   Engaging & Dynamic - Role-playing, visual aids, activities, discussions: Computer networking, systems security, cyber operations, defense, AI, virtual reality

Idaho National Laboratory Internships - Idaho Falls, ID - 6-Week Paid Program
   Nuclear Energy, Renewable Energy, and/or National Security. Interns apply STEM to solve real-world problems with experts in the nuclear field

Illinois

Argonne National Laboratory - 8-Week - College Bound Research Program
   STEM Lab/lecture w/interactive programs. Students take part in real-world problem-solving. This program is FREE, plus $500 per week stipend.

Cyberpatriot - Air Force Assn National Youth Cyber Education Program - 1 Week
   HS Students - Camp locations include Elmhurst University

GenCyber – 5-day Nat Security Agency-Sponsored Cybersecurity Camp for HS Students - College of Dupage – Taught by Cyber Industry Professionals
   Engaging & Dynamic - Role-playing, visual aids, activities, discussions: Computer networking, systems security, cyber operations, defense, AI, virtual reality

Great Books Summer Program - Northwestern University - Grades 6-8 and 9-12
   Great Books & Big Ideas, Writer's Workshops, and Literary Travel Programs
   Read, Write, & Discuss Big Ideas in Literature and Philosophy with scholars

Illinois Institute of Technology - HS Summer Introduction to Architecture
   2-week - Comprehensive overview; 1-week Exploration in Architecture for middle school students – studio-based, firm visits, field trips, projects.

Northwestern University Center for Talent Development Rigorous/Accel - Grades 9-12
   Medical Pharmacology, Neuroplasticity, Cybersecurity, Data Science, Astrophysics, Quantum Mechanics, IoT, Build Your Own Computer, & Machine Learning

Northwestern University – National High School Institute
   5-week Film & Video, Music, Speech & Debate, Theatre, and Dramaturgy

School of the Art Institute of Chicago – Early College Program for HS Students
1-, 2-, 4-week Residential programs in Painting, Drawing, Animation, Comics/ Graphic Novels, and Fashion Design. Portfolio development programs; earn college credit. Full-tuition scholarships are available.

Southern Illinois University Carbondale – Kid Architecture
1-week Elementary Grades, Middle School & High School Architecture Camp

University of Chicago Creative Writing Immersion - High School Writing Program
"Collegiate Writing: Awakening Into Consciousness"

University of Chicago Research in the Biological Sciences (RIBS) 4 week Intensive
Highly competitive project-based training in molecular, microbiological, & cell biology; weekly writing assignments & lunch seminars; intependent project

University of Illinois at Chicago Architecture - HiArch Summer HS Program
1 & 2 week (July) - Culture of architecture, design, thinking, and artmaking.

University of Illinois at Urbana-Champaign - Women in Engineering - 6th-12th
The Grainger College of Engineering introduces engineering to teenage girls.

Univ of Illinois, Urbana-Champaign - HS Students Discover Engineering Camp
STEM-focused camps - 7th-12th grade - Specialized Aerospace, Chemical Electrical, Computer, Mechanical, Nuclear, Radiological, Materials Science, AI, Programming, Molecule Making camps. 20+ camps from June to August

Young Scholars Summer STEMM Research Programs at Univ of Illinois (UIUC)
6-weeks, Rising 10th-12th graders collaborate on cutting-edge research in cancer, immunology, neuroscience, artificial intelligence, physics, quantum mechanics, bioengineering, electrical engineering - Final Symposium in early August

Indiana

Cyberpatriot - Air Force Assn National Youth Cyber Education Program - 1 Week
HS Students - Camp locations include Ivy Tech Community College

GenCyber – 5-day Nat Security Agency-Sponsored Cybersecurity Camp for HS Students - Purdue Univ. Northwest – Taught by Cyber Industry Professionals
Engaging & Dynamic - Role-playing, visual aids, activities, discussions: Computer networking, systems security, cyber operations, defense, AI, virtual reality

Indiana University Bloomington Summer Science Program - HS Students 5-6 Wks
PBiochemistry and molecular biology research - highly competitive, hands-on, collaborative; mentors; student teams; analysis, scientific writing, presentations

Purdue University Summer Programs for HS Students
Seminar for Top Engineering Prospects (STEP) - 1 Week
Program for rising seniors to explore engineering opportunities
Minority Engineering Program - 7th - 9th Grade Students
This summer camp introduces to engineering careers and the design process.
Summer Science Program - HS Students 5-6 Wks
Biochemistry and molecular biology research - highly competitive, hands-on, collaborative; mentors; student teams; analysis, scientific writing, presentations

Rose-Hulman Institute of Technology - Operation Catapult - 2 Weeks
Engineering projects, robotics, research, and STEM design projects - Rising HS juniors or seniors participate in hands-on engineering activities.

Science and Engineering Apprenticeship Program (SEAP) – US Navy – Crane
8-weeks, 300 openings, 30 research labs nationwide, $4,000-$4,500 salary. HS students must be 16+ years old. Apply starting in August for following summer.

University of Notre Dame Summer Scholars Program - 2-weeks HS Students
Film, Photography, Performing Arts - studios, seminars, and field trips STEM: Climate Change, Artificial Intelligence, Engineering, Chemistry, Medicine

Iowa

Iowa State University – College of Design - Design Camps - HS Students
1-week – Architecture, Studio/Fine Arts, Graphic, Interior, & Industrial Design

Kentucky

GenCyber – 5-day Nat Security Agency-Sponsored Cybersecurity Camp for HS Students - Big Sandy Community & Technical College – Taught by Cyber Industry
Engaging & Dynamic - Role-playing, visual aids, activities, discussions: Computer networking, systems security, cyber operations, defense, AI, virtual reality

Louisiana

Barksdale Air Force Base - Bossier Parish, LA - Air Force Research Labs - 8-12 Weeks
Students participate in mentored ongoing research. Paid internship: comp sci, physics, materials science, & aerospace. Workshops, seminars, presentations.

GenCyber – 5-day Nat Security Agency-Sponsored Cybersecurity Camp for HS Students - Louisiana Tech University – Taught by Cyber Industry Professionals
Engaging & Dynamic - Role-playing, visual aids, activities, discussions: Computer networking, systems security, cyber operations, defense, AI, virtual reality

Science and Engineering Apprenticeship Program (SEAP) – US Navy – New Orleans
8-weeks, 300 openings, 30 research labs nationwide, $4,000-$4,500 salary. HS students must be 16+ years old. Apply starting in August for following summer

Maine

Earthwatch Teen Expeditions - Acadia National Park, Maine - 1 week students must be 16+ years old. Apply starting in August for following summer.
Climate Change: Sea to the Trees science exploration program; understand patterns and make observations regarding how humans are changing the ecosystem; wildlife diversity, bird migration, ocean acidification, sea warming

GenCyber – 5-day Nat Security Agency-Sponsored Cybersecurity Camp for HS Students - Northeastern Univ Portland, Maine – Taught by Cyber Industry Prof
Engaging & Dynamic - Role-playing, visual aids, activities, discussions: Computer networking, systems security, cyber operations, defense, AI, virtual reality

Maryland

GenCyber – 5-day Nat Security Agency-Sponsored Cybersecurity Camp for HS Students - Anne Arundel CC, Harford CC, PGCC – Taught by Cyber Industry
Engaging & Dynamic - Role-playing, visual aids, activities, discussions: Computer networking, systems security, cyber operations, defense, AI, virtual reality

Goddard Space Flight Center (NASA) - High School & College
Summer Aerospace and Climate Change Internship at GISS - Greenbelt, MD Research, Mentorship, Experiential Learning Opportunities

Johns Hopkins Engineering Summer Programs in Innovation Sustainable Energy, and Biomedical Engineering - Online and In-Person
Biomedical, chemical, civil, electrical, environmental, and mechanical

Maryland Institute College of Art (MICA) – 2-, 3-, 5-week - HS Students
Live studio workshops, artist talks, collaboration, feedback, critique, evaluation

National Institute of Health – 8-week Paid Internship – Bethesda, Baltimore, and Frederick. MD Research Group Locations - Apply by mid February
Biomedical research internship for students 17 years or older by June 15th. HS-SIP for high school juniors & seniors - June to August - hands-on research.

National Security Agency (NSA) – Paid Computer Internship – Ft. Meade
Students must be at least a junior in high school with interest in business, engineering, or computer science. Apply between September 1 and October 31.

Naval Academy Summer STEM Program - Annapolis, MD - HS Students
Three week-long sessions for students interested in coding, game design computer projects, robotics, & engineering. Collaborate in world-class labs.

Science and Engineering Apprenticeship Program (SEAP) – US Navy – Bethesda, Patuxent River, Silver Spring, Indian Head, and Annapolis
8-weeks, 300 openings, 30 research labs nationwide, $4,000-$4,500 salary. HS students must be 16+ years old. Apply starting in August for following summer.

Terp Young Scholars - University of Maryland - 3-Week High School Program
Immersion into computer science with projects, exams, and collaboration

University of Maryland – 4-week ESTEEM/SER-Quest Summer Program
Rising seniors undertake engineering-focused projects while conducting research

University of Maryland - Discovering Engineering - 1 week (additional programs also)
Exploration of engineering with faculty to learn about the various disciplines.

United States Naval Academy - Summer STEM Program for Students in 9th - 11th
Design and build STEM projects with USNA Faculty and Midshipmen
1 week residential program, $700, includes lodging, meals, transport from airport

Massachusetts

Bentley University - Wolfram Math/Computer -2 Week - HS Summer Program
Intensive training in programming, computation, & technology. Students produce a project from ideation to completion (Wolfram Emerging Scholars)

Boston College - Boston, MA – Creative Writing Seminar Program
3-week (July) Residential Program – HS Students – nonfiction, fiction, poetry
Create & edit the class literary journal and present writings at a public reading

Boston University Math, Engineering, Technology, Media, and Journalism
AMP - Academy of Media Production – Cinematic/journalistic in visual storytelling (Grades 10 – 12)
Code Breakers – 10th & 11th Grade Females - Cybersecurity, Cryptography, Computer Programming, and Ethical Hacking (Free)
Girls Get Math@BU – 5-day Non-residential summer program for enthusiastic 10th – 11th graders
Journalism Academy – 2-week Writing, Photography, Reporting ages 14-18

PROMYS – **Program in Mathematics for Young Scientists** – 6 weeks 80 high school students 14+ years old (scholarships available); seminars in number theory, cryptography, linear algebra, matroids, graphs, and data visualization.
RISE – **Research in Science & Engineering** - 6-week   Research in Science & Engineering program in astronomy, chemistry, neuroscience, and medicine. Engineering Research Options: Biomedical, Computer, Electrical, Mechanical
U-Design – 2-week Engineering Design Prog – hands-on workshop - 6th - 10th

Forsyth Student Scholars Summer Internship Program - 8-Weeks - 11th & 12th grades
Science research mentor program for underserved Massachusetts HS students

GenCyber – 5-day Nat Security Agency-Sponsored Cybersecurity Camp for HS Students - Assumption University & Cape Cod CC – Taught by Cyber Industry
Engaging & Dynamic - Role-playing, visual aids, activities, discussions: Computer networking, systems security, cyber operations, defense, AI, virtual reality

Great Books Summer Program - Amherst College - Grades 6-8 and 9-12
Great Books & Big Ideas, Writer's Workshops, and Literary Travel Programs
Read, Write, & Discuss Big Ideas in Literature and Philosophy with scholars

Harvard University GSD Design Discovery– Cambridge, MA (Ages 18+)
3-week Residential Program – Architecture, Landscape, Urban Planning & Design
Physical modeling, fabrication, assembly

Harvard Summer Program for High School Students Credit/Non Credit Classes
7-week college credit (campus dorms) include: Creating Comics & Graphic Novels; Advertising, Visual Imagery, Creative Writing, Physics, Chemistry, Biology, Medicinal Topics, Calculus, Economics, and Computer Science

Massachusetts College of Art & Design – 4-Week Art Immersion Program
Students take 3 foundation courses and participate in a closing exhibition

Massachusetts Institute of Technology – HS Students – Cambridge
Beaver Works Summer Institute – 4-week intensive program for first-generation high school juniors. Programs include Autonomous Underwater Vehicles to Quantum Software and to Serious Game Design with AI.

Lincoln Laboratory Radar Introduction for Student Engineers (LLRISE) - FFREE - 2-week project-based workshop to teach students how to build small Doppler and range radar systems. HS Juniors. Applications open in January.

MITES – Minority Introduction to Engineering and Science – Intensive 6-week residential program for 80 high school juniors who intend to enter STEM programs, especially from underrepresented groups. The program is free.

MOTSTEC - Hands-on, in-depth STEM mentorship for HS seniors; courses/projects; present research at 5-day event (FREE) Work w/MIT faculty/researchers. Six-month hybrid learning program with 2-week STEM Immersion June-August.

RSI – Research Science Institute – Free. Competitive/Intensive 6-week program for 70 HS juniors who research/study advanced theory in math, science, & engineering. Distinguished Lectures/Alumni Network. Apply by early December.

THINK Scholars Program - 4 months HS students apply between Nov 1-Jan 1, accepted in Feb, join program in June. Pair with MIT researcher. Summer 4-days at MIT, All Expenses Paid + $1,000. Submit detailed proposals for novel ideas.

WTP – Women's Technology Program – 4-wk engineering focus - EE, ME, EECS

Urbanframe Summer Design - Build Project CAD, drafting, sketching, mapping and context study, historical research, carpentry & construction

Additional MIT Hosted Programs: LaunchX, OSC, iD Tech Camps, National Geographic Student Expeditions

National Institute of Health – Paid Internship - Apply in Feb– Framingham, MA
8-week - Biomedical research internship for students 17 years or older by June. HS-SIP for high school juniors & seniors June to August hands-on research.

Northeastern Univ Young Scholars Program w/field trips - Rising HS Seniors
Intro to Engineering - Chemical, Civil, EE, Computer, Mechanical & Industrial Radar, batteries, energy, robotics, lasers, microwave, biotech, medicine, bldgs

Tufts University – 6-Week Writing Intensive - HS Students - Develop Papers
Writing exercises, evaluation from professors, revise, and build on a theme

Tufts University Summer Accelerator - 2-Weeks for HS Students in 10th-12th
Students take 2 college-level seminars in neuroscience, coding, physiology, criminal justice, international affairs, chaos theory, engineering, artificial intelligence, astrochemistry, and mythology

University of Massachusetts Amherst Pre-College – Amherst, MA
1-, 2-, 3-week Residential Intensives Grades 10-12; 3-D Design, 3-D Animation, Building & Construction Technology; Combatting the Climate Crisis Summer Engineering Institute, Design Academy, Programming for Aspiring Scientists

Wellesley College – 2-week Residential Program - Wellesley, MA
EXPLO Pre-College + Career for Grades 10-12 Three session options; Topics include – AI, Entrepreneurship, Engineering, Medicine, Law, CSI

Wentworth Institute of Technology - 2-4 Week Impact Lab - HS 11th & 12th
On-Campus Comp Sci, Engineering, Info Technology, Architecture, & Construction

WPI Frontiers Program - Worcester Polytechnic Institute - Two 2-Week Sessions
This residential program allows HS students to explore comp sci & data science

Youth Design Boston (AIGA) – Boston, MA
Summer Graphic Design Internship & Mentoring Program

Michigan

Andrews University School of Architecture & Interior Design - Renaissance Kids
Virtual Studio Projects; lecture; community build projects

GenCyber – 5-day Nat Security Agency-Sponsored Cybersecurity Camp for HS Students - Northern MI U. & Oakland U. – Taught by Cyber Industry Professionals
Engaging & Dynamic - Role-playing, visual aids, activities, discussions: Computer networking, systems security, cyber operations, defense, AI, virtual reality

Interlochen Center for the Arts – Summer Arts Camp – 1-6 Weeks
Creative Writing, Dance, Art, Motion Picture, Music, Theatre, Visual Arts

Michigan State University - HS Honors Science, Math, Engineering Program
7-week intensive, hands-on summer research program and engineering projects

National Institute of Health – 8-week Paid Internship - Apply in Feb– Detroit
Research biomedical internship for students 17 years or older by June.
HS-SIP for high school juniors & seniors June to August hands-on research.

University of Michigan – Stamps School of Art & Design – 3-Week BFA Preview
HS Students – Creative retreat w/state-of the art facilities & museum excursions

University of Michigan – Summer Engineering Exploration (SEE) - 1 Week
On-campus - engineering design challenges - Apply Jan-Feb – Grades 10-12

Minnesota

GenCyber – 5-day Nat Security Agency-Sponsored Cybersecurity Camp for HS Students - Alexandria Tech & CC & Lake Superior College – Cyber Industry Prof
Engaging & Dynamic - Role-playing, visual aids, activities, discussions: Computer networking, systems security, cyber operations, defense, AI, virtual reality

Summer Liberal Arts Institute (SLAI) Computer Science Program - HS Jr & Sr
Hands-on, project-based residential program in computational solutions to problems, research, and a final symposium to present findings.

Mississippi

GenCyber – 5-day Nat Security Agency-Sponsored Cybersecurity Camp for HS Students - Univ. of Southern MS – Taught by Cyber Industry Professionals
Engaging & Dynamic - Role-playing, visual aids, activities, discussions: Computer networking, systems security, cyber operations, defense, AI, virtual reality

Science and Engineering Apprenticeship Program (SEAP) – US Navy – Stennis
8-weeks, 300 openings, 30 research labs nationwide, $4,000-$4,500 salary. HS students must be 16+ years old. Apply starting in August for following summer.

Missouri

GenCyber – 5-day Nat Security Agency-Sponsored Cybersecurity Camp for HS Students - Univ. of MO, Kansas City – Taught by Cyber Industry Professionals
Engaging & Dynamic - Role-playing, visual aids, activities, discussions: Computer networking, systems security, cyber operations, defense, AI, virtual reality

Univ of Missouri Kansas City – Dept of Architecture, Urban Planning & Design
Design Discovery Program – Architecture, Interior Design, Landscape Architecture 3-day (July) Non-Residential Program – HS Students/Current College Students

Washington University in St. Louis - HS Programs
Creative Writing Program – 2-weeks - fiction, nonfiction, and poetry; morning writer's workshops –editing and sharing work
Arts & Journalism Program - 5-8 week – Dance, Journalism, Photography, Music, Drama, Photojournalism
Young Scientist Program - Rising Seniors - Summer Focus is an 8-week paid summer research internship
Shaw Institute for Field Training (SIFT) and Tyson Environmental Research **Apprenticeship** (TERA) programs.
BOLD@Olin - 1-week Business Leadership/Entrepreneurship Program

Whiteman Air Force Base - Knob Noster, MO - Air Force Research Labs - 8-12 Weeks
Students participate in mentored ongoing research teams. Paid internship: comp sci, physics, materials science, & aerospace. Workshops, seminars, presentations.

Montana

Cyberpatriot - Air Force Assn National Youth Cyber Education Program - 1 Week
HS Students - Camp locations include Montana State University

GenCyber – 5-day Nat Security Agency-Sponsored Cybersecurity Camp for HS Students - Univ. of Montana, Missoula – Taught by Cyber Industry Professionals
Engaging & Dynamic - Role-playing, visual aids, activities, discussions: Computer networking, systems security, cyber operations, defense, AI, virtual reality

National Institute of Health – 8-week Paid Internship – Hamilton, MT
Biomedical research internship for students 17 years or older by June.
HS-SIP for high school juniors & seniors June to August hands-on research.

Nebraska

Cyberpatriot - Air Force Assn National Youth Cyber Education Program - 1 Week
HS Students - Multiple camp locations include Bellevue University

GenCyber – 5-day Nat Security Agency-Sponsored Cybersecurity Camp for HS Students - Univ. of Nebraska, Omaha – Taught by Cyber Industry Professionals
Engaging & Dynamic - Role-playing, visual aids, activities, discussions: Computer networking, systems security, cyber operations, defense, AI, virtual reality

University of Nebraska College of Architecture – 6-day (June) - Grades 11-12
6-day (June) Residential Program – Grades 11 & 12 – Studio training; architectural design; scholarships

Nevada

AFWERX - Las Vegas, NV - Air Force Research Labs - 8-12 Weeks
Students participate in mentored ongoing research teams. Paid internship: comp sci, physics, materials science, & aerospace. Workshops, seminars, presentations

GenCyber – 5-day Nat Security Agency-Sponsored Cybersecurity Camp for HS Students - University of Nevada, LV – Taught by Cyber Industry Professionals
Engaging & Dynamic - Role-playing, visual aids, activities, discussions: Computer networking, systems security, cyber operations, defense, AI, virtual reality

University of Nevada - Hands-On Engineering & Cybersecurity Camps - HS Students
UNR Engineering Exploration - Projects/activities - design, engineer, build, & test
UNLV Cybersecurity Camp - Interactive labs/projects on cyber threats & defense

New Jersey

New Jersey Institute of Technology – Hillier College of Architecture & Design
1-week (July) Residential Program – HS Students – Architecture, Interior Design, Industrial Design, Digital Design - Architecture + Design Programs (2 Start Dates)

Princeton Summer Journalism Program (PSJP) - FREE Residential Prog for HS Juniors
Year-long college prep program for HS juniors from low-income backgrounds
Summer intensive at Princeton University (10 days); tours, seminars, writing project

Princeton University Laboratory Learning Program 5-6 Weeks, 16+ years old
Summer science/engineering research for HS students; lab experience; write paper

Science and Engineering Apprenticeship Program (SEAP) – US Navy – Lakehurst
8-weeks, 300 openings, 30 research labs nationwide, $4,000-$4,500 salary. HS students must be 16+ years old. Apply starting in August for following summer.

New Hampshire

Sustainable Summer @ Dartmouth - Environmental Leadership Academy
Students ages 15-18 attend 2-week program; bootcamp, research/development environmental problem, and then convert abstract ideas into real initiatives.

New Mexico

Cyberpatriot - Air Force Assn National Youth Cyber Education Program - 1 Week
HS Students - Multiple camp locations include San Juan College

GenCyber – 5-day Nat Security Agency-Sponsored Cybersecurity Camp for HS Students - San Juan College – Taught by Cyber Industry Professionals
Engaging & Dynamic - Role-playing, visual aids, activities, discussions: Computer networking, systems security, cyber operations, defense, AI, virtual reality

Kirtland Air Force Base - Albuquerque, NM - Air Force Research Labs - 8-12 Weeks
Students participate in mentored ongoing research. Paid internship: comp sci, physics, materials science, & aerospace. Workshops, seminars, presentations.

New Mexico State Summer Science Program - 5-6 Weeks - HS Students
Astrophysics calculations, astronomy, original research program; mentors, workshops; collaborative community - highly selective - transformative

New York

AIA New York – Center for Architecture 1-week (July) – HS Students
Grades 3-12 include Architectural Design Studio, Drawing, Rooftop Dwelling, Dream House, Treehouses, Skyscrapers, Green Island Home, Neighborhood Design, Subway Architecture, Waterfront City, Parks & Playground Design

Brookhaven National Laboratory - Upton, NY - US Dept of Energy - Rising HS Seniors
Ensure America's energy security, environment, nuclear challenges by researching solutions. 6-week High School Research Program (HSRP) STEM research

Brooklyn College STEM Research Academy - Urban Ecology & Design for HS Students
This 6-week environmental science research program includes lab, fieldwork, and methodology. Students dive into data collection and analysis.

Canon Insights Summer Internship – Canon USA – PR/Marketing - Huntington, NY
Public Relations & Marketing Majors – 10 Week Paid Position

City College of New York - STEM Institute Research/Project for HS Students
Build 3D Printers, Robot, Rockets, & Drones - Free Supercharged Program

Columbia U. - SHAPE (3-Wk - Summer HS Program in Technology & Engineering)
Build 3D Printers, Robots, Rockets, & Drones - Free Supercharged Program

Columbia U. - SHAPE (3-Wk - Summer HS Program in Technology & Engineering)
This engineering program is for HS students pursuing technology-focused subjects.

Columbia University - New York, NY – Summer Art Immersion
3-week July-August Residential Program – Architecture, Creative Writing, Drawing, Filmmaking, Photography, Theater, or Visual Arts

Columbia University School of Engineering - HS Maker Lab - 6-Week Program
FREE - Students address a health problem - design, prototype, & test a biomedical device. Final presentation to leading biomedical executives.

Cooper Union - New York, NY – Summer Art Intensive - 4-Week July-August
Residential Prog – Portfolio Devt, Exhibition, Anthology Publication; Drawing Animation, Creative Writing, Photography, Graphic Design, & Stop Animation

Cornell University – 3-Week Transmedia: Image, Sound, Motion Program
3-, 6-, 9-week June-August Residential Program; Drawing and New Media (collage, drawing, digital photography, screen printing, & video)
Architecture: Design Studio, Culture, and Society, Architectural Science & Technology

Cornell University – CURIE Academy High School females entering 11th and 12th
Students who excel in math & science break the rules to make new discoveries.

Cornell University - CATALYST Scholars - 1-Week STEM Academy (diverse students)
Cornell Engineering faculty/students participate in ten field sessions.

Corning Summer Internships for College Students – Corning, NY
Advanced Optics, Gorilla Glass, Emerging Innovations, Life Sciences, Pharmaceuticals Internships Offered in Engineering, Science, and Business

Environmental Studies Summer Youth Inst-Hobart & William Smith Colleges
2-week, college experience for HS Students - Immerse in discussions, fieldwork in the Adirondacks, and projects on the environment and sustainability.

Federal Bureau of Investigation - Future Agents in Training - Teen Academy
FBI classes on terrorism, cyber crime, public corruption, polygraph exams, evidence response, and SWAT. Meet w/special agents and intelligence analysts.

GenCyber – 5-day Nat Security Agency-Sponsored Cybersecurity Camp for HS Students - Mohawk Valley CC, RIT, & SUNY Buffalo – Taught by Cyber Industry
Engaging & Dynamic - Role-playing, visual aids, activities, discussions: Computer networking, systems security, cyber operations, defense, AI, virtual reality

Goddard Institute for Space Studies (GISS) New York City - Climate Change Research Initiative (CCRI) Summer Internship - High School & College
Research, Mentorship, and Experiential Learning Opportunities

Hofstra University Summer Science Research Program (HUSSRP) - 5-Week HS Prog
Students conduct research with matched faculty mentors, culminating in a poster session; students attend weekly seminars.

Jacobs Institute 8-week Paid Biomedical Internship (Apply Nov.-Jan.)
HS Jr/Sr or College Student – Gates Vascular Institute, Buffalo, NY Niagara Medical Campus; Lunch and Learn, Weekly Grand Rounds, Research, Presentations

Lamont-Doherty Earth Observatory Secondary School Field Research Program
6-week - research, lab, and fieldwork - HS students - $1,400 stipend. Students follow through a research process to resolve environmental problems.

Manhattan College Engineering Summer Camp - 1-Week - HS Students
Campers explore five engineering specialties: mechanical, electrical, civil, chemical, and environmental engineering.

Mount Sinai - Icahn School of Medicine - Internship Program - FREE - Rising Senior
African-American/Black or Hispanic/Latino w/demonstrated interest in medicine 6-Week summer program. Dept of Neurosurgery. Applications open in January

New York University Engineering Innovation and Computer Science Programs
Applied Research in Science and Engineering (ARISE) - ARISE is a Free 7-week STEM program focused on Biomedical, Chemical Civil, Computer, Electrical, Mechanical, & Aerospace Engineering
Cyber Security Awareness Week (CSAW) - Cybersecurity Games & Conference NYU Center for Cyber Security - World's largest student-run event for students of all ages, evolving to keep pace w/the changing threat landscape & innovations.
Computer Science for Cyber Security (CS4CS) - 3-week Immersive CS Intro for HS students w/no cybersecurity/programming exp - Learn data usage, hacking, digital forensics, privacy, cryptography, steganography & relevant cyber issues
Innovation, Entrepreneurship and the Science of Smart Cities (ieSoSC) - Advancing Technology & Engineering - FREE 5-week program focused on 'smart city' design, prototypes, & research Lessons: circuits, electronics, coding, complex tasks, team projects/presentation
SPARC - Summer Prog in Automation, Robotics, & Coding - Three 2-week, programs for HS Students in robotics, mechatronics, AR, AI, IoT, computer science, electrical engineering, mechanical eng, machine learning

Pace University - 2-Week STEM Summer Institute for HS Students - In-Person
Coding w/Python, Data Analytics, Design Thinking

Parsons School of Design – New York and Paris - 4-Week Online & On-Campus
Summer programs for students from 3rd grade to 12th NYC - Portfolio building in 3-credit immersive Design, Studio Art, Photography, Illustration, Game Design Paris Program – Design & Mgmt, Explorations in Drawing & Painting, Fashion Design

Purchase College - SUNY SummerTech - HS Students w/day camp & overnight options
This tech camp offers Python, Java, animation, 3D modeling & individual instruction

Rensselaer Polytechnic University – Summer Architecture Program - Troy, NY
2-week Program in July or August, building 3D models, drawings, image editing

Rochester Institute of Technology - FREE - Stipend - Army Laboratory Research Program
Dissect brains, conduct research, meet scientists, interactive lectures - age 16+

Rockefeller University Summer Neuroscience Program - 2-Week, NYC Students
Dissect a brain, research, meet scientists, interactive lectures - 16+ years old

Rome Laboratory - Rome, NY - Air Force Research Labs - 8-12 Weeks
Students participate in mentored ongoing research. Paid internship: comp sci, physics, materials science, & aerospace. Workshops, seminars, presentations.

Roswell Park Cancer Research Institute for HS Juniors - Poster Presentation
Independent research, classroom instruction on cancer, seminars w/invited speakers Cancer biophysics, genetics, pharmacology, cancer therapeutics, tumor immunology

School of Creative & Performing Arts (SOCAPA) – New York (13-18-year-olds)
2-, 3-week - Learn Filmmaking, Screenwriting, Dance, Music, Photography

Sotheby's Summer Institute – Pre-College, Undergrad, Graduate, and Professional
New York, London, and Virtual Programs; Intensives in Painting & Drawing, Curating, Luxury Marketing, Art Crime/Art Law, Fashion, and Art Business

Spotify – Summer Internship with The Journal – New York (Remote Eligible)
Research, Writing, News Stories, Podcast Work: Partnership w/Gimlet and WSJ

Stony Brook University - Simons Summer Research Prog - FREE/Stipend HS Outreach
Simons Fellows conclude the internship by writing a research abstract & poster Weekly faculty talks; research workshops, tours, events, poster symposium

Syracuse University – 2-, 3-, 6-week On-Campus & Online Programs for HS Students
3-D Studio Art; Sculpture; Architecture; Design Studies; Writing Immersion

University at Buffalo School of Pharmacy and Pharmaceutical Sciences (SPPS) Pharmacy Summer Institute (PSI) - 3-days - Buffalo, NY - HS/College Students
Hands-on experiences, exposure to research, career pathways

University of Rochester - Laboratory for Laser Energetics - 16 Rising Seniors Selected
Attend weekly seminars on LLE research, write reports, present research results

Wave Hill Forest Project - 7-week Environmental Proj - HS NYC Resident (16+ yrs old)
Paid Summer Internship/Fieldwork in ecological restoration & urban ecology. Build/maintain wooded trails, remove invasive plant species, fix eroded slopes

North Carolina

Corning Summer Internships for College Students – NW Charlotte, NC
Advanced Optics, Gorilla Glass, Emerging Innovations, Life Sciences, Pharmaceutical Internships Offered in Engineering, Science, and Business

Cyberpatriot - Air Force Assn National Youth Cyber Education Program - 1 Week
HS Students - Multiple camp locations include Central Piedmont CC & Wayne CC

Duke University Summer Workshop in Math (SWiM) - Free - 1-Week Program
Focused on advancing female participation in math, SWiM participants attend 2 math courses, afternoon lectures by professors and social activities.

GenCyber – 5-day Nat Security Agency-Sponsored Cybersecurity Camp for HS Students - NC Central University – Taught by Cyber Industry Professionals
Engaging & Dynamic - Role-playing, visual aids, activities, discussions: Computer networking, systems security, cyber operations, defense, AI, virtual reality

National Institute of Health – 8-week Paid Internship – Research Triangle Park
Biomedical research internship for students 17 years or older by June.
HS-SIP for high school juniors & seniors June to August hands-on research.

North Carolina State University - Residential Engineering Camp for HS Students
11th & 12th Graders explore engineering - Three 1-week Sessions Available
Topics include: robotics, AI, bioenergy, agriculture, sustainability, paper science, industrial & systems eng, textile eng, aerospace, biomedical eng, comp sci, civil eng, ecological, computer networking, chemical eng, & materials science

Science & Engineering Apprenticeship Program (SEAP) – US Navy – Cherry Point
8-weeks, 300 openings, 30 research labs nationwide, $4,000-$4,500 salary. HS students must be 16+ years old. Apply starting in August for following summer.

University of North Carolina Summer Science Program - HS Students 5-6 Wks
> Biochemistry and molecular biology research - highly competitive, hands-on, collaborative; mentors; student teams; analysis, scientific writing, presentations

North Dakota

GenCyber – 5-day Nat Security Agency-Sponsored Cybersecurity Camp for HS Students - Bismarck State College – Taught by Cyber Industry Professionals
> Engaging & Dynamic - Role-playing, visual aids, activities, discussions: Computer networking, systems security, cyber operations, defense, AI, virtual reality

Ohio

Cyberpatriot - Air Force Assn National Youth Cyber Education Program - 1 Week
> HS Students - Camp locations include the National Museum of the U.S. Air Force

Science and Engineering Apprenticeship Program (SEAP) – US Navy – Dayton
> 8-weeks, 300 openings, 30 research labs nationwide, $4,000-$4,500 salary. HS students must be 16+ years old. Apply starting in August for following summer.

Wright-Patterson AF Base - Dayton, OH - Air Force Research Labs - 8-12 Weeks
> Students participate in mentored ongoing research. Paid internship: comp sci, physics, materials science, & aerospace. Workshops, seminars, presentations.

Oklahoma

GenCyber – 5-day Nat Security Agency-Sponsored Cybersecurity Camp for HS Students - Rose State College – Taught by Cyber Industry Professionals
> Engaging & Dynamic - Role-playing, visual aids, activities, discussions: Computer networking, systems security, cyber operations, defense, AI, virtual reality

University of Oklahoma Architecture Summer Academy - HS Students - 1 week
> Residential Program: Architecture, Interior Design, Construction Science Design in Action: Creativity, Innovation, & Sustainability Shaping the Built Environment

Oregon

GenCyber – 5-day Nat Security Agency-Sponsored Cybersecurity Camp for HS Students - Chemeketa CC, Oregon State, Portland CC – Taught by Cyber Industry
> Engaging & Dynamic - Role-playing, visual aids, activities, discussions: Computer networking, systems security, cyber operations, defense, AI, virtual reality

Pennsylvania

Carnegie Mellon University - Art, Math, Science, and Game Design Programs
> **National HS Game Academy - 6-Week Game Design Program** - Design video games from ideation, development, & pitch, to final product
> **AI Scholars Program** - FREE - 4-Week Program for HS Students - AI, seminars, discussions, research, projects, and engagement with tech companies

Pre-College Residential Art Program: 3-, 4-, 6-wk (July-August)
Intensive Studio Studies Portfolio development in Drawing, Sculpture, Animation and Concept Studio Art Chestnut Hill College Global Solutions Lab

Summer Academy for Math & Science (SAMS)-Free Hands-on STEM program for underrepresented students, explore science w/projects & class instruction

Cyberpatriot - Air Force Assn National Youth Cyber Education Program - 1 Week

HS Students - Multiple locations include Univ. of Pittsburgh, Gannon University, Community College of Beaver County, & Pittsburgh Technical College

Drexel University Westphal College of Media Arts & Design – Discovering Architecture

2-week Residential Program – HS Students – Intensive Studio Architecture Program Visit prominent architectural, multi-disciplinary design offices; meet architects

GenCyber – 5-day Nat Security Agency-Sponsored Cybersecurity Camp for HS Students - Indiana U. of Pennsylvania – Taught by Cyber Industry Professionals

Engaging & Dynamic - Role-playing, visual aids, activities, discussions: Computer networking, systems security, cyber operations, defense, AI, virtual reality

Great Books Summer Program - Haverford College - Grades 6-8 and 9-12

Great Books & Big Ideas, Writer's Workshops, and Literary Travel Programs Read, Write, & Discuss Big Ideas in Literature and Philosophy with scholars

Interactive Global Simulation, Electrifying Africa, & UN Sustainable Growth

1-week – HS Students – Intensive collaborative team solutions to big problems

Lehigh University - IGEI (4 Weeks) and SEI (2 Weeks) - HS Programs for 11th & 12th

Iacocca Global Entrepreneurship Intensive(IGEI) - HS Entrepreneurship Program Sustainable design, global citizenship, design challenges, business hackathons, teams

Summer Engineering Institute (SEI) - Intensive classroom study, discussions, team projects, problem-solving, integrated technology

Maywood University Pre-College Summer Workshop School of Architecture

2-week (July) Residential Program – HS Students – Design/Build Your Future

Penn Summer Coding Academy - Univ of Pennsylvania 3-Week HS Program
Students learn HTML, Cascading Style Sheets, JavaScript, and webpage creation

Pennsylvania State University Architecture & Landscape Architecture Summer Camp
1-week (July) – HS Students –Architecture, Graphics, Design, Built Environment

Pennsylvania State University Summer Discovery Program in Engineering & STEM, Also Engineering Ahead (Free 4-Week Program for Minorities)
Students are introduced to engineering disciplines, design, and research.

Science and Engineering Apprenticeship Program (SEAP) – US Navy – Philadelphia
8-weeks, 300 openings, 30 research labs nationwide, $4,000-$4,500 salary. HS students must be 16+ years old. Apply starting in August for following summer.

Temple University Tyler School of Art and Architecture Pre-College Program
2-week (July-August) Residential Program – HS Students – Studio Architecture

University of Pennsylvania 3 Week Engineering Summer Academy at Penn (ESAP)
Rigorous on-campus program for highly motivated HS students on AP, Biotech, Computer Graphics, Computer Science, Nanotechnology, and Robotics

University of Pittsburgh Medical Center - FREE - Hillman Cancer Center Academy
Immersive 7-week mentored medical research program for HS students (15+ yrs) Research in biology, medicine, computer science.

Wistar Institute High School Fellowship in Biomedical Research - Philadelphia
4-week - cancer biology, genetics, vaccine development, infectious diseases, and bioinformatics. Work in state-of-the-art training lab ; literature review.

Rhode Island

Brown University – 1-4 Weeks – Art Themed Courses & the Environmental Leadership Lab (Climate Change 2-week hand's on program for HS Students
Creative Writing, Music, Studio Art, Art History, & Environment/Sustainability

Cyberpatriot - Air Force Assn National Youth Cyber Education Program - 1 Week
HS Students - Multiple camp locations incl. the Comm College of Rhode Island

GenCyber – 5-day Nat Security Agency-Sponsored Cybersecurity Camp for HS Students - Rhode Island College – Taught by Cyber Industry Professionals
Engaging & Dynamic - Role-playing, visual aids, activities, discussions: Computer networking, systems security, cyber operations, defense, AI, virtual reality

Rhode Island School of Design Pre-College School of Design – Providence, RI
6-week (June-July) Residential Program – HS Students – Foundational Art & Design Studies Figure drawing, projects, trips, exhibitions

Roger Williams University High School Summer Academy in Architecture
4-week (July-August) Residential Program – Grades 11 & 12 – Explore Studio Architecture - Seminars, fieldwork, studio, portfolio development

South Carolina

Clemson University Pre-College School of Architecture Program
1-week (July-August) Residential Program – Grades 7-12 - Engineering Design, Mechanical/Civil Engineering, Intelligent Vehicles, Materials Engineering

Cyberpatriot - Air Force Assn National Youth Cyber Education Program - 1 Week
HS Students - Multiple camp locations, including USC Upstate & USC Aiken

GenCyber – 5-day Nat Security Agency-Sponsored Cybersecurity Camp for HS Students - The Citadel – Taught by Cyber Industry Professionals
Engaging & Dynamic - Role-playing, visual aids, activities, discussions: Computer networking, systems security, cyber operations, defense, AI, virtual reality

Science and Engineering Apprenticeship Program – US Navy – Charleston
8-weeks, 300 openings, 30 research labs nation wide, $4,000-$4,500 salary. HS students must be 16+ years old. Apply starting in August for following summer.

University of South Carolina HS Summer Computer Tech & Engineering Programs
Carolina Master Scholars Adventure Series - 1 Week Hands-on design thinking in VEX Robotics, Digital Content Creation, and Green Engineering
Partners for Minorities in Eng & Comp Sci (PMECS) 9th-12th AI, Cyber, Coding

South Dakota

GenCyber – 5-day Nat Security Agency-Sponsored Cybersecurity Camp for HS Students - Dakota State Univ. – Taught by Cyber Industry Professionals
Engaging & Dynamic - Role-playing, visual aids, activities, discussions: Computer networking, systems security, cyber operations, defense, AI, virtual reality

Tennessee

Arnold Air Force Base - Tullahoma, TN - Air Force Research Labs - 8-12 Weeks
Students participate in mentored ongoing research. Paid internship: comp sci, physics, materials science, & aerospace. Workshops, seminars, presentations.

University of Memphis Discovering Architecture + Design - 1-day – HS Students
Design programs on architecture, interior design, and the built environment

University of Tennessee, Knoxville College of Architecture + Design
1-week UT Summer Design Camp (July) Residential – HS Students
Immersive architecture, graphic design, and professional practice program

Vanderbilt Summer Academy – Nashville, TN – 3-Week Program
" Digital Storytelling", "Writing Fantasy Fiction", "Math & Music", "Writing Short Stories"

Texas

AFWERX Air Force Innovation - Austin, TX - Air Force Research Labs - 8-12 Weeks
Students participate in mentored ongoing research teams. Paid intern: comp sci, physics, materials science, & aerospace. Workshops, seminars, presentations.

Aggie STEM Summer Camps - Texas A&M - Grades 6-8 & 9-12 - 1 & 2 Week
STEM topics include robotics, rockets, coding, and engineering design principles. Students also meet professors & tour STEM labs on the TAMU campus.

Baylor Engineering & Computing Summer Academy (BECSA) - 10th - 12th
Focus on rolling, electrical, calculating energy, energy in flight & harvesting energy

Baylor University - CASPER HS Scholars Program - EE/Aerospace - 11th & 12th
Astrophysics, gravitation, condensed matter, plasmas & beam physics

Boeing Summer Internship – HS & College– Lewisville and San Antonio
Hands-on Industry Experience - Aviation and Engineering Internships

Corning Summer Internships for College Students – Keller, TX
Advanced Optics, Gorilla Glass, Emerging Innovations, Life Sciences, Pharmaceuticals Internships Offered in Engineering, Science, and Business

Cyberpatriot - Air Force Assn National Youth Cyber Education Program - 1 Week
HS Students - Locations include Angelo State U. South Texas College, UTEP, Baylor Collaborative, Texas Women's University, St. Philip's College Texas State

GenCyber – 5-day Nat Security Agency-Sponsored Cybersecurity Camp for HS Students - San Antonio College, Texas A&M – Taught by Cyber Industry Prof.
Engaging & Dynamic - Role-playing, visual aids, activities, discussions: Computer networking, systems security, cyber operations, defense, AI, virtual reality

Jacobs Engineering Internship – Summer Internship (College) - Dallas
Civil, Electrical, Environmental, Geotechnical, & Transportation Engineering; Sustainability, Cybersecurity, Mobility, and R&D with worldwide projects.

National Security Agency (NSA) – Paid Computer Internship – San Antonio
Students must be at least a junior in high school with interest in business, engineering, or computer science. Apply between September 1 and October 31.

Rice University Summer Scholars Programs - Middle & High School Students
Aerospace Academy - 12 days - Hands-on in industry facilities w/NASA reps Immersion attend flight school w/flight prep simulation, launch a satellite
Creative Writing Camp - Develop writing skills while living on campus
National Youth Leadership Forum: Medicine & Health Care - 8 days hands-on HS students gain clinical training in medical diagnostics, surgery & first aid
Pre-College Programs - Economics, Entrepreneurship, Genome Engineering, Global Affairs, Law, Physiology, & Psychology
Rice Center for Engineering Leadership (RCEL) Rice ELITE Tech - Real world advanced engineering & technology - AI, IoT, machine learning, data science
Rice U School Mathematics Project (RUSMP) - Summer Math Camps
Tapia Camps - 1 Week on campus - STEM projects, presentations, field trips

SpaceX – Summer Engineering/Co-op Program – Brownsville & McGregor
Paid Internship - Must be in an undergraduate in a STEM subject

Southern Methodist University - STEM Works, Kids Ahead, TEDXKids@SMU
Introduction to Engineering - 7th & 8th - Basic hands-on project approach
Advanced Engineering - 9th & 10th - Project-based engineering design
Engineering Design Experience - 11th & 12th - Civil, EE, Comp Sci, Mechanical

Tesla Internships – Ave. $33/hour – Full-Time Automotive Design/ Engineering
Austin – Manufacturing Engineering; Waco - People Analytics - Vehicle Service Research/Training

Texas Tech Anson L Clark Scholars Program – Research Areas: Advertising, Architecture, Art, Dance, Engineering, or Theatre - 7-week – Grades 11 & 12
Residential Program (must be 17 years old by start date) – no program fee Intensive research-based program; $500 meal card; $750 tax-free stipend

University of Houston & Wonderworks Pre-College Summer Discovery Program
Hines College of Architecture & Design – Intro to Architecture 6-week – HS Students – Design w/hands-on studio, field trips, & portfolio workshop
UH Coding and AI Camp - Hands-on programming with AI applications

University of Texas at Austin Summer Programs for HS Students
Computer Science Summer Academy - 1 Week - HS Students learn C++, project management, machine learning, AI, & Python
My Introduction to Engineering (MITE) - 5-day camp for 11th grade students to work on team-based engineering projects
Digital Design - 2-D Game Design, 3-D Game Design, 3-D Animation/ Motion - School of Design & Creative Technologies - 1-week – HS Students – portfolio development &

3D Game design

STEM Enhancement in Earth Science (SEES) - NASA, Texas Space Grant Consortium, Center for Space Research Summer Program - Interpret NASA satellite remote sensing data while working w/NASA scientists & engineers Field investigation - HS Juniors/Seniors 16+ years old by July 1 - FREE

Utah

Cyberpatriot - Air Force Assn National Youth Cyber Education Program - 1 Week
HS Students - Multiple camp locations, including Utah Valley University

Edwards Lifesciences Summer College Internship Program - Draper, Utah
Currently Enrolled in College - Interested in Healthcare Related Programs Proficient in Engineering Drafting Software, Writing, or Business/Leadership

GenCyber – 5-day Nat Security Agency-Sponsored Cybersecurity Camp for HS Students - Brigham Young University – Taught by Cyber Industry Professionals
Engaging & Dynamic - Role-playing, visual aids, activities, discussions: Computer networking, systems security, cyber operations, defense, AI, virtual reality

Vermont

Columbia Climate School in the Green Mountains - Green Mountains - HS Students
2-week program on Climate and Sustainability - discussions, seminars, fieldwork, hands-on projects, critical thinking, & problem solving

School of Creative & Performing Arts (SOCAPA) – Burlington, VT (13-18-year-olds)
2-week, 3-week - learn Filmmaking, Screenwriting, Dance, Music, Photography

Virginia

Cyberpatriot - Air Force Assn National Youth Cyber Education Program - 1 Week
HS Students - Locations, incl Mtn Gateway CC & Lynchburg Nat Guard Academy

Federal Bureau of Investigation - Future Agents in Training - Teen Academy
FBI classes on terrorism, cyber crime, public corruption, polygraph exams, evidence response, and SWAT. Meet w/special agents and intelligence analysts.

GenCyber – 5-day Nat Security Agency-Sponsored Cybersecurity Camp for HS Students - Marymount Univ. & Virginia Tech - Taught by Cyber Industry Prof.
Engaging & Dynamic - Role-playing, visual aids, activities, discussions: Computer networking, systems security, cyber operations, defense, AI, virtual reality

NASA Langley Research Center Paid Internship Program (16+ years old) 8-10 weeks
Aerospace program in Public Affairs, Multimedia, Statistics, Aerial Robotics, Space Hardware Design, Testing, Mars Surface Habitat, & High Temperature Materials

NASA's Wallops Flight Facility Summer Internship - High School & College
Research, Mentorship, and Experiential Learning Opportunities

Northrop Grumman – Engineering Intern– Space Systems R & D Team
Graduating HS Seniors – Join an engineering team to design, develop and test space systems and satellites; R & D - land, sea, air, space, and cyberspace.

Pentagon - Arlington, VA - Air Force Research Labs - 8-12 Weeks
Students participate in mentored ongoing research. Paid internship: comp sci, physics, materials science, & aerospace. Workshops, seminars, presentations.

Science and Engineering Apprenticeship Program (SEAP) – US Navy Hampton Roads and Dahlgren
8-weeks, 300 openings, 30 research labs nationwide, $4,000-$4,500 salary. HS students must be 16+ years old. Apply starting in August for following summer.

Virginia Commonwealth University (VCUArts) Pre-College - 3-Week
On-Campus Program – 2D Portfolio Devt, Photography; Clay: More Than Just Mud, Sketchbook to Controller, Animation Workshop, Sculpture, Jewelry & Fashion Design, Stage Combat, Musical Theatre, Acting From Page to Stage

Virginia Tech Inside Architecture + Design & Imagination Camp
1-week – HS Students – Hands-on design studio architecture program 1-week - Electrical & Computer Engineering; Drone, Build, & Fly Program

Washington

COPE Scholars Program – Healthcare Internship – 280 Hours Training Locations in Puyallup, Seattle, Spokane, and Tacoma
Health Scholars must be 18+. Students assist w/basic healthcare for medical or nursing school, etc. Certificate of Completion - Keck Graduate Institute

Cyberpatriot - Air Force Assn National Youth Cyber Education Program - 1 Week
HS Students - Multiple camp locations, including Marysville NUROTC

DigiPen Academy – K-12 Animation, Film, Music, Game Design Summer Programs – Redmond, WA
1-week and 2-week programs, including Teen Art & Animation; Film Scoring Music & Sound Design; Video Game Development; Animation Masterclass

GenCyber – 5-day Nat Security Agency-Sponsored Cybersecurity Camp for HS Students - Eastern Washington Univ., Spokane Falls CC, & Whatcom CC – Taught by Cyber Industry Professionals
Engaging & Dynamic - Role-playing, visual aids, activities, discussions: Computer networking, systems security, cyber operations, defense, AI, virtual reality

NatureBridge Summer Programs - Olympic National Park - 1-2 weeks
Environmental science education, & hands-on fieldwork while backpacking for students in 7th - 12th grades. Connect to nature with trail building, habitat restoration, and wilderness exploration.

University of Washington – Seattle, WA – Middle and HS Students
1-Week - Neurotechnology Young Scholars Program, DawgBytes Computer Science Camp, Material Science Camp, and Summer Session Art Classes
STEM - Summer program in Engineering and Technology

Wilderness Awareness School's Summer Camps - 5-days for 6-12 year olds
Nature and environmental activities, including survival skills training in St. Edward State Park, Cougar Mountain Park, Seward Park, Tolt MacDonald Park, and Carnation Farms. These are day camps for kids.

Youth Engaged in Sustainable Systems (YESS) - HS Student Summer Program
This hands-on paid internship includes natural resources, conservation, ecological restoration, & sustainable environmental practices. Replace invasive plant species to restore ecological environments. Highline & Riverview School Districts

West Virginia

NASA Independent Verification and Validation Facility, Fairmont, WV
Research, Mentorship, and Experiential Learning Opportunities
HS Students - Focus on robotics, programming, engineering, & STEM projects

National Youth Science Academy - FREE - Camp Pocahontas, WV - STEAM
Two delegates (HS juniors or seniors) are selected to attend from each state and D.C. attend for 3 weeks. Housing, meals, transportation, and supplies are provided at no cost. Washington, D.C. trip included.

West Virginia Governor's STEM Institute (GSI) - high-achieving 8th & 9th Graders
Hands-on computer science, cybersecurity, & AI program to advance science exp

Wisconsin

Cyberpatriot - Air Force Assn National Youth Cyber Education Program - 1 Week
HS Students - Camp locations include Marquette University

Experimental Aircraft Association - 1 Week Aviation Camps for students 12 - 18
Young Eagles Camp - 12-13-year-olds - Aeromodeling, Wing Construction, basic flight, interactive computer simulator ground school, fly designed missions
Basic Camp - 14-15-year-olds Ground School, Tech Workshop, Models, Demos
Advanced Camp - Action-packed aviation ground instruction & flight experience

GenCyber – 5-day Nat Security Agency-Sponsored Cybersecurity Camp for HS Students - U. of Wisconsin-Whitewater – Taught by Cyber Industry Professionals
Engaging & Dynamic - Role-playing, visual aids, activities, discussions: Computer networking, systems security, cyber operations, defense, AI, virtual reality

University of Wisconsin - Madison - Engineering Summer Program - 11th & 12th
Free, 3-week residential program for students interested in engineering. Mechanical Engineering & Electrical/Computer Engineering

University of Wisconsin Milwaukee School of Architecture & Urban Planning
1-week – HS Students – Online architectural design & interior design activities, lectures, workshops, and interactive architectural concepts and design thinking.

Wyoming

Sierra Club's Summer Outings - Gros Ventre Wilderness - Yellowstone Ecosystem
Trail restoration trip - 7 days - Forest Service personnel drive gear to the trailhead. Hike the rugged landscape to scenic rivers while working on the trail

TAKE ADVANTAGE OF THIS TIME TO EXPLORE

During high school and college, explore your interests through summer programs, skill-building camps, and internships. Try out different fields you might not have considered before. You never really have the same chance to consider alternatives in quite the same way. Learn something new. There are hundreds of career areas you may never have considered. Have some fun while you are at it!

Everything has its beauty, but not everyone sees it.

– Andy Warhol

Make next summer a summer to remember!
Apply early. Some deadlines are in the fall and others fill fast.

CHAPTER 5
UNIVERSITY OPTIONS

"Never doubt that a small group of committed citizens can change the world; indeed, it is the only thing that ever has."

– **Margaret Mead**

Some people insist the best universities are those with large lecture hall classes. However, some students work better in small, project-based classes with hands-on activities and field trips to labs, research centers, and events.

Every student is different. You need to find a school that fits you. Large, fiercely competitive schools can be motivational or they can leave you with a pit in your stomach and a sense of failure. If graduate school is your goal, you may want to attend a university where you can get research opportunities, master your classes, and get involved. Thus, the best university is the one where you will thrive. Fortunately, there are many colleges and variables to consider.

Big picture data for U.S. college students in 2022-2023 include:

- 19.6 million college students
- 2,679 4-year colleges
- 1,303 2-year colleges
- 5.14 million attend private colleges
- 14.5 million attend public colleges

In another interesting statistic, undergraduate enrollment dropped more than 8% from fall 2019 to fall 2022, representing nearly 2,000,000 loss of students during the pandemic. However, in 2024, enrollment grew 1.2% with greatest increase in community colleges. With test-optional admissions opening the door to more students without test scores or who test poorly, more students applied to the top schools. Beware, though, some colleges are moving back to requiring tests.

US NEWS & WORLD REPORT

Best Global Universities for Energy & Fuels in the US (Top 27 in 2024)

1. Stanford University
2. MIT
3. Georgia Tech
4. UC Berkeley
5. University of Maryland
6. University of Washington
7. North Carolina State
8. Northwestern University
9. UT Austin
10. University of Michigan
11. Penn State
12. University of Tennessee
13. University of Colorado
14. Cornell University
15. University of Illinois (UIUC)
16. ASU
17. Texas A&M
18. UC San Diego
19. University of Minnesota
20. Princeton University
21. Colorado School of Mines
22. University of Houston
23. Washington State University
24. Virginia Tech
25. Ohio State University
26. University of Wisconsin
27. Purdue University

EDURANK 2024 – WORLD RANKING (TITLES ABBREVIATED)

Best Universities for Environmental Engineering

1. Tsinghua Univ., China
2. Harbin Inst. of Technology, China
3. Tongji Univ., China
4. Delft U. of Technology, Netherlands
5. Univ. of Queensland, Australia
6. Technical Univ. of Denmark
7. Zhejiang Univ., China
8. Univ. of California, Berkeley, USA
9. National Univ. of Singapore
10. Imperial College London, UK
11. Univ. of Hong Kong, China
12. Univ. of Tokyo, Japan
13. Univ. of Illinois (UIUC), USA
14. Ghent Univ., Belgium
15. Wageningen U., Netherlands
16. Pennsylvania State U., USA
17. Nanyang Technological U., Singapore
18. Univ. of Alberta, Canada
19. Univ. of Toronto, Canada
20. Stanford Univ., USA
21. MIT, USA
22. Tianjin Univ., China
23. Univ. of Texas at Austin, USA
24. Univ. of Florida, USA
25. Nanjing Univ., China
26. Univ. of California, Davis, USA
27. Cornell Univ., USA
28. Univ. of Michigan, USA
29. Univ. of Minnesota, USA
30. Swiss Federal Institute of Technology Zurich, Switzerland
31. Dalian Univ. of Technology, China
32. Univ. of British Columbia, Canada
33. Hunan Univ. China
34. Shanghai Jiao Tong U., China
35. South China U. of Technology, China
36. Univ. of Sao Paulo, Brazil
37. Catholic Univ. of Leuven, Belgium
38. Univ. of New South Wales, Australia
39. Harvard Univ., USA
40. Beijing Univ. of Technology, China
41. Shandong Univ., China
42. Kyoto Univ., Japan
43. Cranfield Univ., UK
44. Peking Univ., China
45. Indian Institute of Technology Roorkee, India
46. Hong Kong Polytechnic Univ., China
47. Virginia Tech, USA
48. Texas A&M Univ., USA
49. Univ. of Waterloo, Canada
50. Univ. of Wisconsin, USA

CONSIDER MORE THAN JUST RANKINGS

Rankings can be a helpful place to start your search. However, they miss important factors. You need to determine whether the school is a good fit for your circumstances. There are many other factors. Some variables include cost of attendance, competitiveness, majors, acceptance rates, housing availability, research opportunities, ability to enroll in required classes, acceptance to graduate school, and size of freshman and sophomore classes, just to name a few.

Note: Colleges where 400 students enroll in first and second year classes often say their "average class size" is somewhere around 25. Also, almost every school says they offer study abroad, though in most cases the study abroad programs are under another school's umbrella and rarely includes students/professors from your university.

Ask students whether they can register for the classes they need, get support for internships/summer programs, and have access to professors and not just graduate school assistants. Below are some lists and charts with additional information.

PROFESSIONAL ORGANIZATIONS IN ENVIRONMENTAL ENGINEERING

American Academy of Environmental Engineers & Scientists (AAEES)

Established in 1955, AAEES started under the umbrella of the American Society of Civil Engineers, pulling together support from multiple organizations. Members are Board-Certified Environmental Engineers & Scientists while also passing an oral exam and review. Members cover engineering areas including Air Pollution Control, Environmental Sustainability, General Environmental Engineering, Hazardous Waste Management, Industrial Hygiene, Radiation Protection, Solid Waste Management and Water Supply/Wastewater Management. The AAEES sponsors awards for achievements in research, excellence, projects, and professionalism.

Contests: Excellence in Environmental Engineering & Science Competition, Environmental Communication Award Competition, and Student Video & Social Media Competition.

Association of Environmental Engineering & Science Professors (AEESP)

AEESP, established in 1963, comprises more than 700 professors worldwide who serve as educators in environmental engineering and science. Headquartered in Washington, D.C. AEESP publishes *Environmental Engineering Science*, a journal that explores policy initiatives along with innovative solutions to environmental problems. AEESP also hosts conferences to exchange information. The organization recognizes outstanding students, research, and practices in the field.

National Association of Environmental Professionals (NAEP)

NAEP is a network of professionals and students across disciplines whose focus is the environment. Headquartered in Seattle, WA, NAEP hosts workshops and conferences to share technical knowledge and practices. The organization also offers scholarships to students.

Air & Waste Management Association (A&WMA)

A&WMA offers a home to professionals and students in the environmental industry with access to resources, networking, conferences, webinars, publication, and career advancement. A&WMA includes more than 5,000 members and 500 student members belonging to 65 chapters worldwide. Full-time students can join for $35.

Contest: Environmental Challenge International - Team-based competition where students provide a solution to an environmental problem and present findings.

Scholarships & Chapter Awards are also offered.

Water Environment Federation (WEF)

WEF is a non-profit professional organization of more than 34,000 members. With headquarters in Alexandria, VA, members focus on diverse areas of water quality, wastewater, and environmental engineering. WEF hosts conferences and meetings and publishes books, reports, journals, and magazines.

NATIONAL/INTERNATIONAL ASSOCIATIONS AND ORGANIZATIONS FOR CHEMISTRY

American Chemical Society – *Improve the world through the transforming power of chemistry.*

Founded in 1876, the American Chemical Society is one of the largest scientific organizations with more than 173,000 members across 140 countries. ACS holds conferences, sponsors clubs, publishes 80+ journals, and supports research, collaboration, diversity, sustainability, and international enterprise. Start a club and get involved. Join: $25 for undergraduate members, $55 for graduate students

ACS opportunities for students include:

High School	Undergraduate Chemistry	Graduate Students in Chem
ACS ChemClub	Student Chapters	Grad & Postdoc Magazine
Chemistry Olympiad	Bridge Project (Diversity)	Grad Student Organizations
ChemMatters Magazine	Chem Demo Videos	Career Planning
Project SEED	Experience/Mentorships	Awards, Fellowships, Travel
ACS Scholars Program	Chemical Science Careers	Meetings & Events
College Planning	Grants/Scholarships/Travel	Securing a Faculty Position
Science Outreach	Graduate School Planning	International Students

Conferences include:

New Orleans, LA	Denver, CO	San Diego, CA	Washington, D.C.
August 18-22, 2024	March 23-27, 2025	August 17-21, 2025	March 2-26, 2026

American Chemistry Council (ACC) – While this organization is primarily for American companies and policy makers, ACC may be valuable in your research. The ACC represents and advocates for people, products, innovation, and policies, and more than 190 companies. The chemical industry produces groundbreaking products that improve the lives of people globally, making the world healthier, safer, more sustainable, and more productive. The ACC provides news, trends, data, and statistics on industry management, plastics, energy, climate, water, air quality, sustainability, cybersecurity, transportation, safety, security, tax, trade, and research.

International Council of Chemical Associations (ICCA) – The ICCA serves as a voice for the chemical industry on the international stage. ICCA's member organizations include associations, federations, and companies which manufacture and distribute life-changing products that mitigate against the world's most pressing challenges.

STUDENT ORGANIZATIONS FOCUSED ON THE ENVIRONMENT

1. Bee Campus USA
2. Campus Sustainability Council
3. Climate Reality Campus Corps
4. Earth Justice Club
5. Eco Club
6. Energy Club
7. Engineers for a Sustainable World (ESW)
8. Environmental Law Society
9. Food Recovery Network
10. Greenpeace
11. Habitat for Humanity
12. Net Impact
13. Oxfam Campus Club
14. Roots & Shoots
15. Sierra Club
16. Solar Energy Club
17. Sustainable Ocean Alliance
18. Wildlife Conservation Society
19. Students for Environmental Action (SEA)
20. Zero Waste Club

TWENTY-FIVE HIGHLIGHTED ENVIRONMENTAL ENGINEERING & ALTERNATIVE ENERGY RESEARCH UNIVERSITIES

Arizona State University
Project: Arizona Center for Algae Technology & Innovation (AzCATI)
Leads: Taylor Weiss and John McGowen
ASU received $34 million, including a Department of Energy grant to fund projects in biofuels, biopower and bioproducts. AzCATI is investigating alternatives to petroleum by creating biomass production for conversion into low-carbon biofuels.

Carnegie Mellon University
Project: Climate Resilient Environmental Systems and Technologies (CREST)
Leads: Ten faculty and Ph.D. students
CREST focuses on three domains that include climate change, adaptation, mitigation, water systems, and innovative environmental technologies.

Columbia University
Project: Learning the Earth with Artificial Intelligence and Physics (LEAP)
Director: Pierre Gentine, Departments of Earth & Environmental Engineering and Earth & Environmental Sciences
LEAP focuses on planning, predictions, and projections using AI. With an interdisciplinary approach, researchers use climate data science, incorporating available data to provide information so people can make better decisions.

Project: Columbia Electrochemical Energy Center
Researchers: Twelve core faculty, plus postdocs/student researchers
This team seeks to develop safe, effective, affordable, fast-charging batteries and fuel cells to provide sustainable energy. The goal is for the batteries to fully charge in minutes.

Cornell University
Project: Cornell Energy Systems Institute (CESI)
Interim Director: C. Lindsay Anderson
With a focus on developing sustainable energy, CESI's research centers around carbon conversion and sequestration, energy and power systems, fusion, and geothermal processes.

Duke University
Project: Duke Center for Water, Sanitation & Hygiene (WaSH-AID)
Principal Investigators: Brian Stoner, Jeffrey T. Glass, Co-Director With 3.6 billion people without safe sanitation and 432,000 who die each year as a result, Duke is developing novel nutrient removal technologies for stormwater, automated waste treatment, and sensors/diagnostics.

Project: Characterization of Coal Mine Drainage Wastes
Principal Investigator: Heileen Hsu-Kim
This project studies the geochemical extraction of critical metals, acid mine drainage fluids, and treatment solids.

Elon University
Project: Triangle Environmental Health Initiative
Founder & Principal: Tate Rogers Elon is testing new materials for phosphorous and nitrogen removal using sorbent materials developed at Duke's WaSH-AID. USAID funded solid waste management in Cambodia. Other projects include dynamic pump screens to service pits and septic tanks filled with thick sludge and water treatment in West Africa.

Georgia Tech
Project: Smart Cities & Inclusive Innovation (SCI2)
Executive Director: Debra Lam
This project researches. analyzes data, and implements an ecosystem approach to sustainable communities and smart cities using cutting-edge technology, connectivity, mobility, engagement, continuous improvement, and data security.

Project: Extraction, Separation, or Refinement of Critical Minerals from Coal-based Resources
This project studies the testing and development of ionic liquids for extraction.

Harvard University
Project: Salata Institute for Climate & Stability
Director: James H. Stock
This environmental science and engineering research focuses on low-carbon energy solutions and climate change mitigation. Projects include energy-efficient windows, climate adaptation, energy systems, methane emission reductions, and corporate net-zero targets.

Johns Hopkins University
Project: Water, Sanitation, & Hygiene (WASH) Challenge - Drinking Water from Aging Infrastructure & Climate Change
Researchers Include: Kellogg Schwab
Environmental engineering innovation projects in water quality improvement and sustainable water resource management, sanitation, sustainability, and security.

Massachusetts Institute of Technology
Project: MIT.nano
Director: Vladimir Bulovic
This multidisciplinary group studies next-gen nano-materials for microelectronics and microsystems. Teams develop quantum topological materials, entanglement structures, nano-materials for pollution control, and sustainable energy.

Project: Parsons Lab
Department Chair: Ali Jadbabaie
Environmental Chemistry, Environmental Fluid Mechanics and Coastal Engineering, Environmental Microbiology, Hydrology and Hydroclimatology

Michigan State University
Project: Center for Sustainable Systems – Environmental Impact of Autonomous Vehicles
Co-Directors: Gregory Keoleian & Joshua Newell
This research assesses the economic and regulatory issues surrounding the environmental sustainability performance of autonomous vehicle systems and fueling/charging options.

North Carolina State University
Project: Climate, Hydrology & Water Resources Modeling & Synthesis Group
Director: Sankar Arumugam
This water resources group sifts through hydrology and climate data to determine social, climate, and management impacts. Overcoming the challenges of clean water, sanitation, and groundwater, the group considers system design, saltwater intrusion, drought planning, and capacity.

Northwestern University
Project: Dirt-Powered Fuel Cell That Runs Forever
Senior Investigator: George Wells
This research team created a soil-powered fuel cell that harnesses energy from microbes in the dirt. Sustainable power in dirt overcomes battery toxicity and supply chain problems to charge underground sensors for agriculture and communications devices.

Oregon State University
Project: PacWave - Wave Energy Testing
Chief Scientist: Burke Hales
DOE provided $25 million for renewable energy from waves, addressing critical power needs and mitigating global climate change. PacWave supports industry in harvesting and testing energy from waves.

Project: Wastewater Conversion to Simultaneously Irrigate & Fertilize Crops
Principal Leader: Xue Jin
With a U.S. Dept of Agriculture grant, Xue Jin's team researches effective treatment technologies to provide safe reclaimed water for agriculture. This wastewater treatment would decrease ecological impacts by reducing the use of chemical fertilizers.

Portland State University
Project: DOE Water Power Technologies Grant - Advancing Wave Energy
Principal Investigator: Jonathan Bird
PSU is testing and validating a new electromagnetic device that can increase power up to tenfold, allowing ocean waves to be harnessed. This renewable and reliable resource will never be depleted, accelerating the transition to a carbon-free electricity grid.

Purdue University
Project: "Forever" Chemicals in Wastewater & Biosolids
Program Head: Linda Lee, Ecological Science & Engineering

This environmental engineering research addresses legacy and emerging challenges related to the occurrence, mobility, transformation, plant uptake, and remediation of unregulated and harmful polyfluoroalkyl chemicals. The project seeks to develop a decision tool and management guidelines for industry and agriculture.

San Diego State University
Project: Efficient Fuel Generation, Electron & Energy Transfer, and Plastic Waste Upcycling
Principal Investigator: Jing Gu
The Gu lab seeks to understand electron transfer, electricity generation, eco-cycle processes, and uses/breakdown of non-biodegradable waste.

Stanford University
Project: Sustainable Systems
Research Group Lead: Ram Rajagopal

This research focuses on improving electric power systems to accelerate grid decarbonization, improve resilience, and enable equity. The group develops scalable solutions and sustainable built environments using data science optimization and machine learning.

Project: Generation – Hydrogen Initiative
Co-Managing Directors: Naomi Boness & Jimmy Chen
This group focuses on carbon-negative geologic hydrogen production with the goal of developing inexpensive methods to generate green hydrogen at scale without greenhouse gas emissions.

Texas Tech
Project: Center for Nanophotonics
Principal Investigators: Hongxing Jiang & Jingyu Lin
This project increases efficiency by incubating next-generation clean energy, semiconductor neutron detectors, in-situ hydrogen production, and developing technologies to produce tens of mega-electron volts.

University of California, Berkeley
Project: Regenerative Agriculture Practices
Principal Investigators: Timonthy Bowles, Brian Staskawicz, & Miguel Altieri
Agriculture produces 23 percent of global greenhouse gases, reducing available habitats and polluting the environment. Yet, regenerative practices can mitigate against declining biodiversity, soil damage, and climate change. Data on soil health, biodiversity, and scaling opportunities can remove barriers to sustainable practices.

University of California, Irvine
Project: UCI Combustion Laboratory (UCICL) and Advanced Power & Energy Program (APEP)
Director: Vince McDonnell
This UCICL and APEP seek to improve the efficiency of combustion turbines fueled with pure hydrogen. UCI is advancing experimentation, tools, and diagnostics.

University of Central Florida
Project: Center for Advanced Turbomachinery and Energy Research (CATER)
Principal Investigator: Jayanta Kapat
CATER seeks to resolve problems in turbomachinery for power generation, aviation, and space propulsion. His team considers alternative energy, aerodynamics, optimization, and liquid ammonia as a clean fuel for air travel.

Project: Resilient, Intelligent, & Sustainable Energy Systems (RISES)
Founding Director: Zhihua Qu
RISES focuses on sustainable energy systems by creating autonomous vehicles, power systems, smart cities, transportation networks, and smart grids to address today's challenges.

University of Houston
Project: Repurposing Offshore Infrastructure for Clean Energy (ROICE) Project
UH Energy Center Officer – ROICE-Research Team: Ram Seetharam
ROICE installs floating wind turbines, repurposing offshore oil and gas infrastructure in the Gulf of Mexico for clean energy projects like green wind power, hydrogen generation, and carbon sequestration. Another project is a Houston Hydrogen Transportation Pilot, which aims to optimize hydrogen supply.

University of Illinois, Urbana-Champaign
Project: Sustainable and Resilient Infrastructure Systems (SRIS) Program
Director of New Research Initiatives: Ana Pinheiro Privette

This research includes hydrosystems, structural engineering, sanitation, eco-hydraulics, wind engineering, and the Illinois Autonomous/Connected Track (I-ACT).

University of Southern California
Project: Energy & Sustainability Initiative – Rewater Center
Principal Investigator: Amy Childress
The Center conducts research on sustainable water reuse, purification, conservation, contaminant and pathogen detection, as well as energy-efficient water and waste treatment processes.

Project: Center for Sustainability Solutions
Principal Investigator: Mahta Moghaddam
His initiative addresses urban environmental challenges in Southern California, including water management, air pollution, and soil nutrient testing.

ADMISSIONS DATA TO CONSIDER

The Ivy League Schools
Comparison of Early vs Regular Decision Admit Rates and Waitlist Data

Ivy League University	ED Admit Rate – Class of 2027	RD Admit Rate – Class of 2027	ED Admit Rate – Class of 2026	RD Admit Rate – Class of 2026	Number Waitlist Admits
Brown	13%	4%	14.6%	3.71%	15
Columbia	11.3%	3%	10.3%	3%	N/A
Cornell	18%	6%	21.4%	6.7%	260
Dartmouth	19.2%	5%	20%	4.8%	N/A
Harvard	7.6%	3%	7.9%	2.34%	65
UPenn	15%	4%	15.6%	4.2%	N/A
Princeton	Princeton did not publish its data				
Yale	10%	3%	11%	3.4%	N/A

ADMISSIONS DATA FOR TOP SCHOOLS - EARLY VS. REGULAR DECISION

University	ED1/EDII/EA Admit Rate – Class of 2027	RD/Total % Admit Rate – Class of 2027	ED/EDII/EA Admit Rate – Class of 2026	RD/Total % Admit Rate – Class of 2026	Number Waitlist Admits
Amherst	26%	9%	32%	6.1%/7%	36
Boston College	30%	19%/15.1%	28%	16.7%	13
Boston Univ	29%	18.9%/10.7%	26%/25.3%	13.4%/14.15%	3
Cal Poly SLO	N/A	28.1%	N/A	30%	345
Claremont McK	32%	11%	28.2%/29.5%	7.5%/10.3%	11
Colgate Univ	22.4%	12%	25.2%	11.1%/17%	0
Colorado College	40%/22%	19.9%	49.3%/26%/15%	11%/13.6%	2
Duke Univ	16.5%	4.8%	21.3%	4.3%/4.9%	N/A
Emory Univ	37.4%/11.7%	10%	36.5%/14%	9.5%/10.7%	107
Georgetown	11.8%	13%	10%	12.11%	40
GWU	66%	50%	66.1%/65%	48.2%/49%	N/A
Georgia Tech	40%(in-state) 10,5% (out)	16%	39% (in-state) 12% (out)	17.14%	41
Harvey Mudd	21%	10%	19.1%	12.6%/13%	17
Johns Hopkins	19.7%	8%/6.3%	21%/14.8%	5.9%/7.2%	0
MIT	5.7%	4%/4.7%	4.7%	4%	0
Northeastern	39% ED	6%	32.6%/6%	6%/6.8%	N/A
Northwestern	21%	6%	22.1%/12.8%	5.6%/7.2%	83
Notre Dame	15.2%	10%/12%	17.3%	13%	N/A
NYU	38%	8%	38%	12.2%/12.4%	N/A
Rice	18%	7%	24%/18.8%	7.7%/8.6%	0
SMU	N/A	53%	70.9%	50%/51.6%	2
Stanford	N/A	5%	N/A	3.7%	8
Texas Christian	N/A	41%	70.4%	55.3%/56%	2
Tufts	N/A	9.5%	N/A	9.7%	183
Tulane	60%/15%	13%	67.9%/17%	7.9%/8.4%	3
UChicago	N/A	5%	N/A	5.4%	N/A
Univ of Miami	61%/37%	19%/28%	56.7%	17.6%/18.9%	115
Univ of So Cal	6%	9.9%	N/A	11.9%/12%	N/A
Univ of VA	31% (in-state) 12.4% (out)	15%/16.3%	37.8% (in-state) 18.1% (out)	18.7%	N/A
Vanderbilt	15.7%	4%/5.6%	24%/17.6%	5.3%/6%	~200
Wash U St Louis	35%	11%	26.2%/17.6%	9.3%/11.3%	168
Wesleyan	41%	12.4%/15.7%	44%/31%	13.9%	81
William & Mary	45%	42% (in-state) 28% (out)	N/A	42% (in-state) 28% (out)	4
Williams	27%	8%	31%	8.5%	0

UNIVERSITY OF CALIFORNIA

The University of California Fact Sheet data below from UC Admissions, says, "Data are Subject to Change". Nonetheless, here is a comparison between admissions to the class of 2024 and admission to the classes of 2026 and 2027.

The increase in applications to the University of California is in large part due to changes in testing requirements. Policies, prices, and class sizes also allowed for more students to be admitted. Note: Some of the University of California, Berkeley's classes have more than 1,000 students.

UNIVERSITY OF CALIFORNIA ADMISSIONS DATA				
University of California Campus	Residency of Applicants	Number of Applications		
		Class of 2024	Class of 2026	Class of 2027
Berkeley	California	50,223	72,417	72,656
	Out-of-State	20,659	32,580	31,309
	International	17,114	23,195	21,909
	Total	88,026	128,192	125,874
Davis	California	54,570	65,367	65,109
	Out-of-State	6,505	10,748	11,402
	International	15,798	18,610	18,098
	Total	76,873	94,725	94,609
Irvine	California	72,391	84,743	86,409
	Out-of-State	8,000	14,309	15,410
	International	17,525	20,113	19,255
	Total	97,916	119,165	121.074
Los Angeles	California	67,877	91,544	90,747
	Out-of-State	23,016	34,627	33,066
	International	17,944	23,608	22,069
	Total	108,837	149,779	145,882
Merced	California	22,244	22,516	21,854
	Out-of-State	598	1,319	1,271
	International	1,534	2,208	2,605
	Total	24,376	26,043	25,730
Riverside	California	43,151	46,456	47,823
	Out-of-State	1,173	2,492	2,807
	International	4,628	5,417	5,832
	Total	49,252	54,365	56,462
San Diego	California	66,350	84,326	84,910
	Out-of-State	14,364	23,778	23,951
	International	19,320	23,112	21,969
	Total	100,034	131,226	130,830
Santa Barbara	California	63,269	73,575	74.902
	Out-of-State	10,988	18,432	18,390
	International	16,690	18,984	17,569
	Total	90,947	110,991	110,861
Santa Cruz	California	43,893	53,051	54,846
	Out-of-State	3,897	6,878	7,382
	International	7,213	5,937	6,592
	Total	55,003	65,886	68,820

AWARD WINNING COLLEGES AND UNIVERSITIES

2023 American Institute of Aeronautics and Astronautics (AIAA) - Design/Build/Fly Competition

In 2023, 868 university students from 81 teams competed in Tucson, AZ. The competition included students from 14 countries and 27 states including the District of Columbia. The 2023 flight objective required designing, building, and testing a UAV to conduct surveillance and jamming missions for electronic warfare.

Winners

1st Place – RWTH Aachen University, Germany
2nd Place – University of Ljubljana, Slovenia
3rd Place – Embry-Riddle Aeronautical University, Daytona Beach, FL
Best Report Score – University of Washington, Seattle

2023 Spaceport America Cup

Winners & Runner-Ups (different categories)

158 teams (80 National and 78 International)
5,913 rocketeers competed in the 5-day event.

Australian National University (Honorable Mention)
Brigham Young University (Winner 2x and Overall Winner)
Carleton University (Winner)
Cornell University (Winner and Overall Runner-Up)
Ecole de Technologie Superieure (Winner)
Mississippi State University (Runner-Up)
Monash University (Winner 2x)
New York University Abu Dhabi (Runner-Up)
Politecnico di Torino (Winner)
Polytechnique Montreal (Winner & Payload Challenge 2nd Place)
Poznan University of Technology (Winner)
Purdue University (Runner-Up)
Rochester Institute of Technology (Payload Challenge 1st Place)
University of Akron (Runner-Up)
University of California, Berkeley (Honorable Mention)
University of Canterbury (Winner)
University of Florida (Honorable Mention)
University of Illinois at Urbana-Champaign (Runner-Up)
University of Louisville (Runner-Up)
University of Maryland, College Park (Runner-Up)
University of Minnesota, Twin Cities (Winner 2x)
University of New South Wales (Winner)
University of Queensland (Runner-Up)
University of Sao Paulo (Runner-Up)
University of Waterloo (Winner & Runner-Up 2x)
Worcester Polytechnic Institute (Winner & Payload Challenge 3rd Place)
Wroclaw University of Science and Technology (Runner-Up)

NASA's 2023 Student Launch Challenge

800 Students (U.S. and Puerto Rico)
College Winners - Rocketry

Overall Winners
1st Place - University of Alabama, Huntsville
2nd Place – University of North Carolina, Charlotte
3rd Place – Vanderbilt University

3D Printing Award
Iowa State University, Ames

Altitude Award
1st Place – Vanderbilt University
2nd Place – University of North Carolina, Charlotte
3rd Place – University of Alabama, Huntsville

Best-Looking Rocket Award
1st Place – North Carolina State University, Raleigh
2nd Place – Virginia Tech
3rd Place – Auburn University

Payload Award
1st Place – University of Alabama, Huntsville
2nd Place – Washington University, St. Louis
3rd Place – University of North Carolina, Charlotte

Project Review Award
1st Place – University of North Carolina, Charlotte
2nd Place – Vanderbilt University
3rd Place – University of Notre Dame

AIAA Rookie Award
1st Place – U.S. Military Academy, West Point
2nd Place – Angelo State University
3rd Place – University of Central Florida

Safety Award
1st Place – University of North Carolina, Charlotte
2nd Place – University of Alabama, Huntsville
3rd Place – University of Notre Dame

Social Media Award
1st Place – University of Puerto Rico
2nd Place – North Carolina State University, Raleigh
3rd Place – University of North Carolina, Charlotte

STEM Engagement Award
1st Place – Vanderbilt University
2nd Place – University of Notre Dame
3rd Place – University of Alabama, Huntsville

Service Academy Award
U.S. Military Academy, West Point

CubeSat Launch Initiative – U.S. Air Force & U.S. Space Force

2023 University Nanosatellite Program Winners
Florida Institute of Technology
University of the Virgin Islands
University of South Florida
University of New Mexico
Missouri University of Science and Technology
New Mexico State University
Columbia University
Tarleton State University

Association for Uncrewed Vehicle Systems International (AUVSI)

2023 Award Winner for "Xcellence in Academic Research"
University of Colorado, Boulder

CHAPTER 6
COLLEGE DEGREES

"We are all the construction of a story, and it is only at the end that we can assess the value of the plot."

— **Anonymous**

UNDERGRADUATE AND GRADUATE DEGREES

AA – Associate of Arts: 2-year degree

AS – Associate of Science: 2-year degree

BA – Bachelor of Arts: 4-year degree

BArch – Bachelor of Architecture: 5-year professional credential program

BDes – Bachelor of Design: 4-year degree with classes focused on design

BEd – Bachelor of Education: 4-year program focused on teaching & learning

BEng – Bachelor of Engineering: 4-5-year engineering-focused program

BESc – Bachelor of Engineering Science: 4-year science & engineering program

BFA – Bachelor of Fine Arts: 4-year degree with classes focused on art/design

BID – Bachelor of Industrial Design: 4-year Industrial Design-focused degree

BS – Bachelor of Science: 4-year STEM-focused degree

BSCE – Bachelor of Science in Civil Engineering

BS Chem E – Bachelor of Science in Chemical Engineering

BS Comp Sci – Bachelor of Science in Computer Science

BSEE – Bachelor of Science in Electrical Engineering

BSIE – Bachelor of Science in Industrial Engineering

BSME – Bachelor of Science in Mechanical Engineering

EdD – Doctor of Education: 3-5-year program focused on teaching & learning

MA – Master of Arts: 1-2-year specialized degree

MArch – Master of Architecture: 1-3-year professional credential program

MDes – Master of Design: 1-2-year design-focused specialized

MEd – Master of Education: 1-2-year education-focused program

MEng – Master of Engineering: 1-2-year engineering program

MFA – Master of Fine Arts: 1-2-year degree earned after the BA, BS, or BFA

MID – Master of Industrial Design: 1-2-year Industrial Design-focused degree

Minor – Students take 6 to 10 additional classes in an interest area

MS – Master of Science: 1-2-year STEM-focused

MSID – Master of Science in Industrial Design: science-focused Industrial Design

Ph.D. – Doctor of Philosophy: doctorates in any field (typically 3 – 8 years)

AA (ASSOCIATE OF ARTS) & AS (ASSOCIATE OF SCIENCE)

The AA or AS degree is typically a 2-year general studies degree offered online or in-person through a community college. However, some universities offer AA or AS degrees as well. Often, the Associate of Arts degree, while focused on the liberal arts, has no barrier to entry, meaning that students can enter most AA programs with a high school diploma or the equivalent.

The AS degree frequently emphasizes science and math and often has additional requirements. Some students take more or less time to complete the AA based upon their skills upon entering the program, certainty of their direction, and the transfer requirements. For example, students majoring in engineering have additional science and math requirements and need to create an academic plan early in their program to finish in two years.

BA (BACHELOR OF ARTS) & BS (BACHELOR OF SCIENCE)

The BA and BS degrees are 4- or 5-year undergraduate degrees that typically offer a liberal arts foundation along with a major or concentration in a specific subject. The BA and BS degrees frequently require students to take lower-division (first and second-year) liberal arts courses before taking specialized courses focused around a major or concentration in their third and fourth years.

For engineering and architecture, there is typically a fifth year due to the additional experiential requirements. Classes may be taught online or in person. Some students complete their BS in fewer years depending upon AP/IB credit, dual enrollment, and summer/intersession classes.

A BFA is considered a professional arts-focused degree with fewer courses in English, science, math, social science, and the humanities. Thus, the BFA, BDes, BID, BArch are specialist qualifications. The BEng focuses on STEM subjects, while

BEd focuses on education. The BA and BS degrees include significantly more liberal arts classes and thus are more general degrees.

The intention of the BFA, BDes, BID, BArch degrees is for students to pursue a focused curriculum with uniquely tailored courses. Finally, the BA or BS are often interchangeable. Thus, a BFA may be seen as different since there is typically more coursework focused on a specific pursuit with limited broad knowledge and more of a concentration on technical, profession-oriented experiences.

MASTER'S DEGREES & DOCTORAL DEGREES

Both the master's degree and doctorate are specialized, graduate degree programs for students who have completed their bachelor's degree. These degrees can take between one and eight years depending upon coursework, research, practicum, capstone, thesis, qualifying exams, and experiential requirements. Students focus on their field of interest and immerse themselves to gain in-depth practical, coursework, and research training.

A graduate degree in engineering can be helpful in advancing career goals since part of the program typically includes project management, business essentials, and leadership. The additional training combined with internship and networking opportunities may strengthen your resume and career opportunities.

I have nine graduate degrees so far and each set of requirements is distinct. Their programs and processes are designed differently as well. Do not expect standardization. However, one consistency is that you graduate with a much deeper knowledge of the specialty. While admission into these programs is generally selective, planning, preparation, and a good resume of experiences are required. Search for a program that fits your needs. There are numerous options for you to pursue your interests.

THE SEVEN MAJOR DIFFERENCES BETWEEN THE ASSOCIATE, BACHELORS, AND MASTER'S DEGREES

1. Starting Point
2. Academic Discipline
3. Time to Completion
4. Location of the Education
5. Educational Costs
6. Earning Power
7. Professional Opportunities

STARTING POINT

Most students who begin in an Associate of Arts (AA) or Associate of Science (AS) have no college credits. Starting a college education from scratch, students accumulate 60+ units beginning at a community college taking lower division courses. While most students earn AA or AS degrees at the community college, a few earn this degree at a 4-year college or university.

The AA or AS is either a terminal degree, meaning that the student will not continue on with their bachelor's degree or merely a steppingstone to their BA, BS, or BFA. The difference between associate's and bachelor's degrees is just the starting point. Meanwhile, the starting point for the master's degree (MA, MS, or MFA) begins after obtaining a bachelor's degree.

ACADEMIC DISCIPLINE

Every degree encompasses different requirements. Requirements for the AA differ from an AS. Similarly, the requirements for the BA, BS, and BFA also differ. With two additional years of coursework, the BA, BS, and BFA are more thorough. The MA, MS, and MFA build upon the bachelor's degree and pursue topics even deeper. Students studying biology will not take the same classes as those pursuing bioengineering, though some may overlap. While both disciplines are essential to science, the necessary skills for each career area are distinct. Thus, the course requirements are also unique.

Furthermore, two undergraduate students in different majors rarely take the same courses or class sequence. For example, the curriculum requirements for a chemistry degree differ from biology or bioengineering, though there is some

overlap. These degrees may include a different number of credits in math, physics, humanities, and hands-on activities based on the major's course specifications.

TIME TO COMPLETION

Associate of Arts (AA) and Associate of Science (AS) degrees typically take two years, while most BA, BS, and BFA degrees are 4- or 5-year programs, depending upon full-time or part-time status. Students who transfer credits, earn credits through CLEP, or test out can reduce their time to completion.

The time required to earn a bachelor's degree depends upon each student's skills and advanced credit. Still, some students change their chosen major which frequently extends the time to completion based on the additional requirements. According to the National Center for Educational Statistics, college advisors aid students in finishing "on time" though less than half of all students in the United States who start a bachelor's program finish their degree in four years.[1]

Time in college can be reduced. Some students enter bachelor's degree programs with college credits because they were either dual-enrolled or they took college classes outside of school. Some students who earn qualifying scores on AP/IB tests from advanced classes taken in high school are granted credits by the college or university. Policies regarding AP/IB credit vary. Look on each college's website to determine what scores and subjects qualify.

Other ways students can enter at a different starting point include credit-by-exam, CLEP tests, experiential credits, and units granted in the military. Colleges and universities are keenly aware of the challenges students face today with work, illness, and family responsibilities. Thus, many schools of higher education offer flexible enrollment with opportunities for part-time, evening, weekend, and online classes.

LOCATION OF THE EDUCATION

The AA and AS are earned at colleges that grant 2-year degrees. The location may be at a local community college or a university. BA, BS, and BFA programs are offered at a 4-year college or university. However, with online classes, students have the flexibility to take classes from colleges farther away as well. With the

---

1   IEC NCES, "Digest of Education Statistics, Table 326.10," IES NCES, n.d., https://nces.ed.gov/programs/digest/d20/tables/dt20_326.10.asp?referer=raceindica.asp

added variable of students taking classes on multiple campuses, the location in which students study is not as set as it once was. Nevertheless, in-person internships are often situated in corporate hubs and, thus, require grounding in a specific location.

EDUCATIONAL COSTS

Since the AA or AS requires a shorter amount of time and is typically completed at a lower-cost community college, the cost of an associate's degree is typically less than a bachelor's degree. Master's degree programs often cost more per credit but take less time than a bachelor's degree. Don't be surprised. Graduate students in biology, chemistry, physics, and biomedical engineering frequently do not pay tuition since they often receive grants, tuition waivers, fellowships, teaching opportunities, or research assistantships that cover their tuition.

On the other hand, many students can obtain financial aid in the form of grants, loans, and both merit and need-based scholarships. This aid can help pay for school and reduce debt after college.

We must be willing to let go of the life we planned

to have the life that is waiting for us.

- Joseph Campbell

EARNING POWER

Education pays off. According to National Center for Educational Statistics (NCES), the median income for degree attainment is as follows.

- Master's Degree or Higher - $74,600
- Bachelor's Degree - $61,600
- Associate's Degree - $45,000
- High School - $39,700

Median incomes do not tell the whole story since there is significant variation in annual salaries from those who are paid six-digit salaries to those who have a low paying job. Thus, the median salary may seem low since the range is huge.

PROFESSIONAL OPPORTUNITIES

Earning a BA, BS, BEng opens more doors than an AA or AS. Similarly, an MA, MS, or MFA opens more doors than a BA, BS, or BEng along with professional training. You can also obtain some skills through workshops, symposia, and conferences. With a scholarship to pay for college, you might take advantage of professional training, conferences, and study abroad programs to broaden your knowledge. Besides, you will also gain skills that prove to be valuable in your future.

The beautiful thing about learning is that no one can take it from you.

- B.B. King

Professional opportunities depend upon your career interests and country of potential employment. Many engineering and manufacturing companies are also moving into AR, VR, and machine learning. However, some focus on prototyping, lab testing, fieldwork, quality control and manufacturing. Scroll through the firms that hire scientists in your fields of interest or work environment preference to get a sense of the hundreds of professional options available to you.

Company size may also be a factor in your decision-making. While large firms may have more diversity of function and upward mobility, you might also be tasked with a specialized or limited role. On the other hand, a smaller firm may give you the chance to multitask on a wide range of projects and have a greater stake in the big picture of the operation. Whatever you decide, by taking internships in firms large and small, you will discover your preferences and, at a minimum, know the questions to ask during interviews.

Internet of Things (IoT) design combines hardware and software in an integrated system that allows computers to monitor, collect data, relay information, and revise processes. This specialization transforms product ideas from comprehensive strategies into networks that embed, sense, track, and provide more ubiquitous flow of consumer and cloud-based interactions. In addition, individuals and companies will rely increasingly on 3D printed parts for quick repair.

Law school might be another direction you could take your education. One of the biggest challenges facing scientists is the control of intellectual property. While filing for a patent is not terribly difficult, maintaining control of that property is much more challenging. In our copycat world, globalization delivers products worldwide to places that do not conform to international law. Products are taken apart, reconfigured or modified, and put back onto the market. Some firms focus on protecting intellectual property by seeking out and prosecuting violators.

Jump at chances to gain real-world experiences. You may be in the workforce for fifty years. That is a really long time if you do not feel fulfilled. Sure, internships may mean sacrificing a summer holiday for a month somewhere, but it could make a significant difference in your future lifestyle and happiness.

CHAPTER 7
COLLEGE ADMISSIONS

"We have forgotten how to be good guests, how to walk lightly on the earth as its other creatures do."

– **Barbara Ward,** *Baroness Jackson of Lodsworth*

Apply to colleges with the curriculum, clubs, activities, and opportunities that best fit your interests. Georgia Tech, Duke, MIT, SUNY Forestry, Texas A&M, UC Berkeley, Univ of Houston, and UT Austin are eight colleges that stand out for environmental engineering and alternative energy with amazing faculty, excellent facilities, and relatively easy access to job opportunities.

While many students consider colleges where internships abound like those in New York City, Los Angeles, Chicago, and San Francisco, they should not discount other areas around the country. You cannot go wrong by attending schools in other locations like the University of Michigan, UIUC, Carnegie Mellon, or Cornell for their deep dive into the spheres of environmental engineering. These colleges also offer a rigorous course of study and socially responsible projects on the cutting edge of innovation, design, engineering, and forward-thinking optimism.

However, planning is required before you apply. Let's look at a few admissions terms you should know, then move on to community service, connecting with the colleges, and whether or not you should take standardized tests. Then, I offer some data, a checklist, and some tips for applying to and succeeding in college. Best wishes on your journey!!!

ADMISSIONS TERMS TO KNOW

Admissions Tests – These are standardized tests like SAT, ACT, GMAT, GRE, MCAT, etc. that universities use to compare student's aptitude in basic academic skill areas.

Admit Rate – The percent of applicants who are admitted.

Articulation Agreement – This is the agreement between 2-year and 4-year colleges that determines whether credits transfer from one institution to another.

Candidate Reply Date – For freshman admissions, students must reply back to colleges by May 1 with their choice of the college or university they plan to attend from those in which they were accepted.

Class Rank – Most high schools no longer rank students. However, a few still do. This ranking puts students in order of weighted GPA or a combined set of criteria. Some schools rank in percentiles or deciles.

Coalition Application – This application can be sent to multiple schools within their network of approximately 150 colleges. Many of the affiliated colleges also require supplemental applications with additional essays and requirements.

College Credit – Most colleges require 120 – 130 semester credits to graduate with a bachelor's degree. Students earn credits upon successful completion of classes. Colleges may also award college credit for qualifying AP/IB scores, CLEP exams, and military training courses.

Common Application – This standardized digital application can be sent to multiple schools within their network of more than 1,000 colleges. Most colleges also require supplemental applications with additional questions, essays, and requirements.

Deferred Admission – After the EA/ED admissions cycle, students are accepted, denied, or deferred to regular decision. Typically, the chance of being accepted during the regular admissions cycle after being deferred is 5–10%.

Deferred Enrollment – Colleges allow a student to postpone their attendance for up to one year. Note: Not all colleges allow students to defer. If they do, there may be restrictions and other requirements. Check the college's website to be sure.

Domestic Student – U.S. citizens or permanent residents at the time of admission are considered domestic students irrespective of the country in which they live.

Early Action (EA) – EA is an early application submission in which a student also finds out their admission status before regular decisions students. Early action is typically not binding, meaning that students do not need to enroll if accepted. Most EA application due dates are between October 15th and November 15th. Almost all EA decisions come back between December 1st and February 1st with most responses between December 10th – 20th.

Early Decision (ED) – A few colleges have ED whereby a student commits to that school should they be accepted. Students agree to attend when they apply, and they can only apply to one ED school. If admitted, students pay the deposit and withdraw their applications from other schools. ED applications are typically due November 1 and decisions typically come back in mid-December.

Financial Aid – This award is money offered to a student to help pay for school. The amount may be composed of scholarships, grants, loans, and work-study. Financial aid may be granted from the government, college, or private organizations.

First-Generation – Students are 'first-gen' if neither parent earned a four-year college degree. Some colleges specify that that the parents also never attended college. A few students consider themselves first-generation U.S. college students since neither of their parents attended college in the United States. The underlying notion in each case is that these parents lack the knowledge to fully advise their child.

High School GPA – This number is considered or recalculated differently by each college depending upon whether they include 9th – 11th, summers, middle school, AP/IB/Honors credit, college classes, and courses like health, computer applications, leadership, sports, newspaper, MUN, religion etc. Some colleges like the University of California cap their weighted GPA for admissions purposes with only 8 semesters of 'honors' points. No more than 4 of these can be from 10th grade.

In-State – Students are 'in-state' if they have residency in the state with evidence like driver's license, taxes, bills, school attendance, etc. no matter where they physically live. Rules regarding DACA students differ.

International – International applicants are not those who not citizens or permanent residents of the U.S. This designation can vary based upon college/state rules.

Legacy Candidate – A child of a close relative (generally a parent) who graduated from a given college. A few colleges give preference to legacy applicants.

Lower Division – These are courses typically taken during the first two years of college. Most community college classes are lower division. At a university, lower division courses for a BA or BS degree are primarily liberal arts classes.

Need-Aware Admissions – The policy where admissions teams consider financial circumstances in the admissions process.

Need-Blind Admissions – The policy where admissions teams do not consider financial circumstances in the admissions process.

Open Admissions – A college opens enrollment to all students until the seats are filled without consideration of past academic performance or minimum requirements.

Placement Tests – Most colleges require a certain level of mastery before entering a class. Upon enrolling in a college, students take placement tests to determine the level in which they are placed. Since information recall may not be strong from a class taken years before, you should review the material before you take the test. Otherwise, you may need to take one or two additional remedial classes which may prolong graduation.

Portal – This online admissions site, connected to a specific college, is a centralized information area. Students log in to determine next steps, including missing items (transcripts, test scores, portfolio, letters of recommendation, FAFSA, CSS Profile, etc.), financial aid, scholarship opportunities, and admissions status.

Registrar's Office – This is the office of college officials who are responsible for your student records, including recording final grades, checking remaining payments, certifying completion of requirements, and sending transcripts.

Residency – This is the determination of state residency, non-resident U.S., or international status.

Rolling Admission – This is the college policy to accept students as the applications are received rather than waiting for a specific date to review each applicant's records. Many colleges with rolling admissions deliver admissions decisions within a month of receipt of a students application materials.

Summer Melt – The phenomenon whereby students who submit an intent to enroll at a specific college, pay the deposit, and then decide not to attend during the summer. While this situation may have increased during the pandemic, the phenomenon has existed for decades. The primary reasons for summer melt include the inability to pay, illness, family matter, change of heart, acceptance of a job, or getting off the waitlist at another college.

Transfer Student – A student who has taken college classes after completing high school and applies to a 4-year university. Typically, if college classes are taken during high school, students are still considered for freshman admissions.

Upper Division – These are courses typically taken in a student's second two years of college. At a university, upper division courses for a BA or BS degree are primarily major-specific classes.

Waitlist – Admissions offices accept, deny, or waitlist students. Those students on a waitlist must wait until a spot opens. If there is a vacancy, the student may be taken off of the waitlist on a priority basis, ranking system, or admissions review.

Yield – Yield is the percent of admitted students who pay the deposit with the intent to enroll (enrolled/admitted x 100).

PRESIDENT'S VOLUNTEER SERVICE AWARD

Many students support their communities through service activities. These include volunteering in homeless shelters, soup kitchens, food banks, donation centers, schools, concerts for kids, post-disaster cleanups, rescue teams, sports camps, research, nursing homes, Special Olympics, Adopt-a-Family, Habitat for Humanity, Youth Action Team, political campaigns, docent work at theatres, charity 5Ks, concerts, parades, international projects, medical missions, church-sponsored service work, and forest, park, beach, and wetlands cleanups. Some students are recognized for their volunteer contributions with certificates while others serve to contribute to society. By accumulating hours, students can earn one of the following Presidential Volunteer Service Awards.

Hours Required to Earn Awards in Each Age Group

Age Group	Bronze	Silver	Gold	Lifetime Achievement Award
Kids (5–10 years old)	26–49 hours	50–74 hours	75+ hours	4,000+ hours
Teens (11–15)	50–74 hours	75–99 hours	100+ hours	4,000+ hours
Young Adults (16–25)	100–174 hours	175–249 hours	250+ hours	4,000+ hours
Adults (26+)	100–249 hours	250–499 hours	500+ hours	4,000+ hours

COLLEGE ADMISSIONS:

Success in the Face of Uncertainty

There are no guarantees in college admissions. However, planning is essential for success. The most beneficial advice is to pursue your passions with gusto, train to be the best you can be, take advantage of internships and experiences, and meet lots of people along the way.

Remember, "life is a journey, not a destination." Often the journey is more exciting, leading to lessons, friendships, and unforgettable moments. However, the fact is that, in the end, if college is your goal, then you need to remember a few action items to achieve success.

Should you worry about grades in high school? Of course. You should also take classes that challenge you. Colleges pick the best candidates from those who

apply. Students should be academically prepared, socially conscious, and talented in areas in which they are passionate (engineering design, graphic arts, musical instruments, theatre, debate, public speaking, leadership, athletics, community service, computer coding, robotics, construction, etc.).

The college selection process is not much different than companies hiring new employees. While colleges are more or less competitive, companies may have only one job, and a hundred resumes. Discover your unique drive and internal motivation that make you the very best you can be. Be exceptional at what you do academically, personally, and professionally.

Most of all, You Do You!

TALENT FOCUSED

Not all schools require high grades and test scores. Many are simply interested in selecting students who are the most talented, most driven, and the most willing to be team players on the college campus. Thus, you should take a solid set of courses, fulfill the standard curriculum, and develop your talents and interests. Note: Your senior year is not a good time to slack off, even if you completed your requirements.

According to the National Student Clearinghouse Research Center, of the estimated 19 million students enrolled in U.S. undergraduate or graduate courses in 2023, millions attended college with high school GPAs between 2.0 and 3.5. Furthermore, more than ten million college students never took the SAT or ACT.

On the other hand, if you are applying to highly competitive schools, you should take the test. Nevertheless, hundreds of colleges did not require test scores in the 2024-2025 admissions cycle and probably never will in the future.

The National Center for Educational Statistics provides copious data. First, total college enrollment is approximately 19 million, dropping by more than two million since 2010 when enrollment was 21.6 million. Of these students, 11.6 million attend full time and 7.4 million attend part time with 15.8 million undergraduate students and 3.2 million students attending graduate school. Approximately one-third of high school students pursued post-secondary study with 13.7 million students attending public institutions and 5.4 million students attending private institutions. Most college students took distance education classes with 59 percent in one or more virtual courses and 11.2 million students or 30 percent of college students enrolled exclusively in distance education courses.

California has the most college students with 2.72 million; 89.5% attend public institutions; 11.6% leave the state to attend college; 35.8% of full time college students are female.

In approximate numbers, here is some college student data.

DEMOGRAPHIC CHARACTERISTICS

Caucasian – 54.3%
LatinX - 19.3%
Black or African American - 12.6%
Asian or Asian American – 6.8%
American Indian/Alaska Native – 0.66%%
Pacific Islander – 0.26%

Foreign-born – 12%
Women - 55.5%
15 years old or younger – 0.7%
Under 24 years old – 92%
45 years old or older – 1.5%

DEGREES AND MAJORS

4.43 million students graduated from college in 2021

* 24.6% received associate's degrees
* 49.9% received bachelor's degrees
* 20.8% earned master's degrees
* 4.7% earned doctorates/professional degrees

Majors – 58% of all bachelor's degrees are in five areas of study

* 19.1% in business
* 11.9% in health-related professions
* 8% social sciences and history
* 5.9% in psychology
* 5.9% in biological and biomedical sciences

COLLEGE ENROLLMENT (EDUCATIONDATA.ORG)

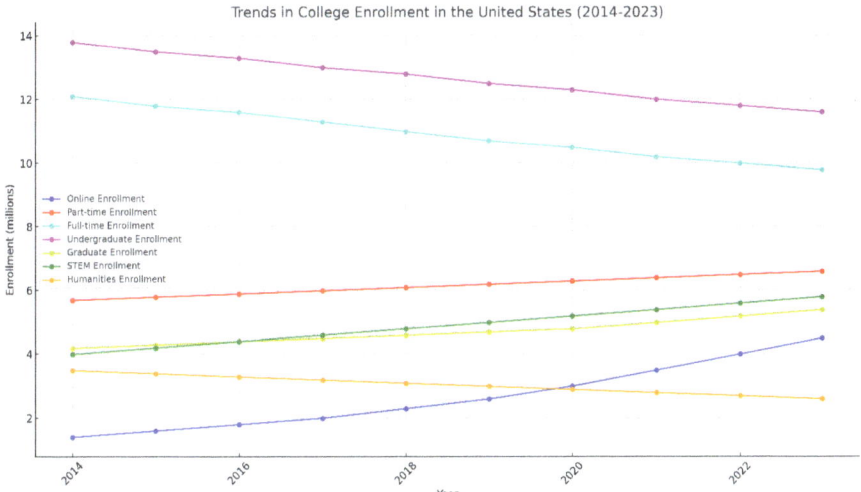

COMPETITIVE COLLEGE ADMISSIONS

A few highly selective colleges seek extraordinary talent over academics, but most zero in on a student's challenging courses and high grades. To gain admission into the most highly selective academic colleges, you must take the most challenging course load you can manage and ace. Highly selective colleges want disciplined scholars AND remarkably talented students.

Determine what you can handle, knowing that some colleges with extremely competitive admission will only take students who have completed more than ten AP, IB, or honors classes over the four years.

The most competitive colleges require classes like AP Calculus, AP Physics, and AP Chemistry because they focus on problem-solving. However daunting these classes may seem, remember, the top colleges have lots of applicants. They need to draw the line somewhere. UCLA had 145,882 applicants for the class of 2027; UC Berkeley had 125,874 applicants. The numbers are truly staggering since neither first-year class will have more than 7,000 freshmen starting in the fall.

College admissions can feel like a rollercoaster of energy and emotion. Creating a portfolio of talent, training, and experience is just the beginning. Meanwhile, some colleges want to see standardized test scores. Applications and essays may seem easy at first, but managing the various requirements and deadlines can be difficult. Therefore, this moment is a good time to get a calendar and organize your tasks.

REQUEST INFORMATION

Almost every college has a link or contact us page where you can request information from the school. If you are considering a particular school, request information from them. In this way, they may send updates, interview dates, scholarship opportunities, application fee waiver, special invites, and other information that could be valuable. While you may loathe receiving even one more e-mail since you are quite possibly receiving them from a few schools anyway, I still recommend that you fill out their form. Then, since you are likely to be inundated with e-mails, make an e-mail file folder for the colleges you are considering. When you get an e-mail from one of those schools, file it away.

STANDARDIZED TESTING

A few schools still require standardized testing. Check first. Many colleges are test-optional. This means that you are not required to take the SAT or ACT. However, if you have a good score, submitting your test results may make all the difference in gaining admission. College admissions officers are studying this topic and considering their future policies. Much of their concern began with test cancellations worldwide due to the pandemic.

School administrators did not want to let possibly infected students onto their campus to take the test, nor were they able to ensure student safety. In addition, social distancing requirements limited the number of students at any testing site.

Yet, for decades, college admissions decisions centered around grades and test scores. This change in the decision-making landscape rattled admissions directors and enrollment managers.

Meanwhile, some colleges proclaim that test-optional truly means that the test is not considered. Yet, evidence proves otherwise. Thus, many students still take the test and work around test preparation and test site hurdles amid the confusion. Competition continues to drive students to present evidence to demonstrate that they are worthy candidates. In the end, colleges need to make a final decision between very good candidates. If one student has a high score, that student may have a higher likelihood of admission depending upon the admissions committee's formal or subliminal decision-making process.

Data show that students who submitted scores within the college's range or higher were accepted at a higher rate than those without a score. Some schools claim to be test blind, saying that they do not consider test scores, yet a few of these colleges still provide a place on the application to input scores. Thus, some are not truly blind. Nevertheless, the decision regarding whether to take the test and submit the score is yours. If the school does not require an admissions test, you can choose to take the test and submit a score as you like. If your academics are solid and you are willing to prepare for the test, you should take the test.

APPLYING EARLY
Early Action (EA), Restricted Early Action (REA), and Early Decision (ED)

With low acceptance rates, the chance to obtain additional scholarship money, and the chaos surrounding cancellations and changes in AP, IB, SAT, and ACT testing, students clamor to apply early to schools. In addition, applications to the top schools increased during the pandemic, resulting in colleges needing to make difficult admissions decisions in their quest to build a diverse, talented, and engaged class of students. Furthermore, students applying early have access to many more scholarship options since some scholarships require test scores. This confluence sent students in droves to apply early. This trend is likely to continue.

In Early Action (EA), Restricted Early Action (REA), and Early Decision (ED), students apply in late summer or early fall to college and generally find out around winter break, though some decisions come out earlier and a few arrive later. This advantage not only gives students a chance for more scholarship money in some cases but the benefit of finding out early reduces the tension of the long waiting period until regular decision results arrive.

Early Action (EA) and Restricted Early Action (REA) are different. In Restricted Early Action, a limitation is placed on either how many or what colleges you can apply to simultaneously. Many REA schools do not allow students to apply to other early action schools, though some will allow students to apply early to public colleges. Check the college websites to be sure. In addition, some schools like Georgetown will allow students to apply EA elsewhere but not apply to a binding Early Decision (ED) program where the student must commit to attending if they are accepted. However, most EA schools do not have these restrictions, and some students apply to a handful of EA schools during the admissions process.

Early Decision (ED) is a binding agreement between the student and college with signatures from the student, the student's parents, and the high school counselor/advisor, ensuring that the student is committed to their first-choice ED school and will attend if accepted. Each of these parties acknowledges and agrees that, if granted admission, the student will fulfill their commitment. There are caveats, though you should go into the agreement fully committing to your ED school.

There are incentives to applying ED. Frequently, acceptance rates are higher. Also, at some schools, a large percentage of their class is filled with students who profess their unequivocal love for their dream school. Students who can commit to a top choice school, fulfilled the necessary admissions prerequisites, and are willing to accept the binding agreement to attend, should apply ED.

COMMON APPLICATION, COALITION APPLICATION, OR COLLEGE-SPECIFIC APPLICATION

Every college's process is unique. However, there are a few commonalities. In 2023, more than 1,000 colleges used the Common App; about 150 colleges used the Coalition App. A few used both. The University of California system has its own application as do the California State Universities and Texas schools. UT Austin and Texas A&M are now on the Common App for the 2024-2025 admissions cycle.

The Common App and Coalition App may be started early. In your junior year, consider getting a head start to review requirements. College-specific questions may change each year. However, the basic application is generally the same and can be created ahead of time. The application rolls over August 1. Toward the end of July, make a copy of the application you completed just in case.

Some schools admit students on a rolling basis. 'Rolling' means that periodically, after all of the materials are received, the admissions committee determines who they will accept, and then sends the notification right away. Some students are accepted as early as August. The thrill of acceptance cannot be overstated.

ESSAYS

The Common Application and Coalition essays are often posted months ahead of time. Since the main essay is required or recommended for nearly all Common Application and Coalition Application schools, the personal statement is an excellent place to start thinking about what you might want to say to colleges.

In addition to the main essay on the Common Application and Coalition Application, about three-fourths of the colleges have their own specific questions or essays. In August, most admissions applications are open and ready for you to dive into the college-specific questions, though many of the essay topics are available earlier, and some schools hold out until later for their big essay reveal.

Essays can be prepared ahead of time too. One popular question is, "What activity is most important to you and why?" Another is "Why did you choose your major?" A third common question is, "Why do you want to attend our school?" For others, you should prepare or at least consider the topics of diversity, adversity, and challenges since these topics have become increasingly important in the admissions process. Everyone has a challenge they needed to overcome. What did you learn from that experience?

Complete the application fully. Think carefully about the optional sections. Typically, universities offer the chance to provide the school with just the right cherry on top of the sundae, allowing you to share something unique about you. If you have absolutely nothing to say, leave it blank. There is also an additional information section on the main Common App, Coalition Application, and University of California application. This location is not a place to write another essay, but you can include information that cannot be adequately explained in the rest of the application.

There are also schools that include scholarship essays within the supplement part of the application. Start early.

TIPS FOR THE COLLEGE ESSAY

Let's look at some step-by-step advice on college entrance essays.

Step 1: Read the Prompt Carefully

Answer the question fully and completely.

Check the word or character count.

Re-read the prompt to understand themes like teamwork, diversity, challenges, community, or goals.

Where do you fit into that college?

What is the intersection of your interests and what they offer?

Step 2: Brainstorm Ideas
- List hobbies, passions, and influences.
- Reflect on your life stories and events.
- What areas fit with the college's culture?
- What were pivotal moments, challenges, or achievements?

Step 3: Find a Unique Angle
- Be creative and interesting but also authentic.
- Do not copy, augment, or adapt someone else's story.
- Going outside of the box is fine, but remember, simple is fine too.
- They just want to get to know you.
- Some students focus on uniqueness at the cost of being relatable.

Step 4: Focus on Key Moments
- Focus on key moments rather than generalities.
- Remember: Show, don't tell.
- Make the story compelling and meaningful.
- What experience changed your perspective?

Step 5: Create an Outline
- This is an essay after all.
- What is your catchy introduction?
- What body paragraphs provide examples for your thesis?
- Conclude with a reflection that ties the story together.

Step 6: Start with a Hook
- A quote, shock, epiphany, or idea can help introduce your story.
- Connect your story to the prompt.

Step 7: Write a Draft and Wrap it with a Bow
- Tie the hook with a story.
- Tie the story to your life experiences.
- Tie the body paragraphs to the prompt.
- Tie the loose ends in a bow and memorable idea.
- Avoid cliches and generalities.

Step 8: Edit for Clarity
- Check spelling, grammar, and ideas.
- Make sure your essay aligns with the college.
- Remember, readers have thousands of essays.

Create smooth paragraph transitions.

Maintain focus.

Sept 9: Seek Feedback

The reader is not a teenager.

What you think is funny or amusing may not appeal to an adult.

However, parents may not be in-tune with colleges.

Think through the feedback. Trust your instincts.

Step 10: Revise, Proofread, and Submit

Remember to use your unique voice.

Format as directed – font, spacing, word count.

Read it over one more time and submit.

Final Notes:

- Optional rarely means optional. In most cases, do it.
- If there is a COVID and Natural Disasters essay, tell your story.
- Write in complete sentences.
- Research the school. Every school is different.
- Do not just write the same essay for each school.
- Don't complain about a teacher, even if it is true.
- Don't lie or tell untruths in your essay or application.

Additional Information Section

Do not put essays in the additional information section, but you can use this section to clarify elements in your application that need explanation, like low grades, a bad semester, family emergencies, or why you did not take a class that you really should have completed.

STUDENT RESUMES FOR COLLEGE ADMISSION

1. Decide on a clean, easy-to-read format
   - One page is best.
   - Most people will only read the first page.
   - Being longwinded and wordy is not helpful.
   - Arial or Times New Roman is best.
   - Font sizes should not be too small.
2. Pictures are okay for a freshman admissions resume
3. Name, E-Mail, and Phone Number
   - Do not include your home address
4. Educational Experiences or Academic Background
   - High School (s), dates, location (s)
   - Colleges Attended, dates, location (s)
   - Academic Programs/Training
   - Languages
5. **Honors, Awards, Certifications**
   - Academic Honors
   - Awards
   - Certificates
6. **Extracurricular Activities**
   - Clubs/Activities
     - Bulletpoint with past tense verbs
     - Focus on achievements/leadership
   - Sports/Athletics – Separate if Extensive
7. Community Service
8. Work Experience
9. Hobbies

Final Notes
- You might add a goal statement at the top or a quote that defines your destiny or vision.
- Avoid writing paragraphs since people will not read these.
- Proofread by double-checking for spelling and errors.
- Ask for feedback.
- If you have time, tailor the resumes to each school.
- Add a LinkedIn URL, Portfolio Link, or Personal Website

LETTERS OF RECOMMENDATION

Most colleges on the Common App and Coalition App, though not all, request letters of recommendation from a counselor and one or more teachers. For engineering programs, university admissions officers may want academic teachers in mathematics, science, or humanities. Plan for this. Occasionally, there is often a section for optional recommendations too. Consider getting a recommendation from a summer program leader or someone with whom you did an internship. If you participated in a sport, there is a location for a coach on about a quarter of the applications. Finally, there may be a supplemental application where you can showcase your talent, projects, writing, or art. For example, SlideRoom often requires separate recommendations and materials reviewed by the college's talent experts.

COLLEGE APPLICATION CHECKLIST

- ☐ Calendar - Keep a calendar of due dates for summer program applications, contests, AP tests, SAT/ACT, applications, scholarships, and financial aid.
- ☐ Career Interest Survey - Take a career interest/aptitude test. Learn more about the majors and career options that best fit your interests and abilities.
- ☐ Consider College Majors – What classes are required in your chosen major? Many students who dislike math are surprised to learn that most business degrees require both calculus and statistics while incorporating math in nearly every class. STEM programs require physics. Research your major.
- ☐ Investigate Colleges – Consider possible schools based on the programs they offer, research opportunities, internships, clubs, activities, sports, and personal interests. Visit if possible. Ask students who are currently in the program.
- ☐ National College Fair – In the spring, colleges send representatives to a couple of dozen cities where you can meet with their admissions staff. These are good to walk around and learn more about the colleges and ask questions.
- ☐ Request Information – Fill out the request for information for each college you are considering so that they keep you informed of opportunities you may not have considered. They may send you a fee waiver or streamlined application.
- ☐ Summer Programs – Summer camps, skill-building, tours, research, internships, and college programs often have deadlines. Apply and consider your options.
- ☐ Narrow Choices – Narrow down your choices in the summer before your senior year so that you have an equal number of target, reach, and safeties.
- ☐ Communicate With Your Counselor – Your counselor can be a helpful guide who not only helps you with course selection but also advocates for you in the admissions process. They often write a recommendation for you and sometimes call admissions officers on your behalf. Get to know them.
- ☐ SAT/ACT – Decide if there is a benefit of taking these tests for the colleges you are considering.
- ☐ Extended Time – Determine if you qualify for extended time on tests.
- ☐ Fee Waivers – Ask your counselor if you qualify for fee waivers for the SAT/ACT, CSS Profile, or college applications.
- ☐ Resume – Create a resume whether or not the college requests one – some do. One day, you may need one for a job anyway. However, a resume allows you to gather your activities and accomplishments in one place for you to see what you want to present to a school.
- ☐ Essays and Short Answer Questions – Determine aspects of your life that stand out. Give colleges the best impression of your interests, inspirations, commitment, and life journey.

- ☐ Counselor Recommendation Form – Determine if your school requires a special form or packet of questions to obtain a counselor recommendation.
- ☐ Recommendations – Ask your teachers in the spring of your junior year or when school starts in your senior year.
- ☐ Early Action/Early Decision – EA and ED applications are due early, typically between October 15th and November 15th.
- ☐ Regional Representative – Some colleges have a regional representative. If you have any specifications, contact your regional representative to answer questions you cannot find the answers to on the website.
- ☐ Transcripts – Order transcripts to be sent to colleges from your high school(s) and any colleges you have attended. Note: Some colleges like the University of California do not want transcripts sent until you are admitted.
- ☐ Deadlines – Keep your eye on the deadlines.
- ☐ Portals – You must log into your portal after you submit your application and then every couple of weeks afterward to see if the college is missing something from your file. Some colleges will close your application if you do not log in while others will move your early application to regular decision.
- ☐ Scholarships – Scholarship due dates vary. Some begin the process of considering students in the spring of your junior year. The Coca-Cola Scholarship is due October 31st. However, due dates for various scholarships occur throughout most of your senior year. Scan www.fastweb.com and www.bigfuture.collegeboard.org/scholarship-search.
- ☐ Regular Decision – Regular decision applications for public colleges vary, but many are due right after Thanksgiving. Regular decision application deadlines for most private schools are the first two weeks of January.
- ☐ FAFSA – Free Application for Federal Student Aid - Apply for federal financial aid (grants, work study, and loans).
- ☐ CSS Profile – About 300 colleges require this form to obtain financial aid.
- ☐ Student Aid Report (SAR) – Approximately 4 weeks after completing your FAFSA you should receive your SAR. Follow the instructions to complete updates or add schools.
- ☐ Update Colleges – Make sure you update colleges with your continued interest.
- ☐ Keep Copies – Keep copies of your application materials in a folder.
- ☐ Visit Colleges – If possible, visit colleges to which you were accepted. Since you are going to live there for four years, you should get a feel for the campus and not just judge a school by its rankings or images on the school's website.
- ☐ Communicate With Students – Find students who currently attend the university who are willing to answer a few questions. How hard is it to change your major? Are students friendly? What do students do on the weekends? Ask your counselor, teachers, or the admissions office if they can refer you to a student who currently attends or just graduated.

- ☐ Waitlisted Schools – Most schools will allow you to write a letter updating them on your accomplishments during your senior year and express your continued interest. Read the instructions since every school has a different format and set of requirements. Demonstrate your commitment.
- ☐ Candidate Reply Date – By May 1st you must choose one school and place a deposit.
- ☐ Senior Year Grades – Colleges rescind admissions offers for students who do poorly in their senior year. Do not slack off. You will regret it.

DECISIONS, DECISIONS: WAITING FOR A RESPONSE

The period between submitting your application and getting your admissions results may not require a tremendous amount of work, but it does require patience and diligence. First, most schools will send you a link to a portal where you will check your results, though the most important reason for checking every couple of weeks is to ensure that the college is not missing something or has not offered you the chance to apply for an extra scholarship.

Check your portal regularly. Additionally, read the college's correspondence sent through your e-mail. Waiting from November until April is agonizing. Students clamor to know the results since their future is on the line. However, colleges typically list the date they will send admissions results on the portal. Other popular sites post decision notification dates too. You will find out soon.

THICK OR THIN ENVELOPE

Students eagerly check each day as winter turns to spring waiting to hear via e-mail, the college portal, or the mail (welcome packet or denial letter). You know spring has come as regular decision admissions results steadily roll in, one at a time. In March, every day seems to last 26 hours, two extra for the period that lingers until that day's announcement. With each school announcing on a different day, the slow drip torture waiting to find out is exacerbated by the uncanny way each college picks a different day in March or April to announce their decision.

At some point, you will know. That statement seems like little solace in the middle of the fray. You have until May 1 to make a decision, though with limited housing available and a first-come, first-served basis of selection, the pressure is on to choose. Visiting the college is vital, despite the fact that AP tests and finals are just around the corner and there seems to be no time. However, this decision influences where you will live, eat, study, make friends, take classes, and get involved for four years. Do you want to base your next four years on a few college-selected pictures and the tweets or feeds of other people?

There are many variables to consider. This is why forward thinking at the beginning of the application process is valuable and even necessary to seek scholarships, merit money, or opportunities for financial aid. This proactive planning is especially needed with the spike in college applications at selective schools and the ever-changing landscape of test-optional admissions. MIT, for example, resumed its test requirement.

Plan ahead. The college application process is not a good time to procrastinate. The fall of your senior year is tough, often with a demanding course load. It is even tougher for athletes who compete in a fall sport. However, throughout your life you will need to work on time management, organization, and goal setting. This is a good time to start so you do not miss thousands of dollars in scholarships. During the pandemic, time management challenged students to adjust their lifestyles in self-paced classes, Zoom meetings, and online assignments.

CELEBRATING ACCEPTANCES AND DEALING WITH REJECTION

Acceptance is not guaranteed. Colleges seek students who are wholly committed to their education, talents, and learning experiences. Unfortunately, even for dedicated students, the probability of acceptance is low at the most highly selective schools. Your commitment, work ethic, and planning make the outcome sweeter when you are accepted and celebrate the next step along your way.

Congratulations! The colleges in which you gain admission go on your list of options. Check your financial aid and scholarship packages too. Money is often an important factor in making your final decision. Even if you cannot visit the campus, ask the college for contact names of students in your major. Many students apply to colleges merely by someone's recommendation, *U.S. News and World Report* ranking, campus photos on Google, or posts on a website.

Nothing replaces the actual campus visit. After all, you will spend a few years there. Be selective about applying. You may decide, after visiting a college that you do not want to apply or attend after all. Understandably, the pandemic's uncertainty and difficulty to travel added more question marks to an already complicated set of admissions processes.

The buzzword for 2020-2030 is resilience. It is never easy to be rejected. However, rejection happens. You will survive this. Note that many colleges still accept applications in April, May, and June, long after most school's applications are closed. If you did not get accepted, look up colleges that still have openings just in case schools you have not considered might be good options for you. In April and May, Google "College Openings Update". You will be surprised to see the colleges that show up on the list that still have open spots.

WAITLISTS: THE ART OF WAITING

Immediately confirm if you are given a waitlist spot and still want to attend. There is often a deadline. You do not want to miss this. If you are no longer interested or have selected another school, go into the portal and turn down the offer. Someone else is bound to be thrilled by your anonymous gift.

If you are still interested, find the location on the portal or site designated by the college to update them on what you have done – accomplishments, awards, extra class, honors, art, shows, or films. You only want to add what they have not yet seen, but if you have taken the initiative to do something more than what you originally stated on the application, by all means, tell them.

You could just wait for their decision, but you are better off being proactive writing an update of what you have accomplished, and showing that you really want to attend their school. Students do get off the waitlists at most schools. How much do you want to attend? Meanwhile, you will have to deposit somewhere else before the May 1st deadline. Stay hopeful. This next year will be a significant step along your journey. Relax!

ACCEPTANCE IS JUST THE BEGINNING

Once you are accepted to college, you begin your journey toward your future. They call graduation "commencement" because the next step you take is a new beginning. You will start this trek on your own path. The decisions you make now are primarily yours with significantly less input from your parents. For better or worse, your parents taught you lessons that you will keep or discard. Going forward, your behaviors, attitudes, internships, study abroad, and career choices will determine what you become.

Warning ahead of time…the path is rarely straight and there are pitfalls along the way. Much like Monopoly, you will roll the dice and move ahead a few squares. You may go back a few spaces as well. You might buy a house or save some money. You might lose a property or an investment too. Life is full of lessons. Successful adults sometimes look back and forget about the wrong turns. Although setbacks sting at the time, they are often dismissed over the years as lessons.

I have literally attended college for fifty years and have degrees that span a multitude of disciplines. I have also taught chemistry, mathematics, engineering, counseling, public relations, and politics. Here are my 21 tips as you go forward.

1. Attend class even when other students don't. Surprisingly, many lecture halls are half empty when there isn't a test. Go anyway. Most college professors know if you attend or can find out from their course assistant.

2. Buy your books and start reading before the semester starts. When classes begin, you live in a blizzard of activities, opportunities, and assignments. Again, surprisingly, most students do not complete their assigned readings. Some get by without reading but getting As that way is tough.

3. Work ahead. Finish your paper or project first, then go out and celebrate your friend's birthday, sports team win, or friend-group's successes. Not only are you more likely to be relaxed, but you might even improve on your work later when you come up with a new idea.

4. Most colleges offer free tutoring. Tutors often read over your papers or assignments and almost always give you valuable assistance that you would never have considered. Return to #3. To get help you must complete your assignments ahead of time.

5. Have a backup plan or two. Murphy's Law says: (1) anything that can go wrong will, (2) nothing is as easy as it looks, (3) everything takes longer than you think it will.

6. Save your digital documents – often. The worst thing is when you lose an entire assignment, your computer turns off, or malware attacks your files. Google Drive and iCloud are fine for some things, but there are pitfalls. Make a file backup if possible, even if your docs are saved in the cloud.

7. Develop solid notetaking and reminder systems that work for you. You will need these for the rest of your life. Small things tend to slip through the cracks. Checklists are extremely helpful.

8. There is never enough time. Bring enough clothes so you do not need to wash them as often. When you do wash them, take them out when they are done or else someone else will and you may never find them again.

9. Register for classes the minute registration opens up for you. Trust me on this one. Otherwise, you get a bad professor at a horrible time that conflicts with your commitments. You might not even get into critical prerequisites which may extend your time in college a semester or a year.

10. Petition to get into a class. Begging is fine. The professor can say no, but at least you tried. Good professors will save your sanity.

11. If you have any academic problem, particularly with an illness, family matter, or emergency, let your professors know immediately. Most will not help you later if you wait a month thinking you can handle it on your own or if you miss an assignment.

12. Make a calendar and keep track of what you need to accomplish. The syllabus is your roadmap. Calendarize dates. Post key dates on your wall.

13. Teamwork is a mantra in college. You will work on teams. A few members are likely to be unmotivated slackers or talented, but extreme procrastinators. Determine this ahead of time and set intermediate goals. Remember, your grade is on the line. It's not fair but go back to #5. In the end, finish the project anyway. The unmotivated slacker will also get an A, which may thoroughly frustrate you, but you will earn an A too.

14. Book prices vary widely. The university bookstore prices are often high but the location is convenient. I have friends who swear by certain online stores where they always buy textbooks, get coupons, and then buy more books. One advantage of buying books in digital format is that you can often use 'Control F' to find on-demand information you need. Sometimes you can also take digital notes, which is impossible with a physical copy. I prefer physical books, but you choose. Also, renting books is okay unless you forget to send the book back.

15. Get involved as soon as you can. Meet students who have similar interests. Join clubs, learn about the school's traditions, try activities you always wanted to learn, ask professors about volunteering on research projects, and get involved with intramural sports.

16. Don't bring a car. A car sounds wonderful, offering you freedom, until your vehicle is broken into, the gas runs out, the car breaks down before a test, or you get a half dozen parking tickets. You will never realize how much trouble a car could be on campus, particularly when there is limited and expensive parking. They can and will hold your transcripts if you do not pay your parking tickets or clear up a violation.

17. Communicate with your professors and TAs. Most of them have office hours. Well, they probably all have office hours, but sometimes professors or teaching assistants are absent. Either drop by during scheduled times or make an appointment. Especially if you have a question or a problem, speak to them. A professor rarely helps a student after they turn in grades but may have excellent advice during the term if you are struggling. Surprisingly, the answer key is occasionally wrong. Sometimes professors are intimidating, standoffish, or mean-spirited. Fortunately, there are only a few bad ones, and even these professors teach important lessons.

18. Don't get so excited about credit cards. Credit card companies will continually hound you to sign up with tempting offers. College students

are prime targets because they do not yet really understand the challenge of paying monthly bills when there is little time and numerous items to purchase. You will probably have to learn the hard way, but credit cards are not the savior they purport to be. Furthermore, you will likely spend more than you imagined, and the interest payments will dig a deep hole in your pocketbook.

19. Drinking and drugs are around you 24/7. It does not matter what school you attend. Rarely is a campus void of alcohol or drugs. However, some colleges have more – much more. Some students will even sell illegal drugs in the dorm. You need to use your own judgment. Be careful. Students consume more than they realize, make judgment errors, get seriously injured, die of overdoses, and spread STDs. This section was not written to scare you but to make you aware of the life-changing realities.

20. During Christmas break of your first year, apply for internships, training opportunities, co-ops, or jobs for the summer. Create a resume. Getting real-world experience cannot be understated if you want to jump on the job market. Career fairs are extremely helpful so you can explore jobs you might want. Every college has a career center. Get to know the people who work there. It may mean the difference in getting a coveted interview.

21. Go boldly into this world and try new things. Thomas Edison once said, "I have not failed. I've just found 10,000 ways that won't work."

CHAPTER 8
FINANCIAL AID & SCHOLARSHIPS

"Environmentally friendly cars will soon cease to be an option...they will become a necessity."

– **Fujio Cho**

Nearly every university in the United States offers money for college. These funds come in the form of grants or scholarships that do not need to be paid back, loans that must be repaid, and 'work study', where students work and are paid for a job associated with the college or university. The grants or scholarships are either need-based or merit-based.

Need-based means that the college or government determines that, based on your income, you will be unable to attend without additional resources. Merit-based means that the college or university offers students money based on some combination of talent, skills, background, experiences, or academic achievement.

NEED-BASED FINANCIAL AID

To obtain need-based financial aid, almost all colleges require the submission of the Free Application for Federal Student Aid (FAFSA). The website address is www.studentaid.gov. Some colleges also require students to complete the College Scholarship Service (CSS) Profile form which is available on the College Board website at www.collegeboard.org.

Both the FAFSA and CSS Profile require the submission of family income based upon the tax returns you and/or your family file with the U.S. federal government.

If your answer is yes to any of the following you do not need to declare your parent's income when filing your FAFSA form. There are nuances to the rules for students who are verifiably independent, ex-pats that have a unique situation, and parents who are unavailable for a variety of reasons. The federal government offers free advice to families if they have a unique case.

1. Will you be 24 or older by Jan. 1 of the school year for which you are applying for financial aid? For example, if you plan to start school in August 2022 for the 2022–23 school year, will you be 24 by Jan. 1, 2022 (i.e., were you born before Jan. 1, 1999)?
2. Are you married or separated but not divorced?
3. Will you be working toward a master's or doctorate degree (such as MA, MBA, MD, JD, Ph.D., Ed.D., etc.)?
4. Do you have children who receive more than half of their support from you?
5. Do you have dependents (other than children or a spouse) who live with you and receive more than half of their support from you?
6. Are you currently serving on active duty in the U.S. armed forces for purposes other than training?
7. Are you a veteran of the U.S. armed forces?
8. At any time since you turned age 13, were both of your parents deceased, were you in foster care, or were you a ward or dependent of the court?
9. Are you an emancipated minor or are you in a legal guardianship as determined by a court?
10. Are you an unaccompanied youth who is homeless or self-supporting and at risk of being homeless?

SCHOLARSHIPS

Merit scholarships are offered through a college/university, private donors, or corporations. These are based upon academic success, talent, background, or life experiences. Scholarships may require additional forms, essays, recommendations, or proof of academic success. Note: A few universities, particularly the highest-ranked schools, do not offer merit scholarships, though most colleges do.

Merit or talent-based scholarships typically require a portfolio, audition, video, performance, research abstract, website, or some other demonstration of your skills. Check the specifications for art, dance, music, writing, debate, theatre, research, robotics, engineering, or other skills/talents to see what the college allows or requires. Each college or university has a different set of rules for what and how you submit your demonstrations of mastery.

Please check out the profile section at the back of this book for scholarships and requirements. Additionally, look up the college website for their financial aid process. To help you get a sense of available scholarships, I selected three schools from the options listed in the profile section.

NORTHWESTERN UNIVERSITY

Northwestern awarded $200 million recently to undergraduate students with half of the students receiving a scholarship. Northwestern provides a chart with the average total aid packages offered to students. More than 90% of students whose families have incomes below $120,000 receive above $50,000 per year in scholarship money to attend. Students from lower-income families receive up to $74,000 per year.

Northwestern participates in the Questbridge College Match Program. The scholarships offered include those for students living in the Chicago area as well as the Northwestern Endowed Scholarship, Founders Scholarship, and Karr Achievement Scholarship. The McCormick School of Engineering website also provides a list of outside scholarships, fellowships, and competitions.

GEORGIA TECH

Georgia Tech's tuition, room, board, and books is relatively low for both in-state and out-of-state students. With an average cost of education half that of attending a private school, this should remind families that the net cost is a key figure. Like other schools, Georgia Tech also refers students to outside scholarships.

Georgia Tech offers a full-ride Stamps President's Scholarship to the top 1% of first-year students. 'Tech's' Provost Scholarship is awarded to 40 first-year, non-resident students which gives an out-of-state tuition waiver for eight semesters. That reduces tuition, room, board, and books for out-of-state students to slightly over $100,000 for all four years.

RICE UNIVERSITY

Rice University offers significant financial aid including full tuition remission for students whose families earn between $75,000-$140,000. Students receive free tuition, room and board if their families earn an annual income is less than $75,000. A half tuition waiver is given for those families whose earn between $140,000-$200,000.

Rice Engineering students were awarded approximately $378,000 in awards and scholarships in a recent year. Rice University practices need-blind admission for domestic students and meets 100% of demonstrated need for undergraduate admitted students.

ENGINEERING SCHOLARSHIPS

Air & Space Forces Association

AFA contributed $230,000/year to Airmen, Guardians, their spouses, and their children through 12 unique scholarships that help fund college tuition, flight school, dental school, Arnold Air Society and Silver Wings, and full rides to universities. Apply between December 1 and April 30 each year.

Air Traffic Control Association

The 2024 Scholarship will open for application submissions in March 2024 and will close on May 1, 2024. ATCA awards $75,000 in scholarships annually; each scholarship recipient receives between $5,000 and $15,000.

Aircraft Electronics Association

Approximately 20 scholarships are given to members of the AEA. See https://aea.net/educationalfoundation/scholarships.asp for list of scholarships.

American Council of Engineering Companies (ACEC) Research Institute Scholarships

Apply through the ACEC Research Institute scholarship portal with more than 100 scholarships totaling $1 million, including a $5,000 award given to one student in every state and D.C. These scholarships are for both undergraduate and graduate study.

American Electric Power Scholarship ($4,000) & ASME Power Division Scholarship ($3,000)

These scholarships are granted to college student members of ASME whose goal is to pursue a career in power engineering. Applications are due in February.

American Institute of Aeronautics and Astronautics

AIAA has given out 1,300 scholarships to students at more than 150 colleges worldwide. Students must be an AIAA student member who has completed 1 year of engineering coursework with a 3.30+ GPA. See website for a list of scholarships.

American Institute of Chemical Engineers (AIChE) Minority Affairs

Minority Scholarship Awards for Underrepresented Chemical Engineering Students (Multiple Awards) are available for applicants who are African-American, Hispanic, Native American, Alaskan Native, Pacific Islander. The $1,000 award is renewable each year.

American Water Works Association

The AWWA supports students who seek a future in preserving, protecting, and providing water to communities. Scholarships of $5,000 are offered to approximately ten students each year, with applications opening in September.

Astronaut Scholarship Foundation

In 2023, ASF awarded 68 scholarships to students from 45 different U.S. universities. Astronaut Scholarships are awarded to students in their junior and senior year of college studying STEM subjects with the intent to pursue research or advance science.

Biomedical Engineering Society Student Design Competition

In addition to student chapter awards and the Rita Schaffer Young Investigator Award, BMES offers Student Design & Research Awards.

Boeing Scholarships

Boeing offers engineering scholarships along with $500,000 for 25 pilot training with Boeing Sisters of the Skies, Boeing Fly-Compton, Aircraft Owners and Pilots Association, Latino Pilots Association. Organization of Black Aerospace Professionals, Sisters of the Skies, and Women in Aviation International
Boeing is also donating $450,000 to Fly Compton, a Los Angeles-based nonprofit that introduces minority youth to career opportunities in aerospace.

Chevron Scholarships - AISES, UNCF, REACH, REC Foundation

Chevron offers scholarships to students (Native American, African American, children of employees, robotics competitors, etc.) with awards of varying amounts.

Environmental Engineering & Science Foundation

Graduate /Masters level scholarships are awarded to students pursuing environmental engineering/science (8 awarded/year).

Experimental Aircraft Association

EAA scholarships encourage aviation enthusiasts to pursue post-secondary education. EAA offers scholarships for college, flight training, and the camp academy. Apply between Nov 1 and March 1.

Eugene C. Figg, Jr. Civil Engineering Scholarship

This $3,000 scholarship is awarded to engineering students who pursue bridge design and construction. Students submit an application, resume, transcripts, recommendations, and an essay regarding bridge design/construction.

Federal Water Quality Association

FWQA provides at least three scholarships for high school students pursuing careers in wastewater and environmental science.

Ford Fund Scholarships for Automotive/Mechanical Engineering

These scholarship are offered to students to assist with laptops, software, tools, books, uniforms, and other supplies.

General Aviation Manufacturers Association

GAMA Edward W. Stimpson Aviation Excellence Award - Awarded to a graduating U.S. high school senior to be enrolled in an aviation degree. $2,000

ICAS Foundation/GAMA Scholarship – $2,000 award is given to students seeking an aviation-related degree, such as professional pilot, maintenance/engineering, or aviation business.

Whirly-Girls Scholarship Fund - Whirly-Girls offers 16 scholarships from $950 to $14,000. Applicants must be a member.

The Aviation Youth Empowerment Fund (AYEF) STEM Scholarship Award – Students are encouraged to apply $4,000 scholarships for aviation, sciences, technology, engineering, and math fields. Students must live in Washington, Oregon, and Northern California.

Google Scholarships
Google Scholarships for Disabled Students
Scholarships for Students in India
Student Veterans; Women Techmakers
Google Travel & Conference Grants
Generation Google Scholarship

Students majoring in Comp Sci, Computer Engineering, or related field and are members of an underrepresented group will receive special consideration. Need-based awards of $10,000 are given to students. Apply in April.

Barry Goldwater Scholarship

Hundreds of scholarships are awarded to college sophomores and juniors pursuing research careers in STEM subjects. A $9 million grant seeks to double the number of awards.

Dan & Vicky Hancock Scholarship - Mechanical Engineering Excellence

One $5,500 scholarship is awarded yearly to applicants pursuing mechanical engineering. Students submit an application, FAFSA form, two letters of recommendation, and demonstrated leadership. Applications are due in March.

Ralph K. Hillquist Honorary SAE Scholarship

This $1,000 award offered every other year at the SAE Noise & Vibration Conference is for junior mechanical engineering majors who are interested in noise, vibration, statics, dynamics, and physics. Applications are due in March.

Institute of Electrical & Electronics Engineers

The IEEE Power & Energy Society (PES) offers $7,000 scholarships toward college expenses while also offering connections, mentoring, and internship opportunities.

Intel Scholarship Program

These scholarships are for students pursuing engineering and computer science. Nearly $2 million distributed annually.

Stephen T. Kugle Scholarship

This $3,000 scholarship is for an active ASME student member who attends college in AZ, AK, CO, LA, NM, OK, TX, UT, or WY. Apps are due in February.

John Lenard Civil Engineering Scholarship

Student members of American Society of Civil Engineers (ASCE) whose primary civil engineering interest is in water supply or environmental engineering can apply in February. Scholarship amounts vary.

Lockheed Martin Scholarships
STEM Scholarship Program

In 2024, Lockheed Martin awarded 100 students, a grant for $10,000 to study at a 4-year college or university. This scholarship is renewable each year. Apply by April 1.

Guglielmo Marconi Engineering Scholarship

This $1,250 engineering scholarship is available to full-time undergraduates who have at least one parent of Italian ancestry. The application is due in April.

John J. McKetta Undergraduate Scholarship

College juniors or seniors who are members of the American Institute of Chemical Engineers and plan to pursue chemical engineering processes can submit an application for this scholarship along with a career essay, transcript, resume, and two letters of recommendation. The application for this $5,000 award is due in June.

Frank & Dorothy Miller Scholarship (2 - $2,000); F.W. "Beich" Beichley Scholarship (1 - $3,000); Garland Duncan Scholarship (2 - $5,000), Irma and Robert Bennett Scholarship (2 - $3,000); John & Else Gracik Scholarships (5 - $5,000); Allen J. Baldwin Scholarship (2 - $3,000); Berna Lou Cartwright Scholarship (2 - $3,000); Sylvia W. Farny Scholarship (2 - $3,000); Agnes Malakate Kezios Scholarship (2 - $3,000); Charles B. Scharp Scholarship (1 - $3,000), Kenneth Andrew Roe Scholarship (1 - $13,000); Melvin R. Green Scholarship (1 - $8,000)

Up to 23 awards are given yearly to college student members of ASME. Considerations include integrity, leadership, academics, and the potential to contribute to the mechanical engineering profession. Applications are due in February.

Microsoft Scholarships, Internships, & Competitions for Students in Computer Science & STEM Disciplines (see link)

https://techcommunity.microsoft.com/t5/educator-developer-blog/microsoft-s-student-opportunities-a-gateway-to-professional/ba-p/3798822

Lawrence W. and Francis W. Cox Scholarship & Robert B.B. and Josephine N. Moorman Scholarship

Applicants for these awards must be student members of ASCE. Students complete an application and essay on why they want to be a civil engineer and how they contributed to ASCE. These applications are due in February.

National Air Transportation Association

Sophomores and juniors interested in aviation and air transportation can apply for the many $1,000 scholarships awarded each year. Applications due in December.

National Oceanic and Atmospheric Administration
Ernest F. Hollings Undergraduate Scholarship Program

Scholars receive up to $9,500/yr during two-yeas of full-time study. During the summer, they participate in oceanic, atmospheric, and science internships paying $700/wk plus travel expenses.

Northrop Grumman
Engineering Scholars Program

These renewable scholarships are for graduating seniors majoring in engineering, computer science, math, or physics. Students must live in CA, IL, MD, NY, OH, or VA.

Donald F. and Mildred Topp Othmer Scholarship Awards (15 Awards)

Undergraduate chemical engineering students may apply for this $1,000 scholarship. The application is due in June.

Recycling Education & Research Foundation Scholarship (Multiple Awards)

These $2,500 scholarships are open to applicants who are college juniors. The application is due in June.

Allen Rhodes Memorial Scholarships

This scholarship is for college student members of the ASME who are interested in pursuing careers in the oil and gas industry. Applications are due in February.

John Rice Memorial Scholarship

This $3,000 scholarship is for students who attend one of nine New York City area colleges. Students will be judged based on their transcript, leadership, integrity, and potential to contribute to the mechanical engineering profession. Applications are due in February.

Udall Undergraduate Scholarship

Future leaders in environmental, Tribal public policy, and healthcare are encouraged to apply for the competitive program with school competitions and a multiday Scholar Orientation. In 2024, the Udall Foundation anticipates awarding 55 scholarships of $7,000 each.

Society of Women Engineers All Together Scholarships

SWE awards 280+ scholarships totaling more than $1,200,000 to students in engineering. College students in all areas of engineering are encouraged to apply.

PRIVATE SCHOLARSHIPS

Some scholarship money does not come directly from the college. Private individuals, corporations, and endowments offer outside scholarships for students who apply. Some of these scholarships are significant. A few offer full tuition. Here are a few of the thousands to consider.

AQHA and AQHF – $25,000 - $35,000 (Dec 1) Quarter Horse Members

A few scholarships for journalism, communications, agricultural studies, and equine research.

Alzheimer's Foundation of America

HS seniors impacted by Alzheimer's disease submit a 1,500-word essay or 4-min video describing the impact of Alzheimer's disease or dementia. Amount: $5,000 Due: April 1.

American Legion National Oratorical Contest

HS juniors/seniors prepare an oration on the U.S. Constitution and citizenship. State Winners: $2,000, National Winner: $20,000 - $25,000.

Ayn Rand Essay Contest - 455,000 student winners; $2,200,000 given out

Read and analyze one of three books (Anthem, Fountainhead, Atlas Shrugged) by Ayn Rand to win this contest. Multiple awards given out. Amount: $2,000 Due: April

Blaze Your Own Trail Scholarship

HS seniors and college students submit a 600-800-word essay describing a challenge you faced, how you overcame it, and your experience. Amount: $1,000 Deadline May

Boren Scholarships ($8,000 - $25,000) and Boren Fellowships ($12,000 -30,000) – Foreign Language Study

The National Security Education Program (NSEP) awards funding for students to study one of about 65 languages the U.S. deems necessary for national security through a study abroad program. Applications open from mid-August to early February. Approximately 300 students are selected.

Brower Youth Awards

Environmental activism awards are granted to 6 winners; each receives $3,000.

Coca Cola Scholarship

1,400 students are selected to receive scholarships. The total amount awarded annually is approximately $3,550,000. 150 students receive $20,000 scholarship each.

Comcast NBCUniversal Leaders and Achievers Scholarship

More than 800 high school student winners each year win a $2,500 scholarship.

Dell Scholars Program – 500 students selected – $20,000 - First-Generation

This scholarship is awarded to students who exhibit grit, potential, and ambition.

Doodle for Google Contest

This art/imagination contest is for K-12 students. Use any medium to describe your wish for the next 25 years. Amount: $5,000 Due: March 14.

Gates Millennium Scholarship

Scholarships covering the full cost of attendance not already covered by other and expected family contributions are granted to 300 African American, American Indian/Alaska Native, Asian Pacific Islander, or Hispanic American student leaders.

GE-Reagan Foundation Scholarship Program $40,000 (10 students)

Another $50,000 is awarded in the Great Communicator Debate Series.

Gloria Barron Prize for Young Heroes

25 students each year ages 8 – 18 receive $10,000 for community service projects.

Grit Award Scholarship

HS seniors with a GPA of 3.0+ must show GPA improvement and describe why they now have academic promise. Amount: $500 Due: May.

Hispanic Scholarship Fund

Approximately 10,000 winners - $30,000,000 awarded annually.

K-12 Educator Scholarship

This scholarship is for children with parents who teach in the K-12 system.

Karcher Founders Scholarship

College-bound HS seniors who live near a Carl's Jr. Award: $10,000 Due: April 4.

LULAC (League of United Latin American Citizens)
Ford Driving Dreams Scholarship, ExxonMobil Scholarship
NBC Universal Scholarship

The LULAC National Scholarship Fund along with corporations (Walmart,

CocaCola, Nissan, Danaher, etc.) provide hundreds of scholarships for high school and college students.

Minecraft Scholarship

HS/college students submit an essay of 500+ words, detailing how Minecraft can be a positive influence on education and careers. Amount: $2,000 Due July 31.

NAACP – National Association for the Advancement of Colored People

African Americans - about 170 students receive awards of $3,000 to $15,000.

NASSP – National Association of Secondary School Principals

600 NHS Scholarships awarded per year, 1 national winner ($25,000 scholarship). 24 national finalists ($5,625 each), 575 national semifinalists ($3,200 each). Apply between October 1 and December 1.

Optimist International Essay Contest

HS students submit a 700-800-word essay on how optimism connects people. Amount: $2,500 Due: February 28.

Parent Employment

Many companies offer scholarships for their employees and their children.

Project Yellow Light Video Contest Scholarship

High school juniors and seniors, plus FT undergrads create a 10 or 25 second video that discourages texting while driving. Award: $8,000 Due: April 1.

Prudential Spirit of Community Award (Prudential Emerging Visionaries)

25 students in grades 5 to 12. Amount: $1,000 - $5,000 award for community service.

Questbridge Scholarship

$200,000 is granted to each of 1,464 students to be used over 4 years.

Race to Inspire Essay Contest

Student runners (5k, 10k, half marathons, or marathons) submit a 1,000-2,000 word essay detailing why you run and your challenges/lessons. Amount: $500 Due August

Rover College Scholarship

HS seniors/college students submit a 400-500-word essay on how growing up with a pet impacted the person you are today. Award: $2,500 Due May 1.

ROTC

These military scholarships are not given to everyone in ROTC. A select group of outstanding candidates is given tuition, fees, textbooks, plus a monthly stipend.

Scholastic Art and Writing Competition

Herblock Award - $1,000 scholarships for editorial cartoons
New York Life Award - $1,000 writing award about personal grief and loss
One Earth Award - $1,000 scholarship for writing about human-caused climate change
Portfolio Scholarships – Up to $10,000 granted for top portfolios
Civic Expression Award - $1,000 scholarships for writing on political and social issues
Best-In-Grade – Juror favorite awards receive $500 scholarships
Art & Writing Scholarships - https://www.artandwriting.org/scholarships/

#ScienceSaves High School Video Scholarship

HS seniors create a 20-30 second video about science and what it does for people. Amount: $10,000 Due May 6

Service/Leadership/Focused Organization Scholarship

Lions Club, Moose Club, Elks Club, Rotary Club, Soroptimists Club, Mensa

Student Veterans of America

These scholarships are awarded to top student veterans. The monies granted to not interfere with GI Bill grants or other financial aid. Scholarships total over $100,000 annually.

Target Scholarship

HBCU Design Challenge for African Americans – Students submit designs for Black History Month. Target Scholars Program – 1,000 students get $5,000 each.

Thurgood Marshall College Fund

African Americans – approximately 500 scholarships per year (average award - $6,200 per year).

Unboxing Your Life Video Scholarship

HS seniors and college students create a 5-min video describing who they are as they unbox their life. Award: $4,000 Due: March 31.

Vegetarian Resource Group Scholarship

HS students who actively promote vegetarianism and peace while demonstrating compassion, courage, and commitment. Amount: $5,000-$10,000 Due Feb 20.

Walgreens Expressions Challenge

High school students between 13 and 18 are challenged to describe your world through words, visual arts, media arts or creative writing. Award: $1,500 - $2,000 Due March

Walmart Scholarship Program

Employees and dependents can obtain up to $13,000 in scholarships to be used over four years. Complete the online application. Qualified candidates will be considered depending on their financial needs and academic performance.

We The Future Contest

HS/college students submit an essay, song, project, film, social media, or PSA on a topic related to the Constitution. Amount $1,000-$5,000 Due May 31.

Note: Like Wal-Mart, many corporations offer scholarships for employees and dependents. Prominent examples include Starbucks, AT&T, & Pepsi. If your parent works for a corporation, check with their human resources department. Also, many organizations like the American Legion, Lions Club, Elks Club, Rotary Club, and the National League of Masonic Clubs offer scholarships.

CHAPTER 9
EMPLOYMENT OUTLOOK

"To be whole. To be complete. Wildness reminds us what it means to be human, what we are connected to rather than what we are separate from."

– Terry Tempest Williams

Environmental scientists and engineers play essential roles in society. Working in offices and in the field, they research, develop, analyze, test, and provide engineering services for companies, organizations, and governmental entities. Environmental scientists and engineers look for opportunities to improve communication, power, and overall systems.

With high demand for environmental action, including recycling, waste reduction, public health, and pollution abatement, environmental engineers address global issues to resolve current problems and minimize future impacts. Environmental engineers are systems thinkers whose job intersects with industry and municipalities in the areas of sustainability, conservation, and human footprints.

According to the *Occupational Outlook Handbook*, employment opportunities in environmental engineering are slated to grow 4% from 2020 to 2030 with approximately 1,900 new jobs expected. Currently, there are approximately 52,300 environmental engineers.

Environmental engineers enter the profession with a bachelor's degree. According to the Bureau of Labor Statistics, the median annual wage in 2021 was $96,820.

Furthermore, with increased advocacy and the rapid development of innovations in many sectors of society, environmental engineers' wages are likely to increase. Environmental engineers may earn their degree in environmental science, applied chemistry, marine biology, forestry, and environmental engineering before focusing their academics and career on the environmental side of organizational operations.

Colleges may list this major under the fields of environmental engineering, sustainability engineering, or civil engineering umbrella, sometimes in a combined Civil & Environmental Engineering department. Applications span fields from power and energy systems to animal science, marine biology, soil science, botany, forestry, oceanography, geography, technology, and safety.

The close relationship between environmental systems and infrastructure construction often links the majors of environmental and civil engineering. Some environmental engineers test and oversee the development of power plants, construction, ocean systems, public health, water conservation, and vehicle exhaust. In the transportation industry, they oversee environmental concerns related to the use of boats, trains, cars, drones, planes, satellites, and rockets.

Licensure is necessary in order to offer services to the public. Entry-level positions require a bachelor's degree. Some continue on to graduate school. Leadership positions in governmental policy, legal frameworks, or construction management typically require a graduate degree in environmental engineering, civil engineering, law, public policy, or business administration.

According to the May 2023 Bureau of Labor Statistics data,

OCCUPATION	JOB SUMMARY	Entry-Level Education	2023 MEDIAN PAY
Aerospace Engineering & Operations Technologists & Technicians	Aerospace engineering and operations technologists and technicians run and maintain equipment used to develop, test, produce, and sustain aircraft and spacecraft.	Associate's Degree	$71,830
Aerospace Engineers	Aerospace engineers design primarily aircraft, spacecraft, satellites, and missiles.	Bachelor's Degree	$130,720
Agricultural Engineers	Agricultural engineers solve problems concerning power supplies, machine efficiency, the use of structures and facilities, pollution and environmental issues, and the storage and processing of agricultural products.	Bachelor's Degree	$88,750

OCCUPATION	JOB SUMMARY	Entry-Level Education	2023 MEDIAN PAY
Architectural & Engineering Managers	Architectural and engineering managers plan, direct, and coordinate activities in the fields of agriculture and engineering	Bachelor's Degree	$165,370
Bioengineers & Biomedical Engineers	Bioengineers and biomedical engineers combine engineering principles with sciences to design and create equipment, devices, computer systems, and software.	Bachelor's Degree	$100,730
Cartographers & Photogrammetrists	Cartographers and photogrammetrists collect, measure, and interpret geographic information in order to create and update maps and charts for regional planning, education, and other purposes.	Bachelor's Degree	$76,210
Chemical Engineers	Chemical engineers apply the principles of chemistry, biology, physics, and math to solve problems that involve the use of fuel, drugs, food, and many other products.	Bachelor's Degree	$112,100
Civil Engineering Technologists & Technicians	Civil engineering technologists and technicians help civil engineers plan, design, and build infrastructure and development projects.	Associate's Degree	$60,700
Civil Engineers	Civil engineers design, build, and supervise infrastructure projects and systems.	Bachelor's Degree	$95,890
Computer Hardware Engineers	Computer hardware engineers research, design, develop, and test computer systems and components.	Bachelor's Degree	$138,080
Drafters	Drafters use software to convert the designs of engineers and architects into technical drawings.	Associate's Degree	$62,530
Electrical & Electronic Engineering Technologists & Technicians	Electrical and electronic engineering technologists and technicians help engineers design and develop equipment that is powered by electricity or electric current.	Associate's Degree	$72.800
Electrical & Electronics Engineers	Electrical engineers design, develop, test, and supervise the manufacture of electrical equipment.	Bachelor's Degree	$117,680
Electro-mechanical & Mechatronics Technologists & Technicians	Electro-mechanical and mechatronics technologists and technicians operate, test, and maintain electromechanical or robotic equipment.	Associate's Degree	$65,080
Environmental Scientists & Specialist	Environmental scientists and specialists use their knowledge of the natural sciences to protect the environment and human health.	Bachelor's Degree	$78,980

OCCUPATION	JOB SUMMARY	Entry-Level Education	2023 MEDIAN PAY
Environmental Engineers	Environmental engineers use the principles of engineering, soil science, biology, and chemistry to develop solutions to environmental problems.	Bachelor's Degree	$100,090
Health & Safety Engineers	Health and safety engineers combine knowledge of engineering and of health and safety to develop procedures and design systems to protect people from illness and injury and property from damage.	Bachelor's Degree	$103,690
Industrial Engineering Technologists & Technicians	Industrial engineering technologists and technicians help engineers solve problems affecting manufacturing layout or production.	Associate's Degree	$62,610
Industrial Engineers	Industrial engineers devise efficient systems that integrate workers, machines, materials, information, and energy to make a product or provide a service.	Bachelor's Degree	$99,380
Landscape Architects	Landscape architects design parks and other outdoor spaces.	Bachelor's Degree	$79,320
Marine Engineers & Naval Architects	Marine engineers and naval architects design, build, and maintain ships, from aircraft carriers to submarines and from sailboats to tankers.	Bachelor's Degree	$100,270
Materials Engineers	Materials engineers develop, process, and test materials used to create a wide range of products.	Bachelor's Degree	$104,100
Mechanical Engineering Technologists & Technicians	Mechanical engineering technologists and technicians help mechanical engineers design, develop, test, and manufacture machines and other devices.	Associate's Degree	$64,020
Mechanical Engineers	Mechanical engineers design, develop, build, and test mechanical and thermal sensors and devices.	Bachelor's Degree	$99,310
Mining & Geological Engineers	Mining and geological engineers design mines to safely and efficiently remove minerals for use in manufacturing and utilities.	Bachelor's Degree	$100,640
Nuclear Engineers	Nuclear engineers research and develop the processes, instruments, and systems used to derive benefits from nuclear energy and radiation.	Bachelor's Degree	$125.460
Petroleum Engineers	Petroleum engineers design and develop methods for extracting oil and gas from deposits below the Earth's surface.	Bachelor's Degree	$135,690

OCCUPATION	JOB SUMMARY	Entry-Level Education	2023 MEDIAN PAY
Surveyors	Surveyors make precise measurements to determine property boundaries.	Bachelor's Degree	$68,540
Urban & Regional Planners	Urban and regional planners develop comprehensive plans and programs for use of land and physical facilities in cities, counties, metropolitan areas, and other jurisdictions.	Master's Degree	$81,800

We know what we are but know not what we may be.

– William Shakespeare

Environmental engineers must earn a bachelor's degree from an ABET (Accreditation Board for Engineering and Technology) program, though many go on to earn an M.S., JD, or MBA. The ABET is required to earn the PE (Professional Engineer) license. The skills an environmental engineering student learns in school include scientific methods, engineering processes, policy development, and project management.

Beginning with coursework focused on math, statistics, chemistry, and physics, they move on to advanced classes in civil engineering, industrial processes, systems engineering, safety, sustainability, and hands-on project development. Many programs are five years and incorporate a co-op program where they work in industry or the government gaining on-the-job training. Environmental engineers research and develop systems to ensure the protection of air, water, and habitats, often with engineers having different backgrounds.

Modernization is at the forefront of the entire engineering umbrella of majors and careers. With new materials, technologies, and policy incentives, there is a tremendous amount of innovation and experimentation within the avenues of process redesign, transportation, communication, production, and sustainability.

The ultimate goal is for an organization to become more effective and achieve improved communication and power delivery. Innovative student engineers and college researchers are working tirelessly to overcome the challenges that face industry, including sticking points with climate change, rising water levels, and changing infrastructure systems. Furthermore, within the next decade, 5G, 6G, and 7G will intersect with drone travel, technological innovation, and efficient renewable energy resources.

To achieve state licensure, environmental engineers must pass the FE (Fundamentals of Engineering) exam, after which they are considered EITs (Engineers in Training) or EIs (Engineer Interns). Subsequently, they must complete a specified number of years of work experience (varies by state) with a licensed engineer and a passing score on the PE (Principles and Practice of Engineering) exam.

Environmental engineers often join organizations like the American Academy of Environmental Engineers and Scientists (AAEES), Association of Civil and Environmental Engineers, Air & Waste Management Association (A&WMA), and Solid Waste Association of North America (SWANA). By joining, members meet professionals in similar lines of work, gain training, and foster relationships within the industry.

WORK ENVIRONMENT, PAY, AND DEMOGRAPHICS

Environmental engineers work full-time in offices and out in the field where they conduct tests and analyze impacts. They research processes often in consultation with other engineers. Those who spend most of their time overseeing projects work additional hours supervising systems, checking procedures, and measuring output to ensure efficient outcomes and professional standards.

Approximately 27% of all environmental engineers work in engineering services, while 19% work in management, scientific, and technical consulting services, 13% work in state government, 5% in local government, and 4% in the federal government.[1] The rest hold a variety of different positions.

The industry is 70.5% male and 29.5% female; 8% describe themselves as LGBTQ+. The average environmental engineer is 42 years old with 71.3% White, 14.9% Asian, 7.4% Hispanic or Latino, 4.0% Black or African American, 0.5% American Indian or Alaskan Native. The remaining are unknown.

Approximately 16% have master's degrees. The majority of environmental engineers work for private companies, though a significant number work in the public sector. Numerous environmental engineers live in either Atlanta, GA or Houston, Texas. San Francisco, CA pays the highest wage in this field with the highest paying in the energy sector.[2]

---

1   Bureau of Labor Statistics, U.S. Department of Labor, Occupational Outlook Handbook, Environmental Engineers, at https://www.bls.gov/ooh/architecture-and-engineering/environmental-engineers.htm

2   Zippia. Environmental Engineer Demographics and Statistics in the US. https://www.zippia.com/environmental-engineer-jobs/demographics/

The fields where annual mean salaries are between 125,000 to $140,000 include Oil and Gas Extraction, Petroleum and Coal Products Manufacturing, Computer Systems Design, Research and Development, and Company Management.[3] Meanwhile, the highest concentration of employees are in these Bureau of Labor Statistics categories: Architectural, Engineering, and Related Services; Pipeline Transportation of Crude Oil, Remediation and Other Waste Management Services, Management, Scientific, and Technical Consulting Services, and Water, Sewage and Other Systems.

Some environmental engineers work on engineering projects abroad. Thus, although difficult to fit travel experiences into a student's packed academic schedule, a semester or summer abroad learning another language or working in a co-op engineering program in another country is helpful.

ROAD TO LICENSURE

The road to licensure after college graduation is typically four years. This should not be discouraging. There are a few steps to take along the way and possibly some certifications that elevate your career and offer you new possibilities. Even so, achieving the goal is rewarding. Encourage those around you. If environmental engineering is the field you want to pursue, pave the road in front of you and drive. Summer internships or apprenticeships each year will only help you in your pursuit of a position at a good firm.

Although some internships are unpaid, you will find that most applicants will have one or more. Some internships pay fairly well. If you are serious, you will make a fantastic career out of your pursuit. Initiative-taking persistence, talent, creativity, and moxie can get you into your desired college program and career. You may have to start at the very bottom of the ladder, but you can climb the rungs methodically one by one.

Companies want to know the work ethic, personality, and professionalism of any employees they choose. An internship allows you to get to know their corporate climate better and allows them to get to know you better too. Thus, many companies hire the interns they feel are the best fit rather than choosing candidates from the piles of resumes that have been submitted from candidates they barely know.

---

3   Bureau of Labor Statistics. Environmental Engineering. https://www.bls.gov/oes/current/oes172081.htm

Education unlocks doors no matter which direction your career takes you. Whatever avenue you pursue, if you lay a foundation, undaunted by the competition, and are unafraid of starting at the bottom, you will do fine. Hard work and creativity go a long way in this industry. Start by getting a solid education.

IMPACT OF COVID-19

The pandemic slowed education and learning with online classes, reduced access to faculty/advising, limited access to labs, inability to attend workshops, retail closures, and fewer conferences, meetings, and trade shows. Health concerns rose to the top of importance as did financial stress, job uncertainty, and social consciousness.

COVID-19 impacted the number of internships and jobs people could get in environmental engineering. A significant drop in opportunities led many engineering students to the internet to post their availability and freelance. The dynamic changed as Pinterest, Instagram, and Facebook became central hubs of activity. While the field is growing with more entrants, training continues to be essential and skill-building can always be improved.

Many students gain work experience to facilitate professional qualifications. Working with the Peace Corps or USAID provides numerous benefits for its service hours, prestige, rewarding work, fieldwork abroad, and opportunities to gain hands-on experience. With the changes in lifestyle and fears about health, safety, and wellness, many bright and talented students developed a fearless sense of autonomy and independence, while for others, the necessary skills ordinarily developed in school were fraught with limitations.

MANAGEMENT AND EMPLOYEE RETENTION

Skills to Know: Management, Industrial Operations, Social Consciousness, Ethics

One of the most significant challenges facing employers in the years from 2022 - 2030 will be locating and retaining talent. Finding talent within the changing hiring atmosphere will require new skills to retain staff. Employees are increasingly looking elsewhere for better opportunities. This development will require managers to earn and harness employee trust and loyalty.

The digital workforce has also placed demands on human resources. While many companies want their employees to work in-person, the convenience of working at home and the drudgery of commuting to work have created an environment where employees seek greater flexibility. Changes are coming. The employee talent challenge is likely to create a more global workforce.

Companies are back to hiring now and good jobs are available in environmental engineering. There is no doubt that the skills you learn in college will be tremendously valuable in the pursuit of your ultimate goals.

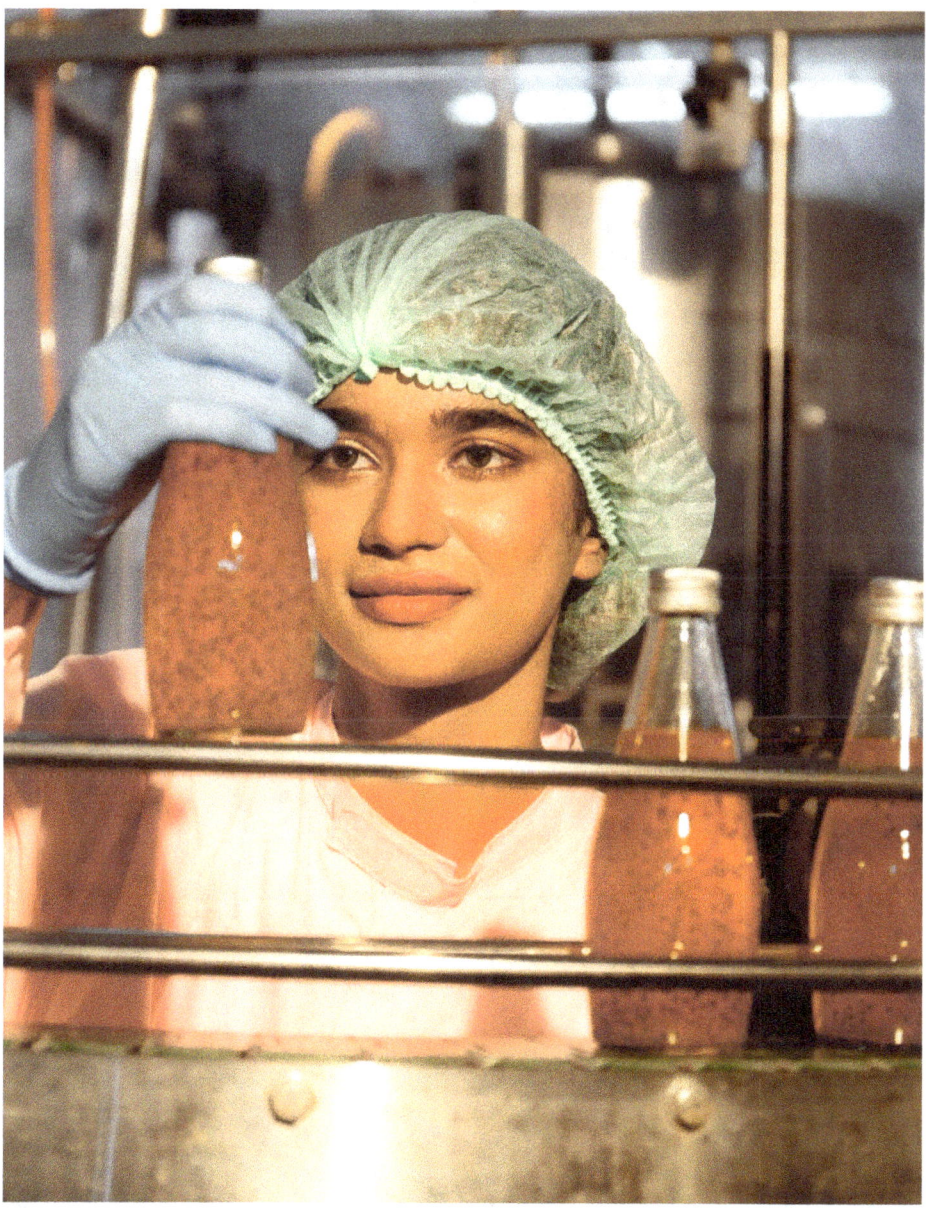

CHAPTER 10
PREPARATION & REAL-WORLD SKILLS

"The Earth does not belong to us; we belong to the Earth."

– **Chief Seattle**

Studying environmental science and engineering offers you the freedom to dive into your studies and experiment dynamically and interactively with your classmates. As you explore the nuances of environmental hazards, conservation, protection, and sustainability, you will engage the creative spirit within you, hungry to emerge. The next step is for you to choose a college where your personality fits into the makeup of the student atmosphere. You will receive personalized, interactive training in college labs infused with inspiration from fellow classmates. Each model you construct will leave a lasting impression.

MAKING CONNECTIONS

Through social media you can instantaneously share your inspirations and projects with millions of people in a matter of moments. The possibilities are limitless. In and out of school, you can engage with groups of socially conscious students, communicate with those similarly-focused on other continents, and aid open-source environments by improving technology and enhancing research.

Connecting with people worldwide, you may discover opportunities in the Metaverse. You might possibly invent processes that were never before possible. The areas of data science, water technology, robotics, and the humanization of computer interfaces offer numerous avenues to pursue. It's unbelievably thrilling.

Studying environmental science and engineering will engage your inventive spirit as outdated monitors and mechanisms are replaced with new technologies. This dynamic, multidimensional field will allow you to infuse your creativity while you learn more on the cutting edge of plastics, pollution, forestry, air flow, water monitoring, and trash management, along with alternative energy solutions like solar, wind, hydroelectric, geothermal, and nuclear power.

You may also become keenly involved with AR, VR, and machine learning as mechanisms to support your endeavors. You are very likely to significantly contribute to the ongoing innovations that will transform interactive technologies. You may invent new sustainable materials or systems.

In some careers, repetitive tasks and uninspiring projects lead employees to loathe their jobs and tick off minutes until their day is done. Yet, your life will undoubtedly be different and ever-changing since the world around you will evolve from moment to moment. Over time, whichever area of environmental engineering or alternative energies becomes your focus, you will earn your way to a career of endless possibilities.

What big ideas do you have that you want to see come to fruition in your lifetime?
- Trash-free ocean?
- Trees planted in towns and cities?
- Beaches, parks, and recreation areas safe for animals and humans?
- Ecofriendly neighborhoods?
- Biodegradable utensils? Methods to prevent environmental damage?
- Teleportation?
- Completely wireless carbon-neutral electric power?
- Nanomaterials that reduce the size of computers to the size of a credit card?
- Natural computer language processing?
- Quantum computing?
- A world free of paper currency?
- Computers that learn tasks like humans and solve problems?
- Working with engineers from other fields, you can collaborate to make your vision of the future come true.

Spend time thinking, even though time sometimes seems short. You may feel that time slips through your fingers like sand in an hourglass. Resist the temptation to upload your ideas before contemplating what you want to express, how you want these to be perceived by your audiences, and the outcome you want to see happen. With your electrified ideas, commitment to school, and a couple of close friends, you can turn your brainstorms into reality.

While social media opens doors to share your vision, truly magical works are created when time stands still and you immerse yourself in a creative state. Today is a precious moment. As you contemplate college choices and tomorrow's future, you will explore your passions. Open doors you never expected and walk inside to discover opportunities that will tantalize and challenge you along the way. In your pursuit, you will capture a new, exciting, and eclectic way of life.

COLLEGE CONNECTIONS

Attending a respected school can help you get noticed. Your next steps will be aided by connections offered by professors, classmates, and alumni. Networking events are also excellent ways to discover opportunities. Conferences, displays, and contests in school, out of school, in the summer, or through social media can help you get noticed. Bring people into your world. Allow them to feel and experience your innovations, interpret their meanings, and give you feedback so you can improve and develop your ideas.

Throughout your varied experiences, you will meet other engineers who may recommend you to employers or inform you about open positions or contract opportunities, even some that are not publicly announced. In addition, many schools have a culminating event like a portfolio, capstone, or symposium where you can put your best foot forward and showcase your work.

OPENING INDUSTRY DOORS

Exposure to industry professionals will open new doors. By interacting with people online or in person you can maintain those connections. Autonomy and freedom to choose the jobs you take by venturing out on your own may seem alluring, freelancing may result in career uncertainty or even limitations. Without a clear track record, potential employers might choose another individual with more experience. Thus, internships, apprenticeships, and related experiences are crucial.

Companies often choose seasoned professionals with work experience in other firms or those people who have risen to proven levels of accomplishment whether or not they have a degree. We live in very fluid times when talent is not always defined by a BS, BSE, MS, or MSE behind your name.

However, if you choose solo contract work, there are ways to mitigate against the lean times by managing multiple projects. Valuable secondary skills include communication, problem-solving, and teamwork. To get paid projects, you might demonstrate mastery, resolve client problems, align your ideology, or initially charge less to earn your way to a higher salary. Despite challenges, put yourself out there.

You could wait for the phone to ring to be discovered. However, you should post ideas, articles, blogs, or availability regularly to industry and professional sites. To be seen, you need to be out and about at contests, conferences, and on social media. Environmental clubs are great places to learn more, collaborate with others, and gain leadership experience.

Some individuals pine away by sending in resumes with the hopes of being selected and then deciding which organization would be a perfect fit. Others only want to work at a specific firm or location. Still others determine they will work for themselves and be their own boss. Yet, sometimes taking any position at the start is a steppingstone to your dream life, commitment to service, and opportunity to put your unique mark on society.

BOLD NETWORKING

Networking takes social skills and a bit of moxie. From elevator speeches and professional encounters to interviews and masterclasses, your job is to find a way to get your talent and abilities in front of people and have employers discover your knowledge of environmental engineering and alternative energy along with leadership potential and willingness to contribute. Present yourself with confidence. You are unique.

Finally, there are professional entities that will welcome your ingenuity, discipline, and impact. How can you be recognized? Meet people. Hand out your resume, give them your business card, ask for their business card, and follow up. Ask if you can call or meet them. Sometimes approaching these professionals may seem uncomfortable. Stay in touch with those you meet, even if your initial interaction is just happenstance or serendipity. Keep a log of each individual's phone, e-mail, and identifying information. Track both the date and location where you met. You never know when you will need it. I put the information on the back of their business card whether I meet those individuals at a conference, meeting, or special evening event.

If you meet people professionally at a workshop, leadership event, or industry conference, even if you do not exchange information, you will quite possibly recognize them at a later date. They may recognize you at a future event too. Keep training. You should always seek ways to improve, irrespective of your experience. Lifelong learning improves your ability to maintain up-to-date skills and transition to new ventures. Furthermore, the outside world's perspective changes more quickly with social media's instant influences.

Though you should not register for workshops just for the sake of meeting people, when you do attend, be present in your quest to lead, serve, and envision. If your focus is not on your learning or professional development, you may appear insincere in your intentions. However, workshops, conferences, and meetings can allow others to see your purpose, vision, and talent.

Big-ticket training does not always mean better trainers or opportunities. Find time to research companies with a focus on sustainability, survey environmental organizations, and notice cultural changes that may determine what people want or need. While gathering new thoughts, remember that humility and open-mindedness go a long way. Defer to the wise and listen. There is much you can learn.

STAY IN TOUCH

Do not annoy busy people, but you can keep in touch every couple of months. Communicating more frequently is overwhelming. However, life is long. People who grow with their craft transition fluidly through life's career phases. In engineering and STEM subjects, contacts are essential in all phases of your career. Also, do not be surprised.

Many go-getters seeking to gain a coveted contract do the following:
1. Keep looking for opportunities.
2. Discipline yourself to create something new.
3. Gain a following on Instagram and Pinterest.
4. Write a newsletter and publish it on LinkedIn and other social media.
5. Link your projects and process to social media.
6. Enter engineering, hacking, and coding contests.
7. Join professional associations and attend their trade shows.
8. Attend social gatherings of potential customers.
9. Keep in touch with your professors.
10. Stay involved with your alumni associations.

DEVELOP LIFELONG FRIENDSHIPS

Friendships matter. Become lifelong colleagues by finding friends who share mutual interests and offer a sounding board or connections to new opportunities. People tend to stay in touch with those people they consider "important". Note to self: Your contemporaries or peers are important people…although possibly not yet. As you form lists of contacts, you are likely to know these people throughout your career.

Be audacious while also being authentic. Networking can sometimes appear fake or forced as if you are going out on a hunt to find people for your own benefit. Worse, the act of networking can appear like stalking for those who incessantly attempt to connect. The mental image of this type of 'networking' conjures the vision of people congregating at the end of a speech or concert for an autograph.

Friendships and the mutual support of allies can be enormously helpful. Note: 20,000 or even 200,000 followers on your website do not mean you are popular or important. However, you can have unexpected meaningful exchanges if you get out, meet people, and live life. Yet, at times, deeply moving, casual conversations in non-professional settings could also turn into significant connections.

Do not lose touch with people or burn bridges along the way. There are only about a thousand or two key policymakers, sustainability activists, and corporate executives who fervently pursue organizational leadership and project development in environmental engineering, environmental science, environmental policy, and alternative energy. This community is not that big, especially in whatever subspecialty you choose. You will continually see extraordinary talent who are just starting out. Encourage them. You never know. They may contact you one day to collaborate or meet for coffee at an event.

COLLEGE AND CAREER CENTERS

Although engineering departments frequently have internal connections to help you secure an internship or job, you might also speak to someone at your campus career center. They often have interesting and possibly new prospective positions you might not find elsewhere. In addition, there may be a specific career liaison for their engineering programs. Connect with them for help in your search process. Besides, you might want a related job that utilizes your analytical, problem-solving, and presentation skills.

Career center coordinators often have excellent ideas of alternative options you may have never considered. Furthermore, they can assist you with creating a professional resume and cover letters for specific industries that are different from the ones you have for environmental engineering, and alternative energy especially if you are considering the possibility of eventually earning an MBA, law degree or Ph.D. or attending leadership development programs.

The staff may also introduce you to past graduates in the industry who make excellent connections. Some of them may have attended your specific engineering major, overcoming the same hurdles you faced. They have been through the ropes, know a few influential people, and may be able to get you an interview or invite you to an industry event. Any contact may help you get your foot in the door or aid you in finding a job to make money in the meantime.

LINKEDIN

LinkedIn is especially helpful for career search. You can locate numerous influential contacts on LinkedIn. After interviews or events, connect with each person you met on LinkedIn. Keep a contact list of individuals you get to know in your area of interest. Do not constantly try to connect with people you do not really know. However, if you have made the connection, occasionally keep in touch.

While some LinkedIn message boxes may be full and you may not get a reply, you can try. Some people have tens of thousands of LinkedIn followers. I have about 20,000 'contacts', which does not necessitate that I am important. It just means that I have connected with 20,000 people. Remember that a big paycheck or lots of friends does not make you more worthy or successful. Worth and value emanate from within your heart. You have the power to improve your life in any way you choose. Your discipline, ingenuity, and dedication will help you stand out from other applicants.

Occasionally on LinkedIn, you hit on a lucky break with a new customer, communicate with a client, or make a close friend. Some professionals prefer LinkedIn to other methods of communication. While that may seem odd, a few people I have known for decades only communicate with me through LinkedIn. Lastly, I do not have time to communicate with everyone. However, I have connected with some of my most inspiring authors, advisors, and intellectual leaders through the LinkedIn platform.

FINALLY

Most people are willing to help you. Five percent will not. Thus, you have a 19 out of 20 chance of interacting with decent people who have the time and are willing to give you advice. Don't lose faith in humanity just because you run into a few people who are too busy to stop for you or are too self-absorbed that they cannot answer your question. They may be consumed with problems of their own that they cannot yet resolve.

Remember that talent is only the beginning. You need to sell yourself. As you organize your goals and responsibilities, remember to think one step ahead of where you want to be by making a game plan. Since actions speak louder than words, take action without complaining and spread kindness along the way. Burned bridges are tough to reconstruct.

Honesty and trustworthiness are worth more than any physical object. Earn this by working hard, being efficient, and telling the truth. In your work, imagine you are the manager, what would you do? One day you may just be a manager and be on the opposite side making decisions.

Exhibit professionalism in your words and deeds. Be productive. Put away all distractions and focus on your tasks. Texts and social media take a surprising amount of time. Get the job done. When you are finished, ask for another project. Do not do this because you are brownnosing, but because you should want your company to be successful. Discipline is achieved by creating a goal and making it happen.

A nice note, card, or gift reminds people you are thinking about them, even when you are incredibly busy. Good friends who have your best interest may know doors that are not yet open for you. Keep in touch with them. Every action you take is a steppingstone to your future.

So, go on a walk, meet people, and live fully. Serendipity happens when you live life. However, your education is immensely valuable. The adage goes - success happens when preparation meets opportunity. Thus, preparation is the best way to generate luck. Finally, even the most disciplined person can be lazy or inefficient . Fight this. Stay active. Make your life happen for you.

Productivity is never an accident.
It is always the result of a commitment to excellence,
intelligent planning, and focused effort.

-Paul J. Meyer

Here are a few things to remember as you go out to pursue your dreams.

- Work ethic is everything.
- Excellence is expected.
- Learn what you do not know on your own time.
- Come to work prepared.
- Take constructive criticism well.
- Be respectful and courteous.
- Keep your cool under pressure.
- Avoid being timid.
- Stay on task.
- Come early.
- Stay late.
- Take your work seriously.
- Do more than expected.
- Be thoughtful and respectful.
- Read your e-mail/texts after hours in case something is important.
- Ask questions. No question is too stupid.
- Maintain a clean workspace.
- Dress and act professionally.
- Don't gossip or complain.
- Play when you are done.
- Avoid frustrating your phenomenally busy supervisor.
- Be straightforward, and don't beat around the bush.

You've Got This!

Be yourself; everyone else is already taken.

- Oscar Wilde

4 Regions

60 Programs

COLLEGE PROFILES AND REQUIREMENTS

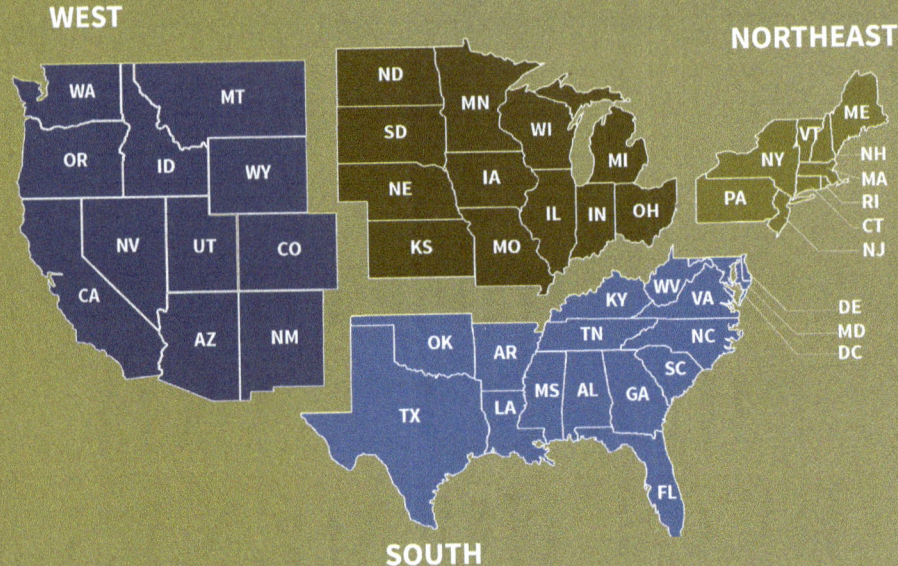

PROGRAMS BY REGION
U.S. CENSUS BUREAU CLASSIFICATIONS

REGION 1 – NORTHEAST
Connecticut, Maine, Massachusetts, New Hampshire, New Jersey, New York, Pennsylvania, Rhode Island, and Vermont

REGION 2 – MIDWEST
Illinois, Indiana, Iowa, Kansas, Michigan, Minnesota, Missouri, Nebraska, North Dakota, Ohio, South Dakota, and Wisconsin

REGION 3 – SOUTH
Alabama, Arkansas, Delaware, District of Columbia, Florida, Georgia, Kentucky, Louisiana, Maryland, Mississippi, North Carolina, Oklahoma, South Carolina, Tennessee, Texas, Virginia, and West Virginia

REGION 4 – WEST
Alaska, Arizona, California, Colorado, Hawaii, Idaho, Montana, Nevada, New Mexico, Oregon, Utah, Washington, and Wyoming

PROFILES OF SELECT ENVIRONMENTAL ENGINEERING & ENVIRONMENTAL SCIENCE PROGRAMS

The 60 programs listed in the following pages include profiles of selected environmental and sustainability focused programs as of December 2024 along with a few additional colleges that offer closely related degrees. Many students interested in the environment and sustainability are often also interested in civil engineering and architecture. Those schools are profiled in other books, though some lists are provided in the back.

Majoring in engineering is not for everyone. Although immensely rewarding, success requires passion, curiosity, and initiative. In college, you will discover your priorities, commitments, and perseverance. You might also choose an alternative path somewhere down the road.

Thus, this book provides you with lists of other programs so you can also explore those options. Keep the book handy. Even after you begin college you may find valuable summer internships and alternative college programs that may catapult you to your career.

Creating lists is often tedious and cumbersome. These lists were gathered to help you with this task. Descriptions of the college programs, tuition, requirements, and deadlines are accurate as of December 2024.

However, the requirements may have changed by the time you purchase this book. Nevertheless, this information is a great place to start!

Note: To simplify the text and fit information into the charts and profiles, abbreviations were used as well as shortened sentences and acronyms. For example, eng = engineering, ctr = center, sys = systems, appl = applied, dev = development, res = research or resources, soc = society, and Amer = American.

CONNECTICUT

MAINE

MASSACHUSETTS

NEW HAMPSHIRE

NEW JERSEY

NEW YORK

PENNSYLVANIA

RHODE ISLAND

VERMONT

CHAPTER 11

REGION ONE

NORTHEAST

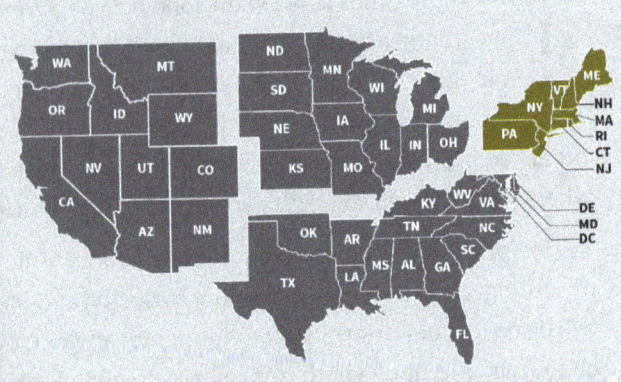

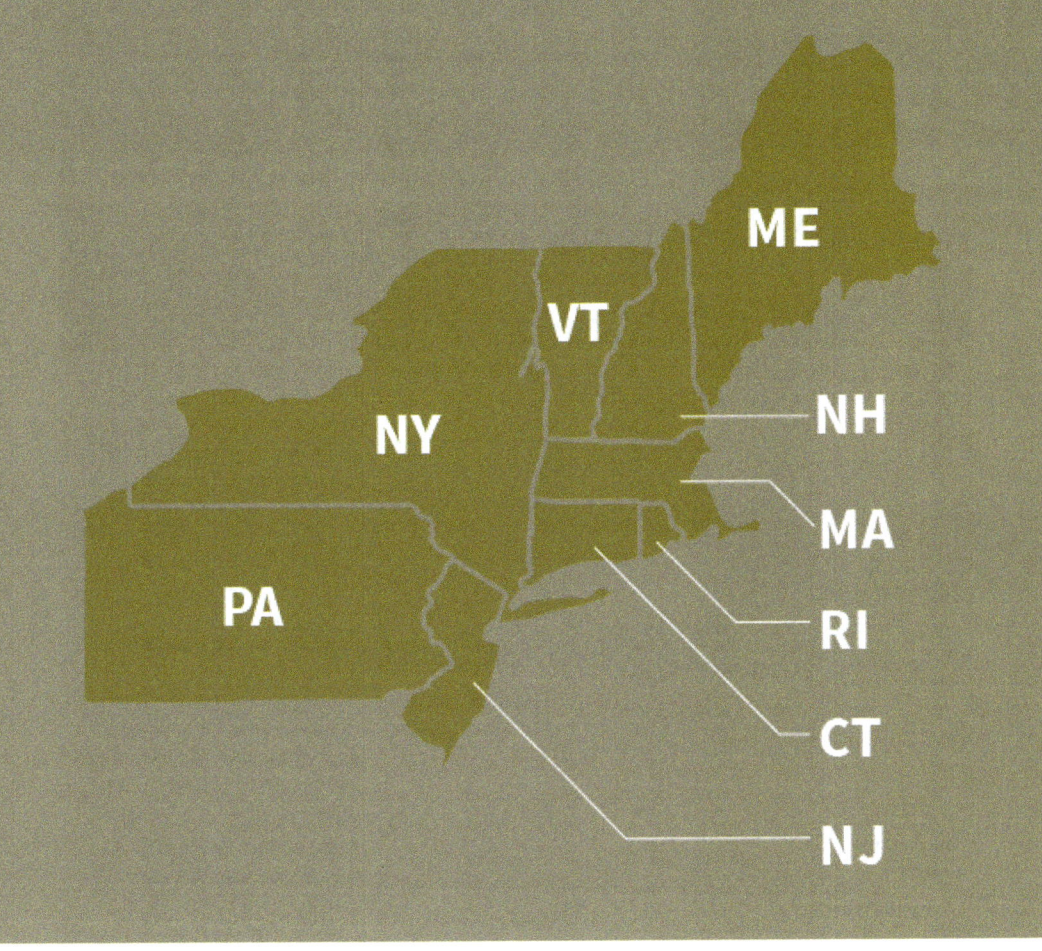

15 Programs | 9 States

1. MA - Massachusetts Institute of Technology (MIT)
2. MA - Tufts University
3. MA - University of Massachusetts, Amherst
4. NJ - Princeton University
5. NJ - Rutgers University
6. NY - Columbia University
7. NY - Cornell University
8. NY - Rensselaer Polytechnic Institute (RPI)
9. NY - SUNY College of Environmental Science and Forestry
10. PA - Bucknell University
11. PA - Carnegie Mellon University
12. PA - Drexel University
13. PA - Lehigh University
14. PA - Pennsylvania State University
15. PA - University of Pittsburgh

ENVIRONMENTAL ENGINEERING & ALTERNATIVE ENERGY PROGRAMS

School	Avg. GPA, SAT ERW, SAT Math (M), and ACT Composite (C) Early Decision (ED)	Admissions Statistics	Related Program(s)
Massachusetts Institute of Technology (MIT) 77 Massachusetts Ave, Cambridge, MA 02139	GPA: N/A SAT (ERW): 740-780 SAT (M): 780-800 ACT (C): 35-36 ED: No, EA: Yes	Admit Rate: 4.8% Undergrad Enrollment: 4,576 Total Enrollment: 11,920	SB, SM, MEng, ScD, Ph.D. Aerospace Eng, Biomedical Eng, Chemical Eng, Civil Eng, Environmental Eng, Const Eng & Mgmt, Environmental Chem, Materials Science & Eng, Robotics & Autonomous Systems, Transplant Eng
Tufts University 419 Boston Ave, Medford, MA 02155	GPA: N/A SAT (ERW): 710-760 SAT (M): 730-790 ACT (C): 33-35 ED: Yes, EA: No	Admit Rate: 10% Undergrad Enrollment: 6,676 Total Enrollment: 13,293	BS, MS, Ph.D. Architectural Studies, Biomedical Eng, Chemical Engineering, Civil Engineering, Computer Engineering, Computer Science, Electrical Eng, Environmental Engineering, Offshore Wind Energy Eng
University of Massachusetts, Amherst 37 Mather Drive Amherst, MA 01003	GPA: 3.93-4.38 SAT (ERW): 650-730 SAT (M): 680-760 ACT (C): 29-34 ED: No, EA: Yes	Admit Rate: 57.7% Undergrad Enrollment: 23,936 Total Enrollment: 34,710	BS, MS, Ph.D. Architecture, Biomedical Eng, Chemical Eng, Civil Eng (Structural Engineering Concentration), Computer Eng, Electrical Eng, Environmental & Water Resources Eng, Industrial Eng, Mechanical Engineering
Princeton University Princeton University, Princeton, NJ 08544	GPA: N/A SAT (ERW): 740-770 SAT (M): 750-800 ACT (C): 33-36 ED: No, REA: Yes	Admit Rate: N/A Undergrad Enrollment: 5,598 Total Enrollment: 8,973	AB, BSE, Ph.D. Aerospace Engineering, Astrophysical Science, Biological Engineering, Chemical Eng, Civil Eng, Environmental Eng, Computer Science, Computer Eng, Electrical Engineering, Financial Eng, Mechanical Eng, Operations Research
Rutgers University 100 Sutphen Road, Piscataway, NJ 08854	SOE GPA: 3.4-3.9 SAT (ERW): 660-740 SAT (M): 690-790 SOE ACT (C): 30-34 ED: No, EA: Yes	Admit Rate: 67% Undergrad NB Enrollment: 36,344 Total Enrollment: 67,620	BS, MS, Ph.D. Biochemical Eng, Biomedical Engineering, Chemical Eng, Cell Biology, Chemical Biology, Computer Eng, Electrical Eng, Materials Science & Engineering, Mechanical Engineering, Neuroscience, Physiology

ENVIRONMENTAL ENGINEERING & ALTERNATIVE ENERGY PROGRAMS

School	Avg. GPA, SAT ERW, SAT Math (M), and ACT Composite (C) Early Decision (ED)	Admissions Statistics	Related Program(s)
Columbia University 1130 Amsterdam Avenue, New York, NY 10027	GPA: N/A SAT (ERW): 740-780 SAT (M): 750-800 ACT (C): 34-35 ED: Yes, EA: No	Admit Rate: 3.9% Undergrad Enrollment: 8,832 Total Enrollment: 33,776	BS, MS, Ph.D. Biomedical Eng, Chemical Eng, Computer Eng, Comp Sci, Earth & Enviro Eng, Materials Science & Eng, Mechanical Engineering, MA Climate & Society, Biotechnology
Cornell University 430 College Ave., Ithaca, NY 14850	GPA: N/A SAT (ERW): 710-770 SAT (M): 740-790 ACT (C): 33-35 ED: Yes, EA: No	Admit Rate: 7% Undergrad Enrollment: 15,735 Total Enrollment: 25,898	BS, MEng, Ph.D. Aerospace & Mechanical Eng, Bio Eng, Biomedical Eng, Chemical Eng, Materials Science & Eng; Minors: Earth & Atmospheric Science, Entrepreneurship & Innovation, Eng Communic.
Rensselaer Polytechnic Institute (RPI) 110 8th Street, Greene Bldg., Troy, NY 12180	GPA: 3.91 SAT (ERW): 620-720 SAT (M): 680-780 ACT (C): 29-34 ED: Yes, EA: Yes	Admit Rate: 57% Undergrad Enrollment: 6,283 Total Enrollment: 7,501	BS, MS, MEng, DEng, Ph.D. Aerospace Eng, Biol Eng, Chem Eng, Civil Eng, Comp Eng, EE, Environmental Eng, Materials Science & Eng, Mechanical Eng, Nuclear Eng, Systems Eng MS, MEng, DEng, Ph.D. Transp Eng, Tech Mgmt
SUNY College of Environmental Science and Forestry One Forestry Dr., Syracuse, NY 13210	GPA: 3.7 SAT (ERW): 570-650 SAT (M): 560-650 ACT (C): 24-30 ED: No	Admit Rate: 60% Undergrad Enrollment: 1,754 Total Enrollment: 2,127	BS, MS, MPS, Ph.D. Chemical Eng, Environmental Biology, Environmental Resources Eng, Environmental Science, Environmental Studies, Landscape Architecture, Sustainable Resource Mgmt
Bucknell University One Dent Dr, Lewisburg, PA 17837	GPA: 3.80 SAT (ERW): 650-730 SAT (M): 660-770 ACT (C): 23-33 ED: Yes, EA: No	Admit Rate: 28% Undergrad Enrollment: 3,925 Total Enrollment: 3,867	BS, MS, Ph.D. Biomedical Engineering, Chemical Engineering, Civil Eng, Computer Engineering, Computer Science, Electrical Eng, Environmental Eng, Mechanical Engineering

NORTHEAST

ENVIRONMENTAL ENGINEERING & ALTERNATIVE ENERGY PROGRAMS

School	Avg. GPA, SAT ERW, SAT Math (M), and ACT Composite (C) Early Decision (ED)	Admissions Statistics	Related Program(s)
Carnegie Mellon University 5000 Forbes Avenue, Pittsburgh, PA 15213	GPA: 3.9 SAT (ERW): 720-770 SAT (M): 770-800 ACT (C): 34-35 ED: Yes, EA: No	Admit Rate: 11% Undergrad Enrollment: 7,509 Total Enrollment: 16,779	BS, MS, BS/MS, MS/MBA, Ph.D. Biomedical Engineering, Chemical Engineering, Civil Eng, Electrical Eng, Materials Science & Engineering, Mechanical Eng; MS Colloids, Polymers, & Surfaces
Drexel University 3141 Chestnut Street Philadelphia, PA 19104	GPA: 3.8 SAT (ERW): 610-700 SAT (M): 620-730 ACT (C): 27-32 ED: Yes, EA: Yes	Admit Rate: 77% Undergrad Enrollment: 12,482 Total Enrollment: 20,845	BS, MS, Ph.D. Architectural Eng, Chemical Eng, Civil Eng, Computer Engineering, Construction Mgmt, EE, Eng Technology, Environmental Eng, Materials Science & Eng, Mechanical Engineering; MS Robotics & Autonomy
Lehigh University 27 Memorial Drive West, Bethlehem, PA 18015	GPA: N/A SAT (ERW): 650-730 SAT (M): 690-760 ACT (C): 30-34 ED: Yes, EA: No	Admit Rate: 25% Undergrad Enrollment: 5,624 Total Enrollment: 7,394	BS, BS/MS, MS, MEng, Ph.D. Bio Eng, Chem Eng, Civil Eng, Computer Science, Computer Eng, EE, Environmental Eng, Materials Science & Eng, Mechanical Engineering, MEng, Ph.D. Structural Eng
Pennsylvania State University (Penn State) 124 Borland Building, University Park, PA 16802	GPA: 3.7 SAT (ERW): 590-680 SAT (M): 620-710 ACT (C): 26-31 ED: No, Rolling: Yes	Admit Rate: 55% Undergrad Enrollment: 41,745 Total Enrollment: 48,765	BS, MS, Ph.D. Aerospace Eng, Biological Eng, Biomedical, Chemical Eng, Civil Eng, Energy Eng, Environmental Eng, Materials Science & Eng, Mechanical Eng, Mining Eng, Nuclear Eng, Petroleum & Nat Gas, Polymer Eng & Science
University of Pittsburgh 4227 Fifth Avenue, Alumni Hall, Pittsburgh, PA 15260	GPA: 4.1 SAT (ERW): 640-720 SAT (M): 640-750 ACT (C): 29-33 ED: No, Rolling: Yes	Admit Rate: 49% Undergrad Enrollment: 19,928 Total Enrollment: 29,178	BS, MS, Ph.D. Biomedical Eng, Chemical Engineering, Civil Engineering, Computer Eng, Computer Science, Electrical Eng, Environmental Eng, Industrial Engineering, Materials Science & Eng, Mechanical Engineering, Nuclear Engineering

- CONNECTICUT
- MAINE
- **MASSACHUSETTS**
- NEW HAMPSHIRE
- NEW JERSEY
- NEW YORK
- PENNSYLVANIA
- RHODE ISLAND
- VERMONT

MASSACHUSETTS INSTITUTE OF TECHNOLOGY (MIT)

Address: MIT School of Engineering, Building 1-206, 77 Massachusetts Avenue, Cambridge, MA 02139-4307
Website: https://engineering.mit.edu/
Contact: https://engineering.mit.edu/contact-us/
Phone: (617) 253-3291
Email: engineering@mit.edu

COST OF ATTENDANCE:
Tuition & Fees: $62,396 | **Addl Exp:** $24,000 | **Total:** $86,396
Financial Aid: https://sfs.mit.edu/

ADDITIONAL INFORMATION:
Available Degree(s)
- SB, SM, MEng, ScD, Ph.D. Aerospace Eng, Aeronautics, Astronautics, Biological Oceanography, BME, Chemical Eng, Chemical Oceanography, Civil Eng, Coastal Eng, Computer Eng, Comp Sci, Construction Eng & Mgmt, Environmental Bio/Chem, Enviro Eng, Environmental Fluid Mechanics, Geotechnical & Geoenvironmental Engineering, Hydrology, Industrial Eng, Materials Science & Eng, Mechanical Eng, Ocean Eng, Robotics Engineering, Structures & Materials

Related Research Centers
Ctr for Adv Urbanism, Ctr for Bits & Atoms, Ctr for Real Estate, Ctr for Global Change Science, Data, Systems, & Society, Entrepreneurship, Environmental Health Sciences, Environmental Solutions Init, Food Systems Lab, Kuwait-MIT Ctr for Natural Resources & Environment, MIT Energy Init, MIT.nano, MIT Portugal Prog, Nuclear Reactor Lab, Ocean Science & Eng, Operations Research Ctr, Soldier Nanotech, Technological Innovation, & World Wide Web Consortium

Scholarships Offered
MIT is need-blind & awards families w/full-need. Approx 60% of MIT students receive aid. For most students w/family incomes under $140,000, MIT ensures scholarship funding, allowing students to attend MIT tuition-free. The average MIT scholarship was $45,146.

Special Opportunities
Passionate students, rigorous education, remarkable professors, cutting-edge research, top reputation, successful graduates, and amazing facilities underscore the reasons to attend MIT. You will study, get stuck, create, collaborate, laugh, and make close bonds with a tight-knit friend group. Though nerdy, quirky, unconventional, and intense MIT offers limitless potential for success.

Orgs: Amer Chemical Soc, Amer Inst of Aeronautics & Astronautics, Amer Inst of Chemical Eng, Amer Nuclear Soc, Biotech Grp, Chem, Energy, & Climate Club, Eng w/o Borders, Hacking Medicine, IEEE, Global Health Alliance, Lab for Chocolate Sci, Medlinks, Microbiome, Science Policy Rev, Science Fiction Soc, Soc of Physics Students, SWE

Teams: Arcturus: Auton. Surface Vehicle & Drone Group, Battlecode, Progr Contests, Combat Robotics, Concrete Canoe, Cubesat, Debate Team, Design-Build-Fly (AIAA Comp), Design for Amer, Driverless/Autonomous Vehicle, Electric Vehicle, eSports, Hyperloop III Team, iGEM (Intl Genetically Eng Mach, Inventors Comp, Lincoln Lab Adv Tech Security & Defense, MADMEC, Marine Robotics, Model Railroad Club, Motorsports, NASA Competitions, Quiz Bowl, Robotics, Rocket Team, Space Devt, Solar Electric Vehicle Team, Spokes Cycling, QL+, Rubik's Cube Club, Science Bowl, Steel Bridge

Notable Alumni
Buzz Aldrin, Colin Angle, Kofi Annan, Satya Atluri, Shiva Ayyadurai, Ben Bernanke, Karel Bossart, Amar Bose, Vanu Bose, Jimmy Doolittle, Mario Draghi, Charles Stark Draper, Esther Duflo, Richard Feynman, Jose Ferre, Carly Fiorina, Jon Kabat-Zinn, Sal Khan, Bill Koch, Charles Koch, Francis Lynch, Thomas Massie, Ronald McNair, Benjamin Netanyahu, Ngozi Okonjo-Iweala, Neri Oxman, Henry Paynter, I.M. Pei, Nicholas A. Peppas, Jonah Peretti, Raghuram Rajan, Claude Shannon, William Shockley, George Shultz, Joseph Stiglitz, Lisa Su, Lawrence Summers, Tom Wolf, and James Woods

TUFTS UNIVERSITY

Address: Tufts University, Science and Engineering Complex, Anderson Hall, Room 105, 200 College Avenue, Medford, MA 02155
Website: *https://engineering.tufts.edu/*
Contact: *https://admissions.tufts.edu/connect-with-us/contact/*
Phone: (617) 627-3237
Email: engineering.inquiry@tufts.edu

COST OF ATTENDANCE:
Tuition & Fees: $67,844 | **Addl Exp:** $22,000 | **Total:** $89,844
Financial Aid: https://students.tufts.edu/financial-services/financial-aid

ADDITIONAL INFORMATION:
Available Degree(s)
- BS, MS, Ph.D. Architectural Studies, Bioengineering (Environmental BiotechTrack) Biomedical Eng, Chemical Engineering, Civil Engineering, Computer Eng, Computer Science, Electrical Engineering, Environmental Engineering, Environmental Health, Offshore Wind Energy Engineering, Materials Science & Engineering, Mechanical Engineering

Related Research Areas
Focus Areas: Climate & Energy, Computer Architecture Lab, Emerging Circuits & Systems, Environmental & Water Resources Engineering, Environmental Health, Extreme Events, Geosystems Engineering, Health & Environment, Nano Lab, Plasma Engineering, Renewable Energy & Applied Photonics, Resilient Systems, Robotic Networks, Signal Processing, Structural Engineering Mechanics

Advanced Materials Center, Applied Brain & Cognitive Sciences, Energy Water, & the Environment, Human Health & Bioengineering, Human-Technology Interface, Intelligent Systems, Neural Science, Disease, & Engineering, STEM Diversity

Scholarships Offered
Tufts meets 100% of demonstrated need regardless of citizenship status. Students with family incomes less than $60,000 typically receive a student aid package with no student loans. Tufts does not award merit-based financial aid.

Special Opportunities
Tufts University's Science & Engineering houses state-of-the-art Advanced Microscopic Imaging Center, Epitaxial Facility and Materials Characterization Lab, Micro Characterization Facility, and the Micro- and Nano-Fabrication Facility.

Orgs: American Society of Chemical Engineers, American Society of Civil Engineers, American Society for Engineering Education, American Society of Mechanical Engineers, Biomedical Engineering Society, BEaCHES, Civil & Environmental Engineering Graduate Student Organization, Engineering Student Council, Engineers w/o Borders, Human Factors & Ergonomics Society, Institute of Electrical & Electronics Engineers, National Society of Black Engineers, oSTEM, Society of LatinX Engineers & Scientists, Society of Women Engineers, Student Teacher Outreach Mentorship Program, Students for the Exploration and Development of Space, Tufts Computer Science Exchange, Women in Computer Science

Teams: Chem-E Car Team, Chess Club, Concrete Canoe Team, Cyber 9/12 Strategy Challenge (annual global cybersecurity policy competition), Debate Society, Electric Racing, Hackathon, iGEM (Genetically Engineered Machines), Jumbo Code, Mock Trial, Model United Nations, Robotics Team, Solar Decathlon, Solar Racing Team, Rubik's Cube, Steel Bridge Team, Tufts MAKE

Notable Alumni
Saleem Ali, Anthony Cortese, Macy DuBois, Margaret Floyd, Robert Kayen, Mark Plotkin, Victor Prather, Eric Rubin, John Trojanowski, and C. David Welch

CONNECTICUT

MAINE

MASSACHUSETTS

NEW HAMPSHIRE

NEW JERSEY

NEW YORK

PENNSYLVANIA

RHODE ISLAND

VERMONT

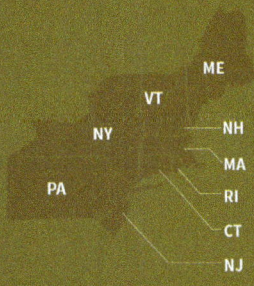

NORTHEAST

- CONNECTICUT
- MAINE
- **MASSACHUSETTS**
- NEW HAMPSHIRE
- NEW JERSEY
- NEW YORK
- PENNSYLVANIA
- RHODE ISLAND
- VERMONT

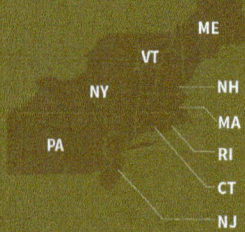

UNIVERSITY OF MASSACHUSETTS, AMHERST

Address: University of Massachusetts College of Engineering, 134 Marston Hall, Amherst, MA 01003
Website: https://engineering.umass.edu/
Contact: https://www.umass.edu/gateway/contact-us
Phone: (413) 545-0160
Email: engineering@umass.edu

COST OF ATTENDANCE:

Tuition & Fees: $17,772 (in-state), $40,449 (out-of-state)
Addl Exp: $20,000 | **Total:** $37,772 (in-state), $60,449 (out-of-state)

Financial Aid: https://www.umass.edu/financialaid

ADDITIONAL INFORMATION:

Available Degree(s)
- BS, MS, Ph.D. Architecture, Biomedical Engineering, Chemical Eng, Civil Eng (Structural Eng Concentration), Computer Engineering, Electrical Eng, Environmental & Water Resources Engineering, Industrial Engineering, Mechanical Engineering

Related Research Areas
Construction, Environmental Eng, Geotechnical Eng, Hydrology, Hydraulics, Materials, Structural Eng, Surveying, Transportation Eng

Drinking Water & Particle Transport, Environmental Bioprocesses, Environmental Microbiology & Biotechnology, Environmental & Water Research Engineering, Fluvial@UMass, Groundwater/Road Salt ISA, Hydrosystems Research, Structural Mechanics, Water & Analytical Chemistry, Water Research & Climate Change, Water Resource Recovery, Sanitation Development

Scholarships Offered
Engineering Scholarships include Merit P. White Endowed Scholarship, Kellogg Scholarship, Perrell Endowed Scholarship, Giziensku Endowed Scholarship, Hendrickson Endowed Scholarship; UMass scholarships are based on merit, financial need, or both; 90% of UMass freshmen receive financial aid

Special Opportunities
Co-ops, internships. Study Abroad: Heriot-Watt Univ (Edinburgh, Scotland), Heriot Watt Univ Malaysia (Malaysia) Univ College Cork. Facilities & equipment include 3D Printing, Design-Build Team Consulting, Additive Manufacturing Workshops w/Industrial-Grade, State-of-the-Art Metal & Polymer 3D Printers, Atomic Force Microscopy, Electron Microscope, CMOS Processing Technology, Nanotech Cleanroom, Fabrication Tech, Sensor Integration, X-ray Scattering. ECE Makerspace, MIE Innovation Lab

Org: American Society of Civil Engineers, Associated General Contractors of America, Association of Computing Machinery, Black Women in Engineering & Computing, Chi Epsilon Civil Engineering Honors Society, Earthquake Engineering Research Institute, Engineers without Borders, Institute of Industrial & Systems Engineers, Institute of Electrical & Electronics Engineers, Institute of Transportation Engineers, National Society of Black Engineers, oSTEM, Society of American Military Engineers, Society of Asian Scientists & Engineers, Society of Hispanic Professional Engineers, Society of Women Engineers, Women in Transportation Seminar

Teams: Chem-E Car Team, Concrete Canoe Team, Cybersecurity Competition Team, Debate Society, Formula SAE Team, HackUMass, MinuteMan Launch Team, Mock Trial Team, Model United Nations, Rocketry Team, Seismic Design Team, Steel Bridge Design Team, Supermileage Vehicle Team, Surveying Team, UMass Robotics, Unmanned Aerial Vehicle Team

Notable Alumni
Roger Biosjoly, Edson de Castro, Renee Elliott, Devang Khakhar, Christopher Ober, Dan Riccio, Matthew Tirrell, and Brian Vibberts

PRINCETON UNIVERSITY

Address: Princeton School of Engineering and Applied Science, Engineering Quadrangle, C207, Princeton, New Jersey 08544
Website: https://engineering.princeton.edu/
Contact: https://engineering.princeton.edu/about
Phone: (609) 258-4554
Email: bogucki@princeton.edu

COST OF ATTENDANCE:

Tuition & Fees: $62,400 | **Addl Exp:** $24,000 | **Total:** $86,400
Financial Aid: https://finaid.princeton.edu/

ADDITIONAL INFORMATION:

Available Degree(s)
- AB, BSE, Ph.D. Aerospace Engineering, Astrophysical Science, Biological Engineering, Chemical Engineering, Civil Engineering Computer Engineering, Computer Science, Electrical Engineering, Environmental Engineering, Materials Science & Engineering, Mechanical Engineering, Operations Research & Financial Engineering
- Minor: Sustainable Energy

Related Research Areas
Applied Physics, Biomechanics & Biomaterials, Control, Robotics, and Dynamical Systems, Climate Science, Electricity Production, Transmission & Storage, Electric Propulsion and Plasma Dynamics Laboratory, Energy Optimization Systems, Fluid Mechanics, Institute for the Science & Technology of Materials, Intelligent Robot Motion Lab, Lithium Extraction/Production, Materials Science, Propulsion & Energy Sciences, Sustainable Energy Production, Wind Institute

Scholarships Offered
Princeton is need-blind w/a no-loan policy that replaces student loans w/grant aid that students do not pay back. Approx. 62% of undergrads receive aid w/an ave grant of $62,200. Families whose income is less than $65,000 do not pay for tuition, room, or board.

Special Opportunities
Internships, Summer Programs, Co-ops, Study Abroad, Seminar Programs, Corporate Research Partnerships; Summer Undergraduate Research Fellows; NSF-Funded Summer REU Program in Biophysics; Machine Learning Theory Summer Program

Orgs: American Institute of Aeronautics & Astronautics, American Institute of Chemical Engineers, American Society of Civil Engineers, American Society of Mechanical Engineering, Assoc for Computing Machinery, Aviation Club Drone Project, Biomedical Eng Society, Eng Council, Engineers w/o Borders, Heirloom Gardens Project, Institute of Electrical and Electronics Engineers, Material Research Society, National Society of Black Engineers, Operations Research Society, Princeton Engineering Education for Kids, Seed Farm, Society of Hispanic Professional Engineers, Society of Women Eng, Students for the Exploration & Development of Space, Women in Computer Science

Teams: Alexa Competition (selected for $100,000 stipend), Amazon Robotics Challenge, Autonomous Underwater Vehicle, Chem-E Car, Chess Team, Concrete Canoe, Cubesat, Electric Car Competition, HackPrinceton, iGEM - International Genetically Engineered Machines, International Math Modeling Competition, IRoM-Lab Robots, Micro-g Neutral Buoyancy Experiment Design Team, Mock Trial, Model Congress, Model United Nations, Princeton Electric Racing, Quiz Bowl, Robotics Competitions, Rocketry Team, Science Olympiad, TigerSats - Satellite Systems, Steel Bridge Team, Unmanned Aerial Vehicle Team

Notable Alumni
James Adamson, Norman Augustine, Ben Baldanza, Daniel Barry, Brian Binnie, Gerald Carr, Charles Coker, Richard Felder, William Ford, Jr., Brian Kernighan, Arthur Levinson, Yueh-Lin Loo, James McDonnell, Red Whittaker, and Ben Zinn

CONNECTICUT

MAINE

MASSACHUSETTS

NEW HAMPSHIRE

NEW JERSEY

NEW YORK

PENNSYLVANIA

RHODE ISLAND

VERMONT

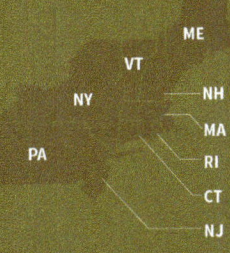

NORTHEAST

CONNECTICUT

MAINE

MASSACHUSETTS

NEW HAMPSHIRE

NEW JERSEY

NEW YORK

PENNSYLVANIA

RHODE ISLAND

VERMONT

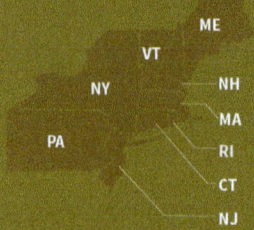

RUTGERS UNIVERSITY

Address: Rutgers University, School of Engineering, Engineering Building, Room B134, 98 Brett Road, Piscataway, NJ 08854-8058
Website: https://soe.rutgers.edu/
Contact: https://soe.rutgers.edu/contact-us
Phone: (848) 445-2212
Email: hello@soe.rutgers.edu

COST OF ATTENDANCE:
Tuition & Fees: $19,683 (in-state), $40,076 (out-of-state)
Addl Exp: $23,000 | **Total:** $42,683 (in-state), $63,076 (out-of-state)

Financial Aid: https://www.rutgers.edu/admissions-tuition/tuition-and-financial-aid

ADDITIONAL INFORMATION:
Available Degree(s)
- BS, MS, Ph.D. Biochemical Eng, Biomedical Eng, Chemical Eng, Civil/Environmental Eng, Computer Eng, Comp Sci, Materials Science & Engineering, Mechanical Eng, Industrial Engineering
- BS Electrical & Computer Engineering, Environmental Chemistry
- MS Applied Industrial & Systems Engineering, Energy Systems Engineering, Packaging Engineering
- Minor: Data Science, Geological Sciences, Military Science – Aerospace Science Track

Related Research Areas
Catalyst Manufacturing Science & Engineering Center, Center for Information Management, Integration & Connectivity, Command, Control, and Interoperability Center for Advanced Data Analysis, Emergent Materials, Energy, Economic, & Environmental Policy, Energy Systems, Environmental Analysis & Communications Group, Geological & Water Survey Core Repository, Green Building, Infrastructure & Transportation, Inst of Earth, Ocean, & Atmospheric Science, National Transit Inst, Remote Sensing & Spatial Analysis, Urban Environmental Sustainability, Urban Policy, Water Resources

Scholarships Offered
Rutgers offers freshman & continuing merit scholarships for 4 years. For engineering scholarships, students must enroll FT & maintain a 3.25 cumulative GPA. A 3.5 or higher is required for the Presidential Scholarship. Honors Program, Alumni Scholarships, California Student Scholarship, and International Student scholarships are also available. Students who apply by December 1 are considered.

Special Opportunities
Double Major Engineering/A&S, Major/Minor, Double Major w/Minor; Study Abroad in Australia, Hong Kong, Ireland, Israel, New Zealand, South Africa, South Korea, Spain, Sweden, & U.K.; Engineering scholarships of up to $1,000 for its student studying abroad during the Fall or Spring semesters who at the time of application has at least a 3.00 cumulative GPA. Engineering Summer Academy

Orgs: American Institute of Aeronautics and Astronautics, American Institute of Chemical Engineers, American Society of Civil Engineers, American Society of Mechanical Engineers, American Water Works Association, Biomedical Engineering Society, Engineering Governing Council, Engineers w/o Borders, Institute of Electrical & Electronics Engineers, Material Advantage, National Society of Black Engineers, Society of Asian Scientists & Engineers, Society of Hispanic Professional Engineers, Society of Women Engineers, Students for the Exploration & Development of Space, Women in Computer Science

Teams: Chem-E-Car, CubeSat, Debate Team, iGEM (Intl Genetically Engineered Machines), Makerspace Club. Mock Trial, Model United Nations, Robotics@Rutgers, Rocket Propulsion Team, Rutgers Formula Racing Team, Solar Car Team, Space Technology Team, Steel Bridge Team, Uncrewed Submarine Team, VexU Robotics

Notable Alumni
Richard Bartha, Stanley Cohen, Louis Gluck, Terry Hart, Mir Imran, Ernest Mario, Daniel Nocera, Peter Schultz, John Scudder, Heather Zichal

COLUMBIA UNIVERSITY

Address: Columbia Engineering, 500 W 120th St., Mudd 510, New York, NY 10027
Website: https://www.engineering.columbia.edu/
Contact: https://www.engineering.columbia.edu/contact
Phone: (212) 854-2993
Email: sfchang@ee.columbia.edu

COST OF ATTENDANCE:
Tuition & Fees: $68,400 | **Addl Exp:** $24,000 | **Total:** $92,400
Financial Aid: https://www.sfs.columbia.edu/fin-aid

ADDITIONAL INFORMATION:

Available Degree(s)
- Fu Foundation SEAS: BS, MS, Ph.D. BME, Chem Eng, Earth & Environmental Eng, Material Science & Eng, Mechanical Engineering, EE, Eng Mgmt Systems, Engineering Mechanics
- BA Applied Mathematics, Applied Physics, Biochemistry, Biology, Biophysics, Chemical Physics, Chemistry
- MA Climate & Society, 3-2 BA/MS Engineering, MS Construction Administration, MS Technology Management, MA Biotechnology, MS Sustainability Management

Related Research Areas
AIDS, Air Quality, Biomechanics, Biomimetics, Carbon Utilization, Catalytic Reaction Eng, Cellular Behavior Predictions, Clean Energy Creation, Climate Change, Electrochemical Energy Storage Solutions, Electron Transport in Molecular Nanostructures, Energy Frontier Res, Genome Eng, Graphene-Based Devices, Microbial Enviro Processes, Nanoscale Science & Eng, Photovoltaic Efficiency Through Molecular Scale Control, Predictive Modeling, Protein Engineering, Renewable Energy, Therapeutics, Tissue Engineering, Transcription & RNA Splicing

Scholarships Offered
Most students from families whose annual income is less than $150,000 attend Columbia tuition-free. Columbia awards more than $177 million annually in scholarships and grants from all sources; 50% of Columbia students receive grants; the average amount awarded is $62,850; Incoming first-year students from low-income families receive a start-up grant of $2,000 to ease their transition to college. Students are expected to borrow $0 to attend Columbia.

Special Opportunities
Internships, Summer Programs, Co-ops, Study Abroad, Seminars, State-of-the-Art Facilities, Corporate Research Partnerships

The cornerstone of Columbia's Fu Foundation is a strong engineering background with a liberal arts core. Columbia's intellectual mission is to provide wide-ranging knowledge in ideas & achievements in literature, philosophy, history, music, art, & science. Students choose from 17 areas enriched by 20 liberal arts minors and 15+ engineering minors.

Orgs: Amer Chemical Soc, Amer Inst of Aeronautics & Astronautics, Amer Inst of Chemical Eng, Amer Medical Students Assoc, American Physician Scientists Association, American Society of Civil Eng, Amer Society of Mechanical Eng, Biomedical Eng Society, Bioethics Soc, Columbia Space Init, Material Advantage, National Society of Black Eng, Neuroscience Society, Pre-Medical Society, Society of Hispanic Prof Eng, Society of Women Engineers, Women in Computer Science

Teams: Chem-E Car Team, Chess Team, CubeSat, Cybersecuity Team, Debate Society, Formula SAE Team, Hackathon for Humanity, MAP Project48 – Data Science Competition, Makerspace Collaboration, Mock Trial, Model Congress, Model United Nations, Quiz Bowl Team, Robotics Club, Science Olympiad Team, Steel Bridge Team

Notable Alumni
Kenneth Bowersox, Shu Chien, Kevin Chilton, Amelia Earhart, Joseph Engelberger, James Fletcher, Herman Hollerith, Gregory Johnson, Rudolf Kálmán, Kai-Fu Lee, John Marchetti, Michael Massimino, Story Musgrave, Stephen Schneider, Eugene Trinh, John Trump, Neil DeGrasse Tyson, and Victor Wouk

CONNECTICUT

MAINE

MASSACHUSETTS

NEW HAMPSHIRE

NEW JERSEY

NEW YORK

PENNSYLVANIA

RHODE ISLAND

VERMONT

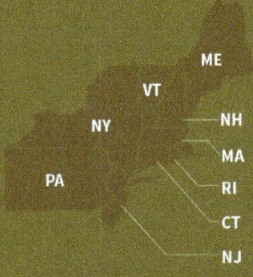

NORTHEAST

CONNECTICUT

MAINE

MASSACHUSETTS

NEW HAMPSHIRE

NEW JERSEY

NEW YORK

PENNSYLVANIA

RHODE ISLAND

VERMONT

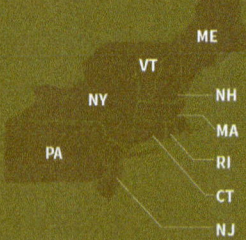

CORNELL UNIVERSITY

Address: Cornell Engineering, Carpenter Hall, 313 Campus Rd., Ithaca, New York 14853
Website: https://www.engineering.cornell.edu/
Contact: https://www.engineering.cornell.edu/contact-us
Phone: (607) 255-4326
Email: engr_generalinfo@cornell.edu

COST OF ATTENDANCE:

Tuition & Fees: $68,380 | **Addl Exp:** $23,000 | **Total:** $91,380
Financial Aid: https://finaid.cornell.edu/

ADDITIONAL INFORMATION:

Available Degree(s)
- BS, MEng, Ph.D. Aerospace Eng, Biological & Biomedical Eng, Chemical Eng, Computer Eng, Comp Sci, Electrical Eng, Environmental Eng, Materials Science & Eng, Mechanical Eng
- Minors: Aerospace Eng, Biomedical Eng, Business for Eng Students, Computer Science, Earth & Atmospheric Science, Entrepreneurship & Innovation, Eng Communication

Related Research Areas
Aerodynamics & Aeroacoustics, Bioenergy, Biomaterials, Biomass Combustion, Combustion Dynamics of Biofuels, Computational Fluid Mechanics, Immunotherapy & Cell Eng, Microfluidic Device Design, Mechanics of Biological Materials, Nano- & Micro-Scale Eng, Robotics & Computer Controlled Machinery, Satellite Systems, Self-Assembling Chemical Reactors, Smart Cities, Solar & Renewable Energy, Sustainable Energy Sys, Thermofluids, Turbulence, Turbines

Scholarships Offered
Most students w/family annual inc less than $150,000 attend Cornell tuition-free. Cornell awards more than $177 million scholarships/grants; 50% of Cornell stud receive grants; ave amount awarded is $62,850; Incoming 1st-year students from low-inc families rec $2,000 startupgrant to ease transition. Students expected to borrow $0.

Special Opportunities
Internships, Summer Programs, Co-ops, Study Abroad, Seminar Programs, State-of-the-Art Facilities, Corporate Partnerships

Orgs: American Chemical Society, American Institute of Aeronautics & Astronautics, American Institute of Chemical Engineers, American Society of Civil Eng, American Society of Mechanical Eng, American Society for Biochemistry & Molecular Biology Society, Bioethics Society, Biomedical Engineering Society, Data Science Club, eMed, Engineers for a Sustainable World, Engineers in Action, Engineers w/o Borders, Eng Ambassadors, Institute of Electrical & Electronics Engineers, National Society of Black Engineers, Hispanic Society of Professional Engineers, Seismic Design, Society of Women Engineers

Teams: Aerial Robotics, AutoBoat Team, Autonomous Bicycle Team, Autonomous Underwater Vehicle Team, Baja SAE Racing, ChemE Car, Combat Robotics@Cornell, Competitive Programming Team, Concrete Canoe Team, Cornell AppDev, Cornell Cup Robotics Team, Custom Silicon Systems (C2S2) Team, Data Science Team, Design Build Fly, Design & Tech Initiative Team, Electric Vehicle Team, eSports, Formula SAE Racing Team, iGEM (Genetically Engineered Machine) Team, GeoData Team, Hack4Impact, Hyperloop Team, Mars Rover Team, Mock Trial, Model United Nations, Rocketry Team, SailBot Intl Robotic Sailboat Regatta, Seismic Design Team, Solar Boat, Speech & Debate Team, Steel Bridge Team, Unmanned Aerial Systems Team, World Health (EWH) Project Team

Notable Alumni
Eric Betzig, Samuel Bodman, Heather Cho, Joseph Coors, Kenneth Derr, Tom Dinwoodie, Pawan Goenka, Leroy Grumman, Jeff Hawkins, Irwin Jacobs, Robert Kennedy, Robert Langer, Douglas Leone, Kenneth Nichols, Spencer Olin, Thomas Reed, Clarence Spicer, John Swanson, Tien Tzuo, David Welch, & Mark Whitacre

RENSSELAER POLYTECHNIC INSTITUTE

Address: School of Engineering, Rensselaer Polytechnic Institute, 110 8th Street Troy, NY 12180 USA
Website: https://eng.rpi.edu/
Contact: https://eng.rpi.edu/contact
Phone: (518) 279-6298
Email: gardes@rpi.edu

COST OF ATTENDANCE:
Tuition & Fees: $62,500 | **Addl Exp:** $22,000 | **Total:** $84,500
Financial Aid: https://admissions.rpi.edu/aid

ADDITIONAL INFORMATION:
Available Degree(s)
- BS, MS, MEng, DEng, Ph.D. Aeronautical Eng, Biomedical Eng, Chemical Eng, Civil Eng, Computer & Sys Eng, Comp Science, Electrical Eng, Environmental Eng, Industrial & Management Eng, Materials Eng, Mechanical Eng, Nuclear Engineering
- MS, MEng, DEng, Ph.D. Transportation Engineering
- ME Systems Engineering & Technology Management
- Ph.D. Decision Science & Engineering Systems, Nuclear Engineering & Science

Related Research Areas
More than 30 research centers, including The Design Lab, Center for Earthquake Engineering Simulation, the Network Science & Technology Center (NeST), & Gaerttner Linear Accelerator Center

Focus Areas: Climate Change, Disease Mitigation, Energy, Water, & Food, Infrastructure, National/Global Security, Resilience, Sustainability

Scholarships Offered
Scholarships available (amts vary): Rensselaer Grant, Rensselaer Leadership Award (outstanding academic/personal achievements), Rensselaer Medal Scholarship; $7,500 nuclear engineering awards

Special Opportunities
Grand Challenges Program, K-12 Outreach, Engineering Ambassadors, Study Abroad, Co-ops, Internships available. Summer and school year internships available.

Orgs: American Helicopter Society, American Institute of Aeronautics & Astronautics, American Institute of Chemical Engineers, American Nuclear Society, American Society of Civil Engineers, American Society of Heating, Refrigeration, & Air Conditioning Engineers, American Society of Mechanical Engineers, Biomedical Engineering Society, Institute of Electrical & Electronics Engineers, National Society of Black Engineers, Rensselaer Aeronautical Federation, Society of Automotive Engineers, Society of Asian Scientists & Engineers, Society of Hispanic Professional Engineers, Students for the Exploration and Development of Space, Society of Women Engineers, Women in Computing

Teams: Call For Code Challenge, Chem-E Car Team, Chess Club, CubeSat, Debate Team, Design-Build-Fly Team, RPI Formula Hybrid Team, Formula SAE Electric Vehicle Team, HackRPI, iGEM (International Genetically Engineered Machines), Model Railroad Society, OSCaR ("Obsolete Spacecraft Capture and Removal"), the semi-autonomous craft, Quiz Bowl, Rensselaer Cybersecurity Collaboratory (first-place in 2023), RPI Rock Raiders, RPISEC "Capture the Flag" Competition Team, Solar Car Racing Team (entered in the North American Solar Challenge and Cross-Australia World Solar Challenge), Terminal Coding Competition

Notable Alumni
Marshall Brain, Leffert Buck, Nicholas Donofrio, Allen DuMont, George Ferris Jr., Joseph Gerber, Lois Graham, William Gurley, Ted Hoff, J. Erik Jonsson, Theodore Judah, Keith Millis, David Noble, Sheldon Roberts, Washington Roebling, Steven Sasson, Robert Scaringe, John Schenck, Bert Sutherland, Massood Tabib-Azar, Raymond Tomlinson, John Waddell, and Robert Widmer

CONNECTICUT

MAINE

MASSACHUSETTS

NEW HAMPSHIRE

NEW JERSEY

NEW YORK

PENNSYLVANIA

RHODE ISLAND

VERMONT

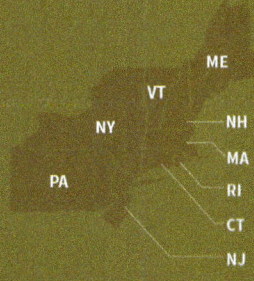

NORTHEAST

CONNECTICUT

MAINE

MASSACHUSETTS

NEW HAMPSHIRE

NEW JERSEY

NEW YORK

PENNSYLVANIA

RHODE ISLAND

VERMONT

SUNY COLLEGE OF ENVIRONMENTAL SCIENCE AND FORESTRY

Address: SUNY Environmental Sciences & Forestry, 1 Forestry Drive, Syracuse, NY 13210
Website: https://www.esf.edu/ere
Contact: https://www.esf.edu/ere/contact.htm
Phone: (315) 470-6500
Email: esfinfo@esf.edu

COST OF ATTENDANCE:

Tuition & Fees: $9,777 (in-state), $22,000 (out-of-state)
Addl Exp: $23,000 | **Total:** $32,777 (in-state), $45,000 (out-of-state)
Financial Aid: https://www.esf.edu/financialaid/

ADDITIONAL INFORMATION:

Available Degree(s)
- BS, MS, MPS, Ph.D. Chemical Engineering, Environmental Biology, Environmental Resources Engineering, Environmental Science & Studies, Landscape Architecture, Sustainable Resource Management
- MS, Ph.D. Ecological Engineering, Environmental Management (MPS), Geospatial Information Science & Engineering, Water Resources Engineering

Related Research Areas
Adirondack Ecological Center, American Chestnut Resource & Restoration Center, Bioregional & Biosphere Reserve Studies, Climate & Applied Forest Resource Institute, Center for Cultural Landscape Preservation, Center for Sustainable Materials Management, Council on Geospatial Modeling & Analysis, Great Lakes Research Consortium, Hydrologic Systems Science, Institute for Sustainable Materials & Manufacturing, Native Peoples & Environment, Northern Forest Institute, Polymer Research Institute, Restoration Science Center, Renewable Materials Institute, SUNY Center for Applied Microbiology, Tropical Timber Information Center, Urban Environment, Wildlife Station, Wood Utilization Service

Scholarships Offered
Presidential and National Scholarships – See site; Other Scholarships – Automatic Consideration (no application necessary) ESF undergraduate merit scholarships awarded to first-year and transfer students based on academic performance.

Special Opportunities
Internships, Summer Programs, Co-ops, Study Abroad, Food Pantry, Blacksmithing, Earth Week, Herpetology, Woodworking

Orgs: Alchemists Society, American Fisheries Society, American Institute of Chemical Engineers, Bee Campus USA, Climbing Club, Engineering for a Sustainable Society, Engineers w/o Borders, Entomology Club, Environmental Health Club, Environmental Resources Engineering Club, Environmental Studies Student Organization, Fly Fishing Club, Forestry Club, Green Campus Initiative, Green Team, New York Water Environment Association, Poetry Club, Science Corps, Society of Ecological Restoration, Sew Knotty, Sustainable Energy Club, Wildlife Society, Veterinary Club

Teams: The National Academy of Engineering's Grand Challenges Scholars Program opportunity to solve global problems impacting humanity and biodiversity. Bass Team, Gaming, Quiz Bowl, Solar Decathlon, Timbersports

Notable Alumni
Ronald Eby, Frank Egler, Jean Frechet, Robin Kimmerer, Michael Kudish, Moshe Levy, Mark Marquisee, Bob Marshall, Joe Martens, Donald Moore, III, James Morrissey, and Clarence Petty

BUCKNELL UNIVERSITY

Address: Bucknell University, College of Engineering, One Dent Drive, 235 Dana Engineering Building, Lewisburg, PA 17837
Website: *https://www.bucknell.edu/academics/college-engineering*
Contact: *https://www.bucknell.edu/azdirectory?t=faculty_staff&s=All*
Phone: (570) 577-2000
Email: engineering@bucknell.edu

COST OF ATTENDANCE:
Tuition & Fees: $67,446 | **Addl Exp:** $21,000 | **Total:** $88,446

Financial Aid: https://www.bucknell.edu/admissions-aid/tuition-fees-financial-aid

ADDITIONAL INFORMATION:
Available Degree(s)
- BS, MS, Ph.D. Biomedical Engineering, Chemical Engineering, Civil Engineering, Computer Engineering, Computer Science, Electrical Engineering, Environmental Engineering, Mechanical Engineering

Related Research Areas
Atmospheric Chem, Biological Eng, Biomaterials, Biotechnology, Chemical Process Engineering, Chemical Transport Computational/Data Science, Environmental Engineering, Hazardous Waste Management, Intelligent Systems, Machine Learning, Materials Engineering, Pharmaceutical Process Engineering, Polymer Science, Predictive Analytics, Product/Process Chemistry, Bucknell Center for Sustainability & the Environment

Scholarships Offered
Merit scholarships-submit Bucknell's scholarship application (same as application deadline. Merit scholarships, renewable for 8 fall/spring terms, awarded at admission (only available for first-year students. Most funding awarded for demonstrate institutional need. A few are awarded to those for merit w/o FAFSA. Scholarships incl: Arts Merit Scholarship, Bucknell Women in Science & Eng, Bauer Scholarship, Community Engagement Schol., Mathematics Schol., Presidential Fellows Schol., PricewaterhouseCoopers Scholarship

Special Opportunities
Industry Collaborations, Study Abroad, Davis United World College Scholars, Grand Challenges Scholars Program. Centers & labs, such as 7th Street Studio & MakerSpace & tech-equipped playgrounds for investigative/innovative minds, outfitted w/vinyl/laser cutters, design software, 3D printers, computer-controlled mills; welding, soldering, woodworking tools, and printed circuit board equipment.

Bucknell's Small Business Development Center hires eng majors as product-devt consultants for eng design, analysis, & prototype development with startups & companies seeking to expand.

The 5-week, on-campus summer Engineering EXCELerator program allows students to attend an Engineering Camp, develop skills in prototyping/fabrication, and get ahead calculus/physics instruction.

Bucknell's facilities, include a research green roof, structural testing lab, and sustainability monitoring center.

Orgs: American Academy of Environmental Engineers & Scientists, American Chemical Society, American Society of Civil Engineers, American Society of Mechanical Engineers, Assoc for Computing Machinery, Biomedical Engineering Society, Engineering Network, Environmental Club, Geological Society, Institute of Electrical & Electronics Engineering, Machine Learning Association, Makers Society, National Society of Black Engineers, Pre-Vet Society, Renewable Energy Scholars, Society of Hispanic Professional Engineers, Society of Women Engineers, Women in STEM Club

Teams: Baja SAE, Case Analysis, Chem-E Car Club, Mock Trial, UTV

Notable Alumni
Steven DeKosky, Dennis Dougherty, Marc Hauser, Marc Lore, Marty Makary, Takeo Shiina, Greg Skibiski, Amos Smith, Trisha Torrey, Bill Westenhofer, and David Wood

CONNECTICUT

MAINE

MASSACHUSETTS

NEW HAMPSHIRE

NEW JERSEY

NEW YORK

PENNSYLVANIA

RHODE ISLAND

VERMONT

NORTHEAST

CONNECTICUT

MAINE

MASSACHUSETTS

NEW HAMPSHIRE

NEW JERSEY

NEW YORK

PENNSYLVANIA

RHODE ISLAND

VERMONT

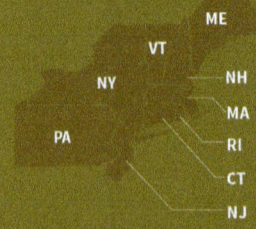

CARNEGIE MELLON UNIVERSITY

Address: 5000 Forbes Avenue, Pittsburgh, PA 15213
Website: https://engineering.cmu.edu/
Contact: https://admission.enrollment.cmu.edu/pages/contact-us
Phone: (412) 268-2354
Email: admission@andrew.cmu.edu

COST OF ATTENDANCE:

Tuition & Fees: $64,596 | **Addl Exp:** $21,000 | **Total:** $85,596
Financial Aid: https://www.cmu.edu/admission/aid-affordability

ADDITIONAL INFORMATION:

Available Degree(s)

- BS, MS, Ph.D. BME, Chemical Eng, Civil Eng, Computer Eng, Computer Science, Electrical Eng, Environmental Eng, Materials Science & Engineering, Mechanical Engineering
- MS Colloids, Polymers, & Surfaces
- MS Energy Science, Technology, & Policy

Related Research Centers

Adv Process Decision-Making, Air, Climate, & Energy, Atmospheric Particle Studies, Climate & Energy Decision-Making, Cognition & Action, Comp On Network Infrastructure for Pervasive Perception, Complex Fluids Eng, Environmental Implications of Nanotech, Green Design, Iron & Steelmaking Research, Manufacturing Futures, Materials Characterization Facility, Mechanics & Engineering of Cellular Systems, Mobility Data Analytics, Next Manufacturing, Smart Infrastructure, Water Quality in Urban Environmental Systems

Scholarships Offered

CMU offers need-based grants & endowed scholarships. Undergrad, graduate, graduate, and alumni awards are available as well. Current students can win design, sustainability, research, and engagement scholarships ($75,000 additional awarded each year).

Special Opportunities

Research proj; first-class facilities; Real-World Eng Program costs are covered by the College of Engineering Dean's Office & the Gupta First-Year Experience program. Travel grants for study abroad.

Orgs: American Institute of Aeronautics & Astronautics, American Institute of Chemical Engineers, American Society of Civil Engineers, American Society of Mechanical Engineers, American Society of Heating, Refrigerating and Air-Conditioning Engineers, Biomedical Engineering Society, Engineers w/o Borders, Engineering Student Council, Green Design Institute, Institute of Electrical & Electronics Engineers, Material Advantage, National Society of Black Engineers, oSTEM, National Robotics Engineering Center, Society of Automotive Engineers, Society of Asian Scientists & Engineers, Society of Hispanic Professional Engineers, Society of Manufacturing Engineering, Society of Women Engineers, Women in Electrical & Computer Engineering

Teams: Abu Dhabi Robotics Challenge, Autonomous Underwater Vehicle Team, Autonomous Aerial Vehicle Team, Build18, Chem-E Car Team, Chess, College Bowl, Concrete Canoe Team, Cubesat, $2 million Defense Adv Research Project Agency (DARPA) Subterranean Challenge (multi-year robotics competition), eSports Team, Formula SAE Electric Car Team, Grand Challenges, Hackathons, iGEM (International Genetically Engineered Machines), Rocket Command (NASA Student Launch Competition, Solar Racing, Model United Nations, Mock Trial, Quiz Bowl, CMU Hacking Team won DEF CON "Superbowl of Hacking" for 6th Time in 2022

Notable Alumni

Alex Acero, Raymond Betler, Gloria Chen, Scott Griffith, Feng-Hsiung Hsu, Anand Iyer, Raj Kapoor, David Kelley, Vinod Khosla, William Lee, William Leone, Leonard Lerman, Candace Matthews, George Mueller, Drew Perkins, Ana Pinczuk, James Rogers, Matt Rogers, Roger Rosner, Jonathan Rothberg, Jane Rudolph, Barb Samardzich, Ivan Sutherland, Daniel Swanson, Carol Williams, Amit Zavery.

DREXEL UNIVERSITY

Address: 3250 Chestnut Street, MacAlister Hall, Suite 4020, Philadelphia, PA 19104
Website: https://drexel.edu/engineering/
Contact: https://drexel.edu/engineering/contact-directories
Phone: (215) 895-2210
Email: engineering@drexel.edu

COST OF ATTENDANCE:

Tuition & Fees: $62,462 | **Addl Exp:** $22,000 | **Total:** $84,462
Financial Aid: https://drexel.edu/drexelcentral/finaid/overview/

ADDITIONAL INFORMATION:

Available Degree(s)
- BS, MS, Ph.D. Architectural Eng, Biomedical Eng, Chemical Engineering, Civil Eng, Computer Engineering, Comp Sci, Electrical Engineering, Environmental Engineering, Materials Science & Engineering, Mechanical Engineering & Mechanics
- MS Robotics & Autonomy
- Minors: Eng Leadership, Eng Policy Analysis, Global Eng, Green Energy & Sustainability, Robotics & Automation
- Certificates: NAE Grand Challenge Scholars Program, Peace Engineering, Reliability Engineering, Systems Engineering, Sustainability & Green Construction

Related Research Centers
A.J. Drexel Nanotechnology Institute, C & J Nyheim Plasma Institute, Center for Electric Power Eng, Expressive & Creative Interaction Tech, Materials Ctr of Excellence, CAD Lab, Design & Manufacturing Lab, Machine Shop, Mesoscale Materials Lab, Multiscale Computational Mechanics & Biomechanics LAB, Theoretical & Appl Mechanics Group

Focus Areas: Air Pollution, Contaminant Hydrology, Environmental Chemistry, Environmental Health, Environmental Risk Management, Hazardous & Solid Waste, Sustainability, Water & Wastewater Infrastructure, Water Resources.

Scholarships Offered
100% of new students were given scholarships at Drexel University, averaging $28,332 per person

Special Opportunities
Students alternate classes w/FT employment through approved employers. Eight different tools are available for internship jobs. Fellowships & volunteer opportunities are also available.

Orgs: Architectural Engineering Institute, Amer Inst of Aeronautics & Astronautics, American Institute of Chemical Engineers, American Society for Engineering Education, American Society of Civil Engineers, American Society of Mechanical Engineers, American Society of Heating, Refrigeration, and Air-Conditioning Engineers, Biomedical Engineering Society, Construction Management Association, Engineers w/o Borders, Icarus Insterstellar, Institute of Electrical & Electronics Engineers, Material Advantage, National Society of Black Engineers, Smart House, Society of Asian Scientists & Engineers, Society of Hispanic Professional Engineers, Society of Manufacturing Engineers, Society of Women Engineers, TechServ

Teams: Aero SAE, Chess, Concrete Canoe Team, CubeSat (Icarus Interstellar), CyberDragons (Cybersecurity Competitions), Debate Union, EarthFest, eSports, Formula SAE Electric Race Car Team, Hackathons, Mock Trial, Model United Nations, Philly Codefest, Robotics Team, Rubik's Cube, Solar Car Team, Steel Bridge Team

Notable Alumni
Sirous Asgari, Paul Baran, Michael Baum, Michael Behe, Lin Bin, Douglas Briggs, Kenneth Dahlberg, Ranjan Dash, Bruce Eisenstein, Lex Fridman, Eli Fromm, David Geiger, Lex Fridman, Walter Golaski, John Gruber, Jon Hall, Vasant Honavar, Moshe Kam, Cynthia Maryanoff, Hiang Mianheng, James Nell, Paul Richards, Alia Sabur, Bernard Silver, and Norman Woodland.

CONNECTICUT

MAINE

MASSACHUSETTS

NEW HAMPSHIRE

NEW JERSEY

NEW YORK

PENNSYLVANIA

RHODE ISLAND

VERMONT

NORTHEAST

LEHIGH UNIVERSITY

Address: P.C. Rossin College of Engineering & Applied Science, 19 Memorial Drive W., Lehigh University, Bethlehem, PA 18015
Website: https://engineering.lehigh.edu/
Contact: https://engineering.lehigh.edu/contact
Phone: (610) 758-4025
Email: engineering@lehigh.edu

COST OF ATTENDANCE:

Tuition & Fees: $64,980 | **Addl Exp:** $20,000 | **Total:** $84,980

Financial Aid: https://www2.lehigh.edu/financial-aid

ADDITIONAL INFORMATION:

Available Degree(s)
- BS, BS/MS, MS, MEng, Ph.D. Biological Eng, Chemical Eng, Civil Eng, Electrical Eng, Enviro Eng, Materials Science & Engineering, Mechanical Engineering, Structural Engineering
- MS, MEng, Ph.D. Polymer Science & Engineering
- Minors: Aerospace Eng, Biotechnology, Business, Chemical & Biomolecular Eng, Computer Sci, Data Science, Electrical Eng, Energy Eng, Engineering Leadership, Entrepreneurship, Environmental Eng, Manufacturing Systems Engineering, Materials Science & Engineering, Mechanics of Materials, Music, Nanotechnology, Polymer Science & Engineering

Related Research Areas
Institute for Cyber Physical Infrastructure & Energy, Institute for Data, Intelligent Systems, & Computation, Institute for Functional Materials & Devices

Scholarships Offered
Lehigh offers renewable merit scholarships – some automatically considered; others require a separate application. Alice P. Gast STEM Scholarship ($12,500 for selected women in STEM careers), Dean's Scholars ($15,000/yr based on academics & leadership), Founder's & Trustees' Scholarships (full or half tuition) Departmental scholarships available. ROTC scholarship includes full tuition, book allowance of $1,200, and a monthly stipend (room & board free for students who commit to becoming an Army officer). Greer Scholars Program provides funding and support network for African American & Hispanic students pursuing engineering at Lehigh.

Special Opportunities
Experiential learning & internships, high-tech research centers, institutes & labs, Lehigh CHOICES Program, & Lehigh Summer Eng Inst for K-12 students. Study abroad options in Belgium, England, France, the Czech Republic, Italy, & China. Winter-term programs have been offered in England, Italy, Costa Rica, Spain, & Ghana.

Orgs: Aerospace Club, American Inst of Aeronautics & Astronautics, American Institute of Chemical Engineers, American Society of Civil Eng, American Society of Mechanical Engineers, Association for Computing Machinery, Biomedical Engineering Society, Eng w/o Borders, Inst of Electrical & Electronics Eng, Material Advantage

Teams: Baja SAE, Chess, Concrete Canoe Team, CubeSat Team, Cyber Security Team, Debate Team, Design-Build-Fly, Formula SAE, F1TENTH Virtual Global Autonomous Racing Comp Head-to-Head Race (1st place in 2022), Hack for Change, Precast/Prestressed Concrete Institute's Engineering Student Design Competition (3rd overall in 2020), Mock Trial Team, Model United Nations, Modeling & Optimization Theory & Applications Competition, National Chem-E Car Competition Team, Rocketry Team, Steel Bridge Team

Notable Alumni
Ali Al-Naimi, William Amelio, Walter Bachman, Stephen Benkovic, William Bowie, Morris Cooke, Stacey Cunningham, Harry Diamond, William Elmore, Martin Faga, Terry Hart, Marc Holtzman, Lee Iacocca, Kevin Kennedy, Andrew Knoll, Reginald Lenna, Judy Marks, Fred Mackenzie, Daniel Moore, John Patrick, Roger Penske, Jordan Ritter, Robert Serber, John Texter, Fred Trump, Jr.

CONNECTICUT

MAINE

MASSACHUSETTS

NEW HAMPSHIRE

NEW JERSEY

NEW YORK

PENNSYLVANIA

RHODE ISLAND

VERMONT

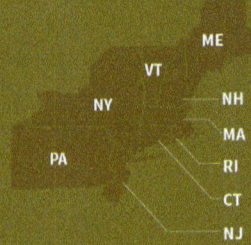

PENNSYLVANIA STATE UNIVERSITY

Address: College of Engineering, Office of the Dean, 101 Hammond Building, University Park, PA 16802
Website: *https://www.engr.psu.edu/*
Contact: *https://www.engr.psu.edu/directory/index.aspx*
Phone: (814) 865-7537
Email: dean@engr.psu.edu

COST OF ATTENDANCE:
Tuition & Fees: $25,738 (in-state), $48,682 (out-of-state)
Addl Exp: $20,000 | **Total:** $45,738 (in-state), $68,682 (out-of-state)
Financial Aid: https://www.psu.edu/tuition-and-financial-aid/

ADDITIONAL INFORMATION:
Available Degree(s)
- BS, MS, Ph.D. Aerospace Eng, Bio Eng, BME, Chemical Eng, Civil/Enviro Eng, Materials Sci & Eng, Mech Eng, Nuclear Eng
- BS Energy Engineering, Mining Engineering, Petroleum & Natural Gas Engineering, Polymer Engineering & Science
- MEng, MS Additive Manufacturing & Design, Engineering Design
- D.Eng. Doctor of Engineering
- Minors: Engineering Leadership Devt, Entrepreneurship & Innovation, Environmental Eng, Intl Eng, Nanotechnology

Related Research Areas
3D Printing & Additive Manufacturing, Adv Manufacturing for Medical & Manufacturing Sciences, Advanced Vehicles, Optimized, & Adaptive Infrastructure, Concrete, Construction, Cyberethics, Cybersecurity, Data Analytics & Data Modeling, Earthquake Engineering, Energy Sourcing & Production, Ethical Water-Energy-Food Policies & Social Responsibility, Food Production Optimization, Infrastructure System Integration, Nanomanufacturing & Biomedical Devices, New Materials, Systems Modeling & Simulation, Transportation & Traffic

Scholarships Offered
To be eligible for any Penn State scholarship, students must submit a FAFSA form. The Provost's Award grants $5,000 for 1st & 2nd years and $7,000 for years 3 and 4 (PA and non-PA residents are considered). The Discover Penn State Award grants $6,000 for 1st & 2nd years and $7,000 for years 3 and 4. Students must be residents of Del., MD, OH, NJ, NY, VA, WV, & DC.

Special Opportunities
Engineering House (E-House), Engineering Student Council, Engineering Leadership Society, Engineering Peer Advising Leaders

Orgs: American Institute of Aeronautics & Astronautics, American Society of Civil Engineers, American Society of Mechanical Engineers, Concrete Institute, Earthquake Eng Research Institute Engineering Ambassadors, Engineering Consulting Collaborative, Engineers for a Sustainable World, Engineers w/o Borders, Global Engineering Fellows, Helicopter Society, Institute of Transportation Eng, Korean-American Scientists & Engineering Association, Lunar Lion, Material Advantage, Materials Research Society, Nat Assn of Home Builders, National Society of Black Engineers, oSTEM, Society for Automotive Engineers, Society of Engineering Science, Society of Hispanic Professional Engineers, Society of Women Engineers, Solar Energy Society, Theme Park Engineering Group, Wind Energy Club

Teams: Advanced Vehicles (Autonomous Vehicles, AutoDrive Challenge), Aero Design-Build-Fly Team, Chess Squad, College Bowl, Concrete Canoe, Cubesat, Formula SAE, HackPSU, Hybrid Electric Vehicle, LionTech Rocket Team, Lunar Lion Google Lunar X Prize Team, Mock Trial, Robotics Club, Robo X, Rubik's Cube Team

Notable Alumni
Elliott Abrams, Guion Bluford, David Bohm, Robert Cenker, Jane Charlton, Shawn Domagal-Goldman, Robert Eberly, Gregory Forbes, Paul Julian, Jim Keller, James Pawelczyk, Jef Raskin, Harry Shoemaker, John Surma, Ben Wang, Paul Weitz, & Patricia Woertz

CONNECTICUT

MAINE

MASSACHUSETTS

NEW HAMPSHIRE

NEW JERSEY

NEW YORK

PENNSYLVANIA

RHODE ISLAND

VERMONT

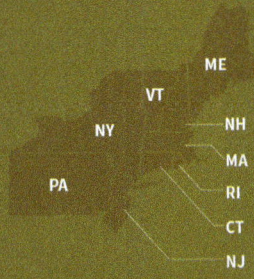

NORTHEAST

CONNECTICUT

MAINE

MASSACHUSETTS

NEW HAMPSHIRE

NEW JERSEY

NEW YORK

PENNSYLVANIA

RHODE ISLAND

VERMONT

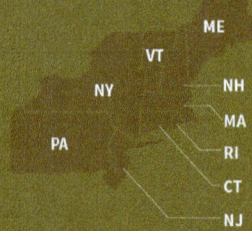

UNIVERSITY OF PITTSBURGH

Address: University of Pittsburgh, Swanson School of Engineering, 151 Benedum Hall, Pittsburgh, PA 15261
Website: https://www.engineering.pitt.edu/
Contact: https://www.engineering.pitt.edu/contact
Phone: (412) 624-9800
Email: ssoeadm@pitt.edu

COST OF ATTENDANCE:

Tuition & Fees: $25,248 (in-state), $44,634 (out-of-state)
Addl Exp: $20,000 | **Total:** $45,248 (in-state), $64,634 (out-of-state)

Financial Aid: https://financialaid.pitt.edu/

ADDITIONAL INFORMATION:

Available Degree(s)
- BS, MS, Ph.D. Biomedical Engineering, Chemical Engineering, Civil Eng, Computer Eng, Computer Science, Electrical Eng, Environmental Engineering, Industrial Engineering, Materials Science & Engineering, Mechanical Eng, Nuclear Engineering
- MS Sustainability Engineering

Related Research Areas
Advanced Imaging, Alzheimer's, Asthma, & Brain Institute, Biologic Imaging, Brain & Spine Injury Center, Cancer Inst, Cardiovascular Institute, Cerebrovascular Neurosurgery Center, Computational Genomics, Craniofacial Regeneration, Center for Bioengineering, Cystic Fibrosis, Digestive Disorders, Drug Discovery, Engineering Res Center on Mobility, Epidemiology, Epilepsy, Genetics, Global Health, Healthcare Data Center, Human Eng Research Lab, Image-Guided Neurosurgery, Liver Diseases, Lung Center, Medical Innovation, Neural Basis of Cognition, Neurophysiology, Nutrition, Obesity, Pharmaceutical Sciences, Regenerative Medicine, Reproductive Physiology, Rheumatoid Arthritis, Spine Research, Sports Medicine, Stroke Institute, Sustainable Innovation, Vaccine Research

Scholarships Offered
All engineering scholarships are posted via the PittFund$Me portal available on my.pitt.edu. Additional Pitt scholarships may have additional criteria and/or specific application dates.

Special Opportunities
Internships, Co-ops, Senior Design Program, Annual First-Year Engineering Conference; Corporate partnerships, global programs for exchange/study abroad/global internships. Numerous state-of-the-art labs, centers, & institutes for research and education.

Orgs: American Institute of Chemical Engineers, American Nuclear Society, American Society of Civil Engineers, American Society of Mechanical Eng, Biomedical Eng Society, Material Advantage, Nat Society of Black Eng, Society of Asian Scientists & Engineers, Society of Astronautics & Rocketry, Society of Automotive Engineers, Society of Hispanic Professional Engineers, Society of Women Engineers

Teams: AERO SAE (remote controlled aircraft competition), Big Idea Competition, ChemE Car Competition, Chess League, Concrete Canoe Team, Energy Team, Formula SAE Racing, 2020 iGEM Gold Medal Winner, Indy Autonomous Vehicle Challenge, Medical Product Eng, Mock Trial, Model United Nations, NASA RASC-AL Mars Ice Competition, Pitt Cyber Team, PropLab (mentored by top aerospace company), Rocket Launch Team, SOAR engineering competitions, Steel Bridge Team, Sustainability Challenge, UNICAMP (12-week summer internship in Sao Paulo), William Pitt Debating Union

Notable Alumni
Engin Arik, Walter Arnheim, Steven Beering, Christine Borgman, Herbert Boyer, Erik Buell, Jingguang Chen, John Choma, David Cleland, Bob Colwell, Sidney Dancoff, William Dietrich, II, Patricia Horoho, Abul Hussam, Paul Lauterbur, Thomas Lynch, Kevin March, Larry Merlo, Kevin McAllister, Brent Saunders, John Simpson, John Swanson, Thomas Usher, Edward Wasp, John Wheatley, Wu Yundong, Tung Chao Yung, and Vladimir Zworykin

ILLINOIS

INDIANA

IOWA

KANSAS

MICHIGAN

MINNESOTA

MISSOURI

NEBRASKA

NORTH DAKOTA

OHIO

SOUTH DAKOTA

WISCONSIN

CHAPTER 12
REGION TWO
MIDWEST

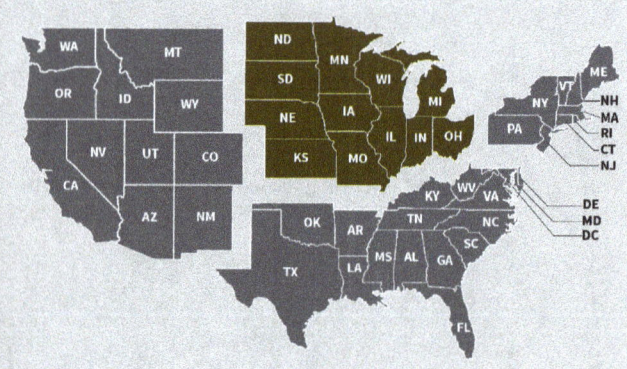

13 Programs | 12 States

1. IL – Northwestern University
2. IL - University of Illinois, Urbana-Champaign
3. IN - Purdue University
4. IN - University of Notre Dame
5. IA - Iowa State University
6. IA - University of Iowa
7. MI - Michigan State University
8. MI - Michigan Technological University
9. MI - University of Michigan
10. MN - University of Minnesota, Twin Cities
11. NE - University of Nebraska
12. OH - The Ohio State University, Columbus
13. WI - University of Wisconsin, Madison

ENVIRONMENTAL ENGINEERING & ALTERNATIVE ENERGY PROGRAMS

School	Avg. GPA, SAT ERW, SAT Math (M), and ACT Composite (C) Early Decision (ED)	Admissions Statistics	Related Program(s)
Northwestern University 633 Clark St, Evanston, IL 60208	GPA: N/A SAT (ERW): 730-770 SAT (M): 760-800 ACT (C): 33-35 ED: Yes, EA: No	Admit Rate: 7% Undergrad Enrollment: 8,776 Total Enrollment: 22,635	BS, MS, Ph.D. Biomedical Eng, Chemical Eng, Civil Eng, Environmental Eng, Computer Engineering, Computer Science, Electrical Engineering, Materials Science & Eng, Mechanical Engineering, MS Biotechnology, Biochem, Manufacturing Eng, Robotics
University of Illinois Urbana-Champaign (UIUC) 901 West Illinois Street, Urbana, IL 61801	GPA: N/A SAT (ERW): 660-740 SAT (M): 680-790 ACT (C): 29-34 ED: No, EA: Yes	Admit Rate: 45% Undergrad Enrollment: 35,120 Total Enrollment: 56,916	BS, MS, Ph.D. Bioengineering, Agricultural & Biological Eng, Chemical & Biomolecular Eng, Civil & Environmental Eng, Computer Eng, Electrical Eng, Industrial & Systems Eng, Materials Science & Eng, Mechanical Engineering
Purdue University Purdue University, West Lafayette, IN 47907	GPA: 367 SAT (ERW): 590-710 SAT (M): 610-760 ACT (C): 27-34 ED: No, EA: Yes	Admit Rate: 53% Undergrad Enrollment: 37.949 Total Enrollment: 50,884	BS, MS, Ph.D. Aeronautical & Astronautical Engineering, Agricultural Eng, Biomedical Eng, Chemical Eng, Civil Eng, Computer Eng, Electrical Eng, Environmental & Ecological Eng, Industrial Eng, Materials Science & Eng, Mechanical Eng
University of Notre Dame University of Notre Dame, Notre Dame, IN 46556	GPA: N/A SAT (ERW): 710-760 SAT (M): 730-780 ACT (C): 32-35 ED: No, REA: Yes	Admit Rate: 11.1% Undergrad Enrollment: 8,968 Total Enrollment: 13,174	BS, BS/MS, MS, Ph.D. Aerospace Engineering, Chemical Engineering, Civil Eng, Computer Engineering, Computer Science, Electrical Eng, Environmental Eng, Mechanical Engineering
Iowa State University 715 Bissell Rd, Ames, IA 50011	GPA: 3.71 SAT (ERW): 480-630 SAT (M): 530-680 ACT (C): 21-28 ED: No, EA: No Rolling: Yes	Overall College Admit Rate: 88% Undergrad Enrollment: 26,843 Total Enrollment: 31,822	BS, MS, MEng & Ph.D. Aerospace Eng, Biomedical Eng, Civil Eng, Computer Eng, Computer Science, Electrical Engineering, Environmental Engineering, Materials Science & Engineering, Mechanical Eng MEng Engineering Mgmt

ENVIRONMENTAL ENGINEERING & ALTERNATIVE ENERGY PROGRAMS

School	Avg. GPA, SAT ERW, SAT Math (M), and ACT Composite (C) Early Decision (ED)	Admissions Statistics	Related Program(s)
University of Iowa Admissions, 2900 University Capitol Centre, Iowa City, IA 52242	GPA: 3.8 SAT (ERW): 560-650 SAT (M): 570-690 ACT (C): 22-28 ED: No, EA: Yes Rolling: Yes	Admit Rate: 86% Undergrad Enrollment: 21,973 Total Enrollment: 30,015	BS, MS, MEng, Ph.D. BME, Chemical Engineering, Civil Eng, Computer Eng, Comp Sci, Electrical Eng, Environmental Eng, Enviro Policy & Planning, Enviro Sci, Geog, Geoscience, Industrial & Systems Eng, Informatics, Mechanical Eng, Naval Science & Tech, Nuclear Medicine Tech, Sustainability
Michigan State University Michigan State University, East Lansing, MI 48824	GPA: 3.74 SAT (ERW): 550-650 SAT (M): 550-690 ACT (C): 24-30 ED: No, EA: Yes	Admit Rate: 76% Undergrad Enrollment: 39,201 Total Enrollment: 50,023	BS, BS/MS, MS, Ph.D. Biosystems Engineering, Chemical Engineering, Civil Eng, Computer Eng, Computer Science, EE, Environmental Engineering, Materials Science & Engineering, Mechanical Eng
Michigan Tech 1400 Townsend Drive, Houghton, MI, 49931	GPA: 3.8 SAT (ERW): 560-660 SAT (M): 570-690 ACT (C): 24-30 ED: No, EA: Yes	Admit Rate: 86% Undergrad Enrollment: 5,710 Total Enrollment: 7,074	BS, MS, Ph.D. Appl Geophysics, Biomedical Engineering, Civil Eng, Computer Eng, Constr Mgmt, Electrical Eng, Enviro Eng, Geological Eng, Geology, Geospatial Eng, Chemical Eng, Materials Science & Eng, Mining Eng, Robotics Engineering
University of Michigan 500 S. State St., Ann Arbor, MI 48109	GPA: 3.87 SAT (ERW): 660-740 SAT (M): 690-790 ACT (C): 31-34 ED: No, EA: Yes	Admit Rate: 18% Undergrad Enrollment: 32,695 Total Enrollment: 51,225	BS, BS/MS, MS, Ph.D. BME, Chemical Eng, Computer Eng, Computer Sci, Electrical Eng, Environmental Eng, Materials Science & Engineering, Nuclear Eng & Radiological Science, Robotics, Space Science Eng
University of Minnesota, Twin Cities 330 21st Ave S., Minneapolis, MN 55455	GPA: 3.57-3.96 SAT (ERW): 660-720 SAT (M): 680-770 ACT (C): 27-32 ED: No, Priority: Yes	Admit Rate: 70% Undergrad Enrollment: 39,248 Total Enrollment: 54,995	BS, MS, Ph.D. Aerospace Eng, Biomedical Eng, Chemical Eng, Civil Eng, Comp Eng, Comp Sci, Environmental Eng, Materials Science & Eng, Mech Eng, MS, Ph.D. Medicinal Chemistry, Molecular Pharmacology, Nuclear Eng

MIDWEST

ENVIRONMENTAL ENGINEERING & ALTERNATIVE ENERGY PROGRAMS

School	Avg. GPA, SAT ERW, SAT Math (M), and ACT Composite (C) Early Decision (ED)	Admissions Statistics	Related Program(s)
University of Nebraska 4th and R St, Lincoln, NE 68588	GPA: 3.6 SAT (ERW): 550-650 SAT (M): 560-670 ACT (C): 22-28 ED: No, Priority: Yes	Admit Rate: 78% Undergrad Enrollment: 20,286 Total Enrollment: 25,108	BS, MS, Ph.D. Agricultural Eng, Architectural Eng, Bio Systems Eng, Chemical Eng, Civil Eng, Comp Eng, Comp Sci, Construction Eng & Mgmt, Data Sci, Electrical Eng, Environmental Eng, Mechanical Eng, Software Eng
The Ohio State University 1849 Cannon Drive, Columbus, OH 43210	GPA: N/A SAT (ERW): 640-710 SAT (M): 670-770 ACT (C): 29-32 ED: No, EA: Yes	Admit Rate: 53% Undergrad Enrollment: 46,123 Total Enrollment: 60,540	BS, BS/MS, MS, Ph.D. Aerosp Eng, BME, Chemical Eng, Civil Eng, Computer Eng, Comp Sci, Environmental Eng, Materials Science & Eng, Mechanical Eng MS, Ph.D. Macromolecular Eng
University of Wisconsin, Madison 702 West Johnson Street, Madison, WI 53715	GPA: 3.87 SAT (ERW): 650-720 SAT (M): 700-790 ACT (C): 28-33 ED: No, EA: Yes	Admit Rate: 49% Undergrad Enrollment: 37,230 Total Enrollment: 49,886	BS, MS, Ph.D. BME, Chemical Eng, Civil Eng, EE, Enviro Eng, Ind Eng, Mat Sci & Eng, Mech Eng, MS, Ph.D. Biophysics, Cancer Bio, Cell & Molecular Path, Computational Biomed Science, Medical Physics

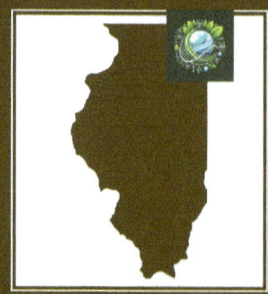

ILLINOIS

INDIANA

IOWA

KANSAS

MICHIGAN

MINNESOTA

MISSOURI

NEBRASKA

NORTH DAKOTA

OHIO

SOUTH DAKOTA

WISCONSIN

NORTHWESTERN UNIVERSITY

Address: Robert R. McCormick School of Engineering and Applied Science Technological Inst, 2145 Sheridan Road, Evanston, IL 60208
Website: https://www.mccormick.northwestern.edu/
Contact: https://www.mccormick.northwestern.edu/contact/index.html
Phone: (847) 491-5220
Email: jm-ottino@northwestern.edu

COST OF ATTENDANCE:

Tuition & Fees: $67,158 | **Addl Exp:** $24,000 | **Total:** $91,158
Financial Aid: https://www.northwestern.edu/admissions/financial-aid-offices.html

ADDITIONAL INFORMATION:

Available Degree(s)
- BS, MS, Ph.D. BME, Chemical Eng, Civil & Enviro Eng, Comp Eng, Comp Sci, EE, Materials Science Engineering, Mech Eng,
- MS Biotech & Biochem, Manuf & Design Engineering, Robotics

Related Research Areas
Argonne Inst & National Security, Atomic & Nanoscale Characterization, Bio-Inspired Energy Science, Catalysis & Surface Science, Center For Nano Oncology, Computationally-Based Imaging of Structure in Materials, Convergence Science & Medicine Institute, Hierarchical Materials Design, Inst For Bioelectronics, Inst For Bionanotechnology, Intl Inst For Nanotech, Life Processes Inst, Materials Research & Eng Ctr, Regenerative Nanomedicine Sleep & Circadian Biology, Northwestern Institute For Nanomedicine, Sustainability & Energy, Synthetic Biology

Scholarships Offered
Most families with incomes under $150,000 receive $48,328. Also, NU offers the NU Scholarship, Northwestern Endowed Scholarship, Good Neighbor, Great University, Questbridge, Founder's Scholarship, Karr Achievement Award, and Chicago Star Scholarship

Special Opportunities
The Technological Inst features 850,000 sq ft w/research facilities, labs, state-of-the-art equipment, clean rooms, robotics lab, & computer labs. NU also offers internships, summer programs, study abroad, and research seminars. Awards for distinguished work incl college honors, major-specific honors, undergrad research grants, & college awards.

Whole Brain Engineering Approach
NU Initiative for Manufacturing Science & Innovation, Design & Manuf Group, Acoustic Microscopes, CLIP 3D Printing, Cyberphysical Manuf, Design Optimization, Fiber-Optic Systems, Functional Surface Texturing, Laser Ultrasonic Systems, mHUB (Innovation center for physical product development & manufactiring) Mass Production Manufacturing, Material Design, Rapid Flexible Manufacturing, Ultrasonic Inspection Systems

Orgs: American Chemical Society, American Institute of Chemical Eng, American Society of Civil Engineers, American Society of Mechanical Engineers, Biomedical Engineering Society, Engineers for a Sustainable World, Engineers w/o Borders, Engineering World Health, Global Water Brigades, Institute of Electrical & Electronics Engineers, Institute of Industrial Engineers, Material Advantage, National Engineering Honor Society, National Society of Black Engineers, National Society of Professional Engineers, Society of Asian Scientists & Engineers, Society of Manufacturing Engineers, Society of Hispanic Professional Engineers, Society of Women Engineers, Supply Chain Management Professionals

Teams: Baja Racing Team, Chess, Computer Science Team, Concrete Canoe, Consulting Competitions, Cubesat Team, Cubing (Rubik's Cube) Cybersecurity Boot Camp, Design for America, Design Competitions, eSports, Mock Trial, Model United Nations, NU Formula Racing, NUSolar Car, Quiz Bowl, Robotics Team, Rocket Team, Science Olympiad, Speech & Debate, Steel Bridge Team, Wildhacks Hackathon

Notable Alumni
Pulickel Ajayan, Deborah Asnis, Cora Brewster, Robert Buethe, Kathryn Bullock, George Crane, Sugun Dawodu, Cheddi Jagan, JacSue Kehoe, Marc Kirschner, Kermit Krantz, Vid Latham, Charles Mayo, Roswell Park, Joseph Rall, Ida Roby, Joan Sherman, Thomas Starzl, Debi Thomas

UNIVERSITY OF ILLINOIS URBANA-CHAMPAIGN

Address: The Grainger College of Engineering, University of Illinois, 306 Engineering Hall MC 266, 1308 West Green Street, Urbana, IL 61801
Website: https://grainger.illinois.edu/
Contact: https://www.admissions.illinois.edu/request-more
Phone: (217) 333-2280
Email: engineering@illinois.edu

COST OF ATTENDANCE:
Tuition & Fees: $22,904 (in-state), $44,664 (out-of-state)
Addl Exp: $20,000 | **Total:** $42,904 (in-state), $64,664 (out-of-state)
Financial Aid: https://admissions.illinois.edu/Invest/financial-aid

ADDITIONAL INFORMATION:

Available Degree(s)
- BS, MS, Ph.D. Agricultural & Biological Engineering, Chemical & Biomolecular Eng, Civil & Environmental Eng, Computer Eng, EE, Industrial & Systems Eng, Materials Science & Engineering, Mechanical Eng, Nuclear, Plasma, & Radiological Engineering
- Minors: Bioeng, Computational Science & Eng, Computer Science, Electrical & Computer Eng, International Minor in Eng, Materials Science & Eng, Physics, Technology & Management

Related Research Centers
Advanced Materials & Eval Lab, AI for Future Resilience, Management, & Sustainability Institute, Human-Centered Design, Institute for Carbon-Neutral Energy Research (improve energy efficiency w/solid oxide fuel cells, polymer membrane-based fuel cells, biomimetic fuels), Materials Research Lab, Institute for Sustainability, Energy, & Environment, Materials Research Science & Engineering Center, Molecular Maker Lab, Nanotechnology Lab, Power Optimization of Electro-Thermal Systems

Scholarships Offered
Applicants are automatically considered for merit-based scholarships. The supplemental form for need-based scholarships may be found at https://secure.osfa.illinois.edu/scholarshipsupp/ Note: 70% of UIUC undergraduates receive aid. Graduate student scholarships, assistantships, hourly positions, eng school opportunities, and loans.

Special Opportunities
K-12 programs include WYSE, I-STEM, and Engineering Ambassadors, internships & co-ops starting the summer of your freshman year.

The College partners with Zhejiang University (ZJU) Campus.

UIUC offers cutting-edge resources, facilities, like the Engineering Library & Idea Lab, Innovation Studio, & MakerLab, & spec. courses, research project, & a joint minor w/the Gies College of Business. UIUC also offers the City Scholars program, study abroad in 50+ countries. Machine Shop: Fab, Precision Machining, Strain Gaging & Load Cells

Orgs: American Chemical Society, American Institute of Chemical Eng, American Society of Civil Engineers, American Soc of Mechanical Eng, ARISE, AWARE, Biomedical Engineering Society, Engineers w/o Borders, Engineering Council, Green Observer, Institute of Electrical & Electronics Eng, Material Advantage, National Society of Black Engineers, National Society of Professional Engineers, Society of Asian Scientists & Eng, Society of Hispanic Professional Engineers, Soc of Women Engineers, Students for Sustainability & the Environment, Women in Engineering

Teams: Chem-E Car Team, Click Beetle Robotics, Eco-Illini Supermileage, eSports Team, EV Concept Car Team, Formula Electric Motorsports, HackIllinois, iGEM (International Genetically Engineered Machines), Illini EV Concept Team, Math Contests, Mock Trial, Midwest Robotics Design Competition, Model United Nations, Off-road Illini, Shell EcoMarathon Americas, Robobrawl (iRobotics Competition) , Solar Car Competition Team, Speech & Debate, contests open to all students.

Notable Alumni
Marc Andreessen, John Bardeen, Arnold Beckman, Eric Bina, Steve Chen, James DeLaurier, Robert Holly, Fazlur Khan, Edwin Krebs, Ray Ozzie, John Roger, D. Sangeeta, H. Gene Slottow, & Kevin Warwick

- ILLINOIS
- INDIANA
- IOWA
- KANSAS
- MICHIGAN
- MINNESOTA
- MISSOURI
- NEBRASKA
- NORTH DAKOTA
- OHIO
- SOUTH DAKOTA
- WISCONSIN

MIDWEST

- ILLINOIS
- **INDIANA**
- IOWA
- KANSAS
- MICHIGAN
- MINNESOTA
- MISSOURI
- NEBRASKA
- NORTH DAKOTA
- OHIO
- SOUTH DAKOTA
- WISCONSIN

PURDUE UNIVERSITY

Address: Purdue University, Neil Armstrong Hall of Engineering, Room 1085, 701 W. Stadium Ave., West Lafayette, IN 47907-2045
Website: https://engineering.purdue.edu/Engr
Contact: https://engineering.purdue.edu/Engr/AboutUs/contact_us
Phone: (765) 494-3975
Email: future-engineers@purdue.edu

COST OF ATTENDANCE:

Tuition & Fees: $12,042 (in-state), $30,844 (out-of-state)
Addl Exp: $20,000 | **Total:** $32,042 (in-state), $50,844 (out-of-state)

Financial Aid: https://www.purdue.edu/dfa/

ADDITIONAL INFORMATION:

Available Degree(s)

- BS, MS, Ph.D. Aeronautic & Astronautic Eng, Agricultural Eng, Biomedical Eng, Bio Eng, Chemical Eng, Civil Eng, Computer Eng, Electrical Eng, Environmental & Ecological Eng, Industrial Eng, Materials Science & Eng, Mechanical Eng, Nuclear Eng
- Humanitarian Eng Conc; Minor in Sustainable Engineering

Related Research Areas
Aviation Sustainability Center, Center for Integrated Systems in Aerospace, Composites Manufacturing & Simulation Center, Consortium on Lyophilization/Freeze-Drying, Flight Dynamics & Control/Hybrid Systems Lab, Institute for Advanced Composites Manufacturing Innovation, Institute for Global Security & Defense Innovation, Value Through Reliability, Safety, & Sustainability

Focus Areas: Aerodynamics, Aerospace Systems Design, Air Traffic Control, Astrodynamics & Space Apps, Autonomy & Control, Cyber-Physical Sys, Multiple Vehicle Sys, Propulsion, Structures & Materials

Scholarships Offered
College of Engineering awards $3.8 million in undergraduate scholarships yearly in addition to institutional and private options.

Special Opportunities
First-Year Eng Prog; Grand Challenges in Aviation & Transportation Tech; internships w/airline industry partners, Project Bloom, Study Abroad, Facilities: Birck Nanotech Ctr (BNC), Bowen Lab, & FlexLab Summer Undergrad Research Fellowship, INSPIRE Research Institute/Pre-College Eng, co-op programs like EPICS, service-learning design; students partner with community orgs; internships available

Orgs: ABE Ambassadors, American Chemical Society, American Institute of Chemical Engineers, Boiler Green Initiative, Biomedical Engineering Society, Engineers w/o Borders, Environmental Science Club, Institute of Electrical & Electronics Engineers, Material Advantage, Nanotechnology Student Advisory Council, Society of Asian Scientists & Eng, Society of Automotive Engineers, Society of Environmental & Ecological Eng, Society of Women Engineers, Sustainability Council

Teams: Aerial Robotics, Algorithmic Prog, Autonomous Motorsports & UAV Team, Boiler Game Mine, Business Case Competitions, Chem-E Car Chess, Concrete Canoe, Cubesat, Cyber Defense, Cyber Security Team, Data Analytics Competition, eSports, Formula SAE & Baja SAE Electric/Solar Car Racing, iGEM (Intl Genetically Engineered Mach), Lunabotics, Mock Trial, Model United Nations, NASA Student Launch, National Marine Energy Collegiate Competition, Purdue Hackers Hack Nights, Quiz Bowl Team, Remotely Operated Underwater Vehicle Team, Rube Goldberg Machine Contest, Rubik's Cube Competitions, Science Olympiad, Speech & Debate Team, TechCrunch Disrupt's Startup Battlefield Business Model Competition, Steel Bridge Team

Notable Alumni
Sue Abreu, Neil Armstrong, Mohammed Atalla, Gregory Ayers, Don Berlin, John Blaha, Stephen Bechtel Jr, Roy Bridges, Mark Brown, John Casper, Eugene Cernan, Roger Chaffee, Paul Cloyd, Richard Covey, Gus Grissom, Guy Gruters, Loral O'Hara, Gary Payton, Mark Polansky, "Sully" Sullenberger, III, Scott Tingle, Janice Voss

UNIVERSITY OF NOTRE DAME

Address: University of Notre Dame, College of Engineering, 257 Fitzpatrick Hall of Engineering, Notre Dame, IN 46556
Website: *https://engineering.nd.edu*
Contact: *https://admissions.nd.edu/visit-engage/request-information/*
Phone: (574) 631-5530
Email: engineer@nd.edu

COST OF ATTENDANCE:
Tuition & Fees: $65,025 | **Addl Exp:** $22,000 | **Total:** $87,025
Financial Aid: https://financialaid.nd.edu/

ADDITIONAL INFORMATION:
Available Degree(s)
- BS, BS/MS, MS, Ph.D. Aerospace Engineering, Chemical Eng, Civil Eng, Computer Engineering, Computer Science, Electrical Engineering, Environmental Engineering, Mechanical Eng
- Ph.D. Bioengineering, Materials Science & Engineering
- Minors: Bioengineering, Computational Eng, Energy Eng, Energy Studies, Eng Corporate Practice, Environmental Earth Sciences, Resiliency & Sustainability of Engineering Systems

Related Research Areas
Aero-Optics Core Facility, Aerospace Research Laboratory, Center for Environmental Science & Technology, Center for Research Computing, Chemical Synthesis & Drug Discovery, Chemical Nitrogen Core, Computer-Aided Molecular Design, Environmental Research Center, Flow Cytometry, Genomics & Bioinformatics Core, Helium Recovery & Liquefaction, Integrated Imaging, Magnetic Resonance Research Center, Mass Spectrometry & Proteomics, Nanofabrication, Nitrogen Core, Molecular Science & Engineering, Multidisciplinary Engineering Research, Radiation Lab/Glassblowing, Turbomachinery Lab

Scholarships Offered
Notre Dame Scholars Program ($25,000/year merit$ for 20 students), Hesburgh-Yusko Scholars Program (350 student scholarships), Notre Dame Stamps Scholarship (full tuition + $12,000 additional money)

Special Opportunities
Community Based Courses, DISC (Dinners for Increased Scholarly Communication), DNA Learning Ctr, Edison Lecture Series, Eng Innovation Hub, Grand Challenges Scholars Program, Integrated Eng & Business Practices Program, Opportunities for K-12 Students/Teachers, *Scientia* (Research Journal), Study Abroad Dublin, Spain, Egypt, Mexico, Chile, London, & Australia, Summer Camps, Google-Sponsored Cybersecurity Carnival (games, contests, prizes)

Orgs: American Chemical Society, American Institute of Aeronautics & Astronautics, American Institute of Chemical Engineers, American Society of Civil Engineers, American Society of Mechanical Engineers, CS for Good, Engineers w/o Borders, Inst of Electrical & Electronics Engineers, E-NABLE ND (biodesign, prosthetics, & assistive tech), Global Medical Brigades, National Society of Black Eng, Society of Hispanic Professional Engineers, NDSeed (empowering rural communities), Society of Women Engineers, Women in Engineering

Teams: Baja SAE Racing Team, ChemE Car, Chess, Concrete Canoe, Cyber Threat Competition Team, Cybersecurity Festival, Debate, Design/Build/Fly Team, eSports, FIRST Robotics, ND Hackathons, Hybrid Electric Car, Hydroplane Team, Innovative Robotics & Interactive Systems, Irish Cubesat, I-Robotics Team, Lego Robotics Team, Mock Trial, Model United Nations, Student Research Challenge (Dronehook - won 2021), Quiz Bowl, Robotic Football Club, Rocketry Team (NASA Student Launch Competition), Science Olympiad Team, Solar Car Team, Steel Bridge Team, Unmanned Aerial Vehicle Team (AUVSI SUAS Mission Team)

Notable Alumni
Joseph Ahearn, Kevin Ford, Michael Good, John Goodwine, Annette Hasbrook, John Henebry, Thomas McMurtry, Dava Newman, Donald Rice, Charles Tucker, Jr., Douglas Vakoch, and Jim Wetherbee

ILLINOIS
INDIANA
IOWA
KANSAS
MICHIGAN
MINNESOTA
MISSOURI
NEBRASKA
NORTH DAKOTA
OHIO
SOUTH DAKOTA
WISCONSIN

MIDWEST

ILLINOIS

INDIANA

IOWA

KANSAS

MICHIGAN

MINNESOTA

MISSOURI

NEBRASKA

NORTH DAKOTA

OHIO

SOUTH DAKOTA

WISCONSIN

IOWA STATE UNIVERSITY

Address: Iowa State College of Engineering, 4100 Marston Hall, 533 Morrill Road, Ames, IA 50011-2103
Website: https://www.engineering.iastate.edu/
Contact: https://www.engineering.iastate.edu/why-iowa-state-engineering/contact-us/
Phone: (515) 294-7186
Email: engineer@iastate.edu

COST OF ATTENDANCE:

Tuition & Fees: $13,000 (in-state), $34,000 (out-of-state)
Addl Exp: $18,000 | **Total:** $31,000 (in-state), $52,000 (out-of-state)

Financial Aid: https://www.financial aid.iastate.edu

ADDITIONAL INFORMATION:

Available Degree(s)
- BS, MS, MEng, Ph.D. Aerospace Engineering, Biomedical Eng, Civil Engineering, Computer Engineering, Computer Science, Environmental Eng, Materials Science & Eng, Mechanical Eng
- MEng Engineering Management
- MS. Ph.D. Environmental Sci, Renewable Resources & Tech
- BS, MS, MEng, and Ph.D. Civil Engineering
- Minors Sustainability, Wind Energy Science, Eng & Policy

Related Research Centers
Advanced Imaging & Noninvasive Operations Ultrasound, Ames Laboratory, Analog & Mixed-Signal VLSI Design Center, Dependable Computing & Networking, Developmental Robotics Lab, Digital Forensics Lab, Distributed Sensing & Decision Making, Electric Power Research Center, Embedded Systems Lab, High-Speed Systems Eng, iCube Sensors, Info Assurance Center, Internet-Scale Event & Attack Generation Environment, Magnetics Research, Microelectronics Research Center, Micro/Nano Systems, Plasmonics & Microphotonics (Biophotonics), Power Infrastructure Cyber Security Lab, Power Systems Eng, Reconfigurable Computing, RF/Microwave Circuits & Systems, Scalable Software Eng, Software Defined Radio Laboratory, Virtual Reality Applications Center, & Wind Energy Systems

Scholarships Offered
Merit scholarships of $2,600/year (in-state), $5,250/year (out-of-state); Kiewit Scholars Program (design & construction engineering); FIRST team member scholarships $1,000; 85% of Iowa State students receive financial aid

Special Opportunities
Ten labs with state-of-the-art equipment including PCB Printer, 3D printers, A/V equipment, laser cutters, mills, lathes, chromatography, electron microscope, tube furnace, vacuums

Co-ops, internships, and career support through Engineering Career Services (ECS); study abroad May in Japan, break in Sydney, semester programs worldwide with engineering classes

Orgs: 4-H, American Institute of Aeronautics & Astronautics, Amer Inst of Chemical Engineers, Amer Soc of Civil Engineers, American Society of Mechanical Engineers, FBLA, Girls Who Compete, IEEE, Material Advantage, Society of Women Engineers, SolidWorks/CAD Club, Transportation Student Association, Wind Energy Student Org

Teams: Cardinal Space Mining, Concrete Canoe Team, Cyclone Rocketry, Design-Build-Fly, Hackathons, Horizon Builders, ISU Robotics, Make-to-Innovate, Power Pullers, Rocketry, SAE International Vehicle Team, Solar Car Team, Steel Bridge Team

Notable Alumni
Clayton Anderson, Dale Anderson, F. Ronald Bailey, Stephen Bales, Arthur Bryson, Jr., Leroy Cain, Vance Coffman, Maj. Gen. Clinton Crosier, Roger Hanson, Prabhat Hajela, Phil Jasper, James Johnson, Sadanand Joshi, Neil Kacena, David Klinger, Paul Kutler, Jang-Moo Lee, Firouz Naderi, Ron Narmi, Kim Pastega, Kevin Petersen, Bion Pierson, Vijaya Shankar, Joseph Steger, John Tannehill, Robert Uhrig, Thornton Wilson, & Donald Young

UNIVERSITY OF IOWA

Address: University of Iowa, Admissions, 2900 University Capitol Centre, Iowa City, IA 52242
Website: *https://admissions.uiowa.edu/academics/engr-comp*
Contact: *https://www.maui.uiowa.edu/maui/pub/admissions/webinquiry/undergraduate.page*
Phone: (319) 335-3500
Email: admissions@uiowa.edu

COST OF ATTENDANCE:

Tuition & Fees: $11,300 (in-state), $34,000 (out-of-state)
Addl Exp: $18,000 | **Total:** $29,300 (in-state), $52,000 (out-of-state)

Financial Aid: https://financialaid.uiowa.edu/

ADDITIONAL INFORMATION:

Available Degree(s)
- BS, MS, MEng, Ph.D. Biomedical Engineering, Chemical Eng, Civil Engineering, Computer Engineering, Computer Science, Electrical Eng, Environmental Engineering, Environmental Policy & Planning, Environmental Science, Geography, Geoscience, Industrial & Systems Engineering, Informatics, Mechanical Eng, Naval Science & Technology, Neuroscience, Nuclear Medicine Technology, Sustainability Science
- Certificate: Artificial Intelligence, Modeling, & Simulation, Entrepreneurial Mgmt, Sustainability, Tech Entrepreneurship

Related Research Centers
Combustion & High-Speed Fluid Mechanics Lab, Ctr for Biocatalysis, Ctr for Bioinformatics & Computational Bio, Ctr for Global & Regional Environmental Research, Center for Health Effects of Environmental Contamination, Ctr for Hydrologic Development, Driving Safety Res Inst, Enviro Health Sci Res Ctr, Genetic Testing Lab, Hydroscience & Eng, IA Geological Survey, IA Initiative for Artificial Intelligence, IA, Init for Biomedical Imaging, IA Flood Ctr, IA Superfund Res Prog, IA Tech Inst, Nanoscience & Nanotechnology Institute, NSF Center for Environmentally Beneficial Catalysis, Occupational Health & Safety

Scholarships Offered
Scholarship offered through the University of Iowa Scholarship Portal, Honors at Iowa link and admissions. Additional competitive scholarships for first-year students to the College of Engineering. Continuing scholarships are also available through merit awards, departmental awards, and need-based awards

Special Opportunities
Lichtenberger Engineering Library, Engineering Career Services, Student Ambassadors, Engineering Visit Day, Involvement & Resources Fair, Trash Crawl, Iowa Engineer Magazine

Orgs: 3D Design Club, Amateur Radio Club, American Institute of Aeronautics & Astronautics, American Institute for Chemical Engineers, American Society of Civil Engineers, American Society of Mechanical Engineers, American Wind Energy Association, Association for Computing Machinery, Biomedical Engineering Society, Earth & Environmental Science Club, Earth Day, Environmental Coalition, Environmental Law Society, Society of Automotive Engineers, Society of Hispanic Professional Engineers, Society of Women Engineers, Women in Computing Sciences

Teams: Bass Fishing Team, BrainHack, Debate Club, Iowa Formula Racing Team, Mock Trial, Model United Nations, Robotics at Iowa, Society of Automotive Eng Baja Racing Team, Scooter Team

Notable Alumni
Hind Al-Abadleh, Archie Alexander, M.M. Ayoub, Alfred Bailey, Theodore Bauer, Mark Boyd, Shirley Briggs, James Cartwright, James Dooge, Mildred Fenton, James Hansen, Silas Hays, Bruce Heezen, Chuck Homer, Marshall Kay, Tom Krimigis, Gregor Luthe, Charles Lynch, Clair Patterson, Richard Schnieders, C. Maxwell Stanley, James Van Allen, Pramod Wangikar, Hugh Wild

ILLINOIS

INDIANA

IOWA

KANSAS

MICHIGAN

MINNESOTA

MISSOURI

NEBRASKA

NORTH DAKOTA

OHIO

SOUTH DAKOTA

WISCONSIN

MIDWEST

ILLINOIS

INDIANA

IOWA

KANSAS

MICHIGAN

MINNESOTA

MISSOURI

NEBRASKA

NORTH DAKOTA

OHIO

SOUTH DAKOTA

WISCONSIN

MICHIGAN STATE UNIVERSITY

Address: Engineering Bldg, 428 S. Shaw Lane, East Lansing, MI 48824
Website: *https://www.egr.msu.edu/*
Contact: *https://www.egr.msu.edu/contact-engineering*
Phone: (517) 355-5113
Email: https://www.egr.msu.edu/contact-engineering

COST OF ATTENDANCE:

Tuition & Fees: $16,844 (in-state), $44,151 (out-of-state)
Addl Exp: $19,000 | **Total:** $35,844 (in-state), $63,151 (out-of-state)
Financial Aid: https://finaid.msu.edu/

ADDITIONAL INFORMATION:

Available Degree(s)
- BS Applied Engineering Science
- BS, BS/MS, MS, Ph.D. Biosystems Engineering, Chemical Eng, Civil Eng, Computational Data Sc, Computer Engineering, Computer Science, Electrical Engineers, Environmental Eng, Materials Science & Engineering, Mechanical Engineering
- MS, Ph.D. Biomedical Engineering
- Concentrations: Global Engineering

Related Research Areas
Automotive Research Experiment Station, BEACON Center for the Study of Evolution in Action, Center for Anti-Counterfeiting & Product Protection, Composite Materials & Structures Center, Connected & Autonomous Networked Vehicles, Fraunhofer Center for Coatings & Diamond Technologies, Geotechnical Engineering, Great Lakes Bioenergy Research Center, Hydrology Systems, Industrial Assessment Center, National Center for Pavement Preservation, Quantitative Health Sciences & Engineering, Structural Engineering, Sustainability Modeling, Transportation Engineering, Water Quality Engineering

Scholarships Offered
MSU Spartan Advantage Program, MSU Student Aid Grant; Eng Scholarships are offered with no additional application required. Students receive notice during the first two weeks of April. MSU College of Engineering offers 300+ scholarships to undergraduate students each year, and numerous graduate scholarships.

Special Opportunities
CoRe Experience – Integrated first-year living-learning engineering academic program (tutoring, peer mentors, professional & recreational field trips, evening presentations, projects, and service opportunities; Engineering Abroad and Future Engineers programs

Global Core - Information & Communication Tech for Development (applying ICT in developing countries with a field experience

Orgs: Amateur Radio Club, American Chemical Society, American Institute of Aeronautics & Astronautics, Amer Institute of Chemical Engineers, American Society of Civil Eng, Amer Society of Mechanical Engineering, Artificial Intelligence Club, Association for Computing Machinery, Audio Enthusiasts & Eng, Biosystems Eng Club, Canvas Soar, Eng Student Council, Engineers for a Sustainable World, Eng w/ Borders, Env Eng Student Society, Inst of Electrical & Electronics Engineers, iOS Club, Leadership Advantage, Material Advantage, MSE Society, National Soc of Black Eng, Science Theatre, Soc of Applied Eng Science, Society of Asian Scientists & Eng, Society of Automotive Eng, Society of Hispanic Prof Eng, Society of Women Eng, Strength Augmenting Robotic eXoskeleton (STARX), Women in Computing

Teams: Baja Racing, Chem-E Car Team, Chess, Concrete Canoe Team, Cubing, Debate Team, FIRST Robotics, Formula Racing, Hackathon, iGEM (Intl Genetically Engineered Machine) Team, Mock Trial, Model United Nations, Rocketry Team, Solar Car Team, SpartaHack, Spartan Aerosystems Team, Spartan Hackers, Steel Bridge Competition Team, Unmanned Systems Team, VEX Robotics

Notable Alumni
Louis Carpenter, Rolla Carpenter, Larry Dalton, Don Jones, Daniel Mindiola, Adrian Ponce, and Ellen Williams

MICHIGAN TECHNOLOGICAL UNIVERSITY

Address: Michigan Technological University,1400 Townsend Drive, Houghton, MI, 49931
Website: https://www.mtu.edu
Contact: https://www.mtu.edu/engineering/about/contact/
Phone: (906) 487-2005
Email: engineering@mtu.edu

COST OF ATTENDANCE:
Tuition & Fees: $18,392 (in-state), $41,433 (out-of-state) |
Addl Exp: $19,000 | **Total:** $37,392 (in-state), $60,433 (out-of-state)
Financial Aid: https://www.mtu.edu/finaid/

ADDITIONAL INFORMATION:

Available Degree(s)
- BS, MS, Ph.D. Biomedical Engineering, Chemical Eng, Civil, Environmental, & Geospatial Engineering, Electrical & Computer Engineering, Geological & Mining Engineering, Manufacturing & Mechanical Engineering, Materials Science & Engineering, Mechanical Eng, Engineering Mechanics

Related Research Areas
Earth, Planetary & Space Science Institute, Ecosystems Science Center, Aerospace Engineering Research Center, Institute of Computing & Cybersystems, Transportation Institute, Health Research Institute, Institute of Materials Processing, Advanced Power Systems Research Center

Scholarships Offered
Students receive generous financial aid offers. Automatic consideration scholarships are available for MI & non-MI residents. Addl scholarships available with a separate application including sponsored scholarships, FIRST scholarships, and service scholarships

Orgs: Airsoft Association, American Indian Science & Engineering Soc, American Institute of Aeronautics & Astronautics, American Institute of Chemical Eng, American Institute of Professional Geologists, American Institute of Steel Construction, ASL Club, American Soc for Engineering Management, American Society of Civil Engineers, American Society of Mechanical Engineers, Arctic Rangers, Arnold Air Society, Association of Students for People, Environment, & Nature, Astronomy Club, Audio Engineering Society, Automotive Enthusiasts, Biochemistry Club, Bioinformatics & Computational Biology, Biomedical Engineering Society, Engineering Ambassadors, Engineers w/o Borders, Geology Club, Human Factors & Ergonomics Society, Institute of Electrical & Electronics, Institute of Transportation Engineers, IPC & Electronics Students, Material Advantage, Materials United, Medlife, Mind Trekkers, National Society of Black Engineers, Optics & Photonics Society, Plant & Gardening Club, Railroad Engineering Club, Smithing Guild, Society for Environmental Engineers, Society for Mining, Metallurgy & Exploration, Society for Technical Communication, Society of American Foresters, Society of Asian Scientists & Engineers, Society of Automotive Engineering, Society of Hispanic Professional Engineers, Society of Manufacturing Engineers, Society of Wetland Science, Society of Women Engineers, Wetland Fire Club, Wildlife Society, Women in Computer Science, Women in Natural Resources

Teams: Aero Design (SAE), Blizzard Baja SAE Team, Chess, DECA, Concrete Canoe Team, Copper Country Robotics, Cubesat Launch Team, CyberCorps, CyberHusky, Cyber Defense Team, D&D, Drone Team, Formula SAE Team, Four Wheelers, Hackathons, Log Rolling, Makers Guild, Model United Nations, Pokemon League, Quiz Bowl, Red Team, Rifle Team, Robot 101 Team, Rocket League, SAE Aero Team, Spacecraft Team, Steel Bridge Team

Notable Alumni
Markus Buehler, Melvin Calvin, David Edwards, Charles Gates, John Hallquist, William Hammack, David Hill, David House, Samson Jenekhe, Martin Lagina, Sarah Rajala, Bhakta Rath, Kanwal Rekhi, Donald Saari, Matthew Songer, Marek Urban

ILLINOIS

INDIANA

IOWA

KANSAS

MICHIGAN

MINNESOTA

MISSOURI

NEBRASKA

NORTH DAKOTA

OHIO

SOUTH DAKOTA

WISCONSIN

MIDWEST

UNIVERSITY OF MICHIGAN

Address: Michigan Engineering, 1221 Beal Ave. Ann Arbor, MI 48109
Website: https://www.engin.umich.edu/
Contact: https://www.engin.umich.edu/about/contact-us/
Phone: (734) 647-7000
Email: engin-info@umich.edu

COST OF ATTENDANCE:

Tuition & Fees: $29,904 (in-state), $57,273 (out-of-state)
Addl Exp: $19,000 | **Total:** $48,904 (in-state), $76,273 (out-of-state)

Financial Aid: https://finaid.umich.edu/

ADDITIONAL INFORMATION:

Available Degree(s)
- BS, BS/MS, MS, Ph.D. Aerospace Eng, Biomedical Engineering, Chemical Engineering, Civil Eng, Climate & Meteorology, Computer Engineering, Computer Science, Data Sci, Electrical Eng, Engineering Physics, Environmental Eng, Industrial & Operations Eng, Materials Science & Engineering, Mechanical Eng, Naval Architecture & Marine Engineering, Nuclear Eng & Radiological Sciences, Robotics, Space Sciences & Engineering

Related Research Areas
Aerodynamics & Propulsion, Autonomous Systems & Control, Autonomous Aerospace Systems Lab, Computational Aerosciences Lab, Plasmadynamics & Electric Propulsion Lab, UM Geophysical Union, Solar Orbiter, Solar & Heliospheric Physics, Solar Probe, Space Instrumentation, Space Systems, Structures & Materials

Scholarships Offered
International Student Scholarships, Merit & Need-Based Scholarships, Study Abroad Scholarship; Approximately 70% of UMich students receive some aid; Ph.D. students receive full funding, which includes a tuition waiver, monthly living stipend, and health insurance

Special Opportunities
Labs & Facilities: Biological Station, Biophysics NMR Center, DNA Sequencing Core Facility, Genomic Diversity Lab, Sustainability, Herbarium, Life Science Inst, Molecular, Cellular, & Developmental Bio Imaging Labs, Molecular Bioscience Core, Scientific Instrument Shop, Single Molecule Analysis in Real-Time Center

Orgs: American Chemical Society, American Institute of Aeronautics & Astronautics, American Institute of Chemical Engineers, Bio-Tech, Entrepreneurship, & Coding Organization, Audio Engineering Society, Biomedical Engineering Society, Blockchain at Michigan, Climate Blue, Eng Elementary Partnerships, Engaging Scientists in Policy & Advocacy, eTrek, FAMNM, Girls Teaching Girls to Code, Genes in Diseases & Systems, Institute of Electrical and Electronics Engineers, INvent, Material Advantage, MECC Consulting, MedLaunch, M-Fab, Michigan Transportation Student Organization, National Org for Business & Eng, National Society of Black Eng, Pre-Med Hub, Society of Women Engineers, Sling Health, Soc of Hispanic Prof Eng, Students for the Exploration & Development of Space, Women in Computing

Teams: Aerial Vehicles, Aerospace Vehicle, Amer Solar Challenge, Autonomous Robotic Vehicles, Baja SAE Racing, Concrete Canoe, Cyber Defense Network Competition Team, Debate Team, Drone Racing Team, Electric Boat Team, Electric Jetski Team, eSports, Formula SAE Electric Car Racing, Green Team, HackBlue, Human-Powered Submarine, Intl Aerial Robotics, iGEM (Intl Genetically Eng Machines), NASA Rocket Launching, MESI Environmental Project Team, M-Fly, M-HEAL, Mars Rover, MHacks, Mock Trial, Model United Nations, Quiz Bowl, Rainworks Challenge, RoboSub, Rubik's Cube, Science Olympiad, Steel Bridge, Vertical Flight Competition Team

Notable Alumni
Frances Allen, Benjamin Bailey, Aisha Bowe, Robert Cailliau, Willian Crossley, Paul Debevec, Tess Hatch, Barbara Johnston, Thomas Knoll, Anne Marinan, Matthew McKeown, Larry Page, Dan Patt, Steve Sandoval, Claude Shannon, Tia Sutton, & Niklas Zennström

- ILLINOIS
- INDIANA
- IOWA
- KANSAS
- **MICHIGAN**
- MINNESOTA
- MISSOURI
- NEBRASKA
- NORTH DAKOTA
- OHIO
- SOUTH DAKOTA
- WISCONSIN

UNIVERSITY OF MINNESOTA, TWIN CITIES

Address: The University of Minnesota, College of Science and Engineering, 117 Pleasant St, Minneapolis MN 55455
Website: *https://cse.umn.edu/*
Contact: *https://cse.umn.edu/college/cse-directories*
Phone: (612) 624-2006
Email: cseinfo@umn.edu

COST OF ATTENDANCE:
Tuition & Fees: $17,190 (in-state), $37,802 (out-of-state)
Addl Exp: $22,000 | **Total:** $39,190 (in-state), $59,802 (out-of-state)
Financial Aid: https://admissions.tc.umn.edu/cost-aid/financial-aid

ADDITIONAL INFORMATION:
Available Degree(s)
- BS, MS, Ph.D. Aerospace Eng, Biomedical Eng, Bioproducts & Biosystems Eng, Chemical Eng, Civil Eng, Computer Eng, Computer Science, Environmental Engineering, Food Science, Geo-Engineering, Industrial & Systems Engineering, Materials Science & Engineering, Mechanical Engineering
- MS, Ph.D. Medicinal Chemistry, Molecular Pharmacology, Nuclear Engineering, Pharmaceutics, Pharmacy

Related Research Centers
BioTechnology Institute, Ctr for Compact & Efficient Fluid Power, Earthquake Engineering Simulation, Catalyst Design Interfacial & Materials Engineering, Energy Science, Institute for Engineering in Medicine, Medical Devices Center, Microfluidic Systems, Robotics Institute, Nanoporous Materials Genome Center, Nanotechnology, Spintronic Materials, Interfaces & Novel Architectures, Plastic Electronics, Renewable Energy, Security, Sustainable Polymers

Scholarships Offered
$50 million awarded in university-wide & major-specific scholarships to freshman each year; no additional form is required for academic scholarships; scholarship opportunities exist for undocumented and international students; 77% of UM students receive some aid.

Special Opportunities
Study Abroad, Volunteer Opp; Internships, Co-ops, Career Services, Summer Camps, Outreach, & K-12 Enrichment Programs

Machine shop with fabrication labs, on-site inspection, SolidWorks Computer-Aided Design, Helium leak detector, silver soldering, stainless steel welding, prototype repair equipment; CAD modeling available materials include aluminum, brass, copper, stainless steel, & miscellaneous engineering plastics. Earthquake Simulation Center, Nanotech Lab, First-in-the-World Ultrafast Electron Microscope

Orgs: American Chemical Society, Amer Indian Sci & Eng Soc, Amer Inst of Aeronautics & Astronautics, American Institute of Chemical Eng, Amer Public Works Assn, American Society of Agricultural & Biological Eng, American Society of Civil Eng, American Society of Mechanical Eng, Amer Society of Heating Refrigeration & AC, Assoc of Computing Machinery, AWM, Biomedical Engineering Soc, Institute of Electrical & Electronics Eng, Institute of Industrial & Systems Engineers, Material Advantage, Nat Soc of Black Eng, oSTEM, Soc for Mining, Metallurgy & Exploration, Society of Asian Scientists & Eng, Society of Hispanic Prof Eng, Soc for Industrial & Applied Math, Society of Women Engineers

Teams: Baja SAE, Bladesmithing Team, Chem-E Car Team, Chess, Collegiate Drone Sports, Concrete Canoe, eSports, Forensics, Gopher Motorsports, iGEM Team, MinneHack, Minn Electric Racing, Mock Trial, Model United Nations, Quiz Bowl, Robotics, Rocketry, Sales Team Championship, Steel Bridge, Solar Vehicle Project

Notable Alumni
J. Edward Anderson, John Barry, Lloyd Berkner, Satish Dhawan, John Eastwood, Robert Gore, Sanjay Mittal, George Prudden, Avtar Saini, Bill Smith, William Stout, and Clarence Syvertson

ILLINOIS
INDIANA
IOWA
KANSAS
MICHIGAN
MINNESOTA
MISSOURI
NEBRASKA
NORTH DAKOTA
OHIO
SOUTH DAKOTA
WISCONSIN

MIDWEST

UNIVERSITY OF NEBRASKA

Address: University of Nebraska, College of Engineering, 114 Othmer Hall/820 N 16th St., P.O. Box 880642, Lincoln, Nebraska 68588-0642
Website: https://engineering.unl.edu/
Contact: http://engineering.unl.edu/about-coe-faculty-staff-contacts/
Phone: (402) 472-3181
Email: engfrontdesk2@unl.edu

COST OF ATTENDANCE:
Tuition & Fees: $10,434 (in-state), $28,584 (out-of-state)
Addl Exp: $22,000 | **Total:** $32,434 (in-state), $50,574 (out-of-state)

Financial Aid: https://financialaid.unl.edu/

ADDITIONAL INFORMATION:
Available Degree(s)
- BS, MS, Ph.D. Agricultural Eng, Architectural Eng, Biological Systems Engineering, Chemical Engineering, Civil Engineering, Computer Eng, Computer Science, Construction Eng, Electrical Eng, Environmental Eng, Mechanical Eng, Software Engineering

Related Research Areas
Center for Biotechnology, Center for Materials & Nanoscience, Energy Science Research Center, Food Processing Center, Industrial Agricultural Products Research Center, Industrial Assessment Center, Innovation Campus, Manufacturing Extension Partnership

Scholarships Offered
UN gives $900,000 in scholarships to first-year and returning students including Kiewit Scholars Program. Submit a scholarship statement - https://admissions.unl.edu/cost/scholarship-statement. Each dept w/i the College of Engineering awards scholarships. The Nebraska Promise states that families w/incomes less than $65,000 may attend tuition free. Numerous graduate fellowships & grants also available.

Special Opportunities
Co-ops, assistantships, Engineering Abroad programs; Peter Kiewit Foundation Engineering Academy, Engineering Readiness Academy, Holland Computer Lab, Multicultural Engineering Program, Women in Engineering Program. Summer/semester internships. Employment includes companies like Archer Daniels Midland, ConAgra, CNH, John Deere, Caterpillar, AGCO, Behlen, USDA, Kawasaki

Design/Fabrication Lab, Holland Computer Center, Nano-Engineering Research Core Facility, Nebraska Innovation Studio, Tractor Test Lab, Transportation Center, UNL Research Core Facilities, Water Sciences Lab

E-Day - Incredible Edible Car Competition for freshmen

CubeSat NASA SpaceX "Cargo Dragon" (sent in space March 25,2024) UNL Big Red Satellite Team
A mentoring program w/the Nebraska Water Environment Association & Nebraska Section American Water Works Association; state-of-the-art surveying and geometric labs; CAD engineering analysis/design; and environmental, geotechnical, structural, hydraulic, water resources and transportation engineering.

Orgs: American Society of Agricultural & Biological Eng, American Society of Civil Eng, American Society of Mechanical Eng, Biomedical Eng Society, Eng w/o Borders, Institute of Transportation Engineers, Inst of Electrical & Electronics Eng, Mechanized Systems Management Club, National Society of Black Eng, Society of Hispanic Professional Eng, Society of Women Engineers, Soil & Water Resources Club, Water Environment Federation, Water Works Assn, Women in Computing

Teams: AEI Competition, Big Red Satellite Team, Chem-E Car Team, Chess Team, Construction Race to Build Competition, CubeSat, Cubing (Rubik's Cube), Debate Team, Engineering Pitch Competition, Ethics in Engineering Team, Fountain Wars Competition Team, Model United Nations, Scale Tractor Team, TEAMS, VEX Robotics Team

Notable Alumni
Bion Arnold, Kay Brummond, Raychelle Burks, Donald Cox, Gladys Dick, Jay Forrester, Charles Purcell, Herbert Webber, Gerald Weinberg, and Evan Williams

ILLINOIS
INDIANA
IOWA
KANSAS
MICHIGAN
MINNESOTA
MISSOURI
NEBRASKA
NORTH DAKOTA
OHIO
SOUTH DAKOTA
WISCONSIN

THE OHIO STATE UNIVERSITY

Address: The Ohio State College of Engineering, 122 Hitchcock Hall, 2070 Neil Ave., Columbus, OH 43210
Website: https://engineering.osu.edu/
Contact: https://engineering.osu.edu/about-college/contacts
Phone: (614) 292-2836
Email: howard.1727@osu.edu

COST OF ATTENDANCE:
Tuition & Fees: $12,859 (in-state), $38,029 (out-of-state)
Addl Exp: $19,000 | **Total:** $31,859 (in-state), $57,029 (out-of-state)
Financial Aid: http://undergrad.osu.edu/cost-and-aid/financial-aid

ADDITIONAL INFORMATION:

Available Degree(s)
- BS, BS/MS, MS, Ph.D. Aerospace Eng, Biochem, BME, Chem, Chem Eng, Civil Eng, Comp Eng, Comp Sci, Electrical Eng, Enviro Eng, Geodetic Eng, Materials Science & Eng, Mech Eng
- Ph.D. Macromolec Eng, Bioethics & Medical Humanities
- Minor in Humanitarian Engineering

Related Research Centers
Accel Maturation of Materials, Advanced Materials & Manufacturing, Aerospace, Aeronautical, & Astronautical, Climate, Energy, & the Environment, Computational Mechanics, Corrosion Ctr, Cosmology & Astroparticle Research, Ergonomics, Gas Dynamics & Turbulence, Gas Turbine Lab, Gear & Power Transmission, Mapping & GIS, Mechatronic/Electromechanical Systems, Occupational Health in Automotive Manufacturing, Polar & Climate Research, Propulsion & Power Center, Satellite Positioning & Inertial Navigation, Simulation Innovation & Modeling, Smart Vehicle Concepts Center, Space Geodesy & Remote Sensing, Spatial & Environmental Statistics, Transportation for Tomorrow's Economy, Turbulence & Combustion Research

Scholarships Offered
Approx 30 scholarships for STEM students w/specialized scholarships for minorities and women in engineering. Study abroad scholarships. Summer Research Fellowships. Approx. 45% of students receive aid.

Special Opportunities
Co-op & internship opps; Buckeye Engineering Career Services (ECS). About 75% of engineering students participate in a co-op or internship before they graduate. OSU selected for multimillion dollar NASA-funded effort to develop commercial human-occupied space stations

Students have access to state-of-the-art facilities: the Scott Lab 080, the Honda Interdisciplinary Lab, a 24-hour lab, corporate partnerships, and Capstone projects. Students may participate in the student-driven Humanitarian Engineering Innovation Lab to research, design, and solve community problems. Specialized initiatives to collaborate on projects in Japan and Tanzania.

Orgs: Amer Chemical Soc, Amer Inst of Aeronautics & Astronautics, Amer Inst of Chemical Eng, Amer Society of Civil Eng, Amer Society of Mechanical Eng, Assoc of Computing Machinery, Biomedical Eng Society, Institute of Electrical & Electronics Eng, Institute of Industrial & Systems Engineers, Material Advantage, National Society of Black Engineers, Society of Asian Scientists & Engineers, Soc of Hispanic Professional Eng, Soc of Women Engineers, Women in Computing

Teams: BajaSAE, Buckeye Solar Racing, Buckeye Space Launch Init, Buckeye Vertical, Chem-E Car, Code 4, Competitive Programming Team, Concrete Canoe, Cyber Security, Design/Build/Fly, EcoCAR Challenge Team, FIRST Robotics, Formula SAE, Maker Club, Science Olympics, Steel Bridge, Tractor Design, Underwater Robotics Team

Notable Alumni
Charles Bassett, Jacqueline Chen, Anjan Contactor, Nancy Currie, Kristen Hammer, Lara Harrington, Christopher Hirata, Robert Lawrence, Jr., Richard Linnehan, Maria Martinez, Ralph Mershon, Margaret Mkhosi, Curtis Moody, Jeff Morosky, Russell Newhouse, Jackie O'Brien, Bob Patel, Ronald Sega, Michael Snyder

ILLINOIS
INDIANA
IOWA
KANSAS
MICHIGAN
MINNESOTA
MISSOURI
NEBRASKA
NORTH DAKOTA
OHIO
SOUTH DAKOTA
WISCONSIN

MIDWEST

ILLINOIS

INDIANA

IOWA

KANSAS

MICHIGAN

MINNESOTA

MISSOURI

NEBRASKA

NORTH DAKOTA

OHIO

SOUTH DAKOTA

WISCONSIN

UNIVERSITY OF WISCONSIN, MADISON

Address: University of Wisconsin-Madison, Department of Engineering, 1415 Engineering Drive, Madison, WI 53706
Website: https://engineering.wisc.edu/
Contact: https://directory.engr.wisc.edu/services/staff/
Phone: (608) 262-3471
Email: contact-us@engr.wisc.edu

COST OF ATTENDANCE:

Tuition & Fees: $12,782 (in-state), $43,270 (out-of-state)
Addl Exp: $19,000 | **Total:** $31,782 (in-state), $62,270 (out-of-state)
Financial Aid: https://financialaid.wisc.edu/

ADDITIONAL INFORMATION:

Available Degree(s)
- BS, MS, Ph.D. Biomedical Engineering, Chemical Eng, Civil Engineering, Computer Eng, Computer Science, Electrical Eng, Environmental Engineering, Geological Eng, Industrial Engineering, Materials Science & Eng, Mechanical Eng
- Certificates: Eng Energy Sustainability, Eng Thermal Energy Systems, Intl Eng, Manufacturing Eng, Nuclear Eng Materials

Related Research Areas
Biomanufacturing, Biomaterials, Biomechanics, Bio-Mechatronics, Engine Research Consortium, Fusion Technology Institute, Health Systems, Immunology, Machine Learning, Nuclear Energy Systems, Neuroengineering, Pathology, Plasma Lab, Power Systems Eng Research Center, Regenerative Medicine, Solid & Hazardous Waste Ed Center, Traffic Operations, Transportation Info Ctr, Water Science & Eng, Wisconsin Electric Machines & Power Electronics Consortium

Scholarships Offered
Engineering Freshman Award, Departmental Scholarships, LEED Scholars Program, Scholarships for Cont Students, STAR Scholarship Program. More via login on the Wisconsin Scholarship Hub (WiSH). Half of the freshman class receives ave aid pkg of approx $16,000.

Special Opportunities
Grainger Institute for Engineering (Incubator for transdisciplinary research), Engineering Student Council, Great Lakes Observing Sys

Facilities: Microelectronics, Nano-Fabrication, Electron Microscopy, Micro-Analysis, Soft Materials Characterization

Orgs: Amateur Radio Society, American Chemical Society, American Institute of Aeronautics & Astronautics, Amer Institute of Chemical Engineers, American Society of Civil Engineers, American Society of Mechanical Engineers, American Society of Heating, Refrigerating & Air-Conditioning Engineers, Association of Computing Machinery, Biomedical Engineering Society, Construction Club, Business & Entrepreneurship, Engineers for a Sustainable World, Environmental Engineering Club, Institute of Electrical & Electronics Eng, Institute of Industrial & Systems Engineering, Insight Washington, Material Advantage, Material Ethics Club, National Society of Black Engineers, Railroad Society, Society of Automotive Engineers, Society of Hispanic Professional Engineers, Society of Women Engineers, Transcend Engineering, *Wisconsin Engineer Magazine*, Women in Computing

Teams: Autonomous Self-Driving Vehicle Team, BadgerHacks, BadgerLoop (pseudo-startup setting), Baja SAE Team, Chess Team, Clean Snowmobile IC & ZE – SAE, Concrete Canoe Team, Collegiate Cyber Defense Team, Electric Vehicle Team, Formula SAE Team, Human-Powered Vehicle, iGEM (International Genetically Engineered Machine), Makerspace - Drones/UAVs, Mock Trial, Model United Nations, NASA Cubesat Team, Robotics Team, Rubik's Cube Team, Science Olympiad, Space Race, Steel Bridge Team, WiscWind (wind-driven power systems for off-grid applications)

Notable Alumni
Robert Bird, Gunter Blobel, William Campbell, Laurel Clark, Michael Dhuey, Louis Friedman, Herbert Gasser, David Geiger, Eric Green, Karl Link, Parry Moon, Newton Morton, Erwin Neher, Richard Rhode, Joseph Sackett, Edward Tatum, Samuel Wonders

ALABAMA

ARKANSAS

DELAWARE

DISTRICT OF COLUMBIA

FLORIDA

GEORGIA

KENTUCKY

LOUISIANA

MARYLAND

MISSISSIPPI

NORTH CAROLINA

OKLAHOMA

SOUTH CAROLINA

TENNESSEE

TEXAS

VIRGINIA

WEST VIRGINIA

CHAPTER 13

REGION THREE
SOUTH

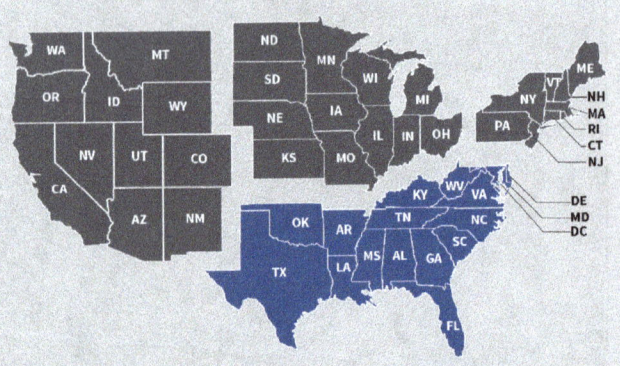

16 Programs | 16 States

1. FL - Florida International University
2. FL - University of Florida, Gainesville
3. GA - Georgia Institute of Technology
4. GA - University of Georgia
5. LA - Louisiana State University
6. MD - Johns Hopkins University
7. MD - University of Maryland, College Park
8. NC - Duke University
9. NC - North Carolina State University
10. SC - Clemson University
11. TN - Vanderbilt University
12. TX - Southern Methodist University
13. TX - Texas A&M University
14. TX - The University of Texas at Austin (UT Austin)
15. VA - University of Virginia
16. VA - Virginia Polytechnic Institute and State University (Virginia Tech)

ENVIRONMENTAL ENGINEERING & ALTERNATIVE ENERGY PROGRAMS

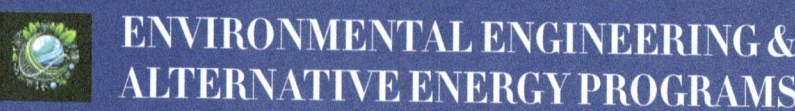

School	Avg. GPA, SAT ERW, SAT Math (M), and ACT Composite (C) Early Decision (ED)	Admissions Statistics	Related Program(s)
Florida International University 11200 SW 8th St Miami, FL 33199	GPA: 3.9 SAT (ERW): 530-610 SAT (M): 530-640 ACT (C): 21-26 ED: No, EA: No, Rolling: Yes	Admit Rate: 64% Undergrad Enrollment: 44,045 Total Enrollment: 54,085	BS, BS/MS, MS, Ph.D. Biomedical Engineering, Civil Eng, Computer Engineering, Computer Science, Construction Mgmt, Electrical Eng, Environmental Engineering, Enterprise & Logistics Eng, Information Science, Materials Eng, Mechanical Engineering
University of Central Florida 4000 Central Florida Boulevard, Orlando, FL, 32816	GPA: 4.18 SAT (ERW): 610-680 SAT (M): 580-670 ACT (C): 25-29 ED: No, EA: No, Rolling: Yes	Admit Rate: 41% Undergraduate Enrollment: 59,548 Total Enrollment: 68,842	BS, MS, Ph.D. Aerospace Eng, Biomedical Eng, Civil Engineering, Computer Eng, Computer Science, Construction Eng, Electrical Engineering, Environmental Eng, Industrial Eng, Information Technology, Materials Science & Engineering, Mechanical Engineering
Georgia Tech Georgia Tech, North Ave NW, Atlanta, GA 30332	GPA: 4.09 SAT (ERW): 670-760 SAT (M): 700-790 ACT (C): 31-35 ED: No, EA: Yes	Admit Rate: 14% Undergrad Enrollment: 18,415 Total Enrollment: 45,296	BS, BS/MS, MS, Ph.D. Aerospace Eng, Biomedical Eng, Chemical Engineering, Civil Engineering, Computer Eng, Computer Science, Electrical Engineering, Environmental Eng, Global Eng, Materials Science & Engineering, Mechanical Eng & Mechanics, Nuclear & Radiological Eng
University of Georgia Dawson Hall, 305 Sanford Dr., Athens, GA 30602	GPA: 4.02 SAT (ERW): 620-710 SAT (M): 600-710 ACT (C): 27-32 ED: No, EA Yes	Admit Rate: 48% Undergrad Enrollment: 29,765 Total Enrollment: 39,147	BS, MS, Ph.D. Agricultural Eng, Biochemical Eng, Biological Eng, Civil Engineering, Computer Eng, Electrical Eng, Environmental Engineering, Materials Science & Engineering, Mechanical Eng, MS Cybersecurity & Privacy
Louisiana State University A&M Baton Rouge, LA 70803	GPA: 3,81 SAT (ERW): 590-670 SAT (M): 560-660 ACT (C): 24-29 ED: No, EA: No, Rolling: Yes	Admit Rate: 74% Undergrad Enrollment: 32,574 Total Enrollment: 39,418	BS, MS, Ph.D. Biomedical Eng, Chem Eng, Civil Eng, Comp Eng, Electrical Eng, Environmental Eng, Mech Eng, Petroleum Eng Ph.D. Bioengineering, Syst Eng Concentration: Smart Oil Fields Minors: Bioprocess Engineering, Environmental Eng, Materials Eng, Tech Commercialization

ENVIRONMENTAL ENGINEERING & ALTERNATIVE ENERGY PROGRAMS

School	Avg. GPA, SAT ERW, SAT Math (M), and ACT Composite (C) Early Decision (ED)	Admissions Statistics	Related Program(s)
Johns Hopkins University 3400 N. Charles St., Mason Hall, Baltimore, MD 21218-2683	GPA: 3.9 SAT (ERW): 750-770 SAT (M): 770-800 ACT (C): 34-35 ED: Yes, EA: No	Admit Rate: 4.6% Undergrad Enrollment: 6,331 Total Enrollment: 28,890	BS/MS, MS, Ph.D. Biomedical Eng, Chemical & Biomolecular Eng, Civil Eng, Computer Eng, Computer Science, Electrical Engineering, Environmental Eng, Materials Science & Engineering, Mechanical Eng, Systems Eng
University of Maryland, College Park 7999 Regents Dr., College Park, MD 20742	GPA: 4.34 SAT (ERW): 670-740 SAT (M): 690-780 ACT (C): 30-34 ED: No, EA: Yes	Admit Rate: 44% Undergrad Enrollment: 30,922 Total Enrollment: 41,272	BS/MS, MS, Ph.D. Aerospace Eng, Bioengineering, Chemical Eng, Civil Eng, Computer Engineering, Computer Science, Cyber-Physical Systems Engineering, Electrical Eng, Environmental Engineering, Materials Science & Engineering, Mechanical Eng
Duke University Duke University, Durham, NC 27708	GPA: N/A SAT (ERW): 720-770 SAT (M): 750-800 ACT (C): 34-35 ED: Yes, EA: No	Admit Rate: 5.1% Undergrad Enrollment: 6,948 Total Enrollment: 16,518	BS, BS/MS, MS, Ph.D. BME, Civil Eng, Comp Eng, Comp Sci, EE, Environmental Eng, Mech Eng MS, Ph.D. Materials Sci & Eng Minors: Machine Learning & Artificial Intelligence, Electrical & Computer Eng, Energy Eng
North Carolina State University (NC State) 50 Pullen Road, Raleigh, NC 27695	GPA: 3.8 SAT (ERW): 620-710 SAT (M): 630 740 ACT (C): 25-31 ED: No, EA: Yes	Admit Rate: 46% Undergrad Enrollment: 26,254 Total Enrollment: 36,700	BS, MS, Ph.D. Aerospace Eng, Agricultural Eng, Biological Eng, Biomedical, Chemical Eng, Civil Eng, Computer Eng, Computer Science, Electrical Eng, Enviro Eng, Materials Science & Eng, Mech Eng, Paper Sci, Textile Eng
Clemson University 101 Calhoun Dr, Clemson, SC 29634	GPA: 4.39 SAT (ERW): 620-700 SAT (M): 610-720 ACT (C): 28-32 ED: No, EA: Yes	Admit Rate: 43% Undergrad Enrollment: 22,566 Total Enrollment: 28,466	BS, MS, Ph.D. Automotive Eng, Biol Eng, Biomedical Data & Info, Biosystems Eng, Chemical Eng, Civil Eng, Comp Eng, Computer Sci, EE, Env Eng, Hydrogeology, Ind Eng, Materials Science & Eng, Mech Eng, Photonics Science

SOUTH

ENVIRONMENTAL ENGINEERING & ALTERNATIVE ENERGY PROGRAMS

School	Avg. GPA, SAT ERW, SAT Math (M), and ACT Composite (C) Early Decision (ED)	Admissions Statistics	Related Program(s)
Vanderbilt University 2305 West End Avenue Nashville, TN 37203	GPA: 3.86 SAT (ERW): 720-770 SAT (M): 750-800 ACT (C): 33-35 ED: Yes, EA: No	Admit Rate: 5.1% Undergrad Enrollment: 7,152 Total Enrollment: 13,456	BS, MS, Ph.D. Biomedical Eng, Chemical & Biomolecular Eng, Civil Engineering, Computer Engineering, Computer Science, Electrical Eng, Engineering Management, Environmental Eng, Materials Science & Eng, Mechanical Engineering
Southern Methodist University (SMU) 6425 Boaz Lane, Dallas, TX 75205	GPA: 3.64 SAT (ERW): 660-730 SAT (M): 660-750 ACT (C): 30-34 ED: Yes, EA: Yes	Admit Rate: 53% Undergrad Enrollment: 7,115 Total Enrollment: 11,842	BS, BS/MS, MS, Ph.D. Civil Eng, Computer Engineering, Computer Science, Data Science, Electrical Eng, Environmental Engineering, Mechanical Eng, Operations Research, Management Science MS Cybersecurity, Data Eng, Info Engineering & Management, Network Engineering, Software Engineering, Systems Engineering
Texas A&M University 400 Bizzell St, College Station, TX 77843	GPA: N/A SAT (ERW): 580-690 SAT (M): 580-800 ACT (C): 26-32 ED: No, EA: No	Admit Rate: 63% Undergrad Enrollment: 57,512 Total Enrollment: 74,014	BS, MS, Ph.D. Aerospace Eng, Architectural Eng, Biomedical Eng, Civil Eng, Computer Eng, Computer Science, Electrical Eng, Environmental Eng, GeoSystems & Hydrogeology, Materials Sci, Mechanical Eng, Petroleum Eng
The University of Texas at Austin (UT Austin) 310 Inner Campus Drive, Austin, TX 78712	GPA: N/A SAT (ERW): 660-740 SAT (M): 650-760 ACT (C): 29-34 ED: No, EA: No	Admit Rate: 31% Undergrad Enrollment: 41,309 Total Enrollment: 52,384	BS, MS, Ph.D. Aerosp Eng, Arch Eng, Biomedical Eng, Civil Eng, Computer Eng, Computer Sci, Electrical Eng, Environmental Eng, GeoSystems Engineering & Hydrogeology, Materials Science & Eng, Mechanical Engineering, Petroleum Engineering
University of Virginia Charlottesville VA, 22904	GPA: N/A SAT (ERW): 690-750 SAT (M): 710-790 ACT (C): 32-35 ED: Yes, EA: Yes	Admit Rate: 16.5% Undergrad Enrollment: 16,793 Total Enrollment: 23,721	BS, MS, Ph.D. Aerospace Eng, Biomedical Engineering, Civil Engineering, Computer Eng, Computer Science, Electrical Engineering, Environmental Engineering, Materials Science & Engineering, Mechanical Eng, Systems Engineering

ENVIRONMENTAL ENGINEERING & ALTERNATIVE ENERGY PROGRAMS

School	Avg. GPA, SAT ERW, SAT Math (M), and ACT Composite (C) Early Decision (ED)	Admissions Statistics	Related Program(s)
Virginia Tech 1325 Perry Street, Blacksburg, VA 24061	GPA: 3.96 SAT (ERW): 600-700 SAT (M): 620-720 ACT (C): 26-32 ED: No, EA: Yes	Admit Rate: 57% Undergrad Enrollment: 30,434 Total Enrollment: 38,170	BS, MS, MEng, Ph.D. Aerospace Engineering, Biomedical Eng, Civil Eng, Computer Engineering, Computer Science, Electrical Eng, Engineering Mechanics, Materials Science & Engineering, Mechanical Engineering, Meteorology, Ocean Engineering

SOUTH

ALABAMA
ARKANSAS
DELAWARE
DISTRICT OF COLUMBIA
FLORIDA
GEORGIA
KENTUCKY
LOUISIANA
MARYLAND
MISSISSIPPI
NORTH CAROLINA
OKLAHOMA
SOUTH CAROLINA
TENNESSEE
TEXAS
VIRGINIA
WEST VIRGINIA

FLORIDA INTERNATIONAL UNIVERSITY

Address: FIU, The Engineering Center, 10555 West Flagler St, Miami, FL 33174
Website: *https://cec.fiu.edu/*
Contact: *https://www.fiu.edu/about/contact-us/index.html*
Phone: (305) 348-2522

COST OF ATTENDANCE:

Tuition & Fees: $6,566 (in-state), $18,964 (out-of-state)
Addl Exp: $20,000 | **Total:** $26,566 (in-state), $38,964 (out-of-state)
Financial Aid: https://onestop.fiu.edu/finances/estimate-your-costs/

ADDITIONAL INFORMATION:

Available Degree(s)
- BS, BS/MS, MS, Ph.D. BME, Civil Eng, Computer Engineering, Computer Science, Construction Management, Electrical Eng, Environmental Eng, Enterprise & Logistics Eng, Information Science, Materials Engineering, and Mechanical Engineering

Related Research Areas
Accelerated Bridge Construction, Advanced Materials Engineering Research Institute, Advanced Self-Power Systems of Integrated Sensors & Tech, Applied Research Center, Center for Adv Technology & Education, Center for Aquatic Chem & the Environment, Center for Personalized NanoMedicine, Center for the Study of Matter at Extreme Conditions, Energy-Efficient Electronics Science, High-Perf Database Res Ctr, Industry Cooperative Res Ctr for Adv Knowledge Enablement, Nanosystems Eng Research Ctr, Telecommunications & Information Technology Institute, Transportation Research Center, Wall of Wind (Smart Structures, Wind Eng, Smart Cities - NSF WOW Natural Hazards Engineering Research Infrastructure Program)

Scholarships Offered
All domestic applicants a considered for scholarship. Average need based financial aid $9,811.

Special Opportunities
6% students in engineering, 37 majors/deg (in Civil & Environmental Eng, 1,000+ undergraduates, 150+ grad students, 80+ doctoral stud), 10 fully online degree programs in eng, 5% out of state, 96% Intl Retention Rate, housing available, 124 tenure-track faculty, 40 patents, $62M in research grants, 26 NSF early career awards, 19 continuing education courses, internships, senior design projects, Alternative Breaks (civic/social engagement) new engineering building development, FIU student paper chosen as Best Paper Award by Elsevier *Engineering Structures Journal*.

Orgs: American Society for Engineering Management, American Inst for Aeronautics & Astronautics, American Society of Civil Engineers, Amer Society of Mechanical Eng, Amer Academy of Environmental Engineers & Scientists, American Concrete Institute, Association for Information Systems, Biomedical Engineering Society, Chemical Society, Civil Eng Honor Society, Code Culture, Developer Student Club, Eco Eng Club, ECO Influencers Biz Club, Engineers w/o Borders, Geology Club, Global Brigades, Green Campus Initiative, Green Energy Society, Institute for Electrical & Electronics Engineers, Institute of Transportation Engineers, Material Advantage, National Society of Black Engineers, Structural Engineering Institute, Society of Hispanic Professional Engineers, Society of Manufacturing Engineers, Society of Women Engineers, Student Association for Wind Engineering, Students for the Exploration & Development of Space, Sustainable Panther Network, Water Environment Federation, Women in Computer Science, Women in CyberSecurity, Women's Transportation Seminar

Teams: AI & Coding Club/Teams, Concrete Canoe Team, Chess, Cubesat, eSports Teams, Cyber Defense Team, Formula SAE/Panther Motorsport, Mock Trial, Panther Gaming, Robotics Team, Spaceport America Cub (SEDS Rocket Competition Team), Steel Bridge Team,

Notable Alumni
Edith Kellnhauser, Elsa Murano, James O'Brien, Carmen Reinhart, David Shor, Bertha Vazquez

UNIVERSITY OF FLORIDA GAINESVILLE

Address: University of Florida, Herbert Wertheim College of Engineering, 300 Weil Hall, 1949 Stadium Road, P.O. Box 116550, Gainesville, FLA 32611-6550
Website: *https://www.eng.ufl.edu/*
Contact: *https://www.eng.ufl.edu/about/contact/*
Phone: (352) 392-0944
Email: info@eng.ufl.edu

COST OF ATTENDANCE:
Tuition & Fees: $6,380 (in-state), $28,658 (out-of-state)
Addl Exp: $15,050 | **Total:** $21,430 (in-state), $43,708 (out-of-state)
Financial Aid: https://www.sfa.ufl.edu/?p=home

ADDITIONAL INFORMATION:
Available Degree(s)
- BS, BS/MS, MS, Ph.D. Aerospace Eng, Biomedical Eng, Civil Eng, Computer Engineering, Computer Science. Electrical Eng, Environmental Engineering, Materials Science & Engineering, Mechanical Eng, Ocean Engineering, Systems Engineering

Related Research Areas
Advanced Computing & Information Systems Lab, Center for Space High-Performance & Resilient Computing, Forida Institute for Cybersecurity Research, Florida Institute for National Security, FL Semiconductor Inst, Institute for the Connected World, Institute for High Energy Physics & Astrophysics, Internet of Things for Precision Agriculture Research Center, Multi-Functional Integrated System Technology, Nanoscience Institute for Medical & Eng Technology

Scholarships Offered
Bright Futures Scholarship, Florida Assistance Grant, UF Grant, First-Gen Matching Grant

Approximately 90% of incoming freshmen receive aid; grants are awarded for those in need; merit scholarships available; academic scholarships are awarded by academic achievement.

Special Opportunities
Study abroad. State-of-the-art facilities include a Biotech lab, prototyping labs, and a global teleconferencing laboratory.

Orgs: American Chemical Society, American Institute of Chemical Engineers, American Society of Civil Engineers, American Society of Mechanical Engineers, Association for Computing Machinery, Biomedical Engineering Society, Engineers w/o Borders, Game Developers' Association, Institute of Electrical and Electronics Engineers, Material Advantage, National Soc of Black Engineers, Packaging Club, Power & Energy Club, Society of Asian Scientists & Eng, Society of Automotive Engineers, Society for Environmental Engineers, Society of Hispanic Professional Engineers, Society of Women Engineers, Students for the Exploration & Development of Space, Theme Park Engineering & Design Organization

Teams: Aggregator Team, Autonomous Maritime System (RobotX Challenge), Battlebots Team, Ceramic Mug Drop Design Team, Chess Club, Concrete Canoe, Concrete Design Team, Cyber Defense Team, Design-Build-Fly Team, Electric Racing/Motorsports Team, Formula SAE Race Car Team, Human-Powered Vehicle Design Team (recumbent bike competition), iGEM Team (Intl Genetically Eng Machine), Info Security Team, Liquid Propulsion Devt Team, Mock Trial, Model United Nations, Quiz Bowl, Roaring Riptide Robotics, Robotics, Rubik's Cube, Science Olympiad, Solar Gator Formula Sun Grand Prix Team, Space Systems Design Team, Speech & Debate, Steel Bridge Team, Swamp Launch Rocket Team, VexU Robotics

Notable Alumni
Andrew Allen, John Anderson, Brian Caffo, Amitava Chattopadhyay, Jack Clemons, Jonathan Earle, William Fisher, Kevin Ford, Fitzhugh Fulton, Ronald Garan, Jesse Garrett, Herbert Gursky, Pramod Khargonekar, Donald Mallick, Bill Nelson, Ronald Parise, Anil Rajvanshi, Michael Reynolds, Lesa Roe, Norman Thagard, and James Thompson

ALABAMA
ARKANSAS
DELAWARE
DISTRICT OF COLUMBIA
FLORIDA
GEORGIA
KENTUCKY
LOUISIANA
MARYLAND
MISSISSIPPI
NORTH CAROLINA
OKLAHOMA
SOUTH CAROLINA
TENNESSEE
TEXAS
VIRGINIA
WEST VIRGINIA

SOUTH

- ALABAMA
- ARKANSAS
- DELAWARE
- DISTRICT OF COLUMBIA
- FLORIDA
- GEORGIA
- KENTUCKY
- LOUISIANA
- MARYLAND
- MISSISSIPPI
- NORTH CAROLINA
- OKLAHOMA
- SOUTH CAROLINA
- TENNESSEE
- TEXAS
- VIRGINIA
- WEST VIRGINIA

GEORGIA TECH

Address: College of Engineering Dean's Office, 225 North Avenue, 3rd Floor Tech Tower, Atlanta, GA 30332-0360
Website: https://coe.gatech.edu/
Contact: https://coe.gatech.edu/about/find-college-engineering
Phone: (404) 894-3350
Email: rbeyah@coe.gatech.edu

COST OF ATTENDANCE

Tuition & Fees: $11,764 (in-state) $32,875 (out-of-state)
Addl Exp: $19,000 | **Total:** $30,764 (in-state) $51,875 (out-of-state)
Financial Aid: http://finaid.gatech.edu/

ADDITIONAL INFORMATION:

Available Degree(s)

- BS, MS, Ph.D. Aerospace Eng, BME, Civil Eng, Computer Eng, Comp Sci, EE, Enviro Eng, Global Eng, Materials Science & Eng, Mechanical Eng & Mechanics, Nuclear & Radiological Eng
- Ph.D. Machine Learning
- Minors in Aerospace Eng, BME, Global Eng Leadership, Eng & Business, Nuclear & Radiological Engineering

Related Research Areas

Aerodynamics & Fluid Mechanics, Aeroelasticity & Structural Dynamics, Ctr for Chemical Evolution, Flight Mechanics & Controls, Relativistic Astrophysics, Radiation Effects on Volatiles & Exploration of Asteroids & Lunar Surfaces, Sustainable Systems, Manufacturing Institute, Institute for Materials, People & Technology, Propulsion & Combustion, Robotics & Intelligent Machines, Space Technology, Graphics, Visualization, & Usability Center, Science & Technology of Advanced Materials & Interfaces, Strategic Energy Institute, Structural Mechanics & Materials, & Systems Design & Optimization

Scholarships Offered

Georgia Tech awards $105+ million in need & merit-based aid to undergrads; 66% rec aid w/an average financial aid pkg of $20,131. The Provost Scholarship awards 40 1st-year, non-resident students an out-of-state tuition waiver for 8 sem. Georgia Tech's 4-year, full-ride Stamps President's Scholarship - top 1% of 1st-year stud. The Gold Scholarship - top 2% of 1st-year students. Also, many in-state students are eligible for the Hope & Zell Miller merit scholarships.

Special Opportunities

Georgia Tech's Co-op Program is a five-year, academic program w/ paid practical work experience. GT's Internship Program provides "real world" applications. Georgia Tech also has a campus in France.

Orgs: Amer Inst of Aeronautics & Astronautics, Amer Soc of Civil Eng, American Society of Mechanical Engineers, American Society of Highway Engineers, Assoc for Computing Machinery, Association of Environmental Engineers and Scientists, Construction Engineering Association, Earthquake Engineering Research Institute, Engineers for a Sustainable World, Engineers w/o Borders, Geotechnical Society, Inst of Electrical & Electronics Eng, Inst of Transportation Engineers, Material Advantage, Students for the Expl & Development of Space, Water Environment Fed, Women's Transportation Seminar

Teams: ASME-CIE Hackathon, Chem-E Car Team, Cubesat, Cyber Ops Hackathon, Debate Team, HyTech Racing (Formula SAE), EcoCAR (EcoCAR Mobility Challenge), eSports, iGEM (International Genetically Engineered Machines), Mock Trial Team, MUN, Motorsports Racing Team, Nat Security Innovation Network's Visualization (top team), Off-Road (Baja SAE), Robotics (7 world competitions), Rubik's Cube, Solar Car Racing, Wreck Racing (Grassroots Motorsports Challenge)

Notable Alumni

Eric Boe, Michael Clifford, Jan Davis, James Deese, Ben Epps, Gabriel Georgiades, Charlie Hillard, Scott Horowitz, Ellis Johnson, Susan Kilrain, Robert Kimbrough, Charles Kohlhase, Timothy Kopra, Sandra Magnus, William McArthur, Yvonne Pendleton, Alan Poindexter, James Thompson Jr, Joe Thompson, Richard Truly

UNIVERSITY OF GEORGIA

Address: UGA College of Engineering, Driftmier Engineering Center, 597 DW Brooks Drive, Athens, GA 30602
Website: http://www.engr.uga.edu/
Contact: http://www.engr.uga.edu/contact
Phone: (866) 364-7842
Email: info@engr.uga.edu

COST OF ATTENDANCE:

Tuition & Fees: $11,680 (in-state), $31,220 (out-of-state)
Addl Exp: $18,000 | **Total:** $29,680 (in-state), $49,220 (out-of-state)

Financial Aid: https://osfa.uga.edu/

ADDITIONAL INFORMATION:

Available Degree(s)
- BS, BS/MS, MS, Ph.D. Agricultural Eng, Biochemical Eng, Biol Eng, Civil Eng, Computer Systems Eng, Comp Sci, Electrical & Electronics Eng, Environmental Eng, Mechanical Engineering
- MS Biomanufact. & Bioprocessing, Cybersecurity & Privacy
- Ph.D. Dynamic Systems & Controls, Energy Systems, Environment & Water, Fluid & Thermal Systems, Mechanics & Materials, Resilient Infrastructure Systems

Related Research Areas
Advanced Human Wellness, Center for Advanced Computer-Human Ecosystems, Center for Cyber-Physical Systems, Cognition, & Learning, Developing Advanced Material, Device, & Cyber Technologies & Tools, Engineering Education, Informatics Institute, Institute for Resilient Infrastructure Systems, New Materials Institute, Phenomics & Plant Robotics Center, Secure, Resilient, & Sustainable Systems, Transformations Institute, Virtual Reality

Scholarships Offered
The University of Georgia College of Engineering offers more than two dozen scholarships annually for undergraduate students. Research & Teaching Assistantships, College & Diversity Fellowships for graduate students.

Special Opportunities
Study Abroad, Research, Internships & Co-ops available; UGA College of Engineering's Cooperative Experiential Learning and Internship Programs; First-Year Scholars; Engineering Student Ambassadors; Senior Design Capstone

Facilities include the Design & Discovery Lab, Student Fabrication Center, Digital Prototyping Lab, Fab (machine) Shop.

Orgs: American Institute of Chemical Engineers, American Society of Agricultural & Biological Engineers, American Society of Civil Eng, American Society of Heating, Refrigeration, & Air Conditioning Eng, American Society of Mechanical Engineers, Biomedical Engineering Society, Global Engineering Club, Institute of Electrical & Electronics Engineers, National Society of Black Engineers, North American Young Generation in Nuclear, Society of Asian Scientists & Engineers, Society of Environmental Eng, Society of Hispanic Professional Eng, Society of Women Engineers, International Society for Optics & Photonics, Student Ambassadors, Student Aerospace Initiative, Society of Automotive Engineers

Teams: Baja SAE Team, Data Dawgs, Debate Team, eSports, Eventing Team, Hackathons, Human-Powered Machine Team, international Engineering Design Competition, JUMP into STEM, Mock Trial, Model United Nations, NASA Small Satellite Research Laboratory (CubeSat), Robotics Club, UGA Motorsports (Formula SAE)

Notable Alumni
Wyatt Anderson, Cornelia Bargmann, Alfred Blalock, Eugene Booth, James Boyd, A. Jamie Cuticchia, Charles Kenyon, Crawford Long, Eugene Odum, Tomlinson Fort Jr.

ALABAMA
ARKANSAS
DELAWARE
DISTRICT OF COLUMBIA
FLORIDA
GEORGIA
KENTUCKY
LOUISIANA
MARYLAND
MISSISSIPPI
NORTH CAROLINA
OKLAHOMA
SOUTH CAROLINA
TENNESSEE
TEXAS
VIRGINIA
WEST VIRGINIA

SOUTH

- ALABAMA
- ARKANSAS
- DELAWARE
- DISTRICT OF COLUMBIA
- FLORIDA
- GEORGIA
- KENTUCKY
- LOUISIANA
- MARYLAND
- MISSISSIPPI
- NORTH CAROLINA
- OKLAHOMA
- SOUTH CAROLINA
- TENNESSEE
- TEXAS
- VIRGINIA
- WEST VIRGINIA

UNIVERSITY OF LOUISIANA, LAFAYETTE

Address: College of Engineering, University of Louisiana at Lafayette, 131 Rex Street Lafayette, LA 70503
Website: https://engineering.louisiana.edu/
Contact: https://engineering.louisiana.edu/about-us/contact-us
Phone: (337) 482-6685
Email: engineering@louisiana.edu

COST OF ATTENDANCE:

Tuition & Fees: $10,346 (in-state), $38,132 (out-of-state)
Addl Exp: $18,798 | **Total:** $29,144 (in-state), $42,872 (out-of-state)

Financial Aid: https://financialaid.louisiana.edu/

ADDITIONAL INFORMATION:

Available Degree(s)
- BS, MS Chemistry & Chemical Engineering, Civil Engineering, Computer Eng, Computer Science, Electrical Engineering, Environmental Engineering, Industrial Design, Materials Engineering, Mechanical Engineering, Petroleum Engineering
- MS Informatics
- Ph.D. Bioengineering, Systems Engineering (specialization in Petroleum Engineering) Concentration: Smart Oil Fields
- Minors: Bioprocess Engineering, Environmental Engineering, Materials Eng, Technology Commercialization, Pre-MBA

Related Research Areas
Accelerator Center, Alternative Energy, Bit Corrosion, Deep Water Development, Ecology Center, Energy, Efficiency, & the Environment, Environmental Protection, Fracking Technology, Horizontal Wells, Critical Infrastructure & Cybersecurity, Low-Permeability Reservoirs, Multi-Lateral Wells, Petroleum Data Tech Consortium, Reservoir Characterization, Sustainable Energy, Synthetic Oil-Based Muds, Visual Decision Informatics, Watershed Flood Center

Scholarships Offered
The Department of Engineering offers 25-35 scholarships per semester from alumni and companies like Citgo, Cabot, & Monsanto another 20+ scholarships are for Petroleum Engineering students

Special Opportunities
100% job placement for Petroleum Engineering graduates (only 14 petroleum engineering programs in the US); a few companies include Chevron, ConocoPhillips, Baker Hughes, Weatherford, Stone Energy, Petro Bras America, and Schlumberger

U.S.-Brazil Program, Apprenticeship Program, Engineering Ambassadors, Research funding available from multiple sources

Expos & Exhibits, Industry Volunteer Opportunities, State-of-the-Art Labs, Engineering Living Learning Community; E&T Expo High School Comps. Community Jobs, Co-ops, Internships through the Engineering Student Career Development Program

Poster Competition, Presentation Competition, Engineering and Technology Week

Orgs: American Association of Drilling Engineers, American Institute of Chemical Engineers, Americorps, CampusCats, Designing Leaders, Association of Computing Machinery, Engineering Ambassadors, Geaux Bike, Habitat for Humanity, Horticulture Club, Institute for Electrical & Electronics Engineers, International Association of Drilling Contractors, Louisiana Engineering Society, National Society of Black Engineers, Society of Petroleum Engineers, Society of Petrophysicists & Well Log Analysts, Society of Women Engineers, Students for Sustainability

Teams: BreakFix, CAPE Satellite Student Team, Chem-E Car Team, Concrete Canoe Team, CubeSat, eSports, Formula SAE Ragin' Cajun Racing Team, Hack-a-Thons, Moot Court, PetroBowl Competition Team, Robotics Team, Speech & Debate Team, Steel Bridge Team

Notable Alumni
Ibrahim Al-Alawi, Abdullah Al-Saadan, Albert Crews, Kowsik Guruswamy, Jay F. Honeycutt, Alex McCool, and Wilma Subra

JOHNS HOPKINS UNIVERSITY

Address: Johns Hopkins University, Whiting School of Engineering, 3400 North Charles Street Baltimore, MD 21218
Website: *https://engineering.jhu.edu/*
Contact: *https://engineering.jhu.edu/contact/*
Phone: (410) 516-4050
Email: wsecommunications@jhu.edu

COST OF ATTENDANCE:
Tuition & Fees: $63,340 | **Addl Exp:** $23,000 | **Total:** $86,340
Financial Aid: https://www.jhu.edu/admissions/financial-aid/

ADDITIONAL INFORMATION:
Available Degree(s)
- BS, BS/MS, MS, Ph.D. BME, Chemical & Biomolecular Eng, Comp Eng, Computer Science, Electrical Eng, Environmental Eng, Materials Science & Engineering, Mechanical Eng
- MS/MSE Bioengineering Innovation & Design, Technical Mgmt

Related Research Areas
Bioengineering Innovation & Design, Cardiovascular Diagnostic & Treatment Center, Computational Biology, Computational Sensing & Robotics, Engineering in Healthcare, Imaging Science, Institute for Computational Medicine, Institute for Nanobiology, Language & Speech Processing, Mammalian Biomanufacturing Innovation Center, Neuroscience Discovery Institute, Sustainable Energy Inst

Scholarships Offered
JHU meets 100% need; most grants are need-based including the Clark Scholarship & Hodson Gilliam Success Scholarship; merit-based awards including The Hodson Trust Scholarship, Charles R. Westgate Scholarship in Eng, National Fellowships Program, ROTC

Special Opportunities
Design Studios for prototyping, testing products (aesthetic, financial, material, theoretical, environmental, and practical), Design Day, Hoptoberfest, Lighting of the Quads, Research Fairs

Orgs: American Association for the Advancement of Science, Amer Chemical Society, American Institute of Chemical Engineers, Amer Physics Society, American Society for Biochemistry & Molecular Biology, American Society for Mass Spec, American Society of Civil Engineers, American Society of Mechanical Eng, Association for Computing Machinery, Biomedical Engineering Society, Biophysical Society, Civil & Systems Engineering Graduate Association, Earthquake Engineering Research Center, Engineers' Council, Engineers w/o Borders, Habitat for Humanity, Institute of Electrical & Electronics Engineers, Materials Research Society, National Society of Black Engineers, NOBCChE, OSA, oSTEM, Students for the Exploration & Development of Space, Society for Biological Engineers, Society of Hispanic Professional Engineers, Society of Women Engineers, Women in Computer Science

Teams: AstroJays, Blue Jay Racing Team, BME Healthcare Design Team, Chem-E Car Competition, Collegiate Inventors Competition, Concrete Canoe Team, Cubesat Team, Design-Build-Fly, Freshman Mechanical Engineering Design Competition, JHU Hackathons, HopHacks, Hopkins Baja SAE, HopStart Competition, Humanitarian Design Hackathon, IDIES Hackathon, IEEEXtreme Programming Competition, Information Security Inst Competition, JHU Business Plan Competition, JHU Robo Challenge, Leading Innovation Design Team, MedHacks, Mock Trial, Model United Nations, Quiz Bowl, Robotics Team, Rocketry Competition Team, Rubik's Cube, Science Olympiad, Steel Bridge Team, Sustainable Solutions Competition, Tower of Power Competition, Unmanned Aerial Vehicle Team

Notable Alumni
Peter Agre, Richard Axel, David Bredt, Jared Cohon, Paul Emmett, Joseph Erlanger, Andrew Fire, Herbert Gasser, William George, Paul Greengard, Carol Greider, Haldan Hartline, Thomas Morgan, Daniel Nathans, Nina Patel, Martin Rodbell, Francis Rous, Hamilton Smith, Morris Tanenbaum, Erika Taylor, George Whipple, and Bang Wong

ALABAMA
ARKANSAS
DELAWARE
DISTRICT OF COLUMBIA
FLORIDA
GEORGIA
KENTUCKY
LOUISIANA
MARYLAND
MISSISSIPPI
NORTH CAROLINA
OKLAHOMA
SOUTH CAROLINA
TENNESSEE
TEXAS
VIRGINIA
WEST VIRGINIA

SOUTH

UNIVERSITY OF MARYLAND, COLLEGE PARK

Address: University of Maryland, 3110 Jeong H. Kim Engineering Building, 8228 Paint Branch Dr., College Park, MD 20742
Website: https://eng.umd.edu/
Contact: https://eng.umd.edu/contact
Phone: (301) 405-8335
Email: futureengineer@umd.edu

COST OF ATTENDANCE:

Tuition & Fees: $11,505 (in-state), $40,306 (out-of-state)
Addl Exp: $19,000 | **Total:** $30,505 (in-state), $59,306 (out-of-state)

Financial Aid: https://financialaid.umd.edu/

ADDITIONAL INFORMATION:

Available Degree(s)
- BS, BS/MS, MS, Ph.D. Aerospace Eng, Chem Eng, Civil Eng, Comp Eng, Comp Sci, EE, Env Eng, Mat Sci & Eng, Mech Eng
- BS Embedded Systems & Internet of Things
- MS Fire Protection Engineering, Systems Engineering
- MS, Ph.D. Reliability Eng; MS, MEng, Ph.D. Project Mgmt

Related Research Areas
Bridge Eng Software & Tech Center, Ctr for Adv Life Cycle Eng, Ctr for Adv Transportation Tech, Ctr for Disaster Resilience, Center for Eng Concepts Dvlt, Center for Minorities in Science & Eng, Ctr for Risk & Reliability, Center for Tech & Systems Mgmt, NanoCenter, Robotics Center, Rotorcraft Inst for Systems Research, Transportation Inst

Scholarships Offered
Ave need-based scholarship - $11,838. Merit Scholarships -apply by Nov 1; Banneker/Key Scholarship – Full tuition, room/board, fees, book allowance, & admit to Honors College; President's Scholarship – 4-yr awards ($2,000 - $12,500) for in-state & out-of-state students; Dean's Scholarship ($1,500 - $4,500) only for in-state students.

Special Opportunities
Alternative Spring Break, Workshops; Keystone Program. Pre-college and K-12 programs; state-of-the-art labs & centers.

Orgs: American Institute of Aeronautics & Astronautics, American Institute of Chemical Engineers, American Helicopter Society, Amer Society of Civil Engineering, American Society of Engineers of Indian Origin, American Society of Mechanical Eng, Amer Soc of Heating, Refrigeration & AC Eng, Asian Eng Students Association, Black Eng Society, Biomedical Engineering Society, Electrochemical Society, Engineering Student Council, Eng w/o Borders, Engineering World Health, Google Developer Student Club, Institute of Electrical & Electronics Engineers, Material Advantage, Materials Engineering Society, Net Impact STEM, oSTEM, Society of Asian Scientists & Eng, Society of Automotive Engineering, Society of Fire Protection Eng, Society of Hispanic Professional Engineers, Society of Women Engineers, Students for the Exploration & Development of Space, Undergraduate Quantum Association, Women in Aeronautics & Astronautics, Women in Electrical and Computer Engineering

Teams: 5G Protocol, Autonomous Micro Air Vehicle, Bitcamp, Chem-E Car Team, Code: Black, CompuTerps, Concrete Canoe, Cybersecurity Team, Equals Hackathon, FIRST Robotics, Formula SAE Team, Game Developers Club, Hack4Impact, Helicopter Design Comp Team, Hovercraft Competition, Hyperloop Team, iGEM (Intl Genetically Eng Machines), Info Challenge Competition, Mock Trial, Model United Nations, Open Sourcery, Parliamentary Debate Soc, Racing Team, Robotics@Maryland, Robotic Exploration of Solar System (RASC-AL), Solar Decathlon, Steel Bridge, Technica, Terps Hackers, Terps Racing, Terrapins Rocket Team, WiCyS, XR Club

Notable Alumni
Richard Arnold, Frederick Billig, Sergey Brin, James Clark, Jeanette Epps, Kevin Greenaugh, Michael Griffin, Elaine Harmon, Chris Kubasik, Tobin Marks, William McCool, Aracely Quispe Neira, Judith Resnik, Paul Richards, Alex Severinsky, and Barbara Williams

- ALABAMA
- ARKANSAS
- DELAWARE
- DISTRICT OF COLUMBIA
- FLORIDA
- GEORGIA
- KENTUCKY
- LOUISIANA
- MARYLAND
- MISSISSIPPI
- NORTH CAROLINA
- OKLAHOMA
- SOUTH CAROLINA
- TENNESSEE
- TEXAS
- VIRGINIA
- WEST VIRGINIA

DUKE UNIVERSITY

Address: Pratt School of Engineering, Duke University, 305 Nello L. Teer Engineering Building, Box 90271, Durham, NC 27708-0271
Website: *https://pratt.duke.edu/*
Contact: *https://pratt.duke.edu/directory*
Phone: (919) 660-5386
Email: prattdeansoffice@duke.edu

COST OF ATTENDANCE:
Tuition & Fees: $69,140 | **Addl Exp:** $24,926 | **Total:** $94,066
Financial Aid: https://financialaid.duke.edu/

ADDITIONAL INFORMATION:
Available Degree(s)
- BS, BS/MS, MS, Ph.D. BME, Civil Eng, Comp Eng, Electrical Engineering, Environmental Eng; Mechanical Engineering
- Minors: Machine Learning & Artificial Intelligence, Electrical & Computer Eng, Energy Engineering, Materials Science & Eng

Related Research Areas
AI & Machine Learning, Big Data & Data Anal, Biomedical Imaging, Biophotonics, Children's Environmental Health, Comput. Modeling, Computer Syst & Architecture, Duke MEDx, Info Processing, Meta-Imaging, Nanoelectric Materials & Devices Group, Neural Eng, Phototonics, Population-Scale Screening, Pulmonary Medicine & Engineering, Quantum Computing, Tissue Engineering, Trustworthy Computing, Water, Sanitation, Hygiene & Infectious Diseases

Scholarships Offered
21% of the first-year class attends tuition-free and meets 100% of their demonstrated need. Other expenses include study away, summer study, and equipment. Merit scholarships are awarded by Duke's Financial Aid & Pratt; A. James Clark Scholars (10 4-year scholarships), Baquerizo Innovation Grant ($20,000 grants)

Special Opportunities
Student Founders - Innovation Venture Program
Duke Innovation & Entrepreneurship Institute - Duke Engineering Entrepreneurship (Signature Experience) – develop an entrepreneurial mindset with advice, education, resources, & connections; Duke-In Global Education – 6 continents, International Internships & Research

Orgs: American Chemical Society, American Institute of Aeronautics & Astronautics, American Institute of Chemical Engineers, American Society of Civil Eng, Amer Society of Mechanical Engineers, ASHRAE, Assoc for Computing Machinery, Biomedical Engineering Society, Duke Aviators, *DukEngineer* Magazine, Duke Conservation Tech, Duke Undergrad Machine Learning, Eng Student Govt, Engineering World Health, Engineering & Science, Engineers for International Development, Engineers w/o Borders, Females Excelling More in Math, Girls Engineering Change, Institute of Electrical & Electronics Engineers, National Society of Black Engineers, Pratt Peer Advisors, Quantum Information Society, Society of Hispanic Professional Engineers, Society of Women Engineers, Students for the Exploration and Development of Space, Tech for Equity, Women in Computing

Teams: Chess, Combat Robotics Team, Concrete Canoe, Conservation Tech, Cyber Defense Team, Debating Society, Design for America, Duke Aero (Spaceport America Cup), Duke Aviators, *DukEngineer* Magazine, Economics Comp Team, eNable, Electric Vehicle Team, eSports Team, HackDuke, Hyperloop, iGEM (International Genetically Engineered Machines), Innoworks, Math Computation & Modeling Competitions, MEDesign, Mock Trial, Model Aeronautics Team, Model United Nations, Motorsports Team, Quiz Bowl, Robotics Team, Project Tadpole, Runway of Dreams, Science Olympiad, Smart Home, Steel Bridge Team

Notable Alumni
Luis von Ahn, Adrian Bejan, John Browne, Lewis Campbell, George Church, Daniel Clancy, Tim Cook, Eddy Cue, William DeVries, Fred Ehrsam, William Hawkins, Mark Humayun, Cassie Kozyrkov, Robert Malkin, Aubrey McClendon, Rick Wagoner, Blake Wilson

ALABAMA
ARKANSAS
DELAWARE
DISTRICT OF COLUMBIA
FLORIDA
GEORGIA
KENTUCKY
LOUISIANA
MARYLAND
MISSISSIPPI
NORTH CAROLINA
OKLAHOMA
SOUTH CAROLINA
TENNESSEE
TEXAS
VIRGINIA
WEST VIRGINIA

SOUTH

- ALABAMA
- ARKANSAS
- DELAWARE
- DISTRICT OF COLUMBIA
- FLORIDA
- GEORGIA
- KENTUCKY
- LOUISIANA
- MARYLAND
- MISSISSIPPI
- **NORTH CAROLINA**
- OKLAHOMA
- SOUTH CAROLINA
- TENNESSEE
- TEXAS
- VIRGINIA
- WEST VIRGINIA

NORTH CAROLINA STATE UNIVERSITY

Address: North Carolina State College of Engineering, Fitts-Woolard Hall, 915 Partners Way, Raleigh, NC 27695-7901
Website: *https://www.engr.ncsu.edu/*
Contact: *https://www.engr.ncsu.edu/about/contact/*
Phone: (919) 515-3263
Email: engineering@ncsu.edu

COST OF ATTENDANCE:

Tuition & Fees: $9,105 (in-state) $31,976 (out-of-state)
Addl Exp: $17,000 | **Total:** $26,105(in-state), $48,976 (out-of-state)
Financial Aid: https://studentservices.ncsu.edu/your-money/financial-aid/

ADDITIONAL INFORMATION:

Available Degree(s)
- BS, MS, Ph.D. Aerospace Eng, Agricultural Eng, Biological Eng, Biomedical Eng, Chemical Eng, Civil Eng, Computer Eng, Computer Science, Electrical Engineering, Environmental Engineering, Forestry Engineering, Materials Science & Engineering, Mechanical Eng, Paper Science & Engineering, Textile Engineering

Related Research Centers
Adv Regenerative Manufacturing, Agromedicine, Animal & Poultry Waste Management, Bioindustrial Manufacturing, Bioinformatics, Comp Med, Dairy Foods Research, Dielectrics & Piezoelectrics, Environmental & Human Health Effects, Forestry, Fungal Research, Genetic Engineering, Human Health & the Environment, Innovation in Manufacturing Biopharmaceuticals, Marine Science, Nutrition Research, Pest Management, Regulatory Science in Agriculture, Textile Protection & Comfort, Water Resources Research Institute

Scholarships Offered
Scholarships via PackAssist. Freshman engineering scholarships: Park Scholarship, General Hugh Shelton Leadership Initiative Scholarship, Chancellor's Leadership Scholarship, Goodnight Scholars Prog; Caldwell Fellows Program for continuing students.

Special Opportunities
Several programs through The Engineering Place and summer camp for K-12 students are held on campus.

Academic enrichment includes the Living and Learning Villages and the Grand Challenges-Focused Research Experiences for Teachers (RET) with Stratified Teaming Program.

NCSU's Clean Energy Center offers students opps to incorporate renewable energy, clean power, industrial efficiencies, clean transportation, policy options, and sustainability into their projects.

Orgs: Air/Waste Management Association, American Chemical Society, American Concrete Institute, American Indian Science & Eng Society, American Inst of Chemical Eng, American Railway Engineers, American Society of Biochemistry and Molecular Biology, American Society of Civil Engineers, American Society of Highway Engineers, American Society of Mechanical Engineers, American Society of Heating, Refrig, & AC Engineering, American Water Research Association, Associated of General Contractors, Coasts, Oceans, Ports & Rivers Inst, Earthquake Eng Research Institute, Engineering Ambassadors, Engineering Entrepreneurs Program, Engineers w/o Borders, Engineers' Council, Institute of Transportation Engineers, Material Advantage, National Association of Home Builders, National Society of Black Engineers, Society of Asian Scientists & Engineers, Society of Hispanic Professional Eng, Society of Women Engineers, Student Energy Club

Teams: Aerial Robotics, AquaPack Robotics (Underwater Vehicle) Biomed Robotics, Concrete Canoe Team, eSports Team, HackPack, High-Powered Rocketry, Pack Motorsports Team, Rubik's Cube, SolarPack (Sun Grand Prix), Steel Bridge Team, VEXU Robotics

Notable Alumni
Anthony Barr, Carol Durham, Donald Farish, James Goodnight, Wes Jackson, Dean Kamen, Trudy Mackay, Jackie Moreland, Rajendra Pachauri, Hugh Shelton, Anand Shimpi, and Charles Stevens

CLEMSON UNIVERSITY

Address: Engineering, Computing and Applied Sciences, Riggs Hall, Clemson, South Carolina 29634
Website: https://www.clemson.edu/cecas/
Contact: https://www.clemson.edu/admissions/undergraduate-admissions/contact-us.html
Phone: (864) 656-3202
Email: agramop@clemson.edu

COST OF ATTENDANCE

Tuition & Fees: $15,558 (in-state) $39,502 (out-of-state)
Addl Exp: $19,000 | **Total:** $34,558 (in-state), $58,502 (out-of-state)
Financial Aid: http://www.clemson.edu/financial-aid/types/

ADDITIONAL INFORMATION:

Available Degree(s)
- BS, MS, Ph.D. Automation Eng, Bio Eng, Biomedical Data & Informatics, Biosystems Eng, Chemical Engineering, Civil Eng, Comp Eng, Computer Science, Electrical Eng, Environmental Eng, Human-Centered Comp, Hydrogeology, Industrial Eng, Materials Science & Eng, Mechanical Eng, Photonics Science

Related Research Areas
Ctr for Adv Eng Fibers & Films, Ctr for Adv Materials for Thermoelect Energy Conversion, Ctr for Optical Materials Science & Engineering Technologies, Construction Industry Cooperative Alliance, Institute for Global Road Safety & Sec, Inst for Innovation in Bldg Materials, Institute for Modeling & Simulation Applications, Micro Fabrication Facility, National Brick Research Center, Nuclear Environmental Eng Sciences & Radioactive Waste Mgmt, Real-Time Power & Intelligent Systems, SC Bioeng Center of Regeneration & Formation of Tissues

Scholarships Offered
Clemson's merit scholarships include the Freshman Academic Recruiting scholarships, the Michelin Annual Scholarship Program, material science scholarships, and the Barry Goldwater Scholarship. Approximately 87% of students receive financial assistance. FAFSA req. Apply by Jan 3 for first-year, transfer, and named scholarships.

Special Opportunities
On-Campus Internship Prog, Co-Op Programs, faculty research, lab positions. Students can access Clemson's Advanced Materials Ctr, the Built Environment Lab, & the Biosystems Research Complex. Students have 24-hour access to workstations, graphic systems, virtual reality sys, network labs, & computer clusters. The Palmetto Cluster is one of the largest supercomputers in the US, ranking 4th on U.S. academic systems Top 500 list with its $1 million upgrade.

National Instruments NI-Elvis II teaching platforms w/functionality of 12 trad test instruments & versatile graphical user interfaces. NI-Elvis II couples w/electronic circuit simulator, Multisim, making it easy to draw schematics, simulate electronic circuits, and compare results to measurements made on actual circuits built on the integrated prototyping board. Workstations include engineering software tools such as LabVIEW, Matlab, PSpice, and Multisim.

Orgs: Amer Inst of Chemical Eng, Amer Soc of Heating Refrigeration & AC Eng, Amer Soc of Civil Eng, Amer Soc of Mechanical Eng, Assoc of Computing Machinery, Human Factors & Ergonomics Soc, Inst of Electrical & Electronics Eng, Institute of Industrial & Systems Eng, Material Advantage, Materials Research Society, NOBCChE, SHPE, Soc of Automotive Eng, Society of Manufacturing Eng, SWE, WICE

Teams: BMES Design Challenge, Concrete Canoe Team, CubeSat Team, CUHackit, Cyber Defense Competition, Debate Society, Formula SAE, Grand Prix Comp, Mock Trial, MUN, Robotics & Rocket Teams, SoutheastCon Hardware Team, Spark Challenge, Steel Bridge, UAV/Drone Team, VEXU, Virtual Students Cluster Competition (Comp Eng)

Notable Alumni
Charlie Blackwell-Thompson, J. Richard Cottingham, Harvey Gantt, Matt Kelley, Mike Mansuetti, Tony Mathis, Gary Parsons, Thomas Phifer, Elizabeth Sloan, and Paul Steelman

ALABAMA
ARKANSAS
DELAWARE
DISTRICT OF COLUMBIA
FLORIDA
GEORGIA
KENTUCKY
LOUISIANA
MARYLAND
MISSISSIPPI
NORTH CAROLINA
OKLAHOMA
SOUTH CAROLINA
TENNESSEE
TEXAS
VIRGINIA
WEST VIRGINIA

SOUTH

ALABAMA
ARKANSAS
DELAWARE
DISTRICT OF COLUMBIA
FLORIDA
GEORGIA
KENTUCKY
LOUISIANA
MARYLAND
MISSISSIPPI
NORTH CAROLINA
OKLAHOMA
SOUTH CAROLINA
TENNESSEE
TEXAS
VIRGINIA
WEST VIRGINIA

VANDERBILT UNIVERSITY

Address: Vanderbilt University, School of Engineering, 2301 Vanderbilt Place, PMB 351826, Nashville, TN 37235-1826
Website: https://engineering.vanderbilt.edu/
Contact: https://engineering.vanderbilt.edu/contact/
Phone: (615) 343-3773
Email: Michele.bender@vanderbilt.edu

COST OF ATTENDANCE:

Tuition & Fees: $68,426 | **Addl Exp:** $30,000 | **Total:** $98,426
Financial Aid: https://www.vanderbilt.edu/financialaid/

ADDITIONAL INFORMATION:

Available Degree(s)
- BS, BS/MS, MS, Ph.D. Biomedical Eng, Chem & Biomolecular Eng, Civil Eng, Computer Eng, Computer Science, Electrical Engineering, Eng Management Environmental Engineering, Materials Science & Engineering, Mechanical Engineering
- MS Engineering Management, Risk, Surgery & Intervention
- Minors: Eng Mgmt, Mat Sci & Eng, Nanoscience & Nanotech

Related Research Areas
Adv Robotics & Mechanism Applications, Assistive Technology, Big Data Science, Cyber-Physical Systems, Data Science Institute, Electro-Mechanical Devices, Mechanical Robot Architectures, Micro/Macro Telemanipulators, Modeling Cardiovascular System, Multiscale Modeling & Simulation Center, Nanotechnology, Piezoelectrically-Actuated Small-Scale Mobile Robots, Rehabilitation, Risk, Reliability, & Resilience, Software Integrated Systems, Space & Defense Systems, Transportation & Operational Resiliency, Vocal Fold Vibration for Surgical Implantation for Voice Disorders

Scholarships Offered
250 Merit-Based Scholarship Winners/yr - After applying submit: Ingram Scholars (Dec 1–Full Tuition) civic-minded, entrepreneurial spirit, innovation, & leadership; Cornelius Vanderbilt Scholarship (Dec 1–Full Tuition) - outstanding academic achievement w/strong leadership & contributions; Chancellor's Scholarship (Dec 1–Full Tuition) bridging economic, social, & racially diverse groups & demonstrated interest in diversity, education, tolerance, & social justice, Carell Family Scholarship – worked part time in high school, demonstrate need (Full Tuition); Clark Scholars Program - $15,000/year + summer aid for eng students; Curb Leadership Scholarship - $8,000/year – students transforming communities

Special Opportunities
Freshman Mentor Program, Internships, Robotics, Study Abroad

Orgs: American Chemical Society, American Institute of Chemical Engineers, American Society of Civil Engineers, American Society of Mechanical Engineers, American Society for Metals, Association of Computing Machinery, Biomedical Engineering Society, Engineering Council, Engineers w/o Borders, Engineering World Health, Institute of Electrical & Electronics Eng, International Society of Optics & Photonics, National Society of Black Engineers, Society of Automotive Engineers, Society of Hispanic Professional Engineers, Society of Engineering Science, Society of Women Engineers

Teams: Aerospace Design Team, Baja SAE, Chess, Concrete Canoe, Cubesat, Data Science Team, Debate, eSports, Formula SAE Electric Vehicle, iGEM (Intl Genetically Eng Machine), Mock Trial, Model UN, Motorsports Team, Quiz Bowl, Robotics, Rubik's Cube, Rocketry (NASA Student Launch Competition), Steel Bridge, U.S. Department of Energy competition - 2023 Electric Challenge Winner, Vanderbilt Rocketeers, VandyHacks, xTechBOLT Competition (1st place in 2022)

Notable Alumni
James Barnard, Kimberly Bryant, Yvonne Clark, Baratunde Cola, Robert Collins, William Davis Jr., William Dobelle, Eric Eidsness, Jordan French, Harold Moses, Jodi Nunnari, Thiago Olson, Philip Porter, Amy Rosemond, Norman Shumway, J. Robert Sims, Bruce Tromberg, Douglas Vahoch, Rhonda Voskuhl, and Li Yang

SOUTHERN METHODIST UNIVERSITY

Address: Southern Methodist University, Lyle School of Engineering, PO Box 750339, Dallas, TX 75205
Website: *https://www.smu.edu/lyle*
Contact: *https://www.smu.edu/Lyle/About-Lyle/Get-in-Touch*
Phone: (214) 768-3050
Email: dean@lyle.smu.edu

COST OF ATTENDANCE:

Tuition & Fees: $67,038 | **Addl Exp:** $22,700 | **Total:** $89,738
Financial Aid: https://www.smu.edu/EnrollmentServices/FinancialAid

ADDITIONAL INFORMATION:

Available Degree(s)
- BS, BS/MS, MS, Ph.D. Civil Engineering, Computer Eng, Comp Sci, Data Sci, Electrical Eng, Environmental Engineering, Mechanical Engineering, Operations Research/Mgmt Science
- MS Cybersecurity, Data Eng, Datacenter Systems Eng, Info Eng & Mgmt, Network Eng, Software Eng, Systems Eng

Related Research Areas
Antenna Chamber, Aqueous & Soil Chemistry Res Lab, Atomic Force Microscopy, AT&T Virtualization Ctr, Autonomous Systems, Center for Digital & Human-Augmented Manufacturing, Center for Engineering Leadership, Circuit Fabrication Lab, Drone Wireless Facility, Electrical Systems, Geotechnical Engineering Lab, Integrated Circuits & Systems Lab, Institute for Cyber Security, Institute for Engineering & Humanity, Metrology Instruments, Near Field Scanning Optical Microscope, Photolithography, Semiconductor Research, Transportation Research

Scholarships Offered
77% of undergrads receive financial aid. Merit scholarships incl the President's Scholars (full tuition & fees & study abroad); Thrive Scholars, Hunt Leadership Scholars $46,000/yr plus airfare & tuition for intl leadership exp (addl essay req); Founders, Second Century Scholarship, SMU Distinguished Scholarship, Provost Scholarships for students who demonstrate outstanding academic success.

Special Opportunities
SMU-in-Taos, with skiing, hiking, and a stunning New Mexico forest backdrop, engages the body, mind, and spirit. Small class sizes and a "classroom without walls" philosophy encourages deep dives into subjects w/tight bonds with faculty and classmates.

Jan Term (France, Morocco, Spain), May Term, Summer Term

Orgs: 3D Printed Prosthetics Club, American Society of Civil Eng, Artificial Intelligence Club, Biomedical Engineering Soc, Blockchain Club, Caruth Institute for Engineering Education, Computer Science Club, Cyber Security Club, Earth First, Engineers w/o Borders, Global Medical Brigades, Hart Center for Engineering Leadership, Hunt Institute for Engineering & Humanity, Inst of Electrical & Electronics Engineers, MedLife, National Society of Black Engineers, Operations & Analytics Club, Paper for Water, Society for Automotive Engineers. Society of Hispanic Professional Engineers, Society of Women Eng, Statistics & Data Science Club, Women in Science & Engineering

Teams: Atlantic Engineering Competition, Chess Club, Cyber Defense Competition Team, Debate Team, eSports Team, HackTheChains, Hilltop Motorsports (Formula SAE), Mock Trial, Model United Nations, Public Debate (International Champions in 2022) Robo-Collaboration, TECHACK, Unmanned Aircraft Systems (UAS) University Innovation Showcase (2nd Place in 2022)

Notable Alumni
Michael Bunnell, Richard Clemmer, Robert Dennard, Aart J. de Geus, Whitney Herd, Keith Jackson, Jack James, Jerry Junkins, Erie Nye, Mark Shepherd, Robert Taylor, Donald

ALABAMA
ARKANSAS
DELAWARE
DISTRICT OF COLUMBIA
FLORIDA
GEORGIA
KENTUCKY
LOUISIANA
MARYLAND
MISSISSIPPI
NORTH CAROLINA
OKLAHOMA
SOUTH CAROLINA
TENNESSEE
TEXAS
VIRGINIA
WEST VIRGINIA

SOUTH

ALABAMA
ARKANSAS
DELAWARE
DISTRICT OF COLUMBIA
FLORIDA
GEORGIA
KENTUCKY
LOUISIANA
MARYLAND
MISSISSIPPI
NORTH CAROLINA
OKLAHOMA
SOUTH CAROLINA
TENNESSEE
TEXAS
VIRGINIA
WEST VIRGINIA

TEXAS A&M UNIVERSITY

Address: Zachry Engineering Education Complex, 125 Spence St., Suite 481, 3127 TAMU, College Station, TX 77843-3127
Website: https://engineering.tamu.edu/
Contact: *https://engineering.tamu.edu/contact/index.html*
Phone: (979) 845-7200
Email: easa@tamu.edu

COST OF ATTENDANCE:

In-State Tuition & Fees: $13,012 (in-state) $41,607 (out-of-state)
Addl Exp: $21,000 | **Total:** $34,012 (in-state), $62,607 (out-of-state)
Financial Aid: https://financialaid.tamu.edu/

ADDITIONAL INFORMATION:

Available Degree(s)
- BS, MS, Ph.D. Aerospace Eng, Architectural Eng, Biological & Agricultural Engineering, Biomedical Engineering, Civil Eng, Computer Engineering, Computer Science, Electrical Eng, Environmental Eng, GeoSystems Engineering & Hydrogeology, Industrial Engineering, Interdisciplinary Engineering, Materials Science & Engineering, Mechanical Engineering, Nuclear Engineering, Ocean Engineering, Petroleum Engineering
- Minor: Cybersecurity, Game Design & Development

Related Research Centers
Algorithms, AI, Computational Fabrication, Computer Architecture, Computer Vision, Cyber-Physical Systems, Cybersecurity, Electronic Design Automation & VSLI, Embedded Systems, Gaming, Graphics & Visualization, Health, Human-Centered Systems, Human-Computer Interactions, Human-Robot Connections, Intelligent Systems, Machine Learning, Robotics, Technical Reporting

Scholarships Offered
20+ Endowed Engineering/Comp Sci/Data Sci Scholarships, Travel Grants, Continuing Student Scholarships, Corporate-Sponsored Scholarships; 81% receive aid; 64% receive grants or scholarships

Special Opportunities
Orgs: 12th Astronaut Lab, Aggie Aerospace Women in Engineering, AggieSat Lab, Aggies Communicate through Eng, Aggie Club of Eng, American Institute of Aeronautics & Astronautics, Amer Concrete Institute, American Society of Civil Engineering, American Society of Mechanical Engineers, American Water Resources Association, Association of Environmental Engineering Students, Civil Materials Student Org, Council for Undergraduate Research in Engineering, Engineering Honor Society, Engineers Serving the Community, Engineers w/o Borders, Freshmen Reaching Excellence in Eng, Geo-Institute of ASCE, Institute of Transportation Engineers, Marine Technology Society, Material Advantage, National Society of Black Engineers, oSTEM, Society of Civil Engineers, Society of Flight Test Engineers, Soc of Naval Architects & Marine Eng, Society of Women in Space Exploration, Society of Mexican Americans in Engineering & Scientists, Student Engineers' Council, Society of Asian Scientists & Engineers, Society of Hispanic Professional Engineers, Society of Women Engineers, Students for the Exploration & Development of Space, Structural Engineering Association of Texas, T-Minus, Women in Computing, Women in Cybersecurity

Teams: AERO Design Team, Aggie Robotics, AggieSat, Baja SAE Team, Concrete Canoe Team, Cybersecurity Competitions, DOE CyberForce, Embedded Security Systems Team, eSports Team, Formula Electric Car, G-I GeoWall Competition, High-Altitude Balloon, Human-Powered Submarine, iGEM (International Genetically Eng Machines), Mock Trial, Model United Nations, Robotics Team, Rocket Engine Design Team, Robomaster Robotics, Speech & Debate Team, Solar Motorsports Team, Sounding Rocketry Team, Vertical Flight Society

Notable Alumni
Khalid Al-Falih, Richard Battin, Michael Fossum, Joe Foster, John Junkins, Mavis Kelsey, Jack Kilby, John Kinealy, Edward Knipling, Byran Lunney, Frank Malina, William Pailes, Steven Swanson

UNIVERSITY OF TEXAS AT AUSTIN

Address: The University of Texas at Austin, 301 E. Dean Keeton St. C2100, Austin, Texas 78712-2100
Website: https://cockrell.utexas.edu/
Contact: https://cockrell.utexas.edu/contact
Phone: (512) 471-1166
Email: mbcates@mail.utexas.edu

COST OF ATTENDANCE:

Tuition & Fees: $11,698 (in-state), $41,070 (out-of-state)
Addl Exp: $21,000 | **Total:** $32,698 (in-state), $ 62,070 (out-of-state)
Financial Aid: https://finaid.utexas.edu/

ADDITIONAL INFORMATION:

Available Degree(s)
- BS, MS, Ph.D. Aerospace Eng, ArchEng, BME, Chem Eng, Civil Eng, Comp Eng, Comp Sci, EE, Enviro Eng, GeoSystems Eng & Hydrogeol, Mat Sci & Eng, Mechanical Eng, Petroleum Eng
- MS, Ph.D. Environmental & Water Resource Engineering, Operations Research & Industrial Engineering

Related Research Centers
Center for Additive Manufacturing & Design Innovation, Center for Aeromechanics Research, Center for Electromechanics, Center for Energy & Environmental Res, Center for Engineering Education, Center for Mechanics of Solids, Structures, & Materials, Center for Nanomanufacturing Systems for Mobile Computing & Mobile Energy Tech, Center for Subsurface Energy & the Environment, Ctr for Space Research, Center for Transportation Res, Center for Water & the Environment, Construction Industry Inst, Energy Inst, Inst for Cellular & Molecular Biology, Microelectronics Research Ctr, Texas Materials Institute, Wireless Networking & Communications Group

Scholarships Offered
UT offers over 3,000 scholarships to incoming and current students. To be considered for merit-based scholarships, complete the Engineering Honors Program Application by December 1.

Special Opportunities
UT Institute for Computational Engineering & Sciences
interdisciplinary program in computational sciences & engineering, modeling, software engineering & computational visualization

UT Center for Predictive Engineering & Computational Sciences
tools/techniques to make reliable predictions of complex systems

Orgs: American Chemical Society, American Institute of Aeronautics & Astronautics, American Institute of Chemical Engineers, American Association of Drilling Engineers, American Society of Biochemistry & Molecular Biology, American Society of Civil Engineers, American Society of Mechanical Engineers, Biomedical Engineering Society, Biomedical Outreach & Leadership, Global Medical Brigades, Institute of Electrical & Electronics Engineers, Material Advantage, Society of Petroleum Engineers, Society of Petrophysicists & Well Log Analysts, Women in Biomedical Engineering, Women in Mechanical Engineering, Women in ECE, Women in Petroleum & Geosystems Engineering

Teams: Aerial Robotics Team, Chem-E Car Team, Chess, Computer Programming Team, Concrete Canoe Team, U.S. Dept of Energy CyberForce Competition, Cyber Policy Team, Design/Build/Fly (AIAA RC Aircraft), HackTexas Hackathon, Longhorn Electric Vehicle Racing, Longhorn Rocketry Association, Makeathon, Model United Nations, Texas Rocket Engineering Lab, Solar Racing, Steel Bridge Team, Texas Spacecraft Lab, UAV (Autonomous Flight) Team

Notable Alumni
Michael Baker, Alan Bean, Robert Crippen, Kenneth Cockrell, Gary Kelly, Phil Ligrani, Paul Lockhart, Carl Meade, Frederick Leslie, Austin Ligon, Andreas Mogensen, "Poppy" Northcutt, Karen Nyberg, H. Grady Rylander, James Truchard, Neil deGrasse Tyson, Michael Webber, Neil Woodward, Stephanie Wilson

ALABAMA
ARKANSAS
DELAWARE
DISTRICT OF COLUMBIA
FLORIDA
GEORGIA
KENTUCKY
LOUISIANA
MARYLAND
MISSISSIPPI
NORTH CAROLINA
OKLAHOMA
SOUTH CAROLINA
TENNESSEE
TEXAS
VIRGINIA
WEST VIRGINIA

SOUTH

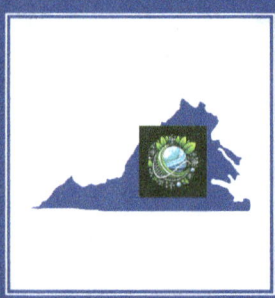

- ALABAMA
- ARKANSAS
- DELAWARE
- DISTRICT OF COLUMBIA
- FLORIDA
- GEORGIA
- KENTUCKY
- LOUISIANA
- MARYLAND
- MISSISSIPPI
- NORTH CAROLINA
- OKLAHOMA
- SOUTH CAROLINA
- TENNESSEE
- TEXAS
- **VIRGINIA**
- WEST VIRGINIA

UNIVERSITY OF VIRGINIA

Address: Thornton Hall, Room A124, 351 McCormick Rd., P.O. Box 400246, Charlottesville, VA 22904-4246
Website: https://engineering.virginia.edu/
Contact: https://engineering.virginia.edu/about/visit-us
Phone: (434) 924-3593
Email: engrdean@virginia.edu

COST OF ATTENDANCE:
Tuition & Fees: $22,323 (in-state), $58,950 (out-of-state)
Addl Exp: $21,000 | **Total:** $43,323 (in-state), $79,950 (out-of-state)
Financial Aid: https://sfs.virginia.edu/

ADDITIONAL INFORMATION:

Available Degree(s)
- BS, MS, Ph.D. Aerospace Engineering, Biomedical Engineering, Civil Engineering, Computer Eng, Computer Science, Electrical Engineering, Environmental Engineering, Materials Science & Engineering, Mechanical Engineering, Systems Engineering

Related Research Centers
Center for Advanced Logistic Systems, Center for Adv Manufacturing, Center for Laser & Plasma, Ctr for Res in Intelligent Storage & Processing in Memory, Ctr for Transportation Studies, Center for Visual & Decision Informatics, Multi-Functional Integrated Systems Tech, nanoSTAR Institute, Nanosystems Eng Center for Advanced Self-Powered Systems of Integrated Sensors & Technology, Rolls-Royce Technology Center

Scholarships Offered
UVA Student Financial Services (SFS) offers privately endowed (individual & foundations) need-based scholarships; several awards include merit aid. In most cases, students are automatically considered. Scholarships for current engineering students as well as hardship scholarships are available.

Special Opportunities
UVA Engineering provides free, scheduled on-demand tutoring with student tutors. 3-D Bioprinting, Industry-Quality Distillation Column, Machine Shops, Microfab Laboratories, Nanoscale Materials Characterization Facility, flight simulator, and rapid prototyping

Study Abroad: Eng/commerce design in Argentina; engineering in Spain; "Exploring German Engineering" - Mercedes-Benz, Bosch, Max Planck Institutes, & research labs; real-world sustainability in Sweden.

Orgs: 3D Printing Club, American Institute of Aeronautics & Astronautics, American Institute of Chemical Engineers, American Society of Civil Engineers, Association for Computing Machinery, Biomedical Engineering Society, Computer Network Security Club, Engineers Going Global, Engineering Student Council, Genomics Society, Gizmologists, Institute of Electrical & Electronics Engineers, Material Advantage, Mechatronics & Robotics Society, National Society of Black Engineers, oSTEM, Society of Asian Scientists & Engineers, Society of Hispanic Professional Engineers, Society of Women Engineers, Spectra, SURE, Student Game Developers, Women in Computing Sciences

Teams: Academic Competitions, Aero Design "Hoos Flying" Team, Chem-E Car Team, Chess, Collaborative Robotics Lab, Coop of autTOnomous Robots; CubeSat, Cyber Defense Team, High-Powered Rocketry Team, HooHacks, Human-Powered Vehicle Team, iGEM (Intl Genetically Engineered Machines); Mock Trial, Model United Nations Team, National Cybersecurity Competition; NSF I-Corps; Pike Eng Entrepreneurship Challenge, Programming Competitions, Robotics Team, Smart-City Innovation, Solar Car Team, Speech & Debate Team, Virginia Motorsports (Formula SAE)

Notable Alumni
Eric Anderson, Daniel Barringer, Algernon Buford, Richard Byrd, W. Graham Claytor, Jr., Norman Crabill, Heber Curtis, Patrick Forrester, Elmer Gaden, Robert Hagood, Karl Henize, Thomas Marshburn, Leland Melvin, Edward Ney, Bill Nelson, Gregory Olsen, William Page, Samuel Spencer, Kathryn Thornton, Robert Young

VIRGINIA TECH

Address: Virginia Tech College of Engineering, 212 Hancock Hall, Blacksburg, VA 24061
Website: https://eng.vt.edu/
Contact: https://vt.edu/academics/contacts/major-contact-general-engineering-1.html
Phone: (540) 231-3244
Email: engris@vt.edu

COST OF ATTENDANCE:
Tuition & Fees: $15,478 (in-state), $36,090 (out-of-state)
Addl Exp: $21,000 | **Total:** $36,478 (in-state), $57,090 (out-of-state)
Financial Aid: https://finaid.vt.edu/

ADDITIONAL INFORMATION:
Available Degree(s)
- BS, MS, MEng, Ph.D. Aerospace Eng, Biomedical Eng. Civil Eng, Computer Engineering, Computer Science, Electrical, Engineering Mechanics, Materials Science & Engineering, Mechanical Engineering, Meteorology, Ocean Engineering
- MS, MEng, Ph.D. Mining & Minerals Eng, Nuclear Engineering

Related Research Centers
Aero-Hydrodynamics, Autonomous Systems, Computational Mechanics, Cyber-Physical Security, Dynamics, Control, & Estimation, Environmentally Responsible Systems, Fabrication, Prototyping, & Additive Manufacturing, National Security, Propulsion, Renewable Energy, Small Satellites & Space-Based Sensing, Space Engineering, Structures & Materials

Scholarships Offered
Davenport Leadership Scholarships ($7,000/year – separate appl), Merit & Need-Based Scholarships (General University Scholarship Application), A. James Clark Scholars Program for engineering students. More than 70% receive aid; a typical package is $17,634.

Special Opportunities
The Frith Lab: first-year students learn by dissecting, designing, making, & analyzing engineering products. Other facilities include the InVents Studio, Ware Lab, & Advanced Engineering Design Lab.

International Research Experiences: Global Eng Ambassador, International Internships, Rolls-Royce International Internship Program, Engineering Research Experience in China, Global Design & Construction in Rwanda, Coastal Engineering in Australia, Semester Abroad in Switzerland; Partnership w/Hamburg University junior spring semester abroad to study German engineering.

Engineering Class: Bridges, Builders & Society class, taught by professors in Spring 2023, includes travel from May 14-26, 2023 to Italy, Austria, & Switzerland. Students travel to Europe with profs.

Orgs: American Indian Scientists & Engineers Society, Amer Institute of Aeronautics & Astronautics, American Institute of Chemical Eng, American Society of Agricultural & Biological Engineers, American Society of Civil Engineers, Amer Society of Mechanical Eng, American Society of Naval Engineers, Association for Computing Machinery, Association for Uncrewed Vehicle Systems International, Association for Women in Computing, Engineers w/o Borders, Inst of Electrical & Electronics Engineers, Material Advantage, National Society of Black Engineers, Society of Hispanic Professional Engineers, Society of Asian Scientists & Engineers, Society of Flight Test Engineers, Soc of Naval Architects & Marine Engineers, Society of Women in Aviation & Space Exploration, Society of Women Engineers, Students for the Exploration & Development of Space, Theme Park Eng & Design Gp

Teams: Baja SAE, Concrete Canoe Team, e-NABLE, Ethics Bowl, Hybrid Electric Vehicle Team, iGEM, Mock Trial, Model United Nations, Robotics Design Team, Rocketry Team, Steel Bridge Team

Notable Alumni
Dave Calhoun, Charles Camarada, Roger Crouch, Regina Dugan, Paige Kassalen, Chris Kraft, Robert Michelson, Enid Montague, and Joseph Ware, Jr.

- ALABAMA
- ARKANSAS
- DELAWARE
- DISTRICT OF COLUMBIA
- FLORIDA
- GEORGIA
- KENTUCKY
- LOUISIANA
- MARYLAND
- MISSISSIPPI
- NORTH CAROLINA
- OKLAHOMA
- SOUTH CAROLINA
- TENNESSEE
- TEXAS
- VIRGINIA
- WEST VIRGINIA

SOUTH

ALASKA

ARIZONA

CALIFORNIA

COLORADO

HAWAII

IDAHO

MONTANA

NEVADA

NEW MEXICO

OREGON

UTAH

WASHINGTON

WYOMING

CHAPTER 14

REGION FOUR

WEST

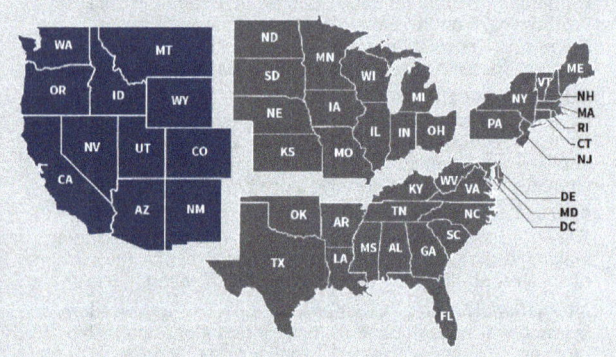

16 Programs | 13 States

1. AZ – Arizona State University
2. CA - California Institute of Technology (CalTech)
3. CA - California Polytechnic State University, San Luis Obispo
4. CA - San Diego State University
5. CA - Stanford University
6. CA - University of California, Berkeley
7. CA - University of California, Davis
8. CA - University of California, Irvine
9. CA - University of California, Los Angeles
10. CA - University of California, Riverside
11. CA - University of California, San Diego
12. CA - University of Southern California
13. CO - Colorado School of Mines
14. CO - University of Colorado, Boulder
15. OR - Oregon State University
16. WA - University of Washington

ENVIRONMENTAL ENGINEERING & ALTERNATIVE ENERGY PROGRAMS

School	Avg. GPA, SAT ERW, SAT Math (M), and ACT Composite (C) Early Decision (ED)	Admissions Statistics	Related Program(s)
Arizona State University 1151 S. Forest Ave. Tempe, AZ 85281	GPA: 3.5 SAT (ERW): 550-680 SAT (M): 570-690 ACT (C): 19-27 ED: No, EA: No, Rolling: Yes	Admit Rate: 88% Undergrad Enrollment: 65,492 Total Enrollment: 80,065	BSE, MS, Ph.D. Aerospace Eng, BME, Chemical Eng, Civil Eng, Comp Eng, Comp Sci, Electrical Eng, Energy Eng, Enviro Eng, Materials Science & Eng, Mech Eng; MS, Ph.D. Construction Mgmt, Sustainable Eng; Accel 5-year, 4+1 BSE/MS Enviro Eng, Robotics & Autonomous Syst
CalTech 383 S. Hill Ave Pasadena, CA 91125	GPA: N/A SAT (ERW): 740-780 SAT (M): 790-800 ACT (C): 35-36 ED: No, REA: Yes	Admit Rate: 7% Undergrad Enrollment: 982 Total Enrollment: 2,401	BS, MS, Ph.D. Biological Eng, Chemical Eng, Computer Eng, Comp Sci, Electrical Eng, Environmental Sci & Eng, Info/Data Science, Material Science & Eng, Mechanical Engineering; MS, Ph.D. Aerospace Eng, Civil Eng, Medical Eng, Space Eng
Cal Poly, San Luis Obispo 1 Grand Avenue, San Luis Obispo, CA 93407	GPA: 4.04-4.25 SAT/ACT Not Considered ED: No, EA: No	Admit Rate 2023 Engineering: 20.4% Undergrad Enrollment: 21,499 Total Enrollment: 22,279	BS, MS, Ph.D. Aerospace Eng, Biomedical Eng, Civil Eng, Computer Eng, Computer Sci, Electrical Eng, Environmental Engineering, Industrial Eng, Materials Science & Engineering, Mechanical Engineering
San Diego State University (SDSU) 5500 Campanile Drive, San Diego, CA 92182	GPA: 3.82 SAT/ACT Not Considered ED: No, EA: No	Admit Rate: 34.2% Undergrad Enrollment: 32,883 Total Enrollment: 37,538	BS, BS/MS, MS, Ph.D. Aerospace Engineering, Civil Engineering, Computer Eng, Construction Engineering, Electrical Eng, Environmental Engineering, Mechanical Engineering Minor: Nuclear Engineering
Stanford University 355 Galvez Street, Stanford, CA 94305	GPA: 3.9 SAT (ERW): 750-780 SAT (M): 750-800 ACT (C): 33-35 ED: No, REA: Yes	Admit Rate: 4% Undergrad Enrollment: 8,049 Total Enrollment: 18,283	BS, MS, Ph.D. Aerospace Eng, Bioengineering, Chemical Eng, Civil Engineering, Computer Eng, Computer Science, Electrical Eng, Environmental Engineering, Materials Science & Engineering, Mechanical Engineering

ENVIRONMENTAL ENGINEERING & ALTERNATIVE ENERGY PROGRAMS

School	Avg. GPA, SAT ERW, SAT Math (M), and ACT Composite (C) Early Decision (ED)	Admissions Statistics	Related Program(s)
University of California, Berkeley Berkeley, CA 94720	GPA: 4.15-4.29 SAT/ACT Not Considered ED: No, EA: No	Admit Rate: 11.6% Undergrad Enrollment: 33,078 Total Enrollment: 45,699	BS Aerosp Eng (new in 2022) BS, MS, Ph.D. Bioengineering, Chemical Eng, Civil Eng, Comp Sci, Data Science, Electrical Eng, Energy Eng, Environmental Eng, Industrial Eng, Mat Sci & Eng, Mechanical Eng, Nuclear Eng
University of California, Davis One Shields Avenue, Davis, CA 95616	GPA: 4.03-4.27 SAT/ACT Not Considered ED: No, EA: No	Admit Rate: 41.8% Undergrad Enrollment: 31,797 Total Enrollment: 39,707	BS, MS, Ph.D. Aerospace Eng, Biochemical Eng, Biological Sys Eng, Biomedical Eng, Chemical Engineering, Civil Engineering, Computer Eng, Computer Science, Electrical Engineering, Environmental Eng, Materials Science & Eng, Mechanical Eng
University of California, Irvine (UCI) 4000 Mesa Rd., Irvine, CA 92697	GPA: 4.07-4.28 SAT/ACT Not Considered ED: No, EA: No	Admit Rate: 25.7% Undergrad Enrollment: 29,503 Total Enrollment: 36,582	BS, MS, Ph.D. Aerospace Eng, Biomedical Engineering, Chemistry, Chemical Engineering, Civil Engineering, Computer Eng, Computer Science, Electrical Engineering, Environmental Engineering, Materials Science & Engineering, Mechanical Engineering
University of California, Los Angeles (UCLA) 405 Hilgard Avenue, Los Angeles, CA 90095	GPA: 4.20-4.31 SAT/ACT Not Considered ED: No, EA: No	Admit Rate: 8.8% Undergrad Enrollment: 33,040 Total Enrollment: 46,678	BS, MS, Ph.D. Aerospace Eng, Chemical Engineering, Civil Eng, Environmental Engineering, Materials Science & Engineering, Mechanical Engineering MS Quantum Science & Technology
University of California, Riverside 900 University Avenue, Riverside, CA, 92521	GPA: 3.76-4.18 SAT/ACT Not Considered ED: No, EA: No	Admit Rate: 70.3% Undergraduate Enrollment: 22,646 Total Enrollment: 26,426	BS, MS Bioengineering, Chemical Engineering, Computer Eng, Computer Science, Data Science, Electrical Engineering, Environmental Engineering, Materials Science & Eng, Mechanical Engineering, Robotics Engineering

WEST

ENVIRONMENTAL ENGINEERING & ALTERNATIVE ENERGY PROGRAMS

School	Avg. GPA, SAT ERW, SAT Math (M), and ACT Composite (C) Early Decision (ED)	Admissions Statistics	Related Program(s)
University of California, San Diego (UCSD) 9500 Gilman Drive, La Jolla, CA 92093	GPA: 4.11-4.29 SAT/ACT Not Considered ED: No, EA: No	Admit Rate: 24.7% Undergrad Enrollment: 33,792 Total Enrollment: 42,376	BS, MS, Ph.D. Aerospacce Eng, Bioengineering, Chemical Eng, Computer Eng, Computer Science, Electrical Engineering, Environmental Eng, Mechanical Engineering, Nano Engineering, Structural Engineering
University of Southern California (USC) Watt Hall, Suite 204, Los Angeles, CA 90089	GPA: 3.9 SAT (ERW): 700-760 SAT (M): 750-790 ACT (C): 32-35 ED: No, EA: Yes	Admit Rate: 9.2% Undergrad Enrollment: 21,000 Total Enrollment: 47,000	BS, MS, Ph.D. Aerospace Eng, Biomedical Eng, Chemical Eng, Civil Eng, Environmental Eng, Industrial & Systems Eng, Intelligence & Cyber Operations, Materials Science & Engineering, Petroleum Engineering
Colorado School of Mines 1812 Illinois Street, Golden, CO 80401	GPA: 3.85 SAT (ERW): 660-720 SAT (M): 670-750 ACT (C): 30-34 ED: No, EA: Yes	Admit Rate: 40% Undergrad Enrollment: 5,852 Total Enrollment: 7,608	BS, MS, Ph.D. Civil Engineering, Computer Science, Electrical Engineering, Environmental Engineering, Geological Eng, Geophysics, Materials Science & Engineering, Mining Eng, Petroleum Engineering
University of Colorado, Boulder Regent Administrative Center, Boulder, CO 80305	GPA: 3.76 SAT (ERW): 550-670 SAT (M): 580-700 ACT (C): 26-31 ED: No, EA: Yes	Admit Rate: 79% Undergrad Enrollment: 30,837 Total Enrollment: 37,153 Eng School: 8,409	BS, MS, Ph.D. Aerospace Eng Science, Architectural Eng, Civil Engineering, Computer Engineering Computer Science, Electrical Engineering, Environmental Engineering, Integrated Engineering Design, Mechanical Engineering
Oregon State University College of Engineering, 101 Covell Hall, Corvallis, OR 97331-2409	GPA: 3.6 SAT (ERW): 23-31 SAT (M): 550-680 ACT (C): 580-700 ED: No, EA: Yes	Admit Rate: 74.9% Undergrad Enrollment: 31,035 Total Enrollment: 36,636	BS, MS, Ph.D. Aerospace Eng, Architectural Eng, Bioeng, Chemical Eng, Civil Engineering, Comp Engineering, Computer Science, Construction Eng, Ecological Eng, Electrical Eng, Energy Systems Engineering, Eng Mgmt, Environmental Eng, Industrial Engineering, Mechanical Eng, Nuclear Eng, MS, Ph.D. AI, Materials Science, Robotics, Water Resources Eng

ENVIRONMENTAL ENGINEERING & ALTERNATIVE ENERGY PROGRAMS

School	Avg. GPA, SAT ERW, SAT Math (M), and ACT Composite (C) Early Decision (ED)	Admissions Statistics	Related Program(s)
University of Washington 1400 NE Campus Parkway, Seattle, WA, 98195	GPA: 3.8 SAT (ERW): 640-740 SAT (M): 660-780 ACT (C): 29-34 ED: No, EA: No	Admit Rate: 48% Undergrad Enrollment: 36,872 Total Enrollment: 53,083	BS, MS, Ph.D. Aerospace Eng, Bioengineering, Bioresource Science & Eng, Chemical Eng, Civil Eng, Computer Engineering, Computer Science, Electrical Eng, Environmental Engineering, Human-Centered Design & Eng, Industrial Eng, Materials Science & Eng, Mechanical Engineering

WEST

ALASKA

ARIZONA

CALIFORNIA

COLORADO

HAWAII

IDAHO

MONTANA

NEVADA

NEW MEXICO

OREGON

UTAH

WASHINGTON

WYOMING

ARIZONA STATE UNIVERSITY

Address: Ira A. Fulton Schools of Engineering, P.O. Box 879309, Tempe, AZ 85287-9309
Website: *https://engineering.asu.edu*
Contact: *https://engineering.asu.edu/contact/*
Phone: (480) 965-2272
Email: FultonSchools@asu.edu

COST OF ATTENDANCE:

Tuition & Fees: $13,500 (in-state), $35,300 (out-of-state)
Addl Exp: $22,000 | **Total:** $35,500 (in-state), $57,300 (out-of-state)
Financial Aid: https://students.asu.edu/financialaid

ADDITIONAL INFORMATION:

Available Degree(s)
- BSE, MS, Ph.D. Aerospace Eng, BME, Chemical Eng, Civil Eng, Computer Eng, Comp Sci, EE, Energy Eng, Environmental Eng, Materials Science & Engineering, Mechanical Engineering
- MS, Ph.D. Construction Mgmt, Sustainable Engineering
- Accel 5-year, 4+1 BSE/MS Enviro Eng, Robotics & Autonomous Sys, Material Science & Engineering or Chemical Engineering

Related Research Centers
Adaptive Intelligent Materials and Systems, Accelerating Operational Efficiency, Complex System Safety, Efficient Vehicles and Sustainable Transportation Systems, Embedded Systems, Human, Artificial Intelligence, and Robot Teaming, Negative Carbon Emissions, Integrated Circuits, Systems, and Sensors, Flexible Electronics and Display, Information Assurance, Infrastructure and Sustainable Engineering, Excellence on Smart Innovations, Power Systems Engineering, Quantum Energy, and Sustainable Solar Technologies, Secure, Trusted, and Assured Microelectronics

Scholarships Offered
ASU's Fulton College of Engineering offers scholarships in addition to the ASU scholarships. Nearly a million dollars are offered to highly academic students. See engineering.asu.edu/scholarships

Engineering Projects in Community Service (EPICS): Design, build, & deploy systems to solve engineering-based probs for nonprofit orgs

Fulton Grand Challenge Scholars Program: Combine classes with cutting-edge, problem-solving research

Fulton Undergraduate Research Initiative provides hands-on lab exp, independent & thesis-based research, & conference travel.

Tooker House: ASU's "dorm built for engineers" has on-site digital classrooms & state-of-the-art maker spaces with 3D printers, laser cutters, and cutting edge tools.

Orgs: Ambassadors, Amer Concrete Inst, Amer Indian Sci & Eng Soc, American Institute of Aeronautics & Astronautics, American Institute of Chemical Eng, American Society of Civil Engineers, American Society of Mechanical Eng, Associated General Contractors of America, Assoc for Computer Systems Security, Biomedical Eng Society, Bridges to Prosperity, Construction Students Abroad, Engineering World Health, Engineers w/o Borders, INFORMS, Institute of Electrical & Electronics Engineers, Material Advantage, National Society of Black Engineers, Society of Automotive Engineers, Society of Hispanic Professional Engineers, Society of Women Eng, SoDA, Women in Computer Science

Teams: Air Devils, Alka Rocketeers, ChemE Car, Combat Robotics, Daedalus Astronautics, DIYBio, Electric Car, Formula SAE, Game Dev Studio, Helios Rocketry, iGEM, Mock Trial, MUN, Motorsports, Next Level Devils, Rossum Rumblers Robotics Team, Satellite Team, Solar Devils, Speech & Debate Team, SunHacks, Underwater Robotics Team

Notable Alumni
Stephen Basila, Robert Bigelow, Stephen DeTommaso, Kent Dibble, Michael Fann, George Geiser, LeRoy Hanneman Jr., Paul Henry, Enamul Hoque, Geza Kmetty, Debra Larson, Hisha Mahmoud, T. Allen McArtor, Harriet Nembhard, Douglas Nicholls, John Nicklow, Valerie S. Roberts, Michael Roy, Janaka Ruwanpura, Francis Scobee, Marylyn Tobey, and Margaret Woodward.

CALIFORNIA INST OF TECHNOLOGY "CAL TECH"

Address: Cal Tech, Division of Engineering and Applied Science, 1200 E. California Blvd., MC 155-44, Pasadena, CA 91125-2100
Website: https://eas.caltech.edu/
Contact: https://eas.caltech.edu/contact
Phone: (626) 395-4101
Email: ugadmissions@caltech.edu

COST OF ATTENDANCE:
Tuition & Fees: $65,740 | **Addl Exp:** $24,000 | **Total:** $89,740
Financial Aid: https://www.finaid.caltech.edu/

ADDITIONAL INFORMATION:

Available Degree(s)
- BS, MS, Ph.D. Biological Eng, Chemical Eng, Computer Eng, Computer Science, Electrical Eng, Environmental Science & Eng, Information/Data Science, Materials Science & Eng, Mech Eng
- MS, Ph.D. Aerospace Eng, Civil Eng, Medical Eng, Space Eng
- Minors: Aerospace, Control/Dynamical Systems, Neurobiology, Structural Mechanics, Visual Culture

Related Research Areas
Autonomous Systems and Technologies, Environmental Microbial Interactions, Artificial Photosynthesis, Quantum Entanglement

Caltech Microanalysis Center, Infrared Processing & Analysis Center, Keck Inst for Space Studies, Laser Interferometer Gravitational-wave Observatory, Owens Valley Radio Observatory, Palomar Observatory, Space Radiation Laboratory, W. M. Keck Observatory

Scholarships Offered
Caltech scholarships depend on demonstrated financial need and can be renewed, though the amount may change. Caltech donors offer scholarships for both need-based and merit-based award.

Special Opportunities
Summer Research & Internships; Summer Programs; with 1,000 undergrads; you will not be anonymous; everyone works hard, takes breaks, & finds an outlet–theatre, sports, 16 NCAA DIII teams, 100 clubs, art, music, competition teams, and 5 NASA facilities

Orgs: A Capella, Amateur Radio Club, Amer Institute of Aeronautics & Astronautics, Anime, American Institute of Chemical Engineers, American Society of Civil Engineers, American Society of Mechanical Engineers, Association for Computing Machinery, Black Scientists & Engineers at CalTech, BlockTech, Computing Club, Engineers w/o Borders, Engineers for a Sustainable World, Institute of Electrical & Electronics Engineers, Latino Association of Students in Engineering and Sciences, MedLife, Origami Club, Sci-Fi, Scuba, Society of Women Engineers, Students for the Exploration & Development of Space

Teams: Amateur Radio, Ballroom Dance, Blocktech, Board Game Competitions, Bridge Club, Caltech Racing Team, Chess, Cubesat, Cybersecurity Bootcamp, Engineering Design Team, Formula SAE Team, Gaming, Hacktech, iGEM Team (Intl Genetically Engineered Machines), Poker, Quiz Bowl, RC Aircraft, Robotics Team, Rocketry Team, Science Olympiad, Solar Decathlon, Speed Cubing, Triathlon

Annual Sumobot Competition - Student teams are challenged to design, build, and field robots for each of the 3 Sumobot categories: (1) Autonomous wheeled, (2) Radio-controlled (R/C) wheeled, and (3) (R/C) Strandbot, i.e., a linkage, mechanism-based walking robot.

Notable Alumni
Mark Adler, Mihran Agbabian, Irving Ashkenas, David Bohm, Frank Borman, David Brin, James Broadwell, Sidney Gottlieb, David Ho, Howard Hughes, Donald Knuth, Fei-Fei Li, Fred Lindvall, Benoit Mandelbrot, John McCarthy, Charlie Munger, Frank Oppenheimer, Linus Pauling, Charles Richter, William Shockley, Peter Shor, Pol Spanos, Kip Thorne, Vito Vanoni, & Stephen Wolfram

ALASKA
ARIZONA
CALIFORNIA
COLORADO
HAWAII
IDAHO
MONTANA
NEVADA
NEW MEXICO
OREGON
UTAH
WASHINGTON
WYOMING

WEST

ALASKA

ARIZONA

CALIFORNIA

COLORADO

HAWAII

IDAHO

MONTANA

NEVADA

NEW MEXICO

OREGON

UTAH

WASHINGTON

WYOMING

CAL POLY SAN LUIS OBISPO

Address: Cal Poly San Luis Obispo, College of Engineering, 1 Grand Avenue, Building 192, Room 301, San Luis Obispo, CA 93407
Website: https://ceng.calpoly.edu/
Contact: https://ceng.calpoly.edu/contact/#contact-our-office
Phone: (805) 756-2131
Email: engineeringdean@calpoly.edu

COST OF ATTENDANCE:

Tuition & Fees: $13,596 (in-state), $34,665 (out-of-state)
Addl Exp: $23,000 | **Total:** $36,596 (in-state), $57,665 (out-of-state)
Financial Aid: https://www.calpoly.edu/financial-aid

ADDITIONAL INFORMATION:

Available Degree(s)
- BS, MS, Ph.D. Aerospace Eng, Biomedical Engineering, Civil Eng, Computer Engineering, Computer Science, Electrical Eng, Environmental Engineering, Industrial Engineering, Materials Science & Engineering, Mechanical Engineering
- MS Fire Protection Engineering

Related Research Centers
CA Cybersecurity Institute, Center for Applications in Biotechnology, Center for Coastal Marine Sciences, Ctr for Construction Engineering, Center for Expressive Technologies, Center for Health Research, Center for Innovation & Entrepreneurship, Center for Sustainability, Electric Power Institute, Global Waste Research Institute, Institute for Advanced Technology & Public Policy, Lab for Global Automatic Identification Technologies, Western Coatings Technology Center

Scholarships Offered
Free Peer-to-Peer Tutoring (Course Assts, Problem Sets, Exam Prep, Gen Study Skills), Group Study Sessions, Supplemental Workshops, Study Skills Library, Research 101, Career Services, Internships, Summer Undergrad Res Prog, Facilities, 80 Labs, Tools/Technology, Plastics, AI, Engineering Student Services, Multicultural Eng Prog, International Exchange Program, Women in Eng Program, 397 Clubs

Orgs: Amateur Radio, American Chemical Society, American Foundry Society, American Indian Science & Engineering Society, American Institute of Aeronautics & Astronautics, American Institute of Chemical Engineers, American Society of Civil Engineers, American Society of Mechanical Engineers, Association for Computing Machinery, Biomedical Engineering Society, Biotech Club, CalGeo Club, Cal Poly Space Systems Club, Computer Engineering Society, Computer Science & AI, Data Science Club, Engineering Ambassadors, Engineering Student Council, Environmental Science Club, Game Development Club, Institute of Electrical & Electronics Engineering, Institute of Industrial & Systems Engineers, Institute of Transport Engineering, Material Advantage, Materials Engineering Student Society, National Society of Black Engineers, oSTEM, PolyHacks, Power & Engineering Society, Quantum Computer Club, Society of Hispanic Professional Engineers, Society of Environmental Engineering, Society of Manufacturing Engineering, Society of Women Engineers, Women Involved in Software and Hardware

Teams: Supermileage Team won 2022 Shell Eco-Marathon, Steel Bridge Team 2nd at ASCE, Concrete Canoe Team wins 6th national title in 2022, Sustainable Packaging Design Team won 1st Place in 2022 national competition, Animal Science Team won 1st Place in ASAS Competition for 3rd consecutive time, Formula SAE, Cal Poly Hackathon, Baja Racing Team, CSU Student Research Competition, Propulsion Technologies (SPT) Team, Debate Team, Mock Trial, Model United Nations, Rockery Team

Notable Alumni
Michael Alsbury, Tory Bruno, Greg Chamitoff, Robert Gibson, Victor Glover, Noel Lee, Mark Lucovsky, Alison Murray, Farid Nazem, Peter Oppenheimer, Aaron Peckham, Burt Rutan, Peter Siebold, Frederick Sturckow, William Swanson

SAN DIEGO STATE UNIVERSITY

Address: SDSU College of Engineering, 5500 Campanile Drive, San Diego, CA 92182
Website: https://www.engineering.sdsu.edu/
Contact: https://www.engineering.sdsu.edu/about/contact-us
Phone: (619) 594-6074
Email: aerospace.sdsu.edu

COST OF ATTENDANCE:
Tuition & Fees: $9,871 (in-state), $19,345 (out-of-state)
Addl Exp: $24,000 | **Total:** $33,871 (in-state), $43,345 (out-of-state)
Financial Aid: https://sacd.sdsu.edu/financial-aid

ADDITIONAL INFORMATION:
Available Degree(s)
- BS, BS/MS, MS, Ph.D. Aerospace Engineering, Civil Engineering, Computer Engineering, Comp Sci, Construction Eng, Electrical Engineering, Environmental Eng, Mechanical Engineering
- Minor: Nuclear Engineering

Related Research Areas
Advanced Methods for Analysis of Composite Structures, Air Quality Monitoring Lab, Astrodynamics, Autonomous Trajectory Planning & Opt, Biomass Eng Lab, Coastal Eng Lab, Data-Informed Construction Engineering, Disturbance Hydrology Lab, Experimental Aerodynamic Design, Geo-Innovations Research Lab, Guidance, Control & Flight Mechanics, Nonlinear Structural Dynamics & Aeroelasticity, Robotic Sensing, Dynamics, & Control, Safe Water Lab, Smart Transportation Analytics Research Lab, Structural Engineering Lab, Urban Water Lab, Visual Lab, Water Innovation & Reuse Lab.

Scholarships Offered
Merit Scholarships ($7,500-$10,000/year), SDSU Advantage Program (non-California resident students), Presidential Scholars Program ($10,000/year), Weber Honors College Scholarship ($1,000-$7,500/yr)

Special Opportunities
Design Day, Senior Gallery

Orgs: 3D4E, American Institute of Aeronautics & Astronautics, Amer Public Works Association, American Society of Civil Engineers, American Society of Mechanical Engineers, American Water Works Assoc, Artificial Intelligence Club, Associated General Contractors, Associated Geology Students, Association of Information Technology Professionals, Aztec Aerospace Design, Aztec Council on Systems Engineering, Biomedical Engineering Soc, Construction Management Association of America, CybOrg (CyberRisk Organization), Data & Design Technology Association, Data Science Initiative, eLeet Coders Club, Engineering Student Council, Engineers w/o Borders, Flying Samaritans, Geography Club, Girls Who Code, Institute of Electrical & Electronics Engineers, Institute of Transportation Engineers, Mechatronics, National Society of Black Engineers, Quality of Life+, Quantum Computing Club, Society of American Military Engineers, Society of Asian Scientists & Engineers, Society of Automotive Eng, Society of Hispanic Professional Engineers, Society of Women Engineers, Space Club, Themed Entertainment Association at SDSU, Women in Science Society, Women of Aeronautics & Astronautics

Teams: Autonomoous Underwater Vehicles (Robosub Team), Baja Racing, Big Data Hackathon, Cyber Defense Team, Design-Build-Fly, Electric Racing, eSports, Forensics Team, Formula Racing, Game Lab, iGEM (International Genetically Engineered Machines), Mock Trial Team, Model United Nations, Quiz Bowl, Robotics Team, Robo Sub, Rocket Team, Speech & Debate Team, Startup Pitch Competition

Notable Alumni
Adelia Coffman, Rick Hamada, Peggy Johnson, Samuel Kounaves, Laurance Doyle, Jacques Gauthier, M. Brian Maple, Gordon Martin, Bridgette Meinhold, Ellen Ochoa, Mark Phillips, J. Michael Scott, Paul Zak

ALASKA
ARIZONA
CALIFORNIA
COLORADO
HAWAII
IDAHO
MONTANA
NEVADA
NEW MEXICO
OREGON
UTAH
WASHINGTON
WYOMING

WEST

ALASKA
ARIZONA
CALIFORNIA
COLORADO
HAWAII
IDAHO
MONTANA
NEVADA
NEW MEXICO
OREGON
UTAH
WASHINGTON
WYOMING

STANFORD UNIVERSITY

Address: Stanford Engineering, 475 Via Ortega, Suite 227, Stanford, CA 94305
Website: https://engineering.stanford.edu/
Contact: https://engineering.stanford.edu/contact-us
Phone: (650) 723-2091
Email: tkenny@stanford.edu

COST OF ATTENDANCE:
Tuition & Fees: $62,484 | **Addl Exp:** $23,000 | **Total:** $85,484
Financial Aid: https://financialaid.stanford.edu/

ADDITIONAL INFORMATION:

Available Degree(s)
- BS, MS, Ph.D. Aerospace Eng, Bioengineering, Chemical Eng, Civil Eng, Computer Eng, Computer Science, Electrical Eng, Environmental Eng, Materials Science & Eng, Mechanical Eng

Related Research Areas
Aerospace Computing, Aerospace Design, Aerospace Robotics, Aircraft Aerodynamics, Air Traffic Management, Autonomous Systems, Extreme Environment Microsystems Lab, Flow Physics & Aeroacoustics Lab, GPS Laboratory, Intelligent & Composites Lab, Mapping & Navigation in Extreme Environments, Morphing Space Structures Lab, Navigation & Autonomous Systems Lab, Planning & Control for Agile Robotic Syst, Reconfigurable Structures, Robotic Transportation Networks, Space Environment & Satellite Systems, Space Rendezvous, Space Robotics, Structures & Composites Lab

Focus: Cities, Energy, Infrastructure, Public Health, Tech, and Water

Scholarships Offered
Families with incomes of $150,000 or less attend college tuition free. Stanford does not offer merit scholarships. Graduate students study for free and receive an additional stipend through a special prog; students are encouraged to apply for the Rhodes, Marshall, and Mitchell Scholarships, Fulbright Grants, Churchill Scholarships, Gates Cambridge Scholarships, German Academic Exchange (DAAD) Awards, and Think Swiss Research Scholarship

Special Opportunities
Global Engineering internships, Cardinal Quarter, Study Tours, Faculty-Initiated Travel Programs, Bing Overseas Study Program (Australia, Berlin, Cape Town, Florence, Madrid, Kyoto, NYC, Oxford, Paris, Santiago), and Chinese Undergraduate Visiting Research Prog

The France-Stanford Ctr for Interdiscip Studies partners w/French Ministry of Foreign Affairs to Humanities, STEM, Business, & Law.

Orgs: American Institute of Aeronautics and Astronautics, American Institute of Chemical Engineers, American Society of Civil Engineers, Assoc for Computing Machinery, Engineers for a Sustainable World, Institute for Electrical & Electronics Eng, Materials Research Society, Nat Soc of Black Eng, Optical Society of America, oSTEM, Product Design Student Assoc, Society of LatinX Eng, Society of Women Eng

Teams: Concrete Canoe Team, Chess, CubeSat, Debate Society, Design-Build-Fly Team, eSports, Formula SAE, iGEM (International Genetically Engineered Machine) Team, Mock Trial, Model United Nations, NASA Student Launch Competition Team, National Collegiate Cyber Defense Competition, Rubik's Cube, Solar Car, Stanford Racing Team, Stanford Student Robotics, Student Space Initiative, Unmanned Aerial Vehicle Team

Notable Alumni
Norman Abramson, Scott Anderson, Ronald N. Bracewell, Robert Cannon, Jr., Eileen Collins, Ray Dolby, Roland Dore, Charles Stark Draper, Charbel Farhat, Mike Fincke, William Fisher, Bill Franke, Owen Garriott, Susan Helms, Michael Hopkins, G. Scott Hubbard, Mae Jemison, Elizabeth Jens, Tamara Jernigan, Stanley Kennedy Sr., Gregory Linteris, A. Louis London, Edward Lu, Bruce McCandless II, John Macready, Barbara Morgan, Raj Reddy, Kathleen Rubins, Ellen Ochoa, Scott Parazynski, Sally Ride, Stephen Robinson, Debbie Senesky, Steve Smith, and Jeff Wisoff

UNIVERSITY OF CALIFORNIA, BERKELEY

Address: UC Berkeley College of Engineering, Dean's Office, 320 McLaughlin Hall, Berkeley, CA 94720-1700
Website: *https://engineering.berkeley.edu/*
Contact: *https://engineering.berkeley.edu/contact/*
Phone: (510) 642-5771
Email: engineeringdean@berkeley.edu

COST OF ATTENDANCE:

Tuition & Fees: $19,500(in-state), $53,000 (out-of-state)
Addl Exp: $23,500 | **Total:** $43,000 (in-state), $76,500(out-of-state)
Financial Aid: https://financialaid.berkeley.edu/

ADDITIONAL INFORMATION:

Available Degree(s)
- BS, MS, Ph.D. Bioengineering, Chemical Eng, Civil Eng, Comp Eng, Computer Science, Data Science, Electrical Eng, Energy Eng, Eng Math/Statistics, Eng Physics, Environmental Eng, Industrial Eng, Materials Science & Engineering, Mechanical Engineering, Nuclear Engineering, Operations Research
- MS Master of Molecular Science & Software Engineering

Related Research Centers
BRAVO Autonomous Vehicle Research, Cool Climate Network, Fire Res Inst, Inst for Energy and the Environment, Institute of Transportation Studies, Jacobs Institute for Design Innovation, Nuclear Science & Security, Pacific Earthquake Engineering Research Center, Partners for Advanced Transportation Tech, Power & Energy Center, SWARM Lab, Team for Research in Ubiquitous Secure Technology, Water Center

Scholarships Offered
Berkeley, Fiat Lux, & Middle-Class Scholarships - no additional app required. Complete the FAFSA or CA Dream Act Application. Regents & Chancellor's - $2,500 for scholars w/o financial need

Special Opportunities
Berkeley Engineering holds classes/research/activities in dozen bldgs using 1,000,000 sq ft w/large-scale facilities, one of the world's largest earthquake simulators. Berkeley Innovators, Eng Research Support Org, The Foundry@CITRIS, Intellectual Property & Industry Research

Labs: Berkeley Research IT, Biomolecular Nanotech Center, Invention Lab, Marvell Nanofabrication Lab, Lawrence Berkeley National Lab, Lawrence Livermore National Laboratory

Orgs: American Chemical Society, American Institute of Aeronautics & Astronautics, American Institute of Chemical Engineers, American Nuclear Society, American Society of Civil Engineers, American Soc of Mechanical Eng, Association for Computing Machinery, Biomedical Eng Society, Engineers for a Sustainable World, Environmental Team, Institute of Electrical & Electronics Engineers, Institute of Industrial & Systems Engineers, Institute of Transportation Engineers, Materials Science & Engineering Association, NAE Grand Challenges Scholars Program, Society of Eng Scientists, Society of Women Engineers

Teams: Bike Builders, Biofuels Tech, Bioprinting@Berkeley, Cal Construction, CalSol, Super Mileage Vehicle Team, Chem-E Car Team, Concrete Canoe, Cyber Security Competition Team, Debate Soc, DOE Cyber Force, Enable Tech, Environmental Team, Extended Reality, Formula SAE Electric Vehicle, Human-Powered Vehicle, iGEM (Intl Genetically Engineered Machines), Mock Trial, Model United Nations, Seismic Design Team, Space Enterprise, Space Technology & Rocketry, Steel Bridge Competition Team, Sustainable Housing at Cal, Transport Team, Unmanned Aerial Vehicle Team, Underwater Robotics Team

Notable Alumni
Thomas Cech, Robert Curl, Andrew Fire, Shafi Goldwasser, Jim Gray, Carol Greider, Alan Heeger, David Julius, Leonard Lademan, Butler Lampson, Yuan Lee, Silvio Micali, Mario Molina, Kary Mullis, Gordon Moore, Loren Ryder, Margret Schmidt, Glenn Seaborg, Henry Taube, Charles Thacker, & Steve Wozniak

ALASKA
ARIZONA
CALIFORNIA
COLORADO
HAWAII
IDAHO
MONTANA
NEVADA
NEW MEXICO
OREGON
UTAH
WASHINGTON
WYOMING

WEST

UNIVERSITY OF CALIFORNIA, DAVIS

Address: University of California, Davis, College of Engineering, One Shields Avenue, Davis, CA 95616
Website: https://engineering.ucdavis.edu/
Contact: https://engineering.ucdavis.edu/about/college-leadership
Phone: (530) 752-1979
Email: engugrad@ucdavis.edu

COST OF ATTENDANCE:

Tuition & Fees: $19,500(in-state), $53,000 (out-of-state)
Addl Exp: $23,500 | **Total:** $43,000 (in-state), $76,500(out-of-state)
Financial Aid: https://financialaid.ucdavis.edu/

ADDITIONAL INFORMATION:

Available Degree(s)
- BS, MS, Ph.D. Aerospace Eng, Biochemical Eng, Biological Systems Engineering, Biomedical Engineering, Chemical Engineering, Civil Eng, Computer Engineering, Computer Science, Electrical Engineering, Environmental Engineering, Materials Science & Engineering, Mechanical Engineering
- MS, Ph.D. Energy Systems
- Minors: Energy Efficiency, Energy Policy, Energy, Science, & Tech, Geographic Info Syst, Precision Agriculture, Tech Mgmt

Related Research Centers
Materials Design Institute, Tahoe Environmental Research Center

Scholarships Offered
Students can apply for $4 million in scholarships ($100 - $14,000). Scholarships awarded on merit basis incl academics, activities, career interests, geographic origin, parents, & perseverance. Students must apply annually. Students do not need to file a FAFSA or Dream Act App. Some merit scholarships do take into account financial need.

Special Opportunities
Facilities: Bioinformatics Core, Biological Electron Microscopy, DNA Techn & Expression Analysis Core, Light Microscopy Imaging, Mass Spectrometry, Metabolomics Core, Nanotech Center, Research Greenhouses, Proteomics Core, UCDNA Sequencing, TILLING Core

BioLaunch Mentor Collective, Bodega Marine Lab, Internships, Student Govt, Study Abroad, Undergrad Research, World Food Inst

Orgs: Adaptive Technology Association, American Chemical Society, American Indian Science & Engineering Society, American Institute of Aeronautics & Astronautics, American Inst of Chemical Eng, American Society of Agricultural & Biological Engineering, American Society of Biochemistry & Molecular Biology, American Society of Civil Eng, American Society of Heating, Refrig, Air-Cond. Eng, American Society of Mechanical Eng, American Water Works Assoc, Bit Project, Black Eng Association, Chicanx & Latinx Engineering & Science Society, Davis Comp Science Club, Google Developer Student Club, Eng w/o Borders, Female Association of Civil Eng, Future Female Electrical Eng, Institute of Electrical & Electronics Engineers, Inst of Transport Engineering, International Society for Pharmaceutical Engineering, Material Advantage, oSTEM, Pilipinx Americans in Science & Engineering, Quantum Computing at Davis, Society of Biological Engineering, Society of Manufacturing Engineers, Society of Women Engineers, Women in Computer Science, Women Machinists' Club

Teams: Aerobrick & Adv Modeling Aeronautics Team, Baja SAE Team, ChemE Car, Concrete Canoe, Debate Team, ECLIPSE Researn Prog, Env Project, eSports Team, Formula Racing, GeoWall, Mock Trial, Model United Nations, OneLoop, RoveCrest, Seismic Design, Steel Bridge, BioInnovation Group, Drone Club, HackDavis, Robotics Club, Solar Boat Team, Solar Car Team, Space & Satellite Systems Team

Notable Alumni
David Abe, Chow Chung-kong, Kaveh Madani, Sig Mejdal, Nelson Pass, Bernard Soriano, Jeffrey Steefel, Adam Steltzner, & Alvin White

ALASKA
ARIZONA
CALIFORNIA
COLORADO
HAWAII
IDAHO
MONTANA
NEVADA
NEW MEXICO
OREGON
UTAH
WASHINGTON
WYOMING

UNIVERSITY OF CALIFORNIA, IRVINE

Address: Samueli School of Engineering, 5200 Engineering Hall Irvine, CA 92697-2700
Website: https://engineering.uci.edu/
Contact: https://engineering.uci.edu/about/got-questions
Phone: (949) 824-4333
Email: ugengr@uci.edu

COST OF ATTENDANCE:
Tuition & Fees: $19,500(in-state), $53,000 (out-of-state)
Addl Exp: $23,500 | **Total:** $43,000 (in-state), $76,500(out-of-state)
Financial Aid: https://www.ofas.uci.edu/index.php

ADDITIONAL INFORMATION:
Available Degree(s)
- BS, MS, Ph.D. Aerospace Eng, BME, Chemistry, Chemical Eng, Civil Eng, Computer Eng, Computer Science, Electrical Eng, Environmental Eng, Materials Science & Eng, Mechanical Eng

Related Research Centers
Adv Power & Energy Prog, Ctr for Advanced Design & Manufacturing of Integrated Microfluidics, Center for Hydrometeorology & Remote Sensing, Laboratory for Fluorescence Dynamics, UCI Combustion Lab

Focus Areas: Aeroaccoustics, Aeroelasticity, Aerospace, Automization & Sprays, Autonomous & Distributed Syst, Biomechanics, Biomedical Flows, Combustion & Emissions, Composites, Comp Fluid Dynamics, Ctrl Thry & Algorithms, Defect Formation/Propagation, Deformation & Failure, Electrosprays, Energy Systems, Fuel Cell Technologies, Heat Transfer, Jet & Rocket Propulsion, Machine Learning, Modeling of Global Air Pollution, Multiphase Flow, Nanomaterials, Navigation & Flight Systems, Reaction Kinetics, Rehabilitation, Renewable Energy, Robotics, Turbomachinery, Uncertainty Quantification

Scholarships Offered
SWE-OC Scholarships; Henry Samueli Endowed Scholarships; Regents' Scholarship, Chancellor's Excellence Scholarship, Director's Scholarship – No additional application necessary

Special Opportunities
3D Printing Club, ANTrepreneurship, Chemistry Field Studies Program, Human Biology Club, UCI BioSci, Wayfinder Incubator

Orgs: 3D Printing Club, American Chemical Society, American Institute of Aeronautics & Astronautics, American Inst of Chemical Engineers, American Academy of Environmental Engineering & Science, American Public Works Association, American Society for Civil Eng, American Society for Mechanical Engineers, Associated General Contractors, Association for Computing Machinery, Biomedical Eng Society, Chinese Engineering Association, Earthquake Engineering Research Institute, Eng Student Council, Engineers w/o Borders, Engineers for a Sustainable World, Filipinos Unifying Student-Engineers in an Organized Network, Global Engineering Brigades, H2Outreach, Institute of Electrical & Electronics Engineers, Ins of Transportation Engineers, Material Advantage, Materials Science Club, Mexican American Engineers & Scientists, National Society of Black Engineers, Society of Hispanic Professional Eng, Society of Women Engineers, Structural Engineers Assoc of So Cal, UCI Triangle, Zotbotics, zotCAMS

Teams: Anteater Racing, Arduino Intelligence Vehicle, ArmBiotics, AI Team, Autonomous Vehicles (Car, Drone, Forklift, Search & Rescue), Baja Racing, Chem-E-Car, Chess, Collegiate Cyber Defense Team, Concrete Canoe, Cubesat, Design at UCI, Electric Car Racing, eSports Team, Formula Racing, Hack at UCI, Hot Air Balloon, Human Gesture Center Robotic Arm, Human Powered Vehicle Competition, Intelligent Ground Vehicle, Mock Trial Team, Model United Nations, Robotics Team, Rocket Team, Solar Car, Solar Plane, Steel Bridge Team, Unmanned Aerial Vehicle Team, Video Game Development

Notable Alumni
Roy Fielding, Patrick Hanratty, Bart Kosko, Lawrence Larmore, James McCaffrey, Paul Mockapetris, Kathie Olsen, and Jim Whitehead

ALASKA
ARIZONA
CALIFORNIA
COLORADO
HAWAII
IDAHO
MONTANA
NEVADA
NEW MEXICO
OREGON
UTAH
WASHINGTON
WYOMING

WEST

UNIVERSITY OF CALIFORNIA, LOS ANGELES

Address: UCLA Samueli School of Engineering, 7400 Boelter Hall, Los Angeles, CA 90095
Website: https://samueli.ucla.edu/
Contact: https://samueli.ucla.edu/contact-us
Phone: (310) 825-9580
Email: engrdean@seas.ucla.edu

COST OF ATTENDANCE:
Tuition & Fees: $19,500 (in-state), $53,000 (out-of-state)
Addl Exp: $23,500 | **Total:** $43,000 (in-state), $76,500 (out-of-state)
Financial Aid: https://financialaid.ucla.edu/

ADDITIONAL INFORMATION:
Available Degree(s)
- BS, MS, Ph.D. Aerospace Eng, Bioengineering, Chemical Eng, Civil Engineering, Computer Engineering, Computer Science, Data Science, Electrical Engineering, Environmental Eng, Materials Science & Eng, Mechanical Eng, Robotics Eng
- MS Computer Networking, Integrated Circuits, Manuf Design, Quantum Sci & Tech, Signal Processing, Structural Materials

Related Research Centers
Breakthrough Tech AI, Ctr for Accel nanoMaterials, Ctr for Domain-Specific Comp, Ctr for Encrypted Functionalities, Ctr of Excellences for Green Nanotech, Ctr for Heterogeneous Integ. & Perf Scaling, Ctr for Info & Computation Security, Media, & Perf, Ctr for Translational Apps of Nanoscale Multiferroic Systems, Inst for Carbon Mgmt, Inst for Tech Law & Policy, Inst for Tech & Advancement, Named Data Networking, Scalable Analytics Institute, Sci Hub for Humanity & AI, Smart Grid Energy Research Center, Western Inst of Nanoelectronics

Scholarships Offered
Regents & Chancellor's Scholarships -$2,500 non-need-based. For need-based scholarships, complete an online "UCLA Scholarship Application" available through MyUCLA & submit a FAFSA or Dream Act application by the March 2 priority deadline EVERY YEAR.

Special Opportunities
UCLA Samueli research labs, Student Creativity Center, & Innovation Lab; Boelter Hall, Engineering-IV, Engineering-V and Engineering-VI

Orgs: American Indian Scientists & Engineering Soc, American Institute of Chemical Eng, Arab American Assoc of Eng & Architects, Assoc for Computing Machinery, American Society of Civil Eng, American Society of Mechanical Eng, Beekeepers, Blockchain @ UCLA, Bruin Consulting, Bruin Entrepreneurs, Bruin Home Solutions, Bruin Space Group, Building Engineers & Mentors, Design Create Solar, Eng Ambassadors, Ecological Restoration Association, Engineering Entrepreneurial Grp, Engineering Society UC, Engineers w/o Borders, exploretech.la, IEEE Electron Devices Society, IEEE Electrics Pkg Society, Inst of Electrical & Electronics Eng, IEEE Women Adv Technology through Teamwork, Institute of Transportation Engineers, Korean-American Science & Engineering Association, LA Blueprint, Materials Research Society, MentorSEAS, National Society of Black Eng, Pilipinos in Engineering & Science (PIES), oSTEM, Renewable Energy Association, Society of Asian Scientists & Engineers, Society of Hispanic Professional Eng, Society of Women Engineering, Women in Tech

Teams: AIAA Design/Build/Fly, Aerial Robotics, Baja SAE, BattleBots, Chess, College Bowl, Comp Sci Team, Concrete CanoeTeam, CubeSat, Cubing, DARPA Challenge, Debate Union, DevX, eSports, DOE Solar Decathlon, Formula SAE Bruin Racing, Hack/Build/Innovate, iGEM Team (Intl Genetically Eng Machines), Logic Competition Team, Mock Trial, Model United Nations, National Collegiate Cyber Defense Team, FIRST Robotics Team, Quiz Bowl, RoboCup (Robotic Soccer Team), Rocket Project, Science Olympiad, Steel Bridge, Supermileage

Notable Alumni
Barry Boehm, Michael Gottlieb, Roberta Gottlieb, David Ho, Howard Judd, Kimberly Lee, Linda Liau, Courtney Lyder, Michael Morhaime, No-Hee Park, Ardem Patapoutian, Frank Pearce, Henry Samueli, Randy Schekman, Taylor Wang, Flossie Wong-Staal, & Mani Zadeh

- ALASKA
- ARIZONA
- **CALIFORNIA**
- COLORADO
- HAWAII
- IDAHO
- MONTANA
- NEVADA
- NEW MEXICO
- OREGON
- UTAH
- WASHINGTON
- WYOMING

UNIVERSITY OF CALIFORNIA, RIVERSIDE

Address: Marlan & Rosemary Bourns College of Engineering, 446 Winston Chung Hall, 900 Univ. Ave. Riverside, CA 92521
Website: https://www.engr.ucr.edu/
Contact: https://mailchi.mp/ucr.edu/bcoemailinglist
Phone: (951) 827-5190
Email: undergrad@engr.ucr.edu

COST OF ATTENDANCE:

Tuition & Fees: $19,500(in-state), $53,000 (out-of-state)
Addl Exp: $23,500 | **Total:** $43,000 (in-state), $76,500(out-of-state)

Financial Aid: https://financialaid.ucr.edu/

ADDITIONAL INFORMATION:

Available Degree(s)
- BS, MS Bioengineering, Chemical Engineering, Computer Engineering, Computer Science, Data Science, Electrical Engineering, Environmental Engineering, Materials Science & Engineering, Mechanical Engineering, Robotics Engineering
- Minors: Earth & Planetary Studies, Environmental Studies, Geology, Neuroscience, Plant Biology, Psychology, Statistics

Related Research Areas
Brain Game Center for Mental Fitness & Well-Being, Catalysis Center, Center for Advanced Neuroimaging, Central Facility for Advanced Microscopy & Microanalysis, Center for Geospatial Sciences, High-Performance Computing Center, Water Resources Engineering

Scholarships Offered
Allen Van Tran Student Award in Engineering, American Honda Science/Engineering Endowed Fund, BCOE-Alumni Scholarship, Gartzke Memorial Endowed Scholarship, Gref Family Endowed Fund for the Advancement of StEM, Babbage Scholarship, Yoo Scholarship
At UCR, 85% of UCR undergraduate students who applied for aid were awarded aid money for college; 97% of undergraduate students who were awarded aid received need-based scholarships and/or grants. UCR students who borrow federal loans have an average student loan debt of $21,500. Summer aid available. Blue & Gold - CA residence whose family income is below $80,000 do not have to pay system-wide tuition and fees. California Dream Act (DACA students; Complete FAFSA

Special Opportunities
Orgs: American Institute of Chemical Engineers, American Society of Mechanical Engineers, Association for Computing Machinery, Biomedical Engineering Society, Cyber@UCR, Engineers without Borders, Environmental Science Club, Game Development Club, Highlander Space Program, Institute of Electrical & Electronics Engineers, Material Research Society, National Society of Black Engineers, Society of Automotive Engineers, Society of Hispanic Professional Engineers, Society of Women Engineers, Women in Computing, Women in Technology

Teams: Chess, CubeSat Team, Cubing, Cyber@UCR, Cyber Defense Competition Team, EcoCAR EV Challenge, eSports, Formula SAE, Gamespawn, Highlander Gaming, Highlander Racing, Mock Trial Team, Model United Nations, National GEICO Hackathon Competition Team, Programming Competitions, Robotics@UCR, Space Team, Sustainable Building Materials Team, UAV/UAS Drone Tech Team

Notable Alumni
Peter Adriaens, Harmohinder Gill, Lynn Gref, Matthew Haughey, Arthur Riggs, Pedram Salimpour, Richard Schrock, Bettie Steinberg, Time White, Jennifer Wilby

ALASKA
ARIZONA
CALIFORNIA
COLORADO
HAWAII
IDAHO
MONTANA
NEVADA
NEW MEXICO
OREGON
UTAH
WASHINGTON
WYOMING

WEST

- ALASKA
- ARIZONA
- **CALIFORNIA**
- COLORADO
- HAWAII
- IDAHO
- MONTANA
- NEVADA
- NEW MEXICO
- OREGON
- UTAH
- WASHINGTON
- WYOMING

UNIVERSITY OF CALIFORNIA, SAN DIEGO

Address: Jacobs School of Engineering, University of California, San Diego, 9500 Gilman Drive, La Jolla, CA 92093-0403
Website: https://jacobsschool.ucsd.edu/
Contact: https://jacobsschool.ucsd.edu/about/contacts
Phone: (858) 534-6237
Email: DeanPisano@eng.ucsd.edu

COST OF ATTENDANCE:

Tuition & Fees: $19,500 (in-state), $53,000 (out-of-state)
Addl Exp: $23,500 | **Total:** $43,000 (in-state), $76,500 (out-of-state)

Financial Aid: https://fas.ucsd.edu/

ADDITIONAL INFORMATION:

Available Degree(s)
- BS, MS, Ph.D. Aerospace Engineering, Bioeng, Chemical Eng,
- Computer Eng, Comp Sci, Data Science, EE, Environmental
- Eng, Mechanical Eng, NanoEngineering, Structural Eng
- MS, Ph.D. Materials Science & Engineering

Related Research Centers
CaliBaja Center for Resilient Materials & Systems, Center for Energy Research, Center for Engineered Natural Intelligence, Ctr for Extreme Events Research, Center for Machine-Intelligence, Computing, & Security, Center for Memory & Recording Res, Center for Microbiome Innovation, Center for Nano-ImmunoEngineering, Center for Visual Computing, Ctr for Wearable Sensors, Contextual Robotics Institute, Deep Decarbonization Initiative, Earthquake Shake Table, Info Theory & Appl Center, Inst of Engineering in Medicine, Institute for the Global Entrepreneur, Institute for Materials Discovery & Design, Power Management Integration Center, Sustainable Power & Energy Center

Scholarships Offered
Regents & Chancellor's Scholarships offer money for scholars w/o financial need; Ellen & Roger Revelle Scholarship. For need-based scholarships, complete addl information in your portal & submit a FAFSA or Dream Act appl by March 2 priority deadline EVERY YEAR.

Special Opportunities
Global industry partnerships; entrepreneurship program; study abroad, research, & internships; pre-college program; multiple scholar program. Facilities include IDEA Engineering Student Center & The EnVision Arts & Engineering Maker Studio - nearly 3,000 sq ft studio providing a wide range of design, fabrication/prototyping tools, both analog & digital. UCSD is the lead in the new $10M NSF Data Science Research Center, EnCORE w/UCLA, UPenn, & UT Austin

Orgs: American Chemical Society, American Institute of Aeronautics & Astronautics, American Inst of Chemical Eng, American Society of Civil Engineers, American Society of Mechanical Eng, Biomedical Engineering Society, EnVisionaries, Engineers for a Sustainable World, Engineering World Health, Global Medical Brigades, Institute of Electrical & Electronics Engineers, National Society of Black Engineers, oSTEM, Society of Asian Scientists & Engineers, Society of Civil & Structural Engineers, Society of Hispanic Professional Engineers, Society of Women Engineers, Students for the Exploration & Development of Space, Women in Computing, Women in Tech

Teams: Aerial Robotics Team, Autonomous Airplane, Baja SAE Team, Bruin Racing (Formula SAE), Chem-E Car Team, Chess, College Bowl, Concrete Canoe, Cubing Club (Rubik's Cube), Cubesat, Design/Build/Fly, Dept of Energy Cyber Force, eSports Team, iGEM (International Genetically Engineered Machines), Mock Trial, Model United Nations, Quantum Processing Team, Quiz Bowl Team, Science Olympiad, Speech & Debate, Steel Bridge Team, Triton RoboSub (UCSD won)

Notable Alumni
Bill Atkinson, Ryan Dahl, Taner Halicioglu, Steve Hart, Gary Jacobs, Brandon Nixon, Greg Papadopoulos, Kate Rubins, Maurizio Seracini, David Shaw, Guy Tribble, Nick Woodman, Edward Wu

UNIVERSITY OF SOUTHERN CALIFORNIA

Address: University of Southern California, Viterbi School of Engineering, Olin Hall, Room 106, 3650 McClintock Ave, L.A., CA 90089
Website: https://viterbischool.usc.edu/
Contact: https://viterbischool.usc.edu/contact-us/
Phone: (213) 740-4488
Email: sath@usc.edu

COST OF ATTENDANCE:
Tuition & Fees: $71,647 | **Addl Exp:** $23,568 | **Total:** $95,225
Financial Aid: https://financialaid.usc.edu/

ADDITIONAL INFORMATION:
Available Degree(s)
- BS, MS, Ph.D. Aerospace Eng, Astronautical Eng, BME, ChemE Civil Eng, Comp Eng, Comp Sci, Construction Eng, Data Sci, Electrical Eng, Enviro Eng, Industrial & Syst Eng, Intelligence & Cyber Ops, Materials Science, Mechanical Eng, Petroleum Eng

Related Research Centers
Airbus Institute for Eng Research, Center for Advanced Manufacturing, Center for Computational Modeling of Cancer, Center for Dark Energy Biosphere Investigations, Center for Intelligent Environments, Center for Interactive Smart Oilfield Technologies, Center for Risk & Economic Analysis of Threats & Emergencies, Center for Systems & Control, Center for Systems & Software Engineering, Center for Technology & Mental Health Core Center of Excellence in Nano Imaging, Energy Institute, M.C. Gill Composites Center, Materials Genome Innovation for Computational Software Center, Institute of Optical Nanomaterials & Nanophotonics, Institute for Collaborative Engineering, Quantum Computation Center, Robotics & Autonomous Systems Center, Signal & Image Processing Institute, Space Engineering Research Center, Systems Engineering Research Center, Visualizing New Narrative Forms through Quantum Physics, Artificial Intelligence, & Sustainability

Scholarships Offered
Merit scholarships are reserved for students w/special qualifications, such as academic, athletic, or artistic talent.

Special Opportunities
Internships, fellowships, summer research; Global Summit, Eng + Program, Grand Challenges; labs, institutes, centers, competition, & entrepreneurship; Viterbi Entrepreneurship Ed (freshman core)

Orgs: 3D4E, American Chemical Soc, ASPEN, ADT, AAEES, American Institute of Aeronautics & Astronautics, American Inst of Chemical Engineers, AISC, Amer Soc of Civil Eng, Amer Soc of Mechanical Eng, AIMC, Biomedical Engineering Society, CAISS++, CybOrg, CTC, CMAA, Global Medical Brigades, Earthquake Eng Research Inst, Engineers w/o Borders, GIT, Institute of Electrical & Electronic Engineers, IISE, KIUEL, Korean Amer Sci & Eng Assn, Nat Soc of Black Eng, QuEST, Rocket Propulsion Lab, Soc of Asian Scientists & Eng, Soc of Hispanic Prof Eng, Society of Women Engineers, Women in Computing, WCHE

Teams: Athena Hacks, ChemE Car Team, Chess, Concrete Canoe Team, CubeSat, Cyber Defense Team, eSports, Formula SAE Car Team, Hack-IoT Team, iGEM, Mock Trial, MUN, MEDesign Team, Quiz Bowl, Recumbent Vehicle Team, Rubik's Cube Team, SC Racing Team, Science Olympiad, Solar Car Team, Steel Bridge, Trojan Debate Squad, Underwater Vehicle Team, USC Makers, VEX Robotics Team 2022 USC AeroDesign Team-4th of 97 teams in AIAA Comp; Maseeh Entrepreneurship Prize Competition (startups), Min Family Challenge; ABC Innovation Prize Competition (atoms, bits, & cells); Global Engineering Design Studio; Viterbi Startup Garage Incubator

Notable Alumni
Neil Armstrong, Wanda Austin, Charles Bassett, II, Karol Bobko, Charles Bolden, Gerald Carr, Nancy Currie, William Dana, Brian Duffy, Andrew Frank, Henry Gordon, Robert Gray, Nathan Lindsay, Jerry Linenger, James Lovell, Carlos Noriega, Kenneth Reightler, Walter Schirra, Shang-Hua Teng, Pierre Thuot, & Andrew Viterbi

ALASKA
ARIZONA
CALIFORNIA
COLORADO
HAWAII
IDAHO
MONTANA
NEVADA
NEW MEXICO
OREGON
UTAH
WASHINGTON
WYOMING

WEST

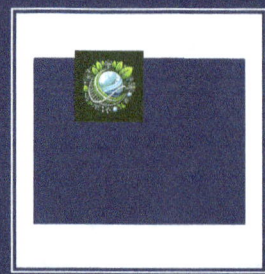

ALASKA

ARIZONA

CALIFORNIA

COLORADO

HAWAII

IDAHO

MONTANA

NEVADA

NEW MEXICO

OREGON

UTAH

WASHINGTON

WYOMING

UNIVERSITY OF COLORADO, BOULDER

Address: University of Colorado, Boulder, College of Engineering & Applied Sciences, 1111 Engineering Dr., 422 UCB, Boulder, CO 80309
Website: https://www.colorado.edu/engineering/
Contact: https://www.colorado.edu/engineering/contact-us
Phone: (303) 492-5071
Email: cueng@colorado.edu

COST OF ATTENDANCE:

Tuition & Fees: $16,958 (in-state), $44,636 (out-of-state)
Addl Exp: $20,000 | **Total:** $36,958 (in-state), $64,636 (out-of-state)

Financial Aid: https://www.colorado.edu/financialaid/

ADDITIONAL INFORMATION:

Available Degree(s)
- BS, MS, Ph.D. Aerospace Engineering, Civil Eng, Computer Engineering, Computer Science, Electrical Eng, Environmental Engineering, Materials Science & Eng, Mechanical Engineering
- Minors: BME, Comp Sci, Comp Eng, Creative Tech & Design, EE, Eng Mgmt, Energy Eng, Global Eng, Quantum Eng, Signals & Sys
- Certificates: Digital Media, Energy, Electrical, Computer & Energy, Eng for Devl Communities, Eng Leadership, Eng Mgmt & Entrepreneurship, Global Eng, Intl Eng, Telecommunications

Related Research Areas
Aerospace Mechanics Research Center, AeroSpace Ventures, ATLAS Institute, Biofrontiers Institute, BioServe Space Technology, Center for Advanced Decision Support for Water & Environmental Systems, Center for Astrodynamics Research, Center for Environmental Mass Spec, Center for Applied of Photopolymerization, Center for Research & Education in Wind, Ctr for Software & Society, Center for Unmanned Aircraft Systems, Joint Inst for Lab Astrophysics, Lab for Atmosphere & Space Physics, Membrane Applied Science & Technology Center, Power Electronics Center, Renewable & Sustainable Energy Institute, Research & Eng Ctr for Unmanned Vehicles, Space Grant Consortium

Scholarships Offered
CUB scholarship application opens Nov 1 - closes Feb 1 or March 1: https://www.colorado.edu/scholarships/cuboulder-scholarship-app

Special Opportunities
Co-Ops, Internships, Service Learning, Senior Design Projects, Earth Lab, Environmental Programs, Entrepreneurship & Engineering, Global Experiences, Leadership, National Center for Women & Information Technology, Space Mobility; Space Weather Technology, Telecommunications Program, Undergraduate Research

Orgs: American Institute of Aeronautics & Astronautics, American Indian Science & Engineering Society, American Institute of Chemical Engineers, American Society of Civil Engineers, American Society of Mechanical Engineers, Architectural Engineering Institute, Associated General Contractors, Association for Computing Machinery, Biomedical Engineering Society, CO Engineer Magazine, Engineering Council, Energy Club, Engineering Fellows, Engineers w/o Borders, Illuminating Engineering Society, Institute of Electrical & Electronics Engineers, International Society for Pharmaceutical Eng, National Society of Black Engineers, Society of Asian Scientists & Engineers, Society of Hispanic Professional Eng, Society of Mexican American Eng & Scientists, Society of Women Engineers, Women in Computing

Teams: Chem-E Car Team, Coding Buffs, Cyber Team, Design-Build-Fly, Drone Racing Team, Formula Baja Racing, Grand Challenge – Our Space, iGEM (Intl Genetically Eng Machines), HackCU, Hyperloop, Mock Trial, Model United Nations, Physics Olympiad, Robotics Team, RoboSub Team, Rover Team, Solar Decathlon, Sounding Rocketry Team, SpaceForce, Speech & Debate, T9hacks

Notable Alumni
Sidney Altman, Steve Chappell, W. Edwards Deming, Jennifer Doudna, Moriba Jah, Alan Kay, Tom Maniatis, Craig Mello, Lou Melton, and Jim Voss

OREGON STATE

Address: Oregon State University, College of Engineering, 101 Covell Hall, Corvallis, OR 97331-2409
Website: *https://engineering.oregonstate.edu/*
Contact: *https://engineering.oregonstate.edu/contact-us*
Phone: *(541) 737-3101*
Email: askengineering@oregonstate.edu

COST OF ATTENDANCE:
Tuition & Fees: $14,391 (in-state), $39,500 (out-of-state)
Addl Exp: $20,000 | **Total:** $34,391 (in-state), $59,500 (out-of-state)
Financial Aid: https://financialaid.oregonstate.edu/

ADDITIONAL INFORMATION:
Available Degree(s)
- BS, MS, Ph.D. Aerospace Eng, Architectural Eng, Bioeng, Chem Eng, Civil Eng, Comp Eng, Comp Science, Constr. Eng Mgmt, Ecological Eng, Electrical Eng, Energy Systems Eng, Eng Mgmt, Environmental Eng, Industrial Eng, Mech Eng, Nuclear Eng
- MS, Ph.D. AI, Materials Sci, Robotics, Water Resources Eng
- Minor: Comp Sci, Geomatics Eng, Humanitarian Eng, Intl Eng
- Certificate: Cybersecurity

Related Research Areas
AI & Robotics, Computer Graphics & Visualization, Computer Science Education, Communications & Signal Processing, Cybersecurity, Data Science & Engineering, Electronic Materials & Devices, Energy Systems, Health Engineering, Integrated Electronics, Networking & Computer Systems, Programming Languages, Soft w are Engineering & Human-Computer Interaction, Theoretical Computer Science

Scholarships Offered
OSU participates in the Western Undergraduate Exchange (WUE) & awards scholarships competitively to a limited number available.

Special Opportunities
Tech Tuesday Seminar Series, AI Seminars, Microwave Lab, EUSES Lab, HCI Lab, Intel Networking Lab, Communications Systems Lab, OSU Materials Innovation Center (OSMIC), Clean Room, Optoelectronics Lab, Novel Materials & Devices Group Lab

Energy Systems & Facility – research/testing on machines/drives, power electronics, hybrid EVs, power systems & renewable energy.

Graphics & Image Technologies Lab – computer graphics & vision, including image & video editing/enhancement, interactive interfaces, special effects, character animation, & 3D geometry representation.

Applied Magnetics Lab – Commercial tools, clean room, microwave lab, machine shop, arbitrary waveform generators, systems for ion beam sputtering

Collaborative Research in Microelectronics (CRiME) Lab – 1000 sq ft facility for communications/RF/mixed-signal research

Orgs: 3D Printing & Additive Manuf Club, Adaptive Tech Eng Network, Amateur Radio Club, American Inst of Aeronautics & Astronautics, American Nuclear Society, American Society of Civil Eng, Amer Soc of Heating, Refrig & Air-Conditioning Eng, American Soc of Mechanical Eng, App Development Club, Architectural Engineering Institute, AI Club, Assoc Gen Contractors, Assoc for Comp Machinery, Audio Eng Club, BMES, Chem, Bio, & Enviro Eng Club, Earthquake Eng Res Inst, Eng That Read, Eng w/o Borders, Future Soft ware Eng, Gen Eng Club, Girls' Empowerment & Outreach, Google Dev Club, Inst of Electrical & Electronic Eng, Inst of Transport. Eng, Linus Users Group, Nat Soc of Black Eng, Power & Eng Soc, Security Club, Soc of Asian Scientists & Eng, Soc of Automotive Eng, Soc of Manufacturing Eng, Soc of Women Eng, Sports Prod Dev Club, Video Game Club, Women in Big Data

Teams: DAM Robotics, Hackathon Club, Human-Powered Sub Team

Notable Alumni
Philip Emeagwali, Paul Emmett, Douglas Engelbart, Milton Harris, Wayne Hubbell, Linus Pauling, Glenn Odekirk, William Oefelein, Michael Waterman

ALASKA
ARIZONA
CALIFORNIA
COLORADO
HAWAII
IDAHO
MONTANA
NEVADA
NEW MEXICO
OREGON
UTAH
WASHINGTON
WYOMING

WEST

- ALASKA
- ARIZONA
- CALIFORNIA
- COLORADO
- HAWAII
- IDAHO
- MONTANA
- NEVADA
- NEW MEXICO
- OREGON
- UTAH
- **WASHINGTON**
- WYOMING

UNIVERSITY OF WASHINGTON, SEATTLE

Address: 371 Loew Hall, 3920 E. Stevens Way NE., Box 352180, Seattle, WA 98195-2180
Website: https://www.engr.washington.edu/
Contact: https://www.engr.washington.edu/about/contact
Phone: (206) 543-0340
Email: coeinfo@uw.edu

COST OF ATTENDANCE:

Tuition & Fees: $13,645 (in-state), $43,997 (out-of-state)
Addl Exp: $21,500 | **Total:** $35,145 (in-state), $65,497 (out-of-state)

Financial Aid: https://www.washington.edu/financialaid/

ADDITIONAL INFORMATION:

Available Degree(s)
- BS, MS, Ph.D. Aeronautics & Astronautics, Bioengineering, Bioresource Science & Engineering, Chemical Engineering, Civil Engineering, Computer Engineering, Computer Science, Electrical Engineering, Environmental Engineering, Human Centered Design & Eng, Industrial & Systems Engineering, Materials Science & Engineering, Mechanical Engineering

Related Research Centers
Boeing Advanced Research Center, Center for Advanced Materials in Transport Aircraft Structures, Center for Intelligent Materials & Systems, Center for the Advancement of Engineering Education, Clean Energy Institute, Human-Computer Interaction & Design, eScience Institute, Initiative for Max Student Diversity, Institute for Nano-Engineering Systems, Molecular Analysis Facility, National Institute of Materials Science, Pacific Earthquake Engineering Research Center, Pacific Marine Energy Center, Pacific NW Transportation Consortium, Supply Chain Transportation & Logistics Center, Turing Center, Urban Form Lab, WA NASA Space Grant Consortium, WA State Transportation Center

Scholarships Offered
About 600 students rec scholarships; UW Undergraduate Academic Excellence Awards – about 100 students, Non-Resident Purple & Gold Scholarships; Honors Program Scholarships; Washington NASA Space Grant; Departmental and institutional scholarships available.

Special Opportunities
Summer camps/programs offered for K-12. Study abroad program. Internships, externships, and career services are available.

Orgs: American Chemical Society, American Institute of Aeronautics and Astronautics, American Institute of Chemical Engineers, American Public Works Association, American Society of Civil Eng, American Society of Mechanical Engineers, Association for Computing Machinery for Women, Engineers w/o Borders, Global Medical Brigades, GRID, HuskyADAPT, Institute of Electrical & Electronics Engineers, Institute of Industrial & Systems Engineering, National Society of Black Engineers, NEXUS Builders, Project Indoor Farm, Science & Engineering Business Association, SeaDawgs Marine Biology Club, Society for Advanced Material Process Engineers, Society for Advanced Rocket Propulsion, Society of Asian Scientists & Engineers, Society of Hispanic Professional Engineers, Synaptech, Society of Women Engineers, Students for the Exploration & Development of Space, WA Wave

Teams: Capture-the-Flag Team (Batman's Kitchen), Chem-E Car Team, ChemE Brew, Chess, Concrete Canoe, Cubesat Team, Cyber Defense Competition Team, Design-Build-Fly, DubHacks, DubsTech, Formula Motorsports Electric Car Racing Team, Human Powered Submarine Team, iGEM (International Genetically-Engineered Machines), Mock Trial, Model United Nations, Satellite Team, Hyperloop Team, Quiz Bowl, Robotics Team, Science Olympiad, Solar Car Team, Sounding Rocket Team, Steel Bridge Team, WOOF3D

Notable Alumni
Jeff Dean, Earl Eisenhower, Muhammad Iqbal, Irving Kanarek, George Martin, Lina Nilsson, and Harley Nygren

CHAPTER 15

PROFILED ENVIRONMENTAL ENGINEERING PROGRAMS

School	School
Arizona State University	Stanford University
Bucknell University	SUNY College of Environmental Science and Forestry
California Institute of Technology (CalTech)	Texas A&M University
California Polytechnic State University, San Luis Obispo (Cal Poly)	The Ohio State University, Columbus
Carnegie Mellon University	The University of Texas at Austin (UT Austin)
Clemson University	Tufts University
Colorado School of Mines	University of California, Berkeley
Columbia University	University of California, Davis
Cornell University	University of California, Irvine
Drexel University	University of California, Los Angeles
Duke University	University of California, Riverside
Florida International University	University of California, San Diego
Georgia Institute of Technology (Georgia Tech)	University of Colorado, Boulder
Iowa State University	University of Florida, Gainesville
Johns Hopkins University	University of Georgia
Lehigh University	University of Illinois, Urbana-Champaign (UIUC)
Louisiana State University	University of Iowa
Massachusetts Institute of Technology (MIT)	University of Maryland, College Park
Michigan State University	University of Massachusetts, Amherst
Michigan Technological University	University of Michigan
North Carolina State University	University of Minnesota, Twin Cities
Northwestern University	University of Nebraska
Oregon State University	University of Notre Dame
Pennsylvania State University	University of Pittsburgh
Princeton University	University of Southern California
Purdue University	University of Virginia
Rensselaer Polytechnic Institute (RPI)	University of Washington
Rutgers University	University of Wisconsin, Madison
San Diego State University	Vanderbilt University
Southern Methodist University	Virginia Tech

CHAPTER 16

ABET ACCREDITED ENVIRONMENTAL ENGINEERING PROGRAMS

School	City/State
Alabama, The University of	Tuscaloosa, AL, USA
Americas, Universidad de las	Quito, Ecuador
Andalas, Universitas	Padang, Indonesia
Andes, Universidad de los	Bogota, Colombia
Arizona State University	Tempe, AZ, USA
Arizona, The University of	Tucson, AZ, USA
Batangas State University, Alangilan Campus	Batangas City, Philippines
Benedict College	Columbia, SC, USA
Brown University	Providence, RI, USA
Bucknell University	Lewisburg, PA, USA
Buffalo, University at, The State University of New York	Buffalo, NY, USA
Cal Poly Humboldt (Formerly Humboldt State University before May 1, 2022)	Arcata, CA, USA
California Polytechnic State University, San Luis Obispo	San Luis Obispo, CA, USA
California, Davis, University of	Davis, CA, USA
California, Irvine, University of	Irvine, CA, USA
California, Merced, University of	Merced, CA, USA
California, Riverside, University of	Riverside, CA, USA
Central Florida, University of	Orlando, Fl, USA
Central State University	Wilberforce, OH, USA
Cincinnati, University of	Cincinnati, OH, USA
Clarkson University	Potsdam, NY, USA
Clemson University	Clemson, SC, USA
Colorado Boulder, University of	Boulder, CO, USA
Colorado School of Mines	Golden, CO, USA
Colorado State University	Fort Collins, CO, USA
Columbia University in the City of New York	New York, NY, USA
Connecticut, University of	Storrs, CT, USA
Cornell University	Ithaca, NY, USA
Delaware, University of	Newark, DE, USA
Drexel University	Philadelphia, PA, USA
Duke University	Durham, NC, USA
Florida Atlantic University	Boca Raton, FL, USA
Florida Gulf Coast University	Fort Myers, FL, USA
Florida International University	Miami, FL, USA
Florida, University of	Gainesville, FL, USA
Gannon University	Erie, PA, USA
Georgia Institute of Technology (Georgia Tech)	Atlanta, GA, USA

School	City/State
Georgia, University of	Athens, GA, USA
Imam Abdulrahman Bin Faisal University	Dammam, Saudi Arabia
Iowa, The University of	Iowa City, IA, USA
Istanbul Technical University	Istanbul, Turkey
Johns Hopkins University	MD, USA
Kennesaw State University	Kennesaw, GA, USA
Lehigh University	Bethlehem, PA, USA
Louisiana State University and A&M College	Baton Rouge, LA, USA
Manhattan College	Riverdale, NY, USA
Mapua University (Formerly Mapua Institute of Technology before Sept 1, 2017)	Manila, Philippines
Miami, University of	Coral Gables, FL, USA
Michigan State University	East Lansing, MI, USA
Michigan Technological University	Houghton, MI, USA
Michigan, University of	Ann Arbor, MI, USA
Middle East Technical University	Ankara, Turkey
Minnesota - Twin Cities, University of	Minneapolis, MN, USA
Missouri University of Science and Technology (Formerly University of Missouri-Rolla before Jan 1, 2008)	Rolla, MO, USA
Montana Technological University (Formerly Montana State University – Bozeman before June 1, 2019)	Butte, MT, USA
Nacional de Ingenieria, Universidad	Rimac, Peru
Nevada, Reno, University of	Reno, NV, USA
New Hampshire, University of	Manchester, NH, USA
New Mexico Institute of Mining and Technology	Socorro, NM, USA
New York at Albany, State University of (SUNY Albany)	Albany, NY, USA
New York College of Environmental Science and Forestry, State University of	Syracuse, NY, USA
New York, City College, City University of (CUNY)	New York, NY, USA
North Carolina State University at Raleigh	Raleigh, NC, USA
Northeastern University	Boston, MA, USA
Northern Arizona University	Flagstaff, AZ, USA
Northwestern University	Evanston, IL, USA
Notre Dame, University of	Notre Dame, IN, USA
Ohio State University, The	OH, USA
Oklahoma, University of Columbus	Norman, OK, USA
Oregon State University	Corvallis, OR, USA
Pennsylvania State University	University Park, PA, USA
Pittsburgh, University of	Pittsburgh, PA, USA

School	City/State
Polytechnic University of Puerto Rico	San Juan, Puerto Rico, USA
Portland State University	Portland, OR, USA
Purdue University at West Lafayette	West Lafayette, IN, USA
Rensselaer Polytechnic Institute	Troy, NY, USA
Rutgers, The State University of New Jersey	New Brunswick, NJ, USA
Saint Francis University	Loretto, PA, USA
San Diego State University	San Diego, CA, USA
Southern California, University of (USC)	Los Angeles, CA, USA
Southern Methodist University (SMU)	Dallas, TX, USA
St. Cloud State University	St. Cloud, MN, USA
Stevens Institute of Technology	Hoboken, NJ, USA
Syracuse University	Syracuse, NY, USA
Tarleton State University	Stephenville, TX, USA
Technological Institute of the Philippines Quezon City	Quezon City, Philippines
Temple University	Philadelphia, PA, USA
Texas A&M University	College Station, TX, USA
Texas A&M University - Kingsville	Kingsville, TX, USA
Texas at Austin, University of (UT Austin)	Austin, TX, USA
Texas Tech University	Lubbock, TX, USA
Toledo, The University of	Toledo, OH, USA
Tufts University	Medford, MA, USA
United States Military Academy	West Point, NY, USA
Utah State University	Logan, UT, USA
Vermont, University of	Burlington, VT, USA
Washington, University of	Seattle, WA, USA
West Texas A&M University	Canyon, TX, USA
Wilkes University	Wilkes-Barre, PA, USA
Wisconsin - Platteville, University of	Platteville, WI, USA
Worcester Polytechnic Institute	Worcester, MA, USA
Zewail City, University of Science and Technology - 6th of October City, City	Egypt

CHAPTER 17

ABET ACCREDITED ENVIRONMENTAL ENGINEERING TECHNOLOGY, FIRE PROTECTION, & ENVIRONMENTAL SCIENCE, HEALTH, & SAFETY

School	City/State
Environmental Engineering Technology	
New York at Canton, State University of	Canton, NY, USA
Northern Illinois University	Dekalb, IL, USA
Vermont State University (Formerly Vermont Technical College before July 2, 2023)	Randolph Center, VT, USA
Wisconsin - Green Bay, University of	Green Bay, WI, USA
Wisconsin - Oshkosh, University of	Oshkosh, WI, USA
Environmental Science	
Hawaii at Manoa, University of	Honolulu, HI, USA
United States Coast Guard Academy	New London, CT, USA
Environmental Health & Safety	
Indiana University of Pennsylvania	Indiana, PA, USA
Millersville University of Pennsylvania	Millersville, PA, USA
North Carolina Agricultural and Technical State University	Greensboro, NC, USA
Oakland University	Rochester Hills, MI, USA
Southeastern Louisiana University	Hammond, LA, USA
Fire Protection Engineering – BS	
University of Maryland	College Park, MD, USA
Fire Protection & Safety Engineering Technology - BS	
Eastern Kentucky University	Richmond, KY, USA
Oklahoma State University	Stillwater, OK, USA

CHAPTER 18

ABET ACCREDITED GEOLOGICAL, MINING, AND OCEAN ENGINEERING PROGRAMS

School	City/State
Geological Engineering	
Alaska Fairbanks, University of	Fairbanks, AK, USA
Colorado School of Mines	Golden, CO, USA
Escuela Superior Politecnica Del Litoral	Guayaquil, Ecuador
Istanbul Technical University	Istanbul, Turkey
Michigan Technological University	Houghton, MI, USA
Middle East Technical University	Ankara, Turkey
Minnesota - Twin Cities, University of	Minneapolis, MN, USA
Mississippi, University of	University, MS, USA
Missouri University of Science and Technology	Rolla, MO, USA
Montana Technological University	Butte, MT, USA
Nacional de Ingenieria, Universidad	Rimac, Peru
Nevada, Reno, University of	Reno, NV, USA
North Dakota, University of	Grand Forks, ND, USA
PetroVietnam University	Baria City, Vietnam
Politecnica de Madrid, Universidad	Madrid, Spain
Pontificia Universidad Catolica del Peru	San Miguel, Peru
South Dakota School of Mines and Technology	Rapid City, SD, USA
Texas at Austin, University of (UT Austin)	Austin, TX, USA
Utah, The University of	Salt Lake City, UT, USA
Wisconsin - Madison, University of	Madison, WI, USA
Geology & Geological Science	
Arkansas at Little Rock, University of	Little Rock, Arkansas, USA
Industrial de Santander, Universidad	Bucaramanga, Colombia
South Dakota School of Mines and Technology	Rapid City, South Dakota, USA
United Arab Emirates University	Al Ain, United Arab Emirates
Mining Engineering	
Alaska Fairbanks, University of	Fairbanks, AK, USA
Arizona, The University of	Tucson, AZ, USA
Colorado School of Mines	Golden, CO, USA
Escuela Superior Politecnica Del Litoral	Guayaquil, Ecuador
Institut Teknologi Bandung	Bandung, Indonesia
Istanbul Technical University	Istanbul, Turkey
Kentucky, University of	Lexington, KY, USA
King Abdulaziz University	Jeddah, Saudi Arabia
Michigan Technological University	Houghton, MI, USA
Middle East Technical University	Ankara, Turkey

Missouri University of Science and Technology	Rolla, MO, USA
Montana Technological University	Butte, MT, USA
Nacional de Ingenieria, Universidad	Rimac, Peru
Nevada, Reno, University of	Reno, NV, USA
Pennsylvania State University	University Park, PA, USA
Politecnica de Madrid, Universidad	Madrid, Spain
Pontificia Universidad Catolica del Peru	San Miguel, Peru
South Dakota School of Mines and Technology	Rapid City, SD, USA
Utah, The University of	Salt Lake City, UT, USA
Virginia Polytechnic Institute & State University (Virginia Tech)	Blacksburg, VA, USA
West Virginia University	Morgantown, WV, USA

Ocean Engineering

Escuela Superior Politecnica Del Litoral	Guayaquil, Ecuador
Florida Atlantic University	Boca Raton, FL, USA
Florida Institute of Technology	Melbourne, FL, USA
Hawaii at Manoa, University of	Honolulu, HI, USA
Istanbul Technical University	Istanbul, Turkey
Massachusetts Institute of Technology (MIT)	Cambridge, MA, USA
New Hampshire, University of	Manchester, NH, USA
Rhode Island, The University of	Kingston, RI, USA
Southern Mississippi, University of	Hattiesburg, MS, USA
Texas A&M University	College Station, TX, USA
United States Naval Academy	Annapolis, MD, USA
Virginia Polytechnic Institute & State University (Virginia Tech)	Blacksburg, VA, USA

CHAPTER 19

ABET ACCREDITED NUCLEAR ENERGY PROGRAMS

School	Degree	Year Accredited
Nuclear & Radiological Engineering		
Air Force Institute of Technology – WPAFB, Ohio	MS Nuclear Engineering	Oct 1, 1964 – Present
University of California, Berkeley – Berkeley, CA	BS Nuclear Engineering	Oct 1, 1983 – Present
University of Florida – Gainesville, FL	BS Nuclear Engineering	Oct 1, 1971 – Present
Georgia Tech – Atlanta, GA	BS Nuclear & Radiological Engineering	Oct 1, 1975 – Present
Idaho State University – Pocatello, ID	BS Nuclear Engineering	Oct 1, 2006 – Present
University of Illinois - Urbana-Champaign, IL (UIUC)	BS Nuclear, Plasma, & Radiological Engineering	Oct 1, 1978 – Present
Jordan University of Science & Technology – Irbid, Jordan	BS Nuclear Engineering	Oct 1, 2014 – Present
King Abdulaziz University – Jeddah, Saudi Arabia	BS Nuclear Engineering	Oct 1, 2007 – Present
University of Massachusetts – Lowell, MA	BS Chemical Engineering: Nuclear Engineering Option	Oct 1, 1999 – Present
Massachusetts Institute of Technology (MIT) – Cambridge, MA	BS Nuclear Science Engineering (Course 22)	Oct 1, 1980 – Present
University of Michigan – Ann Arbor, MI	BSE Nuclear Engineering & Radiological Sciences	Oct 1, 2006 – Present
Missouri University of Science & Technology – Rolla, MO	BS Nuclear Engineering	Oct 1, 1960 – Present
University of New Mexico – Albuquerque, NM	BS Nuclear Engineering	Oct 1, 1984 – Present
North Carolina State University – Raleigh, NC	BS Nuclear Engineering	Oct 1, 1965 – Present
Oregon State University – Corvallis, OR	BS Nuclear Engineering	Oct 1, 2006 – Present
Pennsylvania State University (Penn State) – University Park, PA	BS Nuclear Engineering	Oct 1, 1973 – Present
Purdue University – West Lafayette, IN	BSNE Nuclear Engineering	Oct 1, 1978 – Present
Rensselaer Polytechnic Institute (RPI) – Troy, NY	BS Nuclear Engineering	Oct 1, 1966 – Present
University of Sharjah – Sharjah, UAE	BS Nuclear Engineering	Oct 1, 2015 – Present

School	Degree	Year Accredited
South Carolina State University – Orangeburg, SC	BS Nuclear Engineering	Oct 1, 2005 – Present
University of Tennessee – Knoxville, TN	BS Nuclear Engineering	Oct 1, 1970 – Present
Texas A&M University – College Station, TX	BS Nuclear Engineering	Oct 1, 1969 – Present
United States Military Academy – West Point, NY	BS Nuclear Engineering	Oct 1, 2007 – Present
United States Naval Academy – Annapolis, MD	BS Nuclear Engineering	Oct 1, 2015 – Present
Virginia Commonwealth University (VCU) – Richmond, VA	BS Mechanical Engineering w/a Nuclear Engineering Concentration	Oct 1, 2011 – Present
University of Wisconsin – Madison, WI	BSNE Nuclear Engineering	Oct 1, 2006 – Present
Nuclear Engineering Technology		
Excelsior University (Formerly Regents College)	BS Nuclear Engineering Technology	Oct 1, 1998 – Present
Idaho State University - Pocatello, ID	AA in Energy Systems Nuclear Operations Technology	Oct 1, 2016 – Present
Thomas Edison State University – Trenton, NJ	BS Nuclear Energy Engineering Technology	Oct 1, 2010 – Present

CHAPTER 20

ABET ACCREDITED CIVIL ENGINEERING PROGRAMS

School	Degree	Year Accredited
Alabama A&M University - Huntsville, AL	BSCE	Oct 1, 1998 – Present
Angelo State University - San Angelo, TX	BSCE	Oct 1, 2018 – Present
Arizona State University - Tempe, Arizona	BSE	Oct 1, 1961 – Present
Arkansas State University - Jonesboro, AR	BSCE	Oct 1, 2010 – Present
Auburn University - Auburn, AL	BSE	Oct 1, 1941 – Present
Benedictine College - Atchison, KS	BS	Oct 1, 2017 – Present
Boise State University - Boise, ID	BS	Oct 1, 1997 – Present
Bradley University - Peoria, IL	BSCE	Oct 1, 1963 – Present
Brigham Young University - Provo, UT	BS	Oct 1, 1960 – Present
Brigham Young University - Rexburg, ID	BS	Oct 1, 2013 – Present
Bucknell University - Lewisburg, PA	BSCE	Oct 1, 1936 – Present
California Baptist University - Riverside, CA	BSCE	Oct 1, 2010 – Present
California Polytechnic State U - San Luis Obispo, CA	BS	Oct 1, 1973 – Present
California State Polytechnic U - Pomona, CA	BS	Oct 1, 1970 – Present
California State University - Chico, CA	BS	Oct 1, 1968 – Present
California State University - Fresno, CA	BS	Oct 1, 1968 – Present
California State University - Fullerton, CA	BS	Oct 1, 1985 – Present
California State University - Long Beach, CA	BS	Oct 1, 1963 – Present
California State University - Los Angeles, CA	BS	Oct 1, 1965 – Present
California State University - Northridge, CA	BS	Oct 1, 1994 – Present
California State University - Sacramento, CA	BS	Oct 1, 1965 – Present
Caribbean University - Bayamon, Puerto Rico	BSE	Oct 1, 2013 – Present
Carnegie Mellon University - Pittsburgh, PA	BSCE	Oct 1, 1936 – Present
Carroll College - Helena, MT	BS	Oct 1, 1999 – Present
Case Western Reserve University - Cleveland, OH	BS	Oct 1, 1936 – Present
Catholic University of America - Washington, DC	BSCE	Oct 1, 1938 – Present
Central Connecticut State University - New Britain, CT	BSE	Oct 1, 2011 – Present
Christian Brothers University - Memphis, TN	BS	Oct 1, 1983 – Present
The Citadel – Charleston, SC	BSCE	Oct 1, 1936 – Present
City University of New York, City College – NY, NY	BEng	Oct 1, 1936 – Present
Clarkson University - Potsdam, NY	BS	Oct 1, 1936 – Present
Clemson University - Clemson, SC	BS	Oct 1, 1936 – Present
Cleveland State University - Cleveland, OH	BSE	Oct 1, 1948 – Present
College of New Jersey – Ewing, NJ	BSCE	Oct 1, 2006 – Present
Colorado School of Mines - Golden, CO	BS	Oct 1, 2012 – Present
Colorado State University - Fort Collins, CO	BS	Oct 1, 1938 – Present
Columbia University – NY, NY	BS	Oct 1, 1936 – Present

School	Degree	Year Accredited
Cooper Union - New York, NY	BSCE	Oct 1, 1936 – Present
Cornell University - Ithaca, NY	BS	Oct 1, 1936 – Present
Drexel University - Philadelphia, PA	BSCE	Oct 1, 1936 – Present
Duke University - Durham, North Carolina	BSE	Oct 1, 1936 – Present
Embry-Riddle Aeronautical U - Daytona Beach, FL	BS	Oct 1, 1997 – Present
Fairleigh Dickinson University - Teaneck, NJ	BS	Oct 1, 2019 – Present
Florida A&M U - Florida State U - Tallahassee, FL	BS	Oct 1, 1986 – Present
Florida Atlantic University - Boca Raton, FL	BSCV	Oct 1, 2002 – Present
Florida Gulf Coast University - Fort Myers, FL	BSCE	Oct 1, 2008 – Present
Florida Institute of Technology - Melbourne, FL	BS	Oct 1, 1983 – Present
Florida International University - Miami, FL	BS	Oct 1, 1985 – Present
The George Washington University - Washington, DC	BS	Oct 1, 1940 – Present
Georgia Institute of Technology - Atlanta, GA	BSCE	Oct 1, 1936 – Present
Georgia Southern University - Statesboro, GA	BSCE	Oct 1, 2012 – Present
Gonzaga University - Spokane, WA	BSCE	Oct 1, 1985 – Present
Harding University - Searcy, AR	BS	Oct 1, 2020 – Present
Hofstra University - Hempstead, NY	BS	Oct 1, 2019 – Present
Howard University - Washington, DC	BS	Oct 1, 1936 – Present
Idaho State University - Pocatello, ID	BS	Oct 1, 1998 – Present
Illinois Institute of Technology - Chicago, IL	BS	Oct 1, 1936 – Present
Iowa State University of Science & Technology - Ames, IA	BS	Oct 1, 1936 – Present
Jackson State University - Jackson, MS	BS	Oct 1, 2004 – Present
Johns Hopkins University – Baltimore, MD	BS	Oct 1, 1936 – Present
Kansas State University - Manhattan, KS	BS	Oct 1, 1936 – Present
Kennesaw State University - Kennesaw, GA	BS	May 1, 2012 – Present
King's College - Wilkes Barre, PA	BS	Oct 1, 2019 – Present
Lafayette College - Easton, PA	BS	Oct 1, 1936 – Present
Lamar University - Beaumont, TX	BS	Oct 1, 1961 – Present
Lawrence Technological University - Southfield, MI	BS	Oct 1, 1991 – Present
Lehigh University - Bethlehem, PA	BSCE	Oct 1, 1936 – Present
LeTourneau University - Longview, TX	BS	Oct 1, 2020 – Present
Lipscomb University - Nashville, TN	BS	Oct 1, 2011 – Present
Louisiana State University and A&M College - Baton Rouge, LA	BSCE	Oct 1, 1936 – Present
Louisiana Tech University - Ruston, LA	BSCE	Oct 1, 1948 – Present
Loyola Marymount University - Los Angeles, CA	BSE	Oct 1, 1967 – Present
Manhattan College - Riverdale, NY	BS	Oct 1, 1940 – Present
Minnesota State University - Mankato, MN	BS	Oct 1, 2002 – Present

School	Degree	Year Accredited
Marquette University - Milwaukee, WI	BSCE	Oct 1, 1936 – Present
Marshall University - Huntington, WV	BSCE	Oct 1, 2020 – Present
Merrimack College - North Andover, MA	BS	Oct 1, 1964 – Present
Michigan State University - East Lansing, MI	BS	Oct 1, 1936 – Present
Michigan Technological University - Houghton, MI	BS	Oct 1, 1936 – Present
Milwaukee School of Engineering - Milwaukee, WI	BSCE	Oct 1, 2015 – Present
Mississippi State University - Mississippi State, MS	BS	Oct 1, 1941 – Present
Missouri University of Science & Technology - Rolla, MO	BS	Oct 1, 1936 – Present
Montana Technological University - Butte, MT	BS	Oct 1, 2017 – Present
Montana State University - Bozeman, MT	BS	Oct 1, 1936 – Present
Morgan State University - Baltimore, MD	BS	Oct 1, 1990 – Present
New Jersey Institute of Technology - Newark, NJ	BS	Oct 1, 1936 – Present
New Mexico Institute of Mining & Technology - Socorro, NM	BS	Oct 1, 2006 – Present
New Mexico State University - Las Cruces, NM	BSCE	Oct 1, 1938 – Present
New York University - Brooklyn, NY	BS	Oct 1, 1936 – Present
North Carolina A&T State U - Greensboro, NC	BS	Oct 1, 1990 – Present
North Carolina State University - Raleigh, NC	BS	Oct 1, 1936 – Present
North Dakota State University - Fargo, ND	BS	Oct 1, 1948 – Present
Northeastern University - Boston, MA	BSCE	Oct 1, 1939 – Present
Northern Arizona University - Flagstaff, AZ	BSE	Oct 1, 1974 – Present
Northwestern University - Evanston, IL	BS	Oct 1, 1938 – Present
Norwich University - Northfield, VT	BS	Oct 1, 1936 – Present
Ohio Northern University - Ada, OH	BSCE	Oct 1, 1954 – Present
The Ohio State University - Columbus, OH	BSCE	Oct 1, 1936 – Present
Ohio University - Athens, OH	BSCE	Oct 1, 1951 – Present
Oklahoma State University - Stillwater, OK	BSCE	Oct 1, 1936 – Present
Old Dominion University - Norfolk, VA	BSCE	Oct 1, 1967 – Present
Oregon Institute of Technology - Klamath Falls, OR	BS	Oct 1, 1997 – Present
Oregon State University - Corvallis, OR	BS & HBS	Oct 1, 1936 – Present
Saint Louis University - Saint Louis, MO	BS	Oct 1, 2012 – Present
Pennsylvania State University - University Park, PA	BS	Oct 1, 1936 – Present
Pennsylvania State University, Harrisburg, Middletown, PA	BS	Oct 1, 2010 – Present
Polytechnic University - San Juan, Puerto Rico	BS	Oct 1, 1994 – Present
Portland State University - Portland, OR	BS	Oct 1, 1982 – Present
Prairie View A&M University - Prairie View, TX	BSCE	Oct 1, 1970 – Present
Princeton University - Princeton, NJ	BSE	Oct 1, 1936 – Present
Purdue University - West Lafayette, IN	BSCE	Oct 1, 1936 – Present

School	Degree	Year Accredited
Purdue University - Fort Wayne, IN	BSCE	Oct 1, 2009 – Present
Purdue University Northwest - Hammond, IN	BS	Oct 1, 2010 – Present
Quinnipiac University - Hamden, CT	BS	Oct 1, 2015 – Present
Rensselaer Polytechnic Institute - Troy, NY	BS	Oct 1, 1936 – Present
Rice University - Houston, TX	BSCE	Oct 1, 1936 – Present
Rockhurst University - Kansas City, MO	BS	Oct 1, 2019 – Present
Rose-Hulman Institute of Technology - Terre Haute, IN	BS	Oct 1, 1936 – Present
Rowan University - Glassboro, NJ	BS	Oct 1, 1999 – Present
Rutgers University - New Brunswick, NJ	BS	Oct 1, 1936 – Present
Saint Martin's University - Lacey, WA	BSCE	Oct 1, 1969 – Present
San Diego State University - San Diego, CA	BS	Oct 1, 1964 – Present
San Francisco State University - San Francisco, CA	BS	Oct 1, 1986 – Present
San Jose State University - San Jose, CA	BS	Oct 1, 1959 – Present
Santa Clara University - Santa Clara, CA	BS	Oct 1, 1936 – Present
Seattle University - Seattle, WA	BSCE	Oct 1, 1985 – Present
South Dakota School of Mines & Technology - Rapid City, SD	BS	Oct 1, 1936 – Present
South Dakota State University - Brookings, SD	BS	Oct 1, 1936 – Present
Southern Illinois University Carbondale - Carbondale, IL	BS	Oct 1, 1988 – Present
Southern Illinois University- Edwardsville, IL	BS	Oct 1, 1973 – Present
Southern Methodist University - Dallas, TX	BSCE	Oct 1, 2005 – Present
Southern University and A&M College - Baton Rouge, LA	BSCE	Oct 1, 1970 – Present
Stanford University - Stanford, CA	BS	Oct 1, 1936 – Present
University at Buffalo, SUNY - Buffalo, NY	BS	Oct 1, 1963 – Present
Stony Brook University - New York, NY	BE	Oct 1, 2015 – Present
SUNY, Polytechnic Institute - Utica, NY	BS	Oct 1, 2015 – Present
Stevens Institute of Technology - Hoboken, NJ	BE	Oct 1, 1987 – Present
Syracuse University - Syracuse, NY	BS	Oct 1, 1936 – Present
Tarleton State University - Stephenville, TX	BS	Oct 1, 2016 – Present
Temple University - Philadelphia, PA	BS	Oct 1, 1988 – Present
Tennessee State University - Nashville, TN	BS	Oct 1, 1972 – Present
Tennessee Technological University - Cookeville, TN	BSCE	Oct 1, 1970 – Present
Texas A&M University – College Station, TX	BS	Oct 1, 1936 – Present
Texas A&M University - Kingsville, TX	BSCE	Oct 1, 1980 – Present
Texas Southern University – Houston, TX	BS	Oct 1, 2020 – Present
Texas Tech University – Lubbock, TX	BS	Oct 1, 1937 – Present
Trine University – Angola, IN	BSCE	Oct 1, 1970 – Present
Tufts University – Medford, MA	BS	Oct 1, 1936 – Present

School	Degree	Year Accredited
University of Akron – Akron, OH	BSCE	Oct 1, 1950 – Present
University of Alabama – Tuscaloosa, AL	BSCE	Oct 1, 1936 – Present
University of Alabama – Huntsville, AL	BSCE	Oct 1, 1987 – Present
University of Arizona – Tucson, AZ	BSCE	Oct 1, 1936 – Present
University of Illinois – Chicago, IL	BS	Oct 1, 1985 – Present
University of Iowa - Iowa City, IA	BSE	Oct 1, 1936 – Present
University of Kansas – Lawrence, KS	BSCE	Oct 1, 1936 – Present
University of Rhode Island – Kingston, RI	BSCE	Oct 1, 1936 – Present
University of Texas at Arlington – Arlington, TX	BSCE	Oct 1, 1967 – Present
University of Texas Rio Grande Valley – Edinburg, TX	BS	Oct 1, 2010 – Present
University of Texas - San Antonio, TX	BS	Oct 1, 1986 – Present
University of Toledo – Toledo, OH	BS	Oct 1, 1950 – Present
University of Utah - Salt Lake City, UT	BSCE	Oct 1, 1936 – Present
US Air Force Academy – USAFA, CO	BS	Oct 1, 1967 – Present
US Coast Guard Academy - New London, CT	BS	Oct 1, 1978 – Present
US Military Academy - West Point, NY	BS	Oct 1, 1985 – Present
Universidad Ana. G. Mendez - Gurabo, Puerto Rico	BS	Oct 1, 2015 – Present
University of Alabama – Birmingham, AL	BSCE	Oct 1, 1983 – Present
University of Alaska – Anchorage, AK	BS	Oct 1, 1984 – Present
University of Alaska – Fairbanks, AK	BS	Oct 1, 1940 – Present
University of Arkansas – Fayetteville, AR	BSCE	Oct 1, 1936 – Present
University of California - Berkeley, CA	BS	Oct 1, 1936 – Present
University of California - Davis, CA	BS	Oct 1, 1965 – Present
University of California - Irvine, CA	BS	Oct 1, 1978 – Present
University of California - Los Angeles, CA	BS	Oct 1, 1983 – Present
University of Central Florida – Orlando, FL	BSCE	Oct 1, 1982 – Present
University of Cincinnati – Cincinnati, OH	BS	Oct 1, 1936 – Present
University of Colorado Boulder – Boulder, CO	BS	Oct 1, 1936 – Present
University of Colorado – Denver, CO	BS	Oct 1, 1976 – Present
University of Connecticut – Storrs, CT	BSE	Oct 1, 1940 – Present
University of Dayton – Dayton, OH	BCE	Oct 1, 1951 – Present
University of Delaware – Newark, DE	BCE	Oct 1, 1936 – Present
University of Detroit Mercy – Detroit, MI	BCE	Oct 1, 1936 – Present
University of Evansville – Evansville, IN	BSCE	Oct 1, 1995 – Present
University of Florida – Gainesville, FL	BS	Oct 1, 1936 – Present
University of Georgia – Athens, GA	BSCE	Oct 1, 2014 – Present
University of Hartford - West Hartford, CT	BSCE	Oct 1, 1978 – Present

School	Degree	Year Accredited
University of Hawaii at Manoa – Honolulu, HI	BS	Oct 1, 1951 – Present
University of Houston – Houston, TX	BSCE	Oct 1, 1957 – Present
University of Idaho – Moscow, ID	BSCE	Oct 1, 1936 – Present
University of Illinois (UIUC) - Champaign, IL	BS	Oct 1, 1936 – Present
University of Kentucky – Lexington, KY	BSCE	Oct 1, 1936 – Present
University of Louisiana – Lafayette, LA	BSCE	Oct 1, 1956 – Sep 30, 1963, Oct 1, 1967 – Present
University of Louisville – Louisville, KY	BSCE	Mar 1, 2010 – Present
	MSCE	Oct 1, 1936 – Present
University of Massachusetts – Lowell, MA	BSE	Oct 1, 1977 – Present
University of Maine – Orono, ME	BS	Oct 1, 1936 – Present
University of Maryland - College Park, MD	BS	Oct 1, 1936 – Present
University of Massachusetts – Amherst, MA	BS	Oct 1, 1949 – Present
University of Massachusetts – Dartmouth, MA	BS	Oct 1, 1972 – Present
University of Memphis - Memphis, TN	BSCE	Oct 1, 1971 – Present
University of Miami - Coral Gables, FL	BSCE	Oct 1, 1960 – Present
University of Michigan - Ann Arbor, MI	BSE	Oct 1, 1936 – Present
University of Minnesota, Twin Cities - Minneapolis, MN	BCE	Oct 1, 1936 – Present
University of Minnesota – Duluth, MN	BSCE	Oct 1, 2011 – Present
University of Mississippi – University, MI	BSCE	Oct 1, 1949 – Present
University of Missouri – Columbia, MO	BSCE	Oct 1, 1936 – Present
University of Missouri - Kansas City, MO	BSCIE	Oct 1, 1978 – Present
University of Missouri - St. Louis, MO	BSCIE	Oct 1, 1999 – Present
University of Mount Union – Alliance, OH	BS	Oct 1, 2013 – Present
University of Nebraska – Lincoln, NE	BSCE	Oct 1, 1936 – Present
University of Nevada - Las Vegas, NV	BSE	Oct 1, 1987 – Present
University of Nevada – Reno, NV	BS	Oct 1, 1949 – Present
University of New Hampshire – Durham, NH	BSCivilE	Oct 1, 1936 – Present
University of New Haven - West Haven, CT	BS	Oct 1, 1973 – Present
University of New Mexico – Albuquerque, NM	BS	Oct 1, 1936 – Present
University of New Orleans - New Orleans, LA	BSCE	Oct 1, 1980 – Present
University of North Carolina – Charlotte, NC	BS	Oct 1, 1983 – Present
University of North Dakota - Grand Forks, ND	BSCE	Oct 1, 1936 – Present
University of North Florida – Jacksonville, FL	BS	Oct 1, 2001 – Present
University of Notre Dame - Notre Dame, IN	BS	Oct 1, 1942 – Present
University of Oklahoma – Norman, OK	BS	Oct 1, 1936 – Present
University of Pittsburgh – Pittsburgh, PA	BSE	Oct 1, 1936 – Present

School	Degree	Year Accredited
University of Pittsburgh – Johnstown, PA	BSE	Oct 1, 2018 – Present
University of Portland – Portland, OR	BSCE	Oct 1, 1980 – Present
University of Puerto Rico - Mayaguez, Puerto Rico	BSCE	Oct 1, 1960 – Present
University of South Alabama – Mobile, AL	BS	Oct 1, 1989 – Present
University of South Carolina – Columbia, SC	BSE	Oct 1, 1944 – Present
University of South Florida – Tampa, FL	BSCE	Oct 1, 1984 – Present
University of Southern California (USC)- Los Angeles, CA	BS	Oct 1, 1942 – Present
University of Southern Indiana – Evansville, IN	BSCE	Oct 1, 2019 – Present
University of St. Thomas - Saint Paul, MN	BSCE	Oct 1, 2018 – Present
University of Tennessee – Chattanooga, TN	BSCE	Oct 1, 2006 – Present
University of Tennessee – Knoxville, TN	BS	Oct 1, 1936 – Present
University of Texas– Austin, TX (UT Austin)	BS	Oct 1, 1936 – Present
University of Texas - El Paso, TX	BSCE	Oct 1, 1965 – Present
University of Texas – Tyler, TX	BSCE	Oct 1, 2007 – Present
University of the District of Columbia - Washington, DC	BS	Oct 1, 1988 – Present
University of the Pacific – Stockton, CA	BS	Oct 1, 1971 – Present
University of Vermont – Burlington, VT	BSCE	Oct 1, 1936 – Present
University of Virginia – Charlottesville, VA	BS	Oct 1, 1936 – Present
University of Washington – Seattle, WA	BSCE	Oct 1, 1936 – Present
University of Wisconsin – Madison, WI	BS	Oct 1, 1936 – Present
University of Wisconsin – Milwaukee, WI	BSE	Oct 1, 1969 – Present
University of Wisconsin – Platteville, WI	BS	Oct 1, 1968 – Present
University of Wyoming – Laramie, WY	BSCE	Oct 1, 1941 – Present
Utah State University – Logan, UT	BS	Oct 1, 1936 – Present
Utah Valley University – Orem, UT	BSCE	Oct 1, 2019 – Present
Valparaiso University – Valparaiso, IN	BSCE	Oct 1, 1958 – Present
Vanderbilt University – Nashville, TN	DE	Oct 1, 1939 – Present
Villanova University – Villanova, PA	BSCE	Oct 1, 1941 – Present
Virginia Military Institute – Lexington, VA	BS	Oct 1, 1936 – Present
Virginia Tech – Blacksburg, VA	BSCE	Oct 1, 1936 – Present
Washington State University – Pullman, WA	BSCE	Oct 1, 1936 – Present
Washington State University – Richland, WA	BS	Oct 1, 2018 – Present
Wayne State University – Detroit, MI	BSCE	Oct 1, 1944 – Present
Wentworth Institute of Technology – Boston, MA	BS	Oct 1, 2013 – Present
West Texas A&M University – Canyon, TX	BS	Aug 1, 2013 – Present
West Virginia U Inst. of Technology – Beckley, WV	BS	Oct 1, 1968 – Present
West Virginia University - Morgantown, WV	BSCE	Oct 1, 1936 – Present

School	Degree	Year Accredited
Western Illinois University - Macomb, IL	BSCE	Oct 1, 2020 – Present
Western Kentucky University - Bowling Green, KY	BS	Oct 1, 2003 – Present
Western Michigan University - Kalamazoo, MI	BSE	Oct 1, 2004 – Present
Western New England University - Springfield, MA	BSCE	Oct 1, 2015 – Present
Widener University - Chester, PA	BS	Oct 1, 1988 – Present
William Jewell College - Liberty, MO	BS	Oct 1, 2019 – Present
Worcester Polytechnic Institute - Worcester, MA	BS	Oct 1, 1936 – Present
York College of Pennsylvania - York, PA	BS	Oct 1, 2019 – Present
Youngstown State University - Youngstown, OH	BE	Oct 1, 1959 – Present

CHAPTER 21

ABET ACCREDITED CHEMICAL ENGINEERING PROGRAMS

School	
Akron, University of, Akron, OH	Montana State University, Bozeman, MT
Alabama, University of, Tuscaloosa, AL	Nebraska, University of, Lincoln, NE
Alabama, University of, Huntsville, AL	Nevada, University of, Reno, NV
Arizona, University of, Tucson, AZ	New Hampshire, University of, Durham, NH
Arizona State University, Tempe, AZ	New Haven, University of, New Haven, CT
Arkansas, University of, Fayetteville, AR	New Jersey Institute of Technology, Newark, NJ
Auburn University, Auburn, AL	New Mexico, University of, Albuquerque, NM
Brigham Young University, Provo, UT	New Mexico Institute of Mining and Technology, Socorro, NM
Brown University, Providence, RI	New Mexico State University, Las Cruces, NM
Bucknell University, Lewisburg, PA	New York, City College of the City University of, New York, NY
California, University of, Berkeley, CA	New York, State University of, Buffalo, NY
California, University of, Davis, CA	North Carolina Agricultural & Technical State University, Greensboro, NC
California, University of, Irvine, CA	North Carolina State University, Raleigh, NC
California, University of, Los Angeles, CA	North Dakota, University of, Grand Forks, ND
California, University of, Riverside, CA	Northeastern University, Boston, MA
California, University of, San Diego, CA	Northwestern University, Evanston, IL
California, University of, Santa Barbara, CA	Notre Dame, University of, Notre Dame, IN
California Institute of Technology, Pasadena, CA	Ohio State University, Columbus, OH
California State Polytechnic University, Pomona, CA	Ohio University, Athens, OH
California State University, Long Beach, CA	Oklahoma, University of, Norman, OK
Carnegie Mellon University, Pittsburgh, PA	Oklahoma State University, Stillwater, OK
Case Western Reserve University, Cleveland, OH	Oregon State University, Corvallis, OR
Christian Brothers University, Memphis, TN	Pennsylvania, University of, Philadelphia, PA
Cincinnati, University of, Cincinnati, OH	Pennsylvania State University, University Park, PA
Clarkson University, Potsdam, NY	Pittsburgh, University of, Pittsburgh, PA
Clemson University, Clemson, SC	Polytechnic University, Brooklyn, NY
Cleveland State University, Cleveland, OH	Prairie View A&M University, Prairie View, TX
Colorado, University of, Boulder, CO	Princeton University, Princeton, NJ
Colorado School of Mines, Golden, CO (Chemical and Pet. Ref. Eng.)	Puerto Rico, University of, Mayaguez, PR (5 year program)
Colorado State University, Ft. Collins, CO	Purdue University, West Lafayette, IN
Columbia University, New York, NY	Rensselaer Polytechnic Institute, Troy, NY
Connecticut, University of, Storrs, CT	Rhode Island, University of, Kingston, RI
Cooper Union, New York, NY	Rice University, Houston, TX

School	
Cornell University, Ithaca, NY	Rochester, University of, Rochester, NY
Dayton, University of, Dayton, OH	Rose Hulman Institute of Technology, Terre Haute, IN
Delaware, University of, Newark, DE	Rutgers The State University of New Jersey, New Brunswick, NJ
Detroit Mercy, University of, Detroit, MI	San Jose State University, San Jose, CA
Drexel University, Philadelphia, PA	South Alabama, University of, Mobile, AL
Florida A&M University/Florida State University, Tallahassee, FL	South Carolina, University of, Columbia, SC
Florida Institute of Technology, Melbourne, FL	South Dakota School of Mines and Technology, Rapid City, SD
Florida, University of, Gainesville, FL	South Florida, University of, Tampa, FL
Georgia Institute of Technology, Atlanta, GA	Southern California, University of, Los Angeles, CA
Hampton University, Hampton, VA	Southwestern Louisiana, University of, Lafayette, LA
Houston, University of, Houston, TX	Stevens Institute of Technology, Hoboken, NJ
Howard University, Washington, DC	Syracuse University, Syracuse, NY
Idaho, University of, Moscow, ID	Tennessee, University of, Knoxville, TN
Illinois, University of, Urbana, IL	Tennessee Technological University, Cookeville, TN
Illinois at Chicago, University of, Chicago, IL	Texas, University of, Austin, TX
Illinois Institute of Technology, Chicago, IL	Texas A&M University, College Station, TX
Iowa, University of, Iowa City, IA	Texas A&M University Kingsville, Kingsville, TX
Iowa State University, Ames, IA	Texas Tech University, Lubbock, TX
Johns Hopkins University, Baltimore, MD	Toledo, University of, Toledo, OH
Kansas, University of, Lawrence, KS	Tri State University, Angola, IN
Kansas State University, Manhattan, KS	Tufts University, Medford, MA
Kentucky, University of, Lexington, KY	Tulane University, New Orleans, LA
Lafayette College, Easton, PA	Tulsa, University of, Tulsa, OK
Lamar University, Beaumont, TX	Tuskegee University, Tuskegee, AL
Lehigh University, Bethlehem, PA	Utah, University of, Salt Lake City, UT
Louisiana State University, Baton Rouge, LA	Vanderbilt University, Nashville, TN
Louisiana Tech University, Ruston, LA	Villanova University, Villanova, PA
Louisville, University of, Louisville, KY (5 year master's degree)	Virginia Commonwealth University, Richmond, VA
Maine, University of, Orono, ME	Virginia Polytechnic Institute and State University, Blacksburg, VA
Manhattan College, Riverdale, NY	Virginia, University of, Charlottesville, VA

School	
Maryland, University of, College Park, MD & Baltimore County, MD (1987)	Washington, University of, Seattle, WA
Massachusetts, University of, Amherst, MA	Washington State University, Pullman, WA
Massachusetts, University of, Lowell, MA	Washington University, St. Louis, MO
Massachusetts Institute of Technology (MIT), Cambridge, MA	Wayne State University, Detroit, MI
Michigan, University of, Ann Arbor, MI	West Virginia Institute of Technology, Montgomery, WV
Michigan State University, East Lansing, MI	West Virginia University, Morgantown, WV
Michigan Technological University, Houghton, MI	Widener University, Chester, PA
Minnesota, University of, Minneapolis, MN	Wisconsin Madison, University of, Madison, WI
Minnesota, University of, Duluth, MN	Worcester Polytechnic Institute, Worcester, MA
Mississippi, University of, University, MS	Wyoming, University of, Laramie, WY
Mississippi State University, Mississippi State, MS	Yale University, New Haven, CT
Missouri, University of, Columbia, MO	Youngstown State University, Youngstown, OH
Missouri, University of, Rolla, MO	

CHAPTER 22

ACT-SAT CONCORDANCE TABLE

ACT	SAT	SAT Range
36	1590	1570–1600
35	1540	1530–1560
34	1500	1490–1520
33	1460	1450–1480
32	1430	1420–1440
31	1400	1390–1410
30	1370	1360–1380
29	1340	1330–1350
28	1310	1300–1320
27	1280	1260–1290
26	1240	1230–1250
25	1210	1200–1220
24	1180	1160–1190
23	1140	1130–1150
22	1110	1100–1120
21	1080	1060–1090
20	1040	1030–1050
19	1010	990–1020
18	970	960–980
17	930	920–950
16	890	880–910
15	850	830–870
14	800	780–820
13	760	730–770
12	710	690–720
11	670	650–680
10	630	620–640
9	590	590–610

https://www.act.org/content/dam/act/unsecured/documents/ACT-SAT-Concordance-Information.pdf

Live your dreams today remembering that discipline is the bridge between dreams and achievement!

"We believe in the American Dream that all people rich or poor can go as far in life as their talents and persistence will take them."
– Lizard Publishing Vision

At Lizard, we help you make your dreams come true.

CONTACT INFORMATION

Phone: 949-753-2888

E-mail: collegeguide@yahoo.com

Website: collegelizard.com and Lizard-publishing.com

YOU MAY PURCHASE AVAILABLE BOOKS ON THE FOLLOWING PAGES AT:

https://www.amazon.com/stores/author/B01N5II43V

Email: collegeguide@yahoo.com
Website: collegelizard.com

JOURNEY TO ART, DANCE, MUSIC, THEATRE, FILM, AND FASHION SERIES

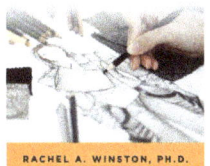

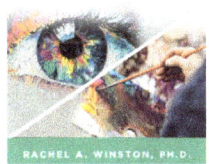

COMPREHENSIVE HEALTH CARE SERIES

 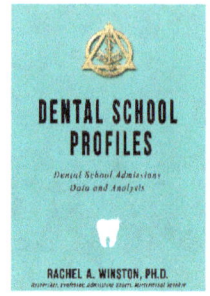  

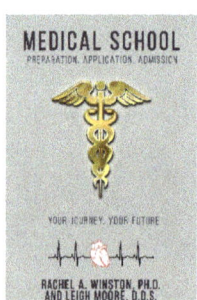  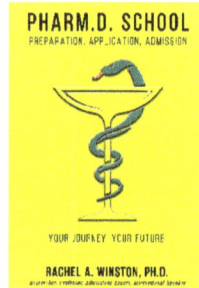 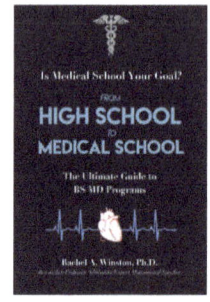

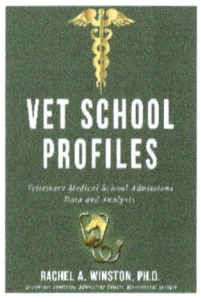   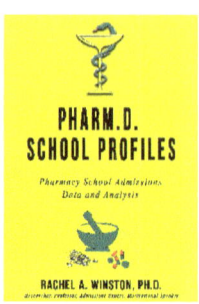

COMPREHENSIVE ENGINEERING SERIES

INDEX

Symbols

3M 17

A

AAEES 89, 165
ABET 6, 7, 164, 276, 280, 282, 286, 290, 300
Academy of Art University 48
Academy of Media Production 62
Accreditation 6, 164
AECOM 40
AEESP 89
Aggie STEM Summer Camps 77
Agriculture 2, 7, 39, 94, 95
AIAA 100, 102, 147, 194, 249, 266, 269
AIChE 147
Aircraft Electronics Association 147
Air Force Institute of Technology 287
Air Pollution 15, 89, 205, 265
Air & Space Forces Association 147
AI Scholars Program 73
Alternative Energy v, vii, 8, 42, 96, 116, 173, 175, 179
American Chemical Society 90, 200, 216, 217, 218, 219, 222, 224, 225, 228, 237, 243, 246, 249, 263, 264, 265, 268, 272
American Chemistry Council 91
American Electric Power 147

American Rocketry Challenge 19
American Water Works Association 147, 198, 226
Anesthesia Summer Institute 51
Angelo State U. 77
Angelo State University 102, 291
Apprenticeship 48, 51, 53, 56, 57, 60, 61, 62, 66, 67, 72, 73, 75, 76, 80
AQHA 153
Arcadis 40
Arcosanti 47
ARISE 70, 217
Arizona State 92, 253, 254, 275, 277, 291, 301
Articulation 116
Artificial Intelligence 60, 92, 221, 222, 243, 247, 258
Associate of Arts 106, 107, 109, 110
Associate of Science 107
Astronaut Scholarship Foundation 148
Auburn University 102, 291, 301
Augmented Reality 36
Australian National University 101
AUVSI 103, 219
A&WMA 90, 165

B

Bachelor of Arts 106
Bachelor of Engineering 106
Bachelor of Fine Arts 106

Bachelor of Science 106
Baylor University 77
Bee Campus USA 91
Biodiversity 14, 95, 202
Bioethics Essay Contest 20
Biofuels 92
BioGENEius Challenge 19
Biomedical Engineering Society 148, 195, 198, 200, 201, 204, 205, 216, 217, 218, 221, 223, 228, 237, 239, 241, 242, 243, 246, 249
Blatch, Nora Stanton 5
Board-Certified 89
Boeing Summer Internship 77
Boise State University 58
Boston College 98
Breakthrough Junior Challenge
Brigham Young University 79, 101, 291, 301
Broadcom 18
Brower Youth Awards 154
Brown University 277, 301
Bucknell University 189, 191, 203, 275, 277, 291, 301
Bureau of Labor Statistics 160, 166, 167
Burns & McDonnell 40

C

CAD 36, 39, 220, 225, 226
California Baptist University 291
California Institute of Technology 6, 253, 275, 301
Cal Poly SLO 98
CalTech 253, 254, 275
Campus Sustainability Council 91
Candidate Reply Date 116, 135
Carbon-neutral 173

Carnegie Mellon 7, 73, 92, 116, 189, 192, 275, 291, 301
Case Western Reserve 7, 291, 301
Catalyst 198, 225
CATALYST Scholars 69
Catholic University 291
Ceramic engineering 7
CES 35
CH2M Hill 40, 41
Checklist 116
Chemical Technology 6
Chevron Scholarships 148
Chichén Itzá, 3
Christian Brothers University 291, 301
Christ the Redeemer 3
Cincinnati, University of 277, 301
Citadel 76
City University of New York 291
Clarkson University 277, 291, 301
Class Rank 116
Clean Energy 96, 199, 244, 272
Clemson University 231, 233, 275, 277, 291, 301
CLEP 110, 116
Cleveland State University 291, 301
Climate Change 2, 7, 10, 39, 41, 47, 92, 93, 94, 95, 156, 164
Climate Reality 91
Coalition Application 116, 127, 128
Coca Cola Scholarship 154
Code Connects 46
College Credit 52, 59, 63, 116
College Fair 133
College of New Jersey 291
Colorado School of Mines 53, 86, 253, 256, 275, 277, 283, 291, 301
Colorado State University 277, 291, 301

Colorado, University of 301
Colosseum 3, 4
Columbia Climate School 79
Columbia University 92, 103, 189, 191, 199, 275, 277, 291, 301
Common Application 117, 127
Competition 17, 19, 21, 89, 100, 125, 148, 156, 196, 197, 199, 201, 204, 206, 208, 217, 218, 219, 222, 224, 226, 236, 239, 240, 241, 242, 245, 246, 247, 248, 249, 250, 259, 260, 261, 262, 263, 265, 266, 267, 269, 272
Computer-Aided Design 225
Computer Science for Cyber Security 70
Computer Science Summer Academy 78
Conferences vi, 38, 89, 90, 112, 168, 175, 176
Conrad Challenge 18
Conservation 15, 91, 243
Consumer Electronics Show 35
Cooper Union 292, 301
Cornell University 5, 92, 101, 189, 191, 200, 275, 277, 292, 302
Corning 69, 72, 77
COVID-19 168
Cox Scholarship 152
Creative Writing 47, 51, 53, 54, 62, 63, 65, 69, 75, 78
CS4CS 70
CSAW 70
CSS Profile 119, 133, 134, 144
CSSSA 48
CubeSat 103, 198, 199, 201, 205, 206, 226, 239, 240, 245, 262, 269
CURIE Academy 69

Cyberpatriot 47, 49, 53, 55, 56, 58, 60, 66, 67, 68, 73, 74, 76, 77, 79, 80, 81, 82
Cybersecurity 47, 48, 49, 53, 54, 56, 57, 58, 60, 61, 62, 63, 65, 66, 67, 68, 69, 70, 72, 73, 74, 75, 76, 77, 79, 80, 81, 82
Cyber Security Awareness Week 70

D

Dartmouth 68, 97, 296
Deferred Admission 117
Deferred Enrollment 117
Dell Scholars 154
Demographics 165, 166
Digital Storytelling 54, 76
Discovery Education 17
Doctor of Philosophy 107
Domestic Student 117
Doodle for Google Contest 154
Drexel University 189, 192, 205, 275, 277, 292, 302
Duke University 92, 231, 233, 243, 275, 277, 292

E

Early Action 117, 126, 134
Early Decision 117, 126, 134, 190, 191, 212, 213, 232, 233, 254, 255
Earth Justice Club 91
Eastern Kentucky University 281
Eastern Washington Univ. 81
Ecole de Technologie Superieure 101
Ecosystem 93
eCYBERMISSION 19
Edwards Lifesciences 49, 79

Egyptian 2
El Mirador 4
Elon University 93
Embry-Riddle Aeronautical University 100
Emissions 95
Employment Outlook 159
Energy Club 91, 207, 237
Engineers for a Sustainable World 91, 200, 207, 216, 222, 228, 238, 263, 265
Environmental Challenge 90
Environmental Law Society 91, 221
Environmental Protection Agency 9, 16
Environmental Science and Forestry 189, 191, 275, 278
Essay Contest 20, 21, 153, 155, 156
Ethiopia 3
Euclid 38
Experimental Aircraft Association 149
ExploraVision 17

F

FAFSA 119, 134, 144, 150, 203, 207, 263, 264, 266, 267, 268
Federal Bureau of Investigation 69, 80
Federal Summer Internship Program 54
Financial Aid 118, 194, 195, 196, 197, 198, 199, 200, 201, 202, 203, 204, 205, 206, 207, 208, 216, 217, 218, 219, 220, 221, 222, 223, 224, 225, 226, 227, 228, 236, 237, 238, 239, 240, 241, 242, 243, 244, 245, 246, 247, 248, 249, 250, 251, 258, 259, 260, 261, 262, 263, 264, 265, 266, 267, 268, 269, 270, 271, 272

First-Generation 118, 154
FIRST Robotics 19, 219, 222, 227, 242
Florida A&M 292, 302
Florida Atlantic University 277, 284, 292
Florida Institute of Technology 103, 284, 292, 302
Florida International University 231, 232, 275, 277, 292
Food Recovery Network 91
Forestry 38, 161, 173
Fullerene 27
Fuller, Thomas 45
Future Agents in Training 69, 80

G

Galileo 43
Gannon University 74, 277
Gates Millennium Scholarship 154
GenCyber 47, 48, 49, 53, 54, 57, 58, 60, 61, 65, 66, 68, 69, 72, 73, 74, 75, 76, 77, 79, 80, 81, 82
General Aviation Manufacturers 149
Genetics Essay Contest 20
Genius Olympiad 19
George Washington University 292
Georgia Institute of Technology 231, 275, 277, 292, 302
Georgia Tech 7, 86, 93, 98, 116, 146, 232, 238, 275, 277, 287
GE-Reagan Foundation 154
Girls Who Code 46
Global Entrepreneurship Intensive 74
Gloria Barron Prize 154
Goddard 70
Goldwater Scholarship 150, 245
Google Scholarship 150

Google Science Fair 17
GPA 116, 118, 147, 154, 190, 191, 192, 198, 212, 213, 214, 232, 233, 234, 235, 254, 255, 256, 257
GPS 262
Grand Canyon University 48
Graphene 26, 199
Great Books 49, 58, 63, 74
Great Wall of China 3
Greenhouse gases 14, 95
Greenpeace 91

H

Habitat for Humanity 91, 241
Hampton University 302
Hancock Scholarship 150
Handbook of Chemical Engineering 6
Harbin Institute 87
Harding University 292
Harvard vi, 46, 63, 87, 93, 97
Harvey Mudd College 50
HDR 41
Hispanic Scholarship Fund 154
Hofstra University 292
Howard University 292, 302
HUSSRP 70

I

ICCA 91
ID Tech 46, 64
Illinois Institute of Technology 58, 292, 302
Imperial College London 87
India 4, 150
Indiana University 60, 281
In-State 118, 248
Interactive Global Simulation 74

International Biology Olympiad 20
International Physics Olympiad 20
Internet of Things 113, 242
IOAA 20
Iowa State University 60, 102, 211, 212, 275, 292, 302
ISEF 17
Istanbul Technical University 278, 283, 284

J

Jacobs 40, 200, 263, 268
Jacobs Institute 263
Jetavanaramaya 5
Johns Hopkins 61
Jordan 4, 16, 206, 246, 287
Jordan University 287
JSHS 18
Jumpstart 55, 56

K

Keck Graduate Institute 49, 50, 57, 80
Kimley-Horn 41
King Abdulaziz University 283, 287
Kugle Scholarship 150

L

Laboratory for Laser Energetics 71
Lalibela 3
Lamar University 292, 302
LaunchX 64
LEED 25, 228
Legacy 118
Lego 219
Lehigh University 74, 189, 192, 206, 275, 278, 292, 302
Leshan Giant Buddha 3

Lexus Eco Challenge 18
Licensure 22, 161
LinkedIn 177, 180, 181
Living Rainforest 21
LLRISE 64
Lockheed Martin 151
Louisiana State 231, 232, 275, 278, 292, 302
Louisiana Tech 61, 292, 302
Lower Division 109, 118
Loyola Marymount 292

M

Machine Learning 95, 113, 173
Machu Picchu 3, 4
MakerBot 35
Manchester Technical School 6
Manhattan College 278, 292, 302
Marconi Engineering Scholarship 151
Marquette University 82, 293
Marshall University 293
Massachusetts Institute of Technology 93, 189, 190, 275, 284, 287, 303
Master of Architecture 106
Master of Arts 106
Master of Design 106
Master of Education 106
Master of Engineering 106
Master of Fine Arts 107
Materials Science 26
MATE ROV
Mayan 4
McKetta Undergraduate Scholarship 151
Merit-Based 144, 195, 217, 238, 241, 249, 259
Metaverse 8, 34, 172
Michigan State 94, 211, 213, 222, 275, 278, 293, 303
Michigan Technological University 211, 223, 275, 278, 283, 293, 303
Microsoft 18, 152
Middle East Technical University 278, 283
Milwaukee School of Engineering 293
Minecraft Scholarship 155
Mississippi State 101, 293, 303
Missouri University 103, 278, 283, 284, 287, 293
MIT 6, 46, 64, 86, 87, 93, 98, 116, 136, 189, 190, 194, 275, 284, 287, 303
Mohenjo Daro 4
Monash University 101
Montana State University 278, 293, 301
Moody's Mega Math 19
Moorman Scholarship 152
Mott MacDonald 41

N

NAACP 46, 155
NAEP 89
Nanoelectronics 266
NASA 17, 21, 61, 78, 79, 101, 194, 204, 208, 218, 219, 224, 226, 227, 228, 239, 259, 262, 272
NASSP 155
National Bioethics Bowl 20
National Center for Educational Statistics 38, 110, 112, 121
National College Fair 133
National HS Game Academy 73
National Institute of Health 66
National Oceanic and Atmospheric Administration 10, 152
National Science Bowl
National Security Agency 53

National Univ. of Singapore 87
NatureBridge Summer Programs 81
Naval Academy 284, 288
NCES ii, 110, 112
Need-Aware 118
Need-Based 50, 111, 144, 204, 217, 221, 241, 242, 250, 259, 266, 267, 268
Need-Blind 146, 194, 197
Net Impact 91, 242
Networking 90, 108, 178
New Jersey Institute of Technology 293, 301
New Mexico Institute 278, 293, 301
New Mexico State University 103, 293, 301
New York, City College of 301
New York, State University of 301
New York University 70, 101, 293
NextGen Boot Camp 46
NOAA 10
Nobel Prize 27
North Carolina State 86, 94, 102, 231, 233, 244, 275, 278, 287, 293, 301
Northeastern University 278, 293, 301
Northrop Grumman 152
Northwestern University 58, 94, 211, 212, 216, 275, 278, 293, 301
Norton, Lewis M. 6
Norwich University 5, 293
NYU 70, 98

O

Occupational Outlook Handbook 160, 166
Ocean Awareness 21
Ohio State University 211, 214, 227, 275, 278, 293, 301
Ohio University 293, 301
Oklahoma State University 281, 293, 301
Olympiad 19, 20, 90, 197, 199, 216, 218, 219, 224, 228, 237, 241, 243, 259, 268, 269, 272
Open Admissions 118
Operation Catapult 60
Optimist International Essay Contest 155
Oregon State University 94, 253, 256, 271, 275, 278, 287, 293, 301
Othmer Scholarship 152
Outlines of Industrial Chemistry 6
Oxfam Campus Club 91

P

Pace University 70
Pandemic 29, 86, 119, 124, 126, 137, 168
Parthenon 4
Pathways Internship Program 54
Pennsylvania State 75, 189, 192, 207, 275, 278, 284, 287, 293, 301
Petra 3, 4
Pharmacy Summer Institute 71
Placement Tests 118
Politecnico di Torino 101
Pollution 2, 7, 39, 40, 93, 160, 173
Polytechnique Montreal 101
Portal 134, 135, 136, 138, 147, 208, 268
Portal 47
Portland State University 94, 279, 293
Potala Palace 3
Poznan University of Technology 101
President's Volunteer Service Award 119
Princeton University 67, 189, 190, 197, 275, 293, 301
Professional Engineer 164
Programs vi, vii, 6, 7, 10, 11, 29, 37, 38,

39, 88, 107, 108, 110, 111, 112, 132, 133, 164, 179, 187, 206, 208, 216, 217, 218, 220, 222, 226, 236, 240, 242, 244, 272
Project-Based 86
Project Yellow Light Video Contest 155
PROMYS 63
Prudential Emerging Visionaries 155
Purdue University 60, 95, 101, 211, 212, 218, 275, 279, 287, 293, 294, 301

Q

Quantum Energy 258
Questbridge Scholarship 155

R

Race to Inspire Essay Contest 156
Rady Children's Hospital 50
Rankings 88
RCEL 78
Recommendation 119, 132, 133, 134, 137, 150, 151
Recycling 15, 152
Regeneron 17
Regional Representative 134
Registrar 119
Regular Decision 117, 126, 134, 136
Rejection 137
Renaissance Kids 65
Renewable Energy 15, 195, 199, 200, 225, 251, 265
Rensselaer Polytechnic 5, 71, 189, 191, 201, 275, 279, 287, 294, 301
Repurpose 15
Research in Science & Engineering 63
Research Science Institute 64
Residency 99, 119

Restricted Early Action 126
Resume 133
Reuse 10, 96
Rice Memorial Scholarship 152
Rice University 78, 146, 294, 301
Ringling College of Art and Design 56
RISE 63
Robots 197, 246
Rochester Institute of Technology 101
Rockefeller University Summer 71
Rocketry 19, 101, 196, 197, 200, 206, 208, 219, 220, 222, 225, 241, 244, 249, 251, 258, 259, 263
Rolling Admission 119
Roots & Shoots 91
Rose-Hulman 294
Roswell Park 216
ROTC 156, 241
Rover College Scholarship 156
Rowan University 294
RSI 64
RUSMP 78
Rutgers 189, 190, 198, 275, 294
RWTH Aachen University 100

S

Sacsayhuamán 5
Saint Louis University 293
Samsung 19
San Diego State University 95, 253, 254, 261, 275, 279, 294
San Jose State University 294, 302
Santa Clara University 294
SASI 51
SAT 116, 121, 124, 126, 133, 190, 191, 192, 212, 213, 214, 232, 233, 234, 235, 254, 255, 256, 257, 304, 305

Scholarships 18, 19, 50, 59, 63, 67, 89, 111, 118, 126, 133, 134, 136, 137, 144, 145, 146, 147, 148, 149, 150, 152, 153, 154, 155, 156, 157, 196, 198, 199, 200, 202, 203, 204, 205, 208, 217, 218, 219, 220, 221, 222, 223, 225, 226, 227, 237, 238, 239, 240, 243, 244, 245, 247, 248, 249, 250, 258, 259, 262, 264, 266, 267, 268, 270, 271, 272
Scholastic Art and Writing 156
Science Bowl 194
Science Camps of America 58
Science Olympiad 197, 199, 216, 218, 219, 224, 228, 237, 241, 243, 259, 268, 269, 272
Sea Levels 9, 14
SEAP 48, 51, 53, 56, 57, 60, 61, 62, 66, 67, 72, 73, 75, 80
SEES 79
Shakespeare 164
Shape 6, 20, 24, 35
Shell Science Lab 18
Sierra Club 91
SMU 78
SMYSP 51
SOCAPA 50, 71, 79
Social media 157, 172, 174, 175, 176, 177, 182
Society for Technical Communication 21, 223
Society of Women Engineers 153, 195, 196, 198, 199, 200, 201, 204, 205, 207, 208, 216, 218, 219, 220, 221, 223, 225, 228, 237, 239, 241, 242, 246, 251, 263, 264, 265, 272
Soil Science 6, 161

Solar Energy Club 91
Sophomore 88
South Dakota School of Mines 283, 284, 294, 302
Southern California Institute of Architecture 51
Southern Illinois University 294
Southern Methodist University 78, 231, 234, 247, 275, 279, 294
SpaceX 51, 78, 226
SPARC 70
SSEA 51
Stamps Scholarship 219
Standardized Testing 124
Stanford University 49, 51, 86, 95, 253, 254, 262, 275, 294
Stantec 41
STEM Enhancement in Earth Science 79
STEM Institute 69, 81
STEMworks 58
Stevens Institute of Technology 279, 294, 302
Stonehenge 5
Stony Brook University 294
Stratasys 35
Student Aid Report 134
Student Science Training Program 56
Students for Environmental Action 91
SUMaC 51
Summer Academy for Math & Science 74
Summer Design Camp 76
Summer Engineering Exploration 65
Summer Liberal Arts Institute 65
Summer Melt 119
Summer Programs 133, 197, 199, 200, 202, 259
Summer Science Program 53, 60, 68, 73

Summet 53
SUNY Buffalo 69
SUNY College of Environmental Science and Forestry 189, 191, 275
Sustainable Ocean Alliance 91
Syracuse University 279, 294, 302
Systems 92, 94, 95, 96, 103, 167, 191, 194, 195, 196, 197, 198, 199, 200, 201, 203, 204, 205, 206, 207, 214, 216, 217, 218, 219, 220, 221, 222, 223, 224, 225, 226, 227, 228, 237, 238, 239, 240, 241, 242, 245, 246, 247, 248, 249, 251, 258, 259, 262, 263, 264, 265, 266, 268, 271, 272, 288

T

Taj Mahal 3
Target Scholarship 156
Tarleton State University 103, 279, 294
TeenNat 51
Temple University 279, 294
Teotihuacan 4
Terp Young Scholars 62
Tesla 78
Tetra Tech 41
Texas A&M 77, 86, 87, 116, 127, 231, 234, 248, 275, 279, 284, 288, 294, 297, 302
Texas Tech 78, 95, 279, 294, 302
Thorpe, Frank H. 6
Thurgood Marshall College Fund 156
TRC Companies 41
Trine University 294
Tri State University 302
Tufts University 189, 190, 195, 275, 279, 294, 302

Tulane University 302
Tuskegee University 47, 302

U

UC Berkeley 52, 86, 116, 123, 263
UCLA v, vi, 123, 255, 266
Udall Undergraduate Scholarship 153
United States Naval Academy 284, 288
University of Arkansas 48
University of California, Berkeley 52, 95, 99, 101, 253, 255, 263, 275, 287
University of California, Davis 253, 255, 264, 275
University of California, Irvine 96, 253, 255, 265, 275
University of California, Los Angeles 253, 255, 266, 275
University of California, San Diego 52, 253, 256, 268, 275
University of Canterbury 101
University of Central Florida 96, 102, 232, 295
University of Chicago vi, 59
University of Cincinnati 295
University of Colorado 53, 103, 253, 256, 270, 275, 295
University of Connecticut 295
University of Dayton 295
University of Delaware 295
University of Florida 101, 231, 237, 275, 287, 295
University of Georgia 231, 232, 239, 275, 295
University of Giessen 6
University of Hartford 295
University of Hawaii 58
University of Houston 96, 296

University of Illinois 96, 101, 211, 212, 217, 275, 287, 295, 296
University of Iowa 211, 213, 221, 275, 295
University of Kansas 295
University of Louisiana 240, 296
University of Louisville 101, 296
University of Maine 296
University of Manchester 6
University of Maryland 41, 62, 101, 231, 233, 242, 275, 281, 296
University of Massachusetts 189, 190, 196, 275, 287, 296
University of Memphis 76, 296
University of Miami 296
University of Michigan 7, 116, 211, 213, 224, 275, 287, 296
University of Minnesota 101, 211, 213, 225, 275, 296
University of Missouri 278, 296
University of Nebraska 211, 214, 226, 275, 296
University of Nevada 67, 296
University of New Hampshire 296
University of New Haven 296
University of New Mexico 103, 287, 296
University of New South Wales 101
University of North Carolina 73, 101, 102, 296
University of North Dakota 296
University of North Florida 296
University of Notre Dame 102, 211, 212, 219, 275, 296
University of Oklahoma 73, 296
University of Pennsylvania 41, 281
University of Pittsburgh 75, 189, 192, 208, 275, 296, 297
University of Puerto Rico 102, 279, 297
University of Queensland 101
University of Rhode Island 295
University of Rochester 71
University of Sao Paulo 101
University of South Alabama 297
University of South Carolina 76, 297
University of Southern California 52, 96, 253, 256, 269, 275, 297
University of South Florida 103, 297
University of Tennessee 288, 297
University of Texas– Austin 297
University of Texas - El Paso 297
University of Texas Rio Grande Valley 295
University of Texas - San Antonio 295
University of Texas – Tyler 297
University of the District of Columbia 297
University of the Virgin Islands 103
University of Toledo 295
University of Tulsa 302
University of Utah 295
University of Vermont 297
University of Virginia 231, 234, 250, 275, 297
University of Washington 7, 100, 253, 257, 272, 275, 297
University of Waterloo 41, 101
University of Wisconsin 82, 211, 214, 228, 275, 288, 297
University of Wyoming 297
Upper Division 119
Urbanization 39
US Air Force Academy 295
US Coast Guard Academy 295
US Military Academy 295
US News & World Report 86

V

Vanderbilt 76
Vanderbilt University 101, 102, 231, 234, 246, 275, 297, 302
Veritas AI Scholars 46
Vestas 42
Villanova University 297, 302
Virginia Commonwealth University 288, 302
Virginia Tech 80, 86, 87, 102, 231, 235, 251, 275, 284, 297
Virtual Reality 34, 36, 245
Volunteer Service Award 119

W

Waitlist 97, 98, 119
Walgreens Expressions Challenge 157
Wallops Flight Facility 80
Walmart Scholarship Program 157
Warhol, Andy 82
Washington University 54, 66, 102, 292, 303
Waste Management 89, 90, 165, 167, 203, 244
Water Environment Federation 90
Water Quality 90, 93
Water Treatment 7, 40, 93
Wave Hill Forest Project 71
Wayne State University 297, 303
WEF 90
Wentworth Institute of Technology 65, 297
Western Michigan University 298
Western New England University 298
West Point 5, 102, 279, 288, 295
West Virginia Institute 303
West Virginia University 284, 297, 303
We The Future Contest 157
Widener University 298, 303
Wildlife Conservation Society 91
Wistar Institute 75
Wonderworks 78
Worcester Polytechnic Institute 65, 101, 279, 298, 303
WPI Frontiers Program 65
Wroclaw University 101
WSP Global 42

Y

Yale University 303
YESS 81
Yield 119
Young Eagles Camp 82
Youngstown State University 298, 303

Z

Zero Waste Club 91

www.ingramcontent.com/pod-product-compliance
Lightning Source LLC
Chambersburg PA
CBHW050301010526
44108CB00040B/1948